William Makepeace Thackeray

William Makepeace Thackeray.
From an unpublished crayon portrait
by Daniel Maclise 1857
(By permission of Major William H. Lambert.)

WILLIAM MAKEPEACE THACKERAY

LEWIS MELVILLE pseud.
of
Lewis S. Benjamin

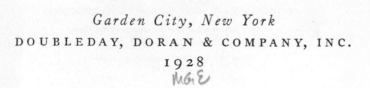

Garden City, New York
DOUBLEDAY, DORAN & COMPANY, INC.
1928

MGE

Printed in Great Britain by Phototype Ltd., Barnet, Herts

To
W. Algernon Locker

PREFACE

"WE all want to know details regarding the men who have achieved famous feats, whether of war, or wit, or eloquence, or endurance, or knowledge," Thackeray said in a Roundabout Paper—'On a Joke I once heard from the late Thomas Hood.' "We want to see this man who has amused and charmed us; who has been our friend, or given us hours of pleasant companionship and pleasant thought." In the same essay he remarked, "If the secret history of books could be written, and the author's private thoughts noted down alongside of his story, how many insipid volumes would become interesting, and dull tales excite the reader."

Thackeray's stories are frequently autobiographical; he often drew upon his experiences, notably in "Pendennis" and "Philip," so that the reader, knowing his life, must certainly find an added pleasure when reading them. His departure from India, his arrival in England, his early school life, the Charterhouse days, Larkbeare, Cambridge, his misfortunes in London, his life in the Paris studios, the newspapers with which he was connected, the people he met, the places he visited are all reproduced under thin disguises. At the same time it has to be borne in mind that his books are no mere transcript from life, and, while often illustrating an incident in the

novelist's career by an extract from his writings, I have
been careful to do so only when there is every reason to
believe that the passages quoted are indeed autobiographical.

There is no lack of material for the biographer. The
primary authorities are, of course, the biographical introductions to an edition of his works, written by his daughter,
Lady Ritchie; and only second in importance is the
memoir by his son-in-law, Sir Leslie Stephen. Next is
the delightful little monograph in the " Great Writers "
series, written by Herman Merivale and Sir Frank T.
Marzials, published in 1891, which contained hitherto
unpublished correspondence. " Thackeray, the Humourist and the Man of Letters," by Theodore Taylor (" John
Camden Hotten "), which appeared in 1864, is merely a
useful compilation. A primary authority is the privately
printed " Memorials of the Thackeray Family," by Jane
Townley Pryme and Alicia Bayne (1879)—the chapter on
the novelist is by Miss Bayne. Sir William Hunter has
written on " The Thackerays in India " (1897); J. F.
Boyes has given his impressions of Thackeray at Charterhouse School (Cornhill Magazine, January 1865); the
Rev. Whitwell Elwin, who also tells of his early period,
carries on the narrative to the time when Thackeray was
in search of a profession (Monthly Review, June, September, October, 1904). Thackeray in a letter to George
Henry Lewes (printed in the " Life of Goethe ") recalls
memories of his stay at Weimar in 1830—Weimar being
the Pumpernickel of " Vanity Fair "; and the " Paris
Sketch Book " and various contributions to the Corsair
and Britannia contain his own accounts of his visits to
Paris. Mr. M. H. Spielmann has given in the " History

of *Punch*" (1895) the story of the novelist's association
with that paper. There are records of Thackeray's
American trips in Thackeray's letters to the Hon.
William B. Reed (" Haud Immemor," 1864), and to the
Baxter family (1904), in Eyre Crowe's "William
Thackeray in America" (1893), and in the biographies
and correspondence of Prescott, Ticknor, Motley, Bancroft, Longfellow, James T. Fields (" Yesterdays with
Authors," 1872), Lester Wallack (" Memoirs of Fifty
Years," 1889). There is much interesting information,
and many letters, portraits, and illustrations, not printed
elsewhere, in General James Grant Wilson's " Thackeray
in the United States" (1904). Thackeray's cor. ection
with the *Cornhill Magazine* has been told by Lady Ritchie
in " The First Number of the *Cornhill*" (*Cornhill
Magazine*, July 1896) and by George M. Smith in
" Our Birth and Parentage" (*Cornhill Magazine*, January
1901).

For the rest, there is Thackeray's correspondence with
the Brookfields, Edward Fitzgerald, Lord Houghton,
Macvey Napier, Professor Aytoun, Abraham Hayward,
Macready, Browning, Tennyson, Longfellow, Dickens,
Edmund Yates, and Dean Hole. There are references to
him in the reminiscences or biographies of Sir Henry Cole,
John Francis, John Hollingshead, George Hodder, Frances
Anne Kemble, Charles Knight, Henry Reeve, Lord
William Pitt Lennox, Frederick Locker-Lampson, David
Masson, George Augustus Sala, R. H. Stoddart, Mrs.
James T. Fields, Bayard Taylor, and Henry Vizetelly;
and also in " Recollections of Thackeray," by his cousin,
Richard Bedingfield (*Cassell's Magazine*, 1870).

The principal collections of Thackeray's works are :

(i) Library Edition (Smith, Elder & Co., 22 vols., 1867–9; with two supplementary volumes, 1885, 1886);

(ii) Edition de luxe (Smith, Elder & Co., 24 vols., 1878–86); with a memoir by Sir Leslie Stephen;

(iii) Works. Edited by Horace E. Scudder (Houghton Mifflin & Co., Boston; 22 vols., 1889);

(iv) Biographical Edition, with Introductions by Lady Ritchie (Smith, Elder & Co.; 13 vols., 1898–9);

(v) Prose Works. Edited, with Introductions by Walter Jerrold and illustrations by C. E. Brock (J. M. Dent & Son, 30 vols., 1901–3);

(vi) Works. Edited, with Introductions by the present writer, the text being that of the first editions, and containing much matter not before included (Macmillan & Co., Ltd.; 20 vols., 1901–7);

(vii) Works. Edited, with Introductions by George Saintsbury (Oxford University Press; 17 vols., 1908);

(viii) Centenary Biographical Edition, with Introductions by Lady Ritchie (Smith, Elder & Co., 26 vols., 1910–11), being a reprint, with additions, of (iv);

(ix) Edition de luxe. Edited, with Bibliographical Introduction by the present writer (Macmillan & Co., Ltd.; 20 vols., 1911), being a reprint of (vi); with the addition of 500 illustrations by Harry Furniss, and an " Artist's Preface " to each volume.

For permission to insert in this work letters written by Thackeray, I am indebted to Messrs. William Blackwood & Sons (two letters from Sir Theodore Martin's " Life of W. E. Aytoun "), Messrs. William Blackwood & Sons (a letter from Mrs. Oliphant's " Annals of a Publishing House," and another from Anthony Trollope's " Autobiography "), Mr. M. H. Spielmann (a letter from " The

Hitherto Unidentified Contributions of W. M. Thackeray to *Punch* "), Sir John Murray (a letter from " The Correspondence of Abraham Hayward "), Lady Reid, Lord Crewe, Messrs. Cassell & Co., Ltd. (three letters from Sir T. Wemyss Reid's " Life of Lord Houghton "), Messrs. Macmillan & Co., Ltd. extracts from Lady Ritchie's " Chapters from Some Memoirs " and " The Letters of Edward Fitzgerald "), and Mr. W. Lawrence Bradbury (two letters in his possession).

LEWIS MELVILLE

LONDON, *August* 1927.

CONTENTS

CONTENTS

ILLUSTRATIONS

XV

I.—B

IN THE TEXT

William Makepeace Thackeray

WILLIAM MAKEPEACE
THACKERAY

CHAPTER I

INTRODUCTORY

The Thackeray family—John de Thackwra—William de Thackwra
—Robert Thackra—Walter Thackeray of Hampsthwaite—Elias
Thackeray—Archdeacon Thackeray—his sons and daughters—the
Rev. Elias Thackeray, Vicar of Dundalk—and Thackeray's tribute
to him in "The Irish Sketch Book"—the Archdeacon's fifth son—
and his family—William Makepeace Thackeray, grandfather of
the novelist—the Thackerays a typical Anglo-Indian family—the
novelist's uncles and aunts—his cousin Sir Richmond Shakespear—
Richmond Thackeray and Anne Becher, the novelist's parents—the
birth of Thackeray.

THE family of the Thackerays has been traced
back to the fourteenth century, when there
was a John de Thackwra who held of the
Abbot of St. Mary of Fountains a dwelling-
house and thirty acres of land at Hartwich in 1336,
and, twenty-five years after, a William de Thackwra,
who was tenant at will of a messuage and twenty-one
acres at the same place. A century later, the family
records note, a Robert Thackra kept the Grange of
Brimham for the convent, and subsequently an Edward

Thacquarye held houses and land from the same convent. They were a prolific race, these de Thackwras,
Thackras, and Thacquaryes, who early in the seven-
teenth century began to adopt the now familiar form of
the surname. Then Walter Thackeray established
himself at Hampsthwaite, a hamlet on the Nidd, near
the forest of Knaresborough, in the West Riding of
Yorkshire, and there for many decades the family remained, until this yeoman branch of the line came to
an end with the death of Thomas Thackeray in 1804,
seven years before the birth of the novelist.

Long before this a scion of the race, one Elias
Thackeray, more restless or more ambitious than the
rest, had left the homestead, and gone to Christ's
College, Cambridge, where fortune smiled upon him,
for, becoming M.A. in 1709, he was two years after
appointed to the living of Hawkerswell in the Archdeaconry of Richmond, Yorkshire. Not unmindful
of the claims of his kindred, he charged himself with
the welfare of a twelve-year-old nephew, Thomas, the
son of his brother Timothy, whom in January 1706 he
contrived to place on the foundation at Eton. There
the lad remained for six years, when he won a foundation scholarship at King's College, Cambridge,
where he proceeded to a fellowship in 1715. Thomas
then, for a while, returned to his old school as an
assistant master, and, after an unsuccessful application
in 1743 for the Provostship of King's, in 1746 was
appointed Headmaster of Harrow. Harrow School, in
spite of traditions dating back for two hundred years,
was at that time in a sad way, having been practically
ruined under the *régime* of a drunken, disorderly, idle

principal; and when Thomas began his reign there were but thirty boys—a number that under his able rule was rapidly increased to one hundred and thirty. "Dr. Thackeray," said Dr. Parr, one of his pupils, "though a strict disciplinarian, possessed much kindness of temper, and much suavity of manner. I have reason to love and revere him as a father as well as a master." He has been described also by Dr. Edmund Pyle, who wrote him down "a great scholar in the Eton way, and a good one in every way; and a true Whig."

The worthy Doctor, in 1730, at the age of thirty-five, had married Ann (a daughter of John Woodward, Lord of the Manor of Butler's Marston, Warwickshire), who, during the next twenty years, bore six sons and ten daughters, and survived until 1797. He was in 1748 appointed chaplain to Frederick, Prince of Wales, and was marked out for further preferment. "The Bishop of Winchester (Benjamin Hoadly) never saw this man in his life, but had heard so much good of him that he resolved to serve him some way or other, if ever he could, but said nothing to anybody," Dr. Pyle wrote in 1753. "On Friday last he sent for this Dr. Thackeray, and when he came into the room my lord gave him a parchment, and told him he had long heard of his good character, and long been afraid he should never be able to give him any serviceable proof of the good opinion he had conceived of him; that what he had put into his hands was the Archdeaconry of Surrey, which he hoped would be acceptable to him, as he might perform the duty of it yearly at the time of his leisure in the Easter holidays. Dr. Thackeray was so surprised and overcome with

this extraordinary manner of doing him a favour, that
he was very near fainting as he was giving him institution." Dr. Thackeray held the archdeaconry for the
remaining seven years of his life.

It is only necessary here to mention three sons of Dr.
Thackeray. The fourth, another Thomas (1736–1806),
practised surgery at Cambridge and left issue fifteen
children ; of whom one daughter, Jane Townley,
married George Pryme, the political economist ; a son
William Makepeace,[1] settled as a physician at Chester,
and another, Elias, took orders and became Vicar
of Dundalk. To this last his relative, the novelist,
paid tribute in " The Irish Sketch Book " :—

> I was so lucky as to have an introduction to the
> Vicar of Dundalk, which that gentleman's kind and
> generous nature interpreted into a claim for unlimited
> hospitality ; and he was good enough to consider
> himself not only bound to receive me, but to give up
> previous engagements abroad in order to do so.
> I need not say that it afforded me sincere pleasure to
> witness, for a couple of days, his labours among his
> people ; and indeed it was a delightful occupation to
> watch both flock and pastor. The world is a wicked,
> selfish, abominable place, as the parson tells us ; but
> his reverence comes out of his pulpit and gives the
> flattest contradiction to his doctrine, busying himself
> with kind actions from morning till night, denying to
> himself, generous to others, preaching the truth to
> young and old, clothing the naked, feeding the
> hungry, consoling the wretched, and giving hope
> to the sick. [2]

The fifth son of Dr. Thackeray was a physician at
Windsor, and in the autobiography of Mrs. Papendiek,

---

[1] The name Makepeace is said to have been derived from an ancestor
who suffered at the stake for his faith in the " good old days " of Queen
Mary.   [2] Chap. xxvi.

Assistant-Keeper of the Wardrobe and Reader to
Queen Charlotte, may be read the story of his run-
away marriage, his early death, and his widow's struggles to bring up her seven children.   One of these was
on the foundation at Eton; another was a midship-
man in the navy; and a third son, George, became
Provost of King's College, Cambridge.

Dr. Thackeray's youngest child, William Makepeace, grandfather of the novelist, born in 1749,
entered the East India Company's service.   After a
preliminary training in book-keeping, proficiency in
which was essential for employment in John Company's service, young William sailed in the *Lord
Camden* for Calcutta.   His career in India was from
the outset successful.   On his arrival, placed in the
Secretary's office with a salary of £80, his zeal at once
attracted the notice of Cartier, Governor of Bengal,
with the result that within twelve months he was made
assistant-treasurer or cash-keeper at a considerably
increased stipend.   In 1771 he was appointed Factor
and Fourth in Council at Dacca, where he set up house
with two sisters whom his advancement enabled him to
summon from home.[1]   Warren Hastings made him

[1] These sisters were Jane and Henrietta, then aged respectively
thirty-two and twenty-two.   Jane married on October 16, 1772, Major
James Rennell, the geographer; and later in the year Henrietta married
from her sister's new home James Harris, the head of the East India
Company's civil service in Eastern Bengal.   The Rennells did not go to
England until 1777, after the loss of their first-born; but the Harrises
returned forthwith.   Harris purchased a country seat near Chelmsford
and a town house in Great Ormond Street, then a more fashionable
district than now; but when he died it was found his extravagance had
made deep inroads into his fortune, although enough was left for his
widow to live comfortably at Hadley, and to provide an excellent education for the children.

Collector of the frontier province of Sylhet, and in 1774 called him back to Dacca as Third in Council.

Two years later William Makepeace married Amelia, daughter of Lieutenant-Colonel Richmond Webb, a descendant of the victor of Weynendal, whom Thackeray has portrayed in "Esmond," and, having during his nine and a half years' sojourn in the East realised a competence, soon after sailed with his eighteen-year-old bride for England. The young couple settled down at Hadley, near Chipping Barnet, and for the rest of their days led a simple, hospitable country life. Mrs. Thackeray died in 1810, and three years later was followed to the grave by her husband, who was buried under the shadow of the church of Monken Hadley, a picturesque building upon the tower of which may still be seen the battered fragments of an old beacon cage.

William Makepeace it was who founded the great Anglo-Indian Thackeray family which, Sir William Hunter says, "formed a typical family of the Bengal Service in the days of John Company, threw out branches into the sister services, military and medical, and by a network of intermarriages created for themselves a ruling connection both in India and in the Court of Directors at home."[1] It has already been mentioned how the sisters who went out to him married Anglo-Indians, and of the twelve children of his marriage, one of whom died in infancy, nine went Eastward Ho! Four sons entered the Madras and Bengal civil services, a fifth entered the Indian army, a sixth became a barrister and journalist at Cal-

[1] Sir W. W. Hunter: *The Thackerays in India.*

cutta; while two daughters married Bengal civilians, and a third became the wife of the Attorney-General in Ceylon.

Of these children. one of them the father of the novelist, brief mention must be made. The eldest, William Makepeace, was born in 1778, and in his twentieth year was sent to Madras, where he was the first civilian to secure a reward (under the rules of 1797, framed for the encouragement of the study of Oriental languages) for proficiency in Telugu. His rise, like that of his father, was rapid. By Lord Clive he was appointed translator at head-quarters; then, assistant to Sir Thomas Munro, Governor of the province; and, later, the first judge of a new court established at Masulipatam. He became a member of the Board of Revenue in 1806, and four years after was promoted to be Chief Secretary to the Madras Government. His health broke down in 1813, and he went to England for a while, when the Court of Directors took the opportunity to commend his services in a despatch. He returned to India in 1816, and was appointed a provisional Member of Council and President of the Board of Revenue in June 1820; but the long sojourn in a tropical climate had undermined his constitution, and he did not live long to enjoy his honours. He died on January 11, 1823, while on a sea voyage undertaken in the hope of restoring his health.

Webb Thackeray, who in 1806, at the age of eighteen, went out to Madras as a writer, died within a year of his arrival. In the same service as the two brothers already mentioned was the fifth son, St. John, who, born in 1791, was one of the first civilians sent out by the East India College that later developed into Haileybury. He went to Madras in 1809, and was killed at Kittur Fort where, hoping to bring the insurgents to terms, he advanced without a flag of truce and was fired upon. Thomas, the fourth son, entered the Bengal army, and was killed in the Nepal War in 1814, in an heroic endeavour to cover the retreat of some British troops with his Light Company against "a strong and overpowering column of Gurkhas," which called forth the highest encomiums in despatches from the commander-in-chief and the Government of India. Charles, the youngest, became a barrister at Calcutta, but obtaining little practice, wrote leading articles for the *Englishman* and other papers. He was the most brilliant of the brothers, but, succumbing to a passion for drink, he sank into an obscure grave in the mid forties. The stay-at-home (sixth) son, Francis (1793–1842), took holy orders, and retired to a Herefordshire parish, where he wrote several books, including a work on the "State of Ancient Britain under the Roman Emperors" and the better known "History of William Pitt, Earl of Chatham," quoted repeatedly by Carlyle in "Frederick the Great," and reviewed by Macaulay, who censured what he considered the author's extravagant praise of his hero.

The two sisters who went out in 1802 to join their brother Richmond married soon after their arrival: Augusta to "her brother's dearest friend," Mr. Elliott, a civilian; Emily (who died in India) to John Talbot Shakespear. Of the latter alliance came nine children, the eldest of whom, Colonel John Dowdeswell Shake-spear, "a noble, chivalrous figure," was regarded by the family as the prototype of Colonel Newcome. A younger son was Colonel Sir Richmond Shakespear, who became Agent to the Governor-General for Central India, and, just before his death in 1861, was appointed by Lord Canning to the Chief Commissionership of Mysore. It was to this cousin that the novelist made appreciative reference in a " Roundabout Paper."

"Can I do anything for you?" I remember the kind fellow asking. He was always asking that question : of all kinsmen ; of all widows and orphans; of all the poor; of young men who might need his purse or his service. I saw a young officer yesterday to whom the first words Sir Richmond Shakespear wrote on his arrival in India were, " Can I do anything for you?" His purse was at the command of all. His kind hand was always open. It was a gracious fate which sent him to rescue widows and captives. Where could they have had a champion more chivalrous, a protector more loving and tender?[1]

Richmond, the second son, and father of the novelist, was born at South Mimms, on September 1, 1781.[2] Sent to Eton at the age of ten, he remained there until 1796, when, being nominated to a writership in the Bengal Civil Service, he left school to go through the usual training in merchants' accounts. He arrived in Calcutta in 1798, studied at Fort William College,

[1] *On Letts's Diary.*
[2] Sir William Hunter has pointed out that the tombstone says Richmond Thackeray died on September 13, 1815, aged thirty-two years, ten months, and twenty-three days, which would make the birth-day October 21, 1782, instead of September 1, 1781, as stated in the Family Book of the Thackerays.

and soon, as a reward for proficiency in Arabic and Persian, was appointed Collector of Midnapur. He was removed to Birbhum in 1803, three years after was appointed Judge of Ramgarh, and in 1807 was promoted to be Secretary of the Bengal Board of Revenue. From this time forth, with the exception of some months during which he acted as Judge of Midnapur, he remained in the capital, where, by virtue of his personal charm and his artistic and musical tastes, he became a noted personage in the little social world that flourished there.

At Calcutta Richmond met, fell in love with, and married on October 13, 1810, one of the reigning beauties, Anne Becher, descended from an old Bengal civilian family, of whom, perhaps, the most distinguished member was Richard Becher, who held high office when Clive ruled India.[1] In the following December Richmond was promoted to be Collector of the Twenty-four Parganas, one of the prizes of the Bengal service, when he and his young wife moved to the official residence at Alipur, which was so close to the city as not to interfere with their social life. There, on July 18, 1811, was born their only child, William Makepeace.

---

[1] Richard Becher retired in 1774, and returned to England, but seven years later lost his fortune in the endeavour to help a friend, whereupon the Court of Directors gave him a compassionate appointment as head of the Calcutta mint. But the blow was too much for him and he died, a disappointed old man, on November 17, 1782. "I wonder," says Sir William Hunter, " if Thackeray had that sad story of his mother's kinsman in mind when he touched off, with so tender a pathos, Colonel Newcome's loss of fortune in old age."

CHAPTER II

CHILDHOOD (1811-1822)

Death of Richmond Thackeray—Thackeray and Richmond Shakespear sent to England, 1817—Thackeray's recollection of India—his subsequent acquaintance with Anglo-Indians—his mother's teachings—their affection for each other—her marriage with Major Carmichael-Smyth—Major and Mrs. Carmichael-Smyth return to England, 1821 —Thackeray's journey from India to England—he sees Napoleon at St. Helena—stays with his guardian, Peter Moore, at Hadley—and afterwards with Mrs. · Becher at Fareham—goes to school at Southampton—his unhappiness there—sent to Dr. Turner's school at Chiswick—Walpole House and Miss Pinkerton's Academy.

FOUR years after the birth of his son Richmond Thackeray died. His widow remained in India and kept the little boy with her until early in the year 1817, when she had to make the sacrifice exacted from all English parents resident in hot climates and send the boy to England. This was William Makepeace's first parting with his mother, and though he was but five years old, not the novelty of the voyage, nor the company of his cousin and playmate, Richmond Shakespear, obliterated the memory of the last good-bye : so deep an impression did it make upon him, that more than two score years after he could still conjure up the moment of his departure.

In one of the stories by the present writer, a man is described tottering "up the steps of the ghaut," having just parted with his child, whom he is despatching to England from India. I wrote this,

13

remembering in long, long distant days, such a
ghaut, or river-stair, at Calcutta ; and a day when,
down those steps, to a boat which was in waiting,
came two children, whose mothers remained on the
shore.   One of these ladies was never to see her boy
more. [1]

The lad carried with him some dim impressions
of the East, of a few people and some places. "My
native Gunga I remember quite well, and the sense of
it as being quite friendly and beautiful," he told
Whitwell Elwin ; [2] but the Anglo-Indians who figure
prominently in some of his novels were, of course,
the outcome of his subsequent acquaintance with
his many relations and friends, civilian and military,
who had passed the greater portion of their lives in
building up the British Empire in that vast southern
peninsula.   Thackeray met them and their kind at the
Oriental Club in Hanover Square, and made no secret
that he drew upon them for some of his characters. " I
see where you got your Colonel Newcome," said Mr.
Fremantle Carmichael to the novelist one day. " To
be sure you would," was the reply, "only I had to
Angelicise the old boys a little." [3]

The principal memory Thackeray brought away from
his birthplace was that of his beautiful, kindly mother,
whose influence remained with him through life.   His
pride of birth and love of romance may have come to
him, through his grandmother, Amelia Richmond
Webb, from the Constables of Richmond and Lords of

---

[1] *On Letts's Diary.*   The "story by the present writer" is " Philip "
(chap. xxviii), the lady who died was Mrs. Shakespear.

[2] Rev. Whitwell Elwin : " Thackeray's Boyhood" (*Monthly Review*,
June, 1904, p. 162).

[3] A. F. Baillie : *The Oriental Club in Hanover Square.*

Burton, although the latter quality was also inherent in his uncle, Francis Thackeray, who delighted the family circle with improvised fairy tales ; his hatred of shams and snobbishness doubtless came to him direct from his distant paternal ancestors of the yeoman stock of Hampsthwaite ; and perhaps the later generations of the Thackerays, men who lived by their brain, built roads and administered justice in a distant land, and fought and died for their country, supplied the stronger fibres of his nature. From his father, it has been suggested, he may have inherited a love for luxury, as well as a taste for art and letters ; from his mother he learnt that reverence for womanhood and the incalculable value of love which was a distinguishing trait of his life and inspired many of the finest passages in his works, perhaps reaching its highest expression in the scene that closes with the death of Helen Pendennis. These principles that he drank in at his mother's knee, when he came to man's estate he was, indeed, never weary of preaching.

> Canst thou, O friendly reader, count upon the fidelity of an artless heart or two, and reckon among the blessings which Heaven hath bestowed upon thee the love of faithful women ? Purify thine own heart, and try to make it worthy of theirs. All the prizes of life are nothing compared to that one. All the rewards of ambition, wealth, pleasure, only vanity and disappointment grasped at greedily and fought for fiercely, and over and over again found worthless by the weary winners.

Thackeray loved his mother and was as proud of her as ever she was of him, and his only complaint was that she would always endeavour to make his friends realise that her son was "the divinest creature in the world." She was, her eldest grand-daughter has told us, a woman of "strong feeling, somewhat imperious, with a passionate love for little children, and with extraordinary sympathy and enthusiasm for anyone in trouble,"[1] and, according to Herman Merivale, who knew her in her later years, she was one of the handsomest old ladies in the world, with great dark eyebrows and beautiful white hair.[2] Thackeray, aged six, wrote little notes to his "dear Mama" in India, and, aged seven, begged her to return to England with Major Henry Carmichael-Smyth, of the Royal (Bengal) Engineers, whom she had recently married. Three years later, in 1821, she came, to his great joy. "He had a perfect memory of me," Mrs. Carmichael-Smyth said, delighted to find him sturdy and tall for his age. "He could not speak, but kissed me again and again." Thackeray's relations with his mother were always intimate, and the only difference that ever arose between them was on religion, Mrs. Carmichael-Smyth belonging to the evangelical section of the Church.

While at Charterhouse Thackeray wrote to her regularly; and from Cambridge and during his continental rambles he never failed to send long letters, usually illustrated with amusing sketches. He named his eldest daughter Anne after her, and when Major Carmichael-Smyth died, his house became her home. She outlived her famous son by a year, and was buried on Christmas Eve 1864, the first anniversary of his death.

[1] Lady Ritchie : *Chapters from Some Memoirs*, p. 15.
[2] Merivale and Marzials : *Thackeray*, p. 39.

Thackeray has placed on record some of his earliest memories, dating so far back as his voyage from India.

When I first saw England, she was in mourning for the young Princess Charlotte, the hope of the Empire.   I came from India as a child, and our ship touched at an island (St. Helena) on the way home, where my black servant took me a long walk over rocks and hills until we reached a garden, where we saw a man walking.   "That is he," cried the black man : "that is Bonaparte ! He eats three sheep every day, and all the children he can lay hands on." There were people in the British dominions besides that poor Calcutta serving-man, with an equal horror of the Corsican ogre.   With the same childish attendant, I remember peeping through the colonnade at Carlton House, and seeing the abode of the great Prince Regent.   I can yet see the Guards pacing before the gates of the Palace.   The palace ! What palace?   The palace exists no more than the palace of Nebuchadnezzar.   It is but a name now.[1]

From the above passage it is possible approximately to fix the date of the little boy's arrival in England : Princess Charlotte died on November 6, 1817.   He was taken at once to his guardian and great-uncle, Peter Moore, the husband of Sarah Richmond Webb (Amelia's sister), Lord of the Manor of Hadley, where there was an Anglo-Indian colony connected with the Thackerays.   William Makepeace the first had settled there, and, after the death of her husband, Mrs. Harris established herself in her brother's neighbourhood, while subsequently another Thackeray became rector of the parish.   Moore, however, was the great man there. In a few years he had made an ample fortune in India and at the age of thirty returned to England, where he

[1] *The Four Georges—George the Third.*

threw himself into the political arena, sided with Burke
and Sheridan against Warren Hastings, was returned
as member of Parliament for Tewkesbury in 1796, and
in 1803, after a contest that cost him £25,000, was
elected at Coventry, which constituency he represented
through six parliaments.   He became known as a most
adroit manager of private bills; but unfortunately he
was careless as to the financial stability of the com-
panies to which he gave the support of his name, and,
when in 1825 there was a general collapse of the
properties with which he was associated, he had to fly
to Dieppe to escape arrest.   He was, however, an
honest man; gave up nearly all his property to the
creditors of the various ventures; and died, "a broken
exile," at Abbeville, on May 5, 1828, aged seventy-five.
Moore was kind to his ward, whose impressions of him
were tender; and doubtless the sudden transformation
of the wealthy and influential Member of Parliament
into the unhappy bankrupt old man, occurring at an
age when a lad is susceptible, supplied some touches
to the narrative of the last days of Colonel Newcome,
and provided the future novelist's first acquaintance
with

> the old old tale
> Of Folly, Fortune, Glory, Ruin.

When Thackeray was not at Hadley he stayed at
Fareham in Hampshire in the care of his mother's
grandmother and aunt—"Aunt Becher," Lady Ritchie
says she called the latter, "but her other name I do
believe was Miss Martha Honeyman."   The contrast
between the splendour of the Hadley mansion and the
simplicity of the house in the Fareham High Street

must have impressed itself on the observant lad, who
began early in life to store up a mass of material
which he was subsequently to turn to such excellent
use ; but he was as happy in one place as the other,
and of the humbler home in the small Cranford-like
town he has left a pretty picture.

She was eighty years of age then. A most lovely
and picturesque old lady, with a long tortoiseshell
cane, with a little puff, or *tour*, of snow-white (or
was it powdered?) hair under her cap, with the
prettiest little black velvet slippers and high heels
you ever saw. She had a grandson, a lieutenant in
the navy ; son of her son, a captain in the navy ;
grandson of her husband, a captain in the navy. She
lived for scores and scores of years in a dear little old
Hampshire town inhabited by the wives, widows,
daughters of navy captains, admirals, lieutenants.[1]

The lad had little to complain of until his education
began, when his lot was unfortunate. He was sent first
to a small school at Southampton.

We Indian children [i.e. Richmond Shakespear
and himself] were consigned to a school of which our
deluded parents had heard a favourable report, but
which was governed by a horrible little tyrant, who
made our young lives so miserable that I remember
kneeling by my little bed of a night, and saying,
" Pray God, I may dream of my mother. "[2]

How he hated the place, and how miserable he was
there, he never forgot to the end of his days, and more
than once towards the end of his life he wrote of it.

That first night at school—hard bed, hard words,
strange boys bullying, and laughing, and jarring
you with their hateful merriment—as for the first
night at a strange school, we most of us remember
what *that* is. And the first is not the *worst*, my boys,

[1] *On a Peal of Bells.*   [2] *On Letts's Diary.*

there's the rub.[1] . . . What a dreadful place that private school was; cold, chilblains, bad dinners, not enough victuals, and caning awful![2]

He was soon taken from this place and sent to a school at Chiswick, kept by a Dr. Turner, a distant relative. From there at the instigation of his aunt, Mrs. Ritchie, who lived close by, he might write to his mother that he was happy because "there are so many good boys to play with"; but, as a matter of fact, so miserable was the sensitive little man that he made an attempt to run away, and, in later days, when driving to Richmond, would point to that end of Chiswick Lane which abuts on the wide road to Hammersmith where, frightened, he turned back, fortunately to arrive at the house without his absence being noted. The school occupied the historic Walpole House, on Chiswick Mall, and figured subsequently as Miss Pinkerton's Academy in "Vanity Fair." An illustration at the end of the first chapter of that novel shows the fine iron gates of the Academy, and, just outside, a coach, with Sambo of the bandy legs hanging on behind, taking away Becky Sharp and Amelia Sedley, and, while little Laura Martin (who was just in roundhand) is weeping because her dear Amelia is leaving, Miss Sharp, her pale face thrust out of the carriage window, is throwing back the copy of Johnson's Dixonary which good-hearted Miss Jemima has just given her. "So much for the Dixonary," she exclaimed. "Thank God, I'm out of Chiswick." Doubtless, when in 1821 little William Makepeace left Dr. Turner's, his feeling was much the same.

[1] *On Two Children in Black.*   [2] *On Being Found Out.*

WALPOLE HOUSE, CHISWICK MALL

CHAPTER III

THE CHARTERHOUSE (1822–1828)

Thackeray goes to the Charterhouse, 1822—Dr. John Russell—Dr. Russell portrayed in " Pendennis "—Thackeray unhappy at the Charterhouse—at the Rev. Edward Penny's house in Wilderness Row —becomes a day-boy and lives at Mrs. Boyes's—his studies—his schoolfellows—his love of reading, and especially of novel-reading— first attempts to write—his earliest verses—his passion for carica- ture—description of him as a schoolboy—his nose broken in a fight —he creates " Grey Friars "—visits his old school—Thackeray the great apostle of " tipping "—the Poor Brethren of the Charterhouse —a prototype of Colonel Newcome—Thackeray's description of Grey Friars in " The Newcomes."

AFTER four years' preliminary training Thack- eray, at the age of ten, was sent in 1822 to Charterhouse School. It was an unpro- pitious time for a small boy to enter that great seminary, for just then the head master, Dr. John Russell,[1] was introducing the " Madras " or " Bell " system, under which a school, to a great extent, teaches itself, the lower forms being taught by *præpositi*—boys of a form just below the Sixth (or, as Russell called it, the First), which bore the name of the *Emeriti*. It was found possible under this system to run the school with only seven assistant-masters, and the saving effected by the reduction of the teaching staff was so consider-

[1] John Russell (1787–1863), head master of Charterhouse 1811–1832 ; then Rector of St. Botolph's, Bishopsgate, until his death.

able that the Governors materially reduced the fees, which resulted in a rush of parents anxious to obtain for their sons the advantages of a first-class school at small expense. Far more boys were taken than could be comfortably accommodated, and the class-rooms and the boarding-houses kept by masters were over-crowded.

Russell, whom Thackeray nicknamed "Rude Boreas" and compared to a hungry lion, was not noted for suaveness of manner, and at his first interview with the new boy did not make a favourable impression. "Take that boy and his box to the matron," he thundered in his big brassy voice to the school janitor, as hough sentencing a culprit for execution, "and make my compliments to the junior master and tell him the boy knows nothing and will just do for the lowest form." This was not a pleasant introduction to public-school life for a timid lad of tender years, but there was worse to come, for Russell would address lengthy and vigorous rebukes to any boy who blundered—a habit which subsequently Thackeray, who had suffered from it, satirised most delightfully.

Pendennis, sir, your idleness is incorrigible, and your stupidity beyond example. You are a disgrace to your school, and to your family, and I have no doubt will prove so in after-life to your country. If that vice, sir, which is described to us as the root of all evil, be really what moralists have represented (and I have no doubt of the correctness of their opinion), for what a prodigious quantity of future crime and wickedness are you, unhappy boy, laying the seed! Miserable trifler! A boy who construes δε *and* instead of δε *but* at sixteen years of age is guilty not merely of folly, and ignorance, and dul-

WILLIAM MAKEPEACE THACKERAY
From a bust by J. Devile, circa 1822

ness inconceivable, but of crime, of deadly crime, of filial ingratitude, which I tremble to contemplate. A boy, sir, who does not learn his Greek play cheats the parent who spends money for his education. A boy who cheats his parent is not very far from robbing or forging upon his neighbour. A man who forges on his neighbour pays the penalty of his crime on the gallows. And it is not such a one that I pity (for he will be deservedly cut off), but his maddened and heart-broken parents, who are driven to a premature grave by his crimes, or, if they live, drag on a wretched and dishonoured old age. Go on, sir, and I warn you that the very next mistake that you make shall subject you to the punishment of the rod.[1]

At first terrified by these admonitions, Thackeray after a while, like the rest of the school, came to bear them more calmly; but before he arrived at that happy state, when thus addressed before his class, he was miserable: shy and retiring, his nature was outraged by such verbal castigations; and when Russell employed the weapon of ridicule, he had hard work to hold back his tears.

Do not laugh at him writhing, and cause all the other boys to laugh. Remember your own young days at school, my friend—the tingling cheeks, burning ears, bursting heart, and passion of desperate tears, with which you looked up, after having performed some blunder, whilst the doctor held you up to public scorn before the class, and cracked his great clumsy jokes upon you, helpless, and a prisoner! Better the block itself, and the lictors, with their fasces of birch-twigs, than the maddening torture of those jokes![2]

[1] *Pendennis*, chap. ii.
[2] *Thorns in the Cushion.*

It must not, however, be thought that Thackeray was systematically ill-treated, for the Doctor, whose bark was much worse than his bite, though unsympathetic, pompous, and stern, was just according to his lights : none the less the lad, especially during his first years at the Charterhouse, was far from happy, and, indeed, the school at that time was a rough training-ground. Who, looking back, cannot remember in his school-days instances of injustice caused by a master's carelessness or ignorance, and recall the deep sense of injury aroused by what in reality was the most trifling incident? That Thackeray never forgot these early troubles is clear from many passages in his works and from the fact that, in one of the last years of his life, he gladly commissioned Mr. Frederick Gale to write for the *Cornhill Magazine* an article on "The Wrongs of My Boyhood,"[1] showing how unjust masters were and how they misunderstood boys.

When Thackeray first went to Charterhouse he was placed in the care of the Rev. Edward Penny, whose house in Wilderness Row, Clerkenwell Road (from which a tunnel ran into the school grounds), still stands, and now boasts a tablet bearing in rudely cut letters the inscription :

WILLIAM MAKEPEACE
THACKERAY
lived here
1822–1824

There he was wretched, and certainly little consideration was shown by this assistant master for the delicately nurtured lads in his custody :

[1] Vol. III, pp. 95-103.

THE REV. EDWARD PENNY'S HOUSE, WILDERNESS ROW, CLERKENWELL
Where Thackeray lived when he was first at the Charterhouse

We were fifty boys in our boarding-house, and
had to wash in a leaden trough, under a cistern, with
lumps of fat, yellow soap floating about in the ice
and water.

Thackeray left Penny's to become a day-boy, when
he stayed with Mrs. Boyes, who lived in Charterhouse
Square, and took in lads belonging to Charterhouse
and Merchant Taylors. Here he was less discontented,
though it seems that the lady was of a hasty temper.
To the last, however, Charterhouse was uncongenial
to Thackeray, and even when he was seventeen years
old, and second monitor in Day-boys, he found cause
for bitter complaint.

If the boy found the master devoid of sympathy,
there can be no doubt the master had reason to consider the boy a not very satisfactory pupil. Placed
originally in the Tenth Form, in 1823 he was in the
Seventh, in the next year in the Sixth, and in 1825 in
the Third;[1] while the Blue Book of May 1826 shows
him in the Second, and that of the following May in
the First Form. He seems to have jumped the *Emeriti*,
the qualification for which was an intimate acquaintance with Horace. His rapid rise, however, may be

---

[1] Among his schoolfellows in 1825 were Edmund Lushington, captain
of the school; Francis Edgworth and Charles Freshwater, monitors;
G. S. Venables, Richard Venables, John Murray, and Martin Tupper,
in the First Form; Ralph Bernal (afterwards Bernal-Osborne), Paken-
ham Edgworth, Francis Beaumont, and John Stewart Horner in the
Second; in the Third, besides Thackeray himself, James Reynolds
Young; and in the Fourth, Henry George Liddell. Henry Ray Freshwater was in the Seventh; Richmond Shakespear and Alfred Gatty in
the Eighth; and in the Twelfth, just entering the school, John Leech
and Alfred Montgomery. Other contemporaries were George Shakespear, George Lock, Robert Curzon, J. F. Boyes, Eubank, Carne,
Stoddart, Garden, and Poynter.

attributed rather to the fact that in 1826 and the following year the school ran down in numbers than to his scholastic attainments. Euclid, we are told, was easy to him, though he made little progress in algebra; but, from the pedagogical point of view, his most serious defect was inaptitude for the study of the classics, and doubtless it was the difficulty he experienced in his efforts to write Latin hexameters and construe Greek that aroused Dr. Russell's ire and embittered the lad's stay at Charterhouse.

> I always had my doubts about the classics. When I saw a brute of a schoolmaster, whose mind was as coarse-grained as any ploughboy's in Christendom; whose manners were those of the most insufferable of Heaven's creatures, the English snob trying to turn gentleman; whose lips, when they were not mouthing Greek or grammar, were yelling out the most brutal abuse of poor little cowering gentlemen standing before him: when I saw this kind of man (and the instructors of youth are selected very frequently indeed out of this favoured class) and heard him roar out praises, and pump himself into enthusiasm for, certain Greek poetry,—I say I had my doubts about the genuineness of the article. A man will thump you or call you names because you won't learn—but I could never take to the proffered delicacy; the fingers that offered it were so dirty. Fancy the brutality of a man who began a Greek grammar with, "τύπτω, I thrash!" We were all made to begin it in that way.[1]

After reading this reminiscence it is not surprising to find that all Thackeray's contemporaries are agreed that he had no school industry: Dean Liddell (whom the novelist subsequently accused of having ruined

[1] *Punch in the East*, III.

his chance of scholarship by doing his verses) thought
he was very lazy in school-work;[1] and J. F. Boyes,
another comrade, has put it on record that, " No one in
those early days could have believed that there was
much work in him, or that he would ever rise to the
top of any tree by climbing." [2]   With the exception of
Horace, whom he came to love, Thackeray was never
intimately acquainted with any Latin or Greek author,
and it may be doubted if, after he left Cambridge,
he ever read their works.   His style was moulded,
not upon these ancient writers, but upon the great
English classics of the eighteenth century, and
especially upon Fielding, Steele (for whom and for
Addison he had great regard as old Carthusians),
Goldsmith, and Sterne, while in many passages of
"Esmond" may be discerned a memory of Addison's
stately prose.   "My English would have been much
better," he said, "if I had read Fielding before I was
ten."

Thackeray, in after-life, was under no illusion as to
his lack of distinction at Charterhouse.

I was not a brilliant boy at school—the only
prize I ever remember to have got was in a kind of
lottery in which I was obliged to subscribe with
seventeen other competitors—and of which the prize
was a flogging.   That I won.   But I don't think I
carried off any other.   Possibly from laziness, or if
you please from incapacity, but I certainly was rather
inclined to be on the side of the dunces.[3]

This account of himself at an early age he put into

[1] G. S. Davies : *Thackeray at Charterhouse.*
[2] *A Memorial of Thackeray's Schooldays.*
[3] *Punch in the East*, III.

the mouth of the "Fat Contributor," and, not long after, in the novel of "Pendennis," he gave an excellent description of himself in his schooldays.[1]

Reading was the boy's great solace, and he was never so happy, in these days, whether at school or in the holidays, as when he had a book in his hand : like Arthur Pendennis, he "had a natural taste for every book which did not fall into his school course." Even in later life, when he had too many calls on his time and too much strain on his mind to permit any great indulgence in this direction, he cherished the intention, when he could afford it, to retire into the country, and, ending as he began, to feast upon books. Works of fiction were his great delight.[2] "Novels are sweets : all people with healthy literary appetites love them—almost all women,—and a vast number of clever, hard-headed men," he declared forty years later ; and in his youth he liked "novels without love or talking or any of that nonsense, but containing plenty of fighting, escaping, robbing and rescuing."[3]

As some bells in a church hard by are making a great holiday clanging in the summer afternoon, I am reminded somehow of a July day, a garden, and a great clanging of bells years and years ago, on the very day when George IV was crowned (July 19, 1821). I remember a little boy, lying in that garden, reading his first novel. It was called "The Scottish Chiefs."[4]

[1] *Pendennis*, chap. ii. See the passage beginning, "Arthur Pendennis's schoolfellows at the Grey Friars school state that, as a boy, he . . ."

[2] Whitwell Elwin : *Thackeray's Boyhood.*

[3] *On a Lazy Idle Boy.*

[4] *On a Peal of Bells.*

That was before he went to Charterhouse, but the
taste remained, and many an hour that should have
been devoted to study was occupied by the surrep-
titious reading of works of fiction.

What is that I see? A boy,—a boy in a jacket.
He is at a desk; he has great books before him—
Latin and Greek books and dictionaries. Yes, but
behind the great books, which he pretends to read,
is a little one, with pictures, which he is really reading.
It is—yes, I can read it now—it is "The Heart of
Midlothian," by the author of "Waverley"—or, no, it
is "Life in London, or, The Adventures of Corinthian
Tom, Jeremiah Hawthorn, and their friend Bob
Logic," by Pierce Egan; and it has pictures—oh,
such funny pictures! As he reads there comes
behind the boy a man, a dervish, in a black gown,
like a woman, and a black square cap, and he has
a book in each hand, and he seizes the boy who is
reading the picture-book, and lays his head upon
one of his books, and smacks it with the other.
The boy makes faces, and so that picture dis-
appears.[1]

Those happy hours spent over entrancing fiction he
was never tired of recalling, and in later days even as
he groaned over the lost illusions of the pantomime,
so he sighed over the never-to-be-repeated raptures
derived from those novels of a bygone age that no
longer had the power to charm the more sophisticated
reader of mature age.

Yonder comes a footman with a bundle of novels
from the library. Are they as good as *our* novels?
Oh! how delightful they were! Shades of Valan-
cour, awful ghost of Manfroni, how I shudder at
your appearance! Sweet image of Thaddeus of

[1] *De Juventute.*

Warsaw, how often has this almost infantile hand tried to depict you in a Polish cap and richly embroidered tights! And as for the Corinthian Tom in the light blue pantaloons and Hessians, and Jerry Hawthorn from the country, can all the fashion, can all the splendour of real life which these eyes have subsequently beheld, can all the wit I have heard or read in later times, compare with your fashion, with your brilliancy, with your delightful grace, and sparkling vivacious rattle? . . . (My eyes) are looking backwards, back into forty years off, into a dark room, into a little house hard by on the Common here, in the Bartlemy-tide holidays. The parents have gone to town for two days : the house is all his own, his own and a grim old maid-servant's, and a little boy is seated at night in the lonely drawing-room—poring over " Manfroni, or, The One-handed Monk," so frightened that he scarce dares to turn round.[1]

From intense admiration of books to the desire to write is in many cases but a step, and Thackeray, though not precocious, felt from an early age a call to authorship. From the first he found no difficulty in expressing himself on paper. "I always feel as if I were at home when I am writing," he said, in excuse for his many lengthy letters to his mother ; and later he took the same fond relative into his confidence in the matter of his ambitious longings. "I have not yet drawn out a plan for my stories, but certain germs thereof are yet budding in my mind which I hope by assiduous application will flourish yet and bring forth fruit." How like is that to the maturer Thackeray, who always dreamt of assiduous application and so rarely succeeded in drawing out a plan for his stories !

[1] *Tunbridge Toys.*

Oh, for a half-holiday, and a quiet corner, and one of those books again! Those books and perhaps those eyes with which we read them ; and, it may be, the brains behind the eyes ! It may be the tart was good ; but how fresh the appetite was ! If the gods would give me the desire of my heart, I should be able to write a story which boys would relish for the next few dozen of centuries.[1]

There was nothing remarkable in this wish, which has been indulged in by many thousand lads before and since, but the vast majority have soon outgrown their desire, and become soldiers, merchants, sailors, clerks, shopkeepers, or followers of the score of other professions or trades. What is distinctive is that in this one case the boy realised his youthful ideal.

Though we have it on the authority of Mr. Boyes that in his schooldays Thackeray's idea was the serious and sublime, and that he spoke "in terms of homage to the genius of Keats that he would not have vouchsafed to the whole tribe of humorists," his first efforts as a juvenile author were humorous. Indeed, among his friends he became known by the ease with which he wrote verses and parodies, and his first known effort has been preserved.

VIOLETS	CABBAGES
(LETITIA ELIZABETH LANDON)	(THACKERAY)
Violets ! deep blue violets !	Cabbages ! bright green cabbages !
April's loveliest coronets :	April's loveliest gifts, I guess,
There are no flowers grown in the vale,	There is not a plant in the garden laid,
Kissed by the sun, woo'd by the gale,	Raised by the dung, dug by the spade,

[1]. *De Juventute.*

None with the dew of the twilight
wet,
So sweet as the deep blue violet.

None by the gardener watered, I
ween,
So sweet as the cabbage, the cabbage green.

I do remember how sweet a breath
Came with the azure light of a
wreath,
That hung round the wild harp's
golden chords,
That rang to my dark-eyed lover's
words,
I have seen that dear harp rolled
With gems of the East and bands
of gold,
But it never was sweeter than
when set
With leaves of the dark blue violet.

I do remember how sweet a smell
Came with the cabbage I loved so
well,
Served up with the beef that beautiful looked,
The beef that dark-eyed Ellen
cooked.
I have seen beef served with radish
of horse,
I have seen beef served with lettice
of cos,
But it is far nicer, far nicer, I
guess,
As bubble and squeak, beef and
cabbages.

And when the grave shall open for
me—
I care not how soon that time may
be—
Never a rose shall bloom on my
tomb,
It breathes too much of hope and
bloom ;
But let me have there the meek
regret
Of the bending and deep blue violet.

And when the dinner-bell sounds
for me—
I care not how soon that time may
be—
Carrots shall never be served on
my cloth,
They are far too sweet for a boy of
my broth ;
But let me have there a mighty
mess
Of smoking hot beef and cabbages.

These verses are noteworthy only as showing the
boy's keen eye for the ridiculous and his natural antipathy to mawkish sentimentality ; but they are interesting as the first fruits of the gift that was later to
produce the amusing lampoon on Lytton and to cul-
minate in the admirable "Novels by Eminent Hands."
"Cabbages" was thought very witty by the Carthusians,
who encouraged the author to further efforts, of which

the most amusing was, by Anthony Trollope, "found hanging in the memory of an old friend, the serious nature of whose literary labours would certainly have driven such lines from his mind, had they not at the time caught fast hold of him." [1]

> In the romantic little town of Highbury
> My father kept a circulatin' library ;
> He followed in his youth that man immortal, who
> Conquered the Frenchmen on the plains of Waterloo.
> Mamma was an inhabitant of Drogheda,
> Very good to darn and to embroider.
> In the famous island of Jamaica,
> For thirty years I've been a sugar-baker ;
> And here I sit, the Muses' 'appy vot'ry,
> A cultivatin' every kind of po'try.

This is more suggestive of the maturer Thackeray in frolicsome moments, with his liking for those disgraceful rhymes of which, so far from being ashamed, he was inordinately proud ; and in the easy flow of these doggerel lines a discerning reader may, perhaps, detect the mettle that was to produce the astonishing description of the famous White Squall in the account of the "Journey from Cornhill to Grand Cairo."

If Thackeray found delight in parody, his supreme joy in those days was caricature, and his sketches, if they did not extort praise from the masters, gave him an enviable fame among his fellows.

> O Scottish Chiefs, didn't we weep over you ! O mysteries of Udolpho, didn't I and Briggs Minor draw pictures out of you. . . . Efforts feeble, indeed, but still giving pleasure to ourselves and our friends.

[1] Anthony Trollope : *Thackeray*, p. 32.

"I say, old boy, draw us Vivaldi tortured in the Inquisition," or "Draw us Don Quixote and the windmills," amateurs would say, to boys who had a love of drawing.[1]

As a child he began to draw, and one of his first letters to his mother contained an attempt at a pen-and-ink portrait of Major Carmichael-Smyth, to whom she was then engaged. "His drawings are wonderful," said his proud parent. At the Charterhouse he ornamented the leaves of his class-books with satirical pictures of his masters and schoolfellows, and he embellished with burlesque illustrations his copies of "Don Quixote," "The Castle of Otranto," "Robinson Crusoe," "Joseph Andrews," and many other stories.

A lad who does not place games above everything in the world, and prefers a book to a ball, is looked at askance in all English public schools; and Thackeray cannot have been popular till he showed himself possessed of qualities that compensated, or almost compensated, for these defects. It has already been said that his powers of caricature attracted the respectful admiration of his schoolfellows, which was not lessened when it was found that the volumes over which he pored provided him with tales to narrate in the dormitory. These accomplishments apart, he was very like other boys. Like all lads worth their salt, he was a

---

[1] *De Juventute.* Many of the drawings done at the Charterhouse have been reproduced in "Thackerayana," edited by Joseph Grego (1875). "Vivaldi" was evidently a favourite subject with Thackeray, for there are two sets of sketches, one reproduced by Lady Ritchie in the biographical edition of her father's works (Vol. xiii), the other by the present writer in the *Connoisseur* (January 1904).

THE CHARTERHOUSE

hero-worshipper, and bowed down before the cock of
the school. "I have never seen the man since, but
still think of him as of something awful, gigantic, mysterious " ;[1] he was good-tempered and sociable, full of
fun, and possessed of the redeeming virtue of an in-
ordinate love of "tuck": it was one of the humorous
laments of his later days that confectioners were not
what they were when he was a lad.

They say that claret is better now-a-days, and
cookery much improved since the days of *my*
monarch—of George IV. *Pastry Cookery* is certainly
not so good. I have often eaten half-a-crown's worth
(including, I trust, ginger-beer) at our school pastrycook's, and that is a proof that the pastry must have
been very good, for could I do as much now? I
passed by the pastrycook's shop lately, having occasion to visit my old school. It looked a dingy old
baker's; misfortunes may have come over him—
those penny tarts certainly did *not* look so nice as I
remember them : but he may have grown careless as
he has grown old (I should judge him to be now
about 96 years of age), and his hand may have lost
its cunning.[2]

Thackeray found pleasure in other schoolboy delights, took part in amateur theatricals—the play was
the now long-forgotten "Bombastes Furioso"—and
joined in the debates. "We are going to have a debate
to-morrow night on the expediency of a standing
army," he wrote to his mother in February 1828.
"We have not yet settled the sides we shall take."[3] He
must have been present at the great fight between the

---

[1] *Men's Wives: Mr. and Mrs. Frank Berry*, chap. i.
[2] *De Juventute.*
[3] Merivale and Marzials : *Thackeray*, p. 45.

prototypes of Berry and Biggs, narrated with much
detail in "Mr. and Mrs. Frank Berry," when, after the
hundred-and-second round, the latter could not come up
to time ; and no doubt he witnessed the severe punishment inflicted upon Reginald Cuff by "Dobbin of
Ours," the full particulars of which all may read in
the fifth chapter of "Vanity Fair." He even himself
indulged in a bout—with dire results. George Stovin
Venables, when they were both boarders at Penny's,
goaded him into combat, and unhappily broke his nose.
The nose was reset, and then deliberately rebroken
by a brutal school bully. "I got at last big enough
and strong enough," Thackeray told his friend Boyes,
the son of the lady with whom he lived, "to give the
ruffian the soundest thrashing a boy ever had."[1]

Thackeray once referred to his schooldays as
"years of infernal misery, tyranny, and annoyance,"
but time naturally softened his feelings towards the
Charterhouse, and although he avenged himself on
Dr. Russell by pillorying him as Dr. Birch and Dr.
Swishtail, in the days of his prosperity he regarded
his old seminary without malice, and the "Slaughter
House School, near Smithfield, London," of "Men's
Wives" became the "Grey Friars" of "The Newcomes." Probably Mr. Whibley is right, however, in
asserting that Thackeray did not love the Charterhouse until he had created it for himself,[2] though this,
of course, never occurred to the great man.

To others than Cistercians, Grey Friars is a
dreary place possibly. Nevertheless, the pupils

[1] J. F. Boyes : *A Memorial of Thackeray's Schooldays.*
[2] *William Makepeace Thackeray*, p. 6.

educated there love to revisit it; and the oldest of
us grow young again for an hour or two as we come
back into these scenes of childhood.[1] . . . Men
revisit the old school, though hateful to them, with
ever so much kindness and sentimental affection.
There was the tree, under which the bully licked
you : here the ground where you had to fag out on
holidays and so forth. . . .[2]

Thackeray left the Charterhouse on April 16, 1828,
but he revisited it frequently, and a recollection of the
first time he went there not as a pupil probably inspired a description of a similar event in the lives of
Arthur Pendennis and Harry Foker, who renewed
acquaintance with some of their old comrades there.

The bell for afternoon-school rang as they were
swaggering about the play-ground talking to their
old cronies.   The awful Doctor passed into school
with his grammar in his hand.   Foker slunk away
uneasily at his presence, but Pen went up blushing
and shook the dignitary by the hand.   He laughed
as he thought that well-remembered Latin Grammar
had boxed his ears many a time.[3]

Thackeray must have received a hearty welcome
from the boys there as elsewhere, for he was the great
apostle of tipping, and always filled his pockets before
paying such a visit.   An old Carthusian who once
accompanied him has related how Thackeray tipped
the first lad he met with a sovereign, proceeded to
empty purse and pocket in tips for the other boys, and,
his resources temporarily exhausted, borrowed every
coin his companion had about him, and distributed

---

[1] *The Newcomes*, chap. lxxv.
[2] *On a Joke I once heard from the late Thomas Hood.*
[3] *Pendennis*, chap. xviii.

E

these too, with the result that, not having the cab-fare left, the two "old boys" had to walk home. Thackeray could never see a boy without wanting to tip him, and there can scarcely have been a lad of his acquaintance who did not profit by his good-nature. On Founder's Day at Charterhouse he would single out a name from the gown-boys' list. "Here's the son of dear old So-and-so," he would say. "Let's go and tip him." "He had a particular delight in boys, and an excellent way with them," Dickens has recorded. "I remember his once asking me with fantastic gravity, when he had been to Eton where my eldest boy was, whether I felt as he did in regard of never seeing a boy without want-ing instantly to give him a sovereign."[1] Arguments against tipping met with short shrift from Thackeray.

> Ah, my dear sir! if you have any little friends at school, go and see them, and do the natural thing by them. Don't fancy they are too old—try 'em. And they will remember you, and bless you in future days ; and their gratitude shall accompany your dreary after-life, and they shall meet you kindly when thanks for kindness are scant. Oh, mercy! shall I ever forget the sovereign you gave me, Captain Bob. . . It is all very well, my dear sir, to say that boys contract habits of expecting tips from their parents' friends, that they become avaricious and so forth. Avaricious! fudge! Boys contract habits of tart and toffee-eating which they do not carry into after-life. On the contrary, I wish I *did* like 'em. What rapture of pleasure one could have now for five-shillings, if one could but pick it off the pastrycook's tray! No. If you have any little friends at school, out with your half-crowns, my friend, and impart to those little ones the fleeting joys of their age.[2]

[1] Charles Dickens : *In Memoriam* (*Cornhill Magazine*, July 1864).
[2] *Tunbridge Toys.*

Though Charterhouse figures prominently in several of Thackeray's books, and though he sent to that establishment young Rawdon Crawley, George Osborne and his son, Arthur Pendennis, Philip Ringwood, Colonel Newcome and Clive, Philip Firmin, and many other lads of his creation, Thackeray earned the title of *Carthusianus Carthusianorum*, not for his mention of the school, but for the immortal picture of the Poor Brethren. A thoughtful boy, the magic of the ancient monastery threw its spell over him, and many a time he must have contemplated with awe those venerable gentlemen in the cloak that is a survival of the old monastic garb of the Carthusians patrolling in the spacious quadrangles and beautiful lawns hemmed in by the quaint one-storied buildings, and have pondered on the sight of the few score veterans fallen upon evil days in their humble quiet lodging, a stone's-throw from the noisiest, busiest part of the noisiest, busiest city in the world. The present writer visited the place not long since, and was so fortunate as to be taken in hand by a mere stripling of sixty-one—he did not look a day more than fifty—who mentioned incidentally that he had come here to end his days. He stated this simply. He was making no bid for sympathy. He had lost his wife. He must have lost his money, too, else he would not have been eligible for nomination as a Pensioner in this home for " gentlemen by descent and in poverty." Yet, though this is a pleasant, peaceful retreat in which to wait until one enters the last Home, none the less, when the writer took leave of his newly acquired friend, there was a catching of his breath as he said "Good-bye" to his courteous host.

How many tragedies, how many broken hearts, disappointed loves, shipwrecked careers, may be sheltered there! If ever a man deserved well of his kind and has earned the meed of gentle thoughts after he has gone to another place, that man, surely, is Thomas Sutton, *Fundator Noster*, who provided this retreat where the weary and unfortunate traveller through the maze of life may end his days in peace and comfort.

"I shall put all this in my book," Thackeray exclaimed while at the Charterhouse on Founder's Day, 1854; and early in the following year he asked John (afterwards Canon) Irvine, then at school there, to introduce him to a "Codd" (a colloquial term for a Poor Brother) because "Colonel Newcome is going to be a 'Codd.'" The lad took him to see Captain Light, an old soldier whom blindness and reduced circumstances had compelled to seek the shelter of the Hospital; and who, after the novelist had been to see him, gleefully exclaimed, "I'm going to sit for Colonel Newcome."

Who that has read will not gladly read again the novelist's account of the ancient institution that concludes with the description of the impressive ceremonies of Founder's Day, when the boys and the old black-gowned pensioners take their seats in the lighted chapel where "Founder's Tomb, with its grotesque monsters, heraldries, darkles and shines with the most wonderful shadows and lights."

We oldsters, be we ever so old, become boys again as we look at that familiar old tomb, and think how the seats are altered since we were here, and how the doctor—not the present doctor, the doctor of *our* time—used to sit yonder, and his awful eye used to

frighten us shuddering boys, on whom it lighted; and
how the boy next us *would* kick our shins during
service time, and how the monitor would cane us
afterwards because our shins were kicked.   Yonder
sit forty cherry-cheeked boys, thinking about home
and holidays to-morrow.   Yonder sit some threescore
old gentlemen pensioners of the hospital, listening to
the prayers and the psalms.   You hear them coughing
feebly in the twilight—the old reverend blackgowns.
Is Codd Ajax alive, you wonder?—the Cistercian lads
called these old gentlemen Codds, I know not wherefore—I know not wherefore—but is old Codd Ajax
alive, I wonder? or Codd Soldier? or kind old Codd
Gentleman? or has the grave closed over them?   A
plenty of candles light up this chapel, and this scene
of age and youth, and early memories, and pompous
death.   How solemn the well-remembered prayers
are, here uttered again in the place where in childhood we used to hear them!   How beautiful and
decorous the rite ; how noble the ancient words of the
supplications which the priest utters, and to which
generations of fresh children and troops of bygone
seniors have cried Amen! under those arches.[1]

Who does not remember the pathetic scenes when
"Codd" Newcome took up his residence in that ancient
foundation, those beautiful sad chapters that end with
the death of this *chevalier sans peur et sans reproche:*

At the usual evening hour, the chapel bell began to
toll, and Thomas Newcome's hands outside the bed
feebly beat time.   And just as the last bell struck,
a peculiar sweet smile shone over his face, and he
lifted up his head a little, and quickly said, "Adsum!"
and fell back.   It was the word we used at school,
when names were called ; and lo! he, whose heart
was as that of a little child, had answered to his name,
and stood in the presence of The Master.[2]

[1] *The Newcomes*, chap. lxxxv.   [2] *Ibid.*, chap. lxxx.

CHAPTER IV

LARKBEARE AND CAMBRIDGE (1828-1830)

Thackeray leaves the Charterhouse—stays with his mother and step-
father at Larkbeare, Ottery St. Mary—prepares for Cambridge—
Larkbeare and Ottery St. Mary in "Pendennis"—"Irish Melody"
—Captain Costigan and Miss Fotheringay—at Cambridge—
Thackeray's good intentions—his studies—his amusements—his
views on history—and on Shelley—speech at the Union on Napoleon
—assists in the formation of an Essay Club—contributes to the
Snob—"Timbuctoo"—"Ramsbottom Papers"—his friendships—
Richard Monckton Milnes—Rev. W. H. Brookfield and his wife—
Edward FitzGerald—Alfred Tennyson.

SHORTLY after his return from India Major
Carmichael-Smyth was appointed Governor of
the East India Company's military college at
Addiscombe; but in 1825 he retired from the
service, and settled down as a gentleman-farmer at
Larkbeare, which was situated on the confines of the
parish of Ottery St. Mary, in the valley of the Otter,
about eleven miles from Exeter. There Thackeray
spent his holidays with his mother and stepfather,
travelling by the Exeter coach, arriving in winter
benumbed with cold; and, because he regarded his
school terms as bondage, anticipating the periods of
temporary emancipation with even greater joy than the
majority of his fellows.

If you are paterfamilias, and a worthy kind gentleman, no doubt you have marked down on your

LARKBEARE OTTERY, ST. MARY
Where Thackeray stayed with Major and Mrs. Carmichael-Smyth

register, 17th December (say), "Boys come home."
Ah, how carefully that blessed day is marked in *their*
little calendars! In my time it used to be,—Wednesday, 13th November, "5 weeks from the holidays";
Wednesday, 20th November, "4 *weeks from the holidays*"; until sluggish time sped on, and we came to
WEDNESDAY, 18th DECEMBER. O rapture![1]

Happy were the days spent at Larkbeare, and none
more pleasant than those during which, the Charterhouse
training ended, the young man prepared himself for
Cambridge. From May 1828 until the following February Major Carmichael-Smyth coached him; and
perhaps with some prototype of Pendennis's tutor,
Smirke, Thackeray "galloped through the Iliad and the
Odyssey, the tragic playwrights and the charming,
wicked Aristophanes (whom he vowed to be the greatest
poet of all)," and, doubtless, like the more brilliant
Arthur Pendennis,

he went at such a pace that, though he certainly
galloped through a considerable extent of the ancient
country, he clean forgot it in after-life, and had only
such a vague remembrance of his early classic course
as a man has in the House of Commons, let us say,
who still keeps up two or three quotations; or a reviewer, who, just for decency's sake, hints at a little
Greek.[2]

The months Thackeray spent at Larkbeare made
their contribution to literature, for the neighbourhood
was reproduced in "Pendennis," the most autobiographical of Thackeray's novels. There is in one of the
sketches illustrating "Pendennis" an unmistakable
representation of the clock-tower of the parish church

[1] *On Letts's Diary.*　　　　[2] *Pendennis,* chap. iii.

of Ottery St. Mary, and the local descriptions clearly
identify Clavering St. Mary, Chatteris, and Baymouth,
as Ottery St. Mary, Exeter, and Sidmouth, while
Larkbeare figures as Fairoaks, although with a
novelist's license, Thackeray placed Fairoaks close by
Ottery, whereas Larkbeare was a mile and a half from
the village.

> Looking at the little town from London Road, as it
> runs by the lodge at Fairoaks, and seeing the rapid
> and shiny Brawl (the Otter) winding down from the
> town, and skirting the woods of Clavering Park, and
> the ancient church tower and peaked roofs of the
> house rising up among trees and old walls, behind
> which swells a fair background of sunshiny hills that
> stretch from Clavering westward towards the sea, the
> place looks so cheery and comfortable that many a
> traveller's heart must have yearned towards it from
> the coach-top, and he must have thought that it was
> in such a calm, friendly nook he would like to shelter
> at the end of life's struggle.[1]

Dr. Cornish, the vicar of Ottery St. Mary, who was
friendly with the lad, has remarked that "the characteristics of 'Pendennis' found no counterpart in the
inhabitants of the locality ";[2] but most readers of the
novel are reluctant to accept this statement. It is more
pleasant to think that the Rev. F. Wapshot of Clavering may have had an original in some master of the
old King's School ; and there is Thackeray's authority
for the statement that Dr. Cornish furnished the model
for Dr. Portman ; while the *County Chronicle and
Chatteris Champion*, to which young Arthur Pendennis
sent his verses to be printed in the poets' corner, must

[1] *Pendennis*, chap. ii.
[2] *Short Notes on the Church and Parish of Ottery St. Mary.*

have been the paper published in Exeter under the splendid title of the *Western Luminary*, in which journal they first appeared in print. Unlike Pendennis, whose poems after he met the Fotheringay "were no longer signed NEP by their artful composer, but subscribed EROS," Thackeray's only identified contribution was no love-song, but an unromantic parody of a speech, which Lalor Sheil intended to deliver at Penenden on October 24, 1828, in favour of Roman Catholic Emancipation, but which, owing to the threatening attitude of the mob, he was unable to do : he had, however, sent copies of the prepared address to the newspapers, where they duly appeared the next morning.

IRISH MELODY

(Air : *The Minstrel Boy*)

Mister Shiel into Kent has gone
  On Penenden Heath you'll find him ;
Nor think you that he came alone,
  There's Doctor Doyle behind him.

"Men of Kent," said the little man,
  "If you hate Emancipation,
You're a set of fools."   He then began
  A cut and dry oration.

He strove to speak, but the men of Kent
  Began a grievous shouting ;
When out of the waggon the little man went,
  And put a stop to his spouting.

"What though these heretics heard me not !"
  Quoth he to his friend Canonical,
"My speech is safe in the *Times*, I wot,
  And eke in the *Morning Chronicle*."

The early chapters of "Pendennis" are, indeed, so autobiographical that it is almost legitimate to wonder if the love-affairs therein so graphically described had not some basis in fact, and if Miss Costigan, known professionally as Miss Emily Fotheringay, had not her prototype in some member of the stock company at the old Exeter theatre. It has been suggested that the Fotheringay was a fancy portrait of the actress, Eliza O'Neill, who in 1819 married William Becher, then M.P. for Mallow and afterwards, on William IV's coronation, created a baronet. Dolphin, who by the offer of a London engagement, lured the Fotheringay from Baymouth, was drawn from the well-known theatrical manager, Alfred Bunn, whom Thackeray nearly a score of years before "Pendennis" was written, had caricatured in "Flore et Zéphyr" and lampooned in the *National Standard*. Certainly, Miss Fotheringay's father, the immortal Costigan, existed, though Thackeray did not meet him till years after he had evolved him out of his inner consciousness.

In the novel of "Pendennis," written ten years ago, there is an account of a certain Costigan, whom I had invented (as I suppose authors invent their personages out of scraps, heel-taps, odds and ends of characters). I was smoking in a tavern parlour one night and this Costigan came into the room—alive —the very man :—the most remarkable resemblance of the printed sketches of the man, of the rude drawings in which I had depicted him. He had the same little coat, the same battered hat, cocked on one eye, the same twinkle in that eye. "Sir," said I, knowing him to be an old friend whom I had met in unknown regions, "Sir," I said, "may I offer you a glass of brandy-and-water?" "*Bedad, ye may,*" says he, "*and I'll sing ye a song, tu!*" Of course, he

spoke with an Irish brogue. Of course, he had been
in the army. In ten minutes he pulled out an Army
Agent's account, whereon his name was written. A
few months after we read of him in a police court.[1]

While "Pendennis," as has been said, is frequently
autobiographical, the chapters of that book which treat
of its hero at the University must not be accepted as
a guide to its author's life at Cambridge. Indeed,
Thackeray was very careful to avoid even the suspicion of personalities. Oxbridge is an obvious com-
pound of Oxford and Cambridge, skip is a word
manufactured from the Oxford scout and the Cambridge
gyp, the river is the Camisis, and the descriptions
of the colleges are deliberately confused; none of
Thackeray's friends of that time are introduced, and
the authorities of Trinity are excluded. Nor is there
any resemblance between the careers of Pendennis
and his creator at the University : Pendennis was a
dandy of the first water—Thackeray, it is true, before
going up, did order " a buckish coat of blue-black
with a velvet collar," but there the resemblance ends.
Pendennis hunted, gambled with (and was plundered
by) card-sharpers, entertained lavishly, and spoke with
great success at the Union : Thackeray did none of
these things, except spend money freely ; and only
resembled the other in the enjoyment he derived from
being his own master, the change from the strict
routine of the Charterhouse being a blessed relief.

Every man, however brief or inglorious may
have been his academical career, must remember with
kindness and tenderness the old university com-

[1] *De Finibus.*

rades and days. The young man's life is just beginning : the boy's leading strings are cut, and he has all the novel delights and dignities of freedom. He has no ideas of care yet, or of bad health, or of roguery, or poverty, or to-morrow's disappointment. The play has not been acted so often as to make him tired. Though the after-drink, as we mechanically go on repeating it, is stale and bitter, how pure and brilliant was that first sparkling draught of pleasure !—How the boy rushes at the cup, and with what a wild eagerness he drains it ! [1]

In February 1829 Thackeray left Larkbeare for Cambridge, accompanied by Major Carmichael-Smyth (even as Major Pendennis went with his nephew Arthur), staying *en route* for a few days in London. They put up at Slaughter's Coffee House in St. Martin's Lane, an establishment patronised by William Dobbin and George Osborne, visited the Charterhouse, and went to see Dr. Turner, upon whom his late pupil now looked with a less unfavourable eye, and Mrs. Ritchie, who recommended the young man to the kind offices of her cousin, Dr. Thackeray, the Provost of King's. There were other Thackerays at Cambridge whom the undergraduate came to know; George, a Fellow of King's, and a third, doctor of medicine, who once prescribed for his young relative, and refused to take a fee. " What !" he demanded ; " do you take me for a cannibal ? "

Thackeray, who had been entered at Trinity College, was put into ground-floor rooms in the Great Court, opposite the Master's Lodge, and on the left of the Great Gate, under those once occupied by Newton.

---

[1] *Pendennis*, chap. xiii (first edition)—other editions, chap. xvii.

TRINITY COLLEGE, CAMBRIDGE. *It is interesting to note that Macaulay*

The rooms that Thackeray occupied are on the ground floor to the left of the great gate. It is interesting to note that Macaulay had the rooms on the other side of the door, whilst those of Isaac Newton were over Thackeray's, the top of the tower being used for his instruments

He went up with the intention to become a reading
man, and to judge from a letter he wrote in March to
his mother, no one could have started better.

> Badger and I are going to read Greek Play to-
> gether from eleven until twelve every day. I am
> getting more and more into the way of reading now.
> I go to Fawcett every other morning from eight to
> nine, to Fisher (the Mathematical lecturer) from nine
> to ten, and to Starr (the Classical one) from ten to
> eleven; then with Badger from eleven till twelve;
> twelve to half-past one Euclid or Algebra, and an
> hour in the evening at some one or other of the
> above, or perhaps at some of the collateral reading
> connected with Thucydides or Æschylus. This is
> my plan, which I trust to be able to keep.[1]

Not long afterwards he told his mother he had been
to see "our library," and had borrowed from it five
stout quartos. He was apparently determined to win
the approval of Whewell, his tutor, and Fawcett, his
coach, whom he described as a "most desperate good-
hearted bore."

> I am just beginning to find out the beauties of
> the Greek Play ; I pursue a plan of reading only the
> Greek without uttering a word of English, and thus
> having the language in itself, which I find adds
> to my pleasure in a very extraordinary manner and
> will, if I pursue it, lead me, I hope, to think in
> Greek, and of course will give me more fluency.[2]

It was doubtless the hope of being able to "think in
Greek " that inspired Thackeray with the desire to
compete for a college prize offered for the best essay on
" The Influence of the Homeric Poems on the Religion,

---

[1] Merivale and Marzials : *Thackeray*, p. 69.　　[2] *Ibid.*, p. 67.

F

the Politics, the Literature and Society of Greece";
but even at the outset he harboured a doubt: "it will
require much reading, which I fear I have not the time
to bestow upon it." He soon found he had not the
time to bestow on it. Indeed, as the novelty wore off,
the new broom did not sweep so thoroughly, and the
"plan which I trust to be able to keep" was soon
abandoned in favour of pursuits more congenial. "If
I get a fifth class in the examination I shall be lucky,"
he wrote home in May; but he was put in the fourth
class where, we have it on the authority of Dr. Thompson, "clever non-reading men were put, as in a limbo."

Thackeray threw himself gleefully into the usual
undergraduate amusements, and never allowed his
studies to interfere with supper-parties, where, "though
not talkative, rather observant," he enjoyed the humour
of the hours and would troll "Old King Cole" and
other favourite ditties; nor was he too occupied to play
chess and practise fencing, or (as he was careful to record) fall asleep over John Galt's "Life and Administra-
tion of Cardinal Wolsey." Reading, however, was still
his principal delight, and he now read poetry as well
as the old English novels. History, too, came in for a
share of his attention, and all the days of his life he
advocated the study of that subject. "Read a tremendous lot of history," he advised a young cousin many
years later; though it must be admitted that, referring
to this same subject, he declared to Cordy Jeaffreson:
"There's nothing new, and there's nothing true, and
it don't much signify";[1] but he realised to the full
its value even after he had become acquainted with the

---

[1] J. C. Jeaffreson: *A Book of Recollections*, Vol. I, p. 211.

sad fact that great deeds arise all too often from mean causes.

The dignity of history sadly diminishes as we grow better acquainted with the materials which compose it. In our orthodox history-books the characters move on as a gaudy play-house procession, a glittering pageant of kings and warriors, and stately ladies, majestically appearing and passing away. Only he who sits very near to the stage can discover of what stuff the spectacle is made. The kings are poor creatures, taken from the dregs of the company; the noble knights are dirty dwarfs in tin foil; the fair ladies are painted hags with cracked feathers and soiled trains. One wonders how gas and distance could ever have rendered them so bewitching.[1]

At the University, as at school, Thackeray, by his love of books, was incited to take an active interest in literature. Shelley was then the rage at Cambridge, and Thackeray, like the rest, was attracted by the magic of that great wonderful poetry.

When I come home I will bring with me "The Revolt of Islam" by Percy Bysshe Shelley [he wrote to his mother]. It is (in my opinion) a most wonderful poem—though the story is absurd, and the republican sentiments conveyed in it, if possible, more absurd.[2]

But soon he altered his mind about introducing a revolutionary work into the peaceful household at Larkbeare.

Shelley appears to me to have been a man of very strong and good feelings, all perverted by the absurd

[1] Review of The "Duchess of Marlborough's Private Correspondence" in the *Times*, January 6, 1838.

[2] Merivale and Marzials: *Thackeray*, p. 70.

creed which he was pleased to uphold; a man of
high powers, which his conceit led him to over-rate,
and his religion prompted him to misuse. . . . I
think I said I should bring home Shelley's "Revolt of
Islam," but I have rather altered my opinion, for it is
an odd kind of book, containing poetry which would
induce me to read it through, and sentiments which
might strongly incline one to throw it into the fire.[1]

However, Shelley still retained his fascination over
the young student, and when the scheme was mooted
of a university magazine to be called the *Chimera*,
Thackeray volunteered an essay on the poet, and wrote
it at Paris in the Long Vacation of 1830; but the
bibliographers have not traced the publication either
of the essay or the periodical.   Thackeray also intended
to speak at the Union when Shelley was the subject of
debate, but the speech was not delivered, for the meeting was adjourned, and the orator's courage failed
him in the interval.   The only recorded instance of
Thackeray taking part in a discussion at the Union
was when the character of Napoleon was the theme.

> I have made a fool of myself [he wrote to his
> mother in March 1829]; I have rendered myself a
> public character: I have exposed myself.   I spouted
> at the Union.

Unhappily no one thought it worth while to record
his attitude towards *le petit Caporal*.   What were his
sentiments at that date towards the great filibuster?
Did he show the average Englishman's hatred of the
French?   Was he carried away by the genius of that
great general and legislator? or did he then in

---

[1] Merivale and Marzials: *Thackeray*, p. 70.

feebler tones pipe the tune that later he sang so clearly?

> He captured many thousand guns;
> He wrote "The Great" before his name;
> And, dying, only left his sons
> The recollection of his shame.
>
> Though more than half the world was his,
> He died without a rood his own,
> And borrowed from his enemies
> Six feet of ground to lie upon.
>
> He fought a thousand glorious wars,
> And more than half the world was his;
> And somewhere now, in yonder stars,
> Can tell, mayhap, *what greatness is.*[1]

Who maun to Cupar maun to Cupar, and Thackeray's desire to write found outlets from the first.

We are going to establish an Essay Club [he told his mother on April 29, 1829]. There are as yet but four of us, Browne, Moody, Young, and myself, all Carthusians. We want no more Charterhouse men; if we get ten we shall scarcely have to write three essays a year, so that it will take up but little of our time.[2]

Though no further record of the Essay Club exists, it seems probable that it came into being, and was taken by its members with great seriousness.

Are we the same men now that . . . delivered or heard those essays and speeches so simple, so pompous, so ludicrously solemn; parodied so artlessly from books, and spoken with smug chubby

[1] *The Chronicle of the Drum* (1841).
[2] Merivale and Marzials: *Thackeray*, p. 67.

faces, and such an admirable aping of wisdom and gravity.[1]

Three essays a year did not exhaust Thackeray's vigour, and he was the mainstay of a small literary club that included John Allen, Henry Alford, William Hepworth Thompson, Robert Hindes Groome, and James Reynolds Young of Caius. "I don't know that we ever agreed upon a name," Dr. Thompson has mentioned. "Alford proposed the 'Covey' because we 'made such a noise when we got up'—to speak, that is ; but it was left for further consideration. I think Thackeray's subject was 'Duelling,' on which there was much diversity of opinion."[2]

Thackeray's chief pleasure was derived from his connection with two little university papers, founded by his fellow-student at Trinity, W. G. Lettsom, later Her Majesty's *chargé d'affaires* in Uruguay. Lettsom (who afterwards declined the dedication of "The Book of Snobs") had early in 1829 projected a little weekly paper, which bore the title, *The Snob: A Literary and Scientific Journal NOT Conducted by Members of THE University*. The word "Snob" was here used, not in reference to "one who meanly admires mean things," but to denote a townsman in contra-distinction to a gownsman. "Though your name be Snob," Thackeray wrote to the editor, in the note pre-fixed to "Timbuctoo," "I trust you will not refuse this tiny poem of a gownsman." The *Snob* was doubtless so called because, as its contents were for the most part harmless squibs directed against the University, it

---

[1] *Pendennis*, chap. xix.
[2] Merivale and Marzials : *Thackeray*, p. 72.

was thought to add to the humour by a pretence that
it was written by those unconnected with *Alma Mater;*
while the explanatory "Literary and Scientific Journal"
was also a poor joke—the contents being solely would-
be-amusing pieces in prose and verse.

Thackeray soon became a contributor, and his skit
on "Timbuctoo," the subject of the English poem for the
Chancellor's medal (won by Alfred Tennyson), attracted
some attention.

> A "poem of mine" hath appeared in a weekly
> periodical here published, and called the *Snob.* . . .
> "Timbuctoo" received much laud. I could not help
> finding out that I was very fond of this same praise.
> The men knew not the author, but praised the poem.
> How eagerly I sucked it in !   "All is vanity" ! [1]

> In Africa (a quarter of the world)
> Men's skins are black, their hair is crisp and curled ;
> And somewhere there, unknown to public view,
> A mighty city lies, called Timbuctoo.

Thus the opening.   Then follows a description of the
fauna and flora of Timbuctoo, of a lion-hunt, of the
home-life of the inhabitants and the misery caused by
the introduction of slavery ; the whole concluding with
a prophecy of dire disaster to Europe.

> The day shall come when Albion's self shall feel
> Stern Afric's wrath and writhe 'neath Afric's steel.
> I see her tribes the hill of glory mount,
> And sell their sugars on their own account,
> While round her throne the prostrate nations come,
> Sue for her rice and barter for her rum. [2]

[1] Merivale and Marzials : *Thackeray*, p. 71.
[2] The *Snob*, April 30, 1829.

It was a feeble production ; and indeed there is little amusement to be derived from a perusal of this and other farcical absurdities contributed to the little paper, which, however, served its purpose in amusing its authors.

On Monday night myself and the editor of the *Snob* sat down to write the *Snob* for Thursday. We began at nine and finished at two ; but I was so afflicted with laughter that I came away quite ill. . . . The *Snob* goeth on and prospereth. I have put "Genevieve" into it with a little alteration. Here is a specimen of my wit in the shape of an advertisement therein inserted :—"Sidney Sussex College. Wanted a few Freshmen. Apply at the Butteries, where the smallest contribution will be gratefully received."[1]

The contributions of Thackeray to the *Snob* and its successor, the *Gownsman*, were neither better nor worse than the average undergraduate production ; and it will suffice to make a passing reference to those letters signed "Dorothea Julia Ramsbottom," inept parodies of Theodore Hook's Mrs. Ramsbottom, which are interesting, only because in them may, perhaps, be detected the germ from which, seven years later, sprang the later correspondence of the erudite Mr. Yellowplush.[2]

Though Thackeray left Cambridge in June 1830 without taking a degree, his residence there was of value to him. He read widely if not deeply, and

---

[1] C. P. Johnson : *Early Writings of Thackeray*, p. 7.

[2] Thackeray's contributions to the *Snob* and the *Gownsman* have been collected by the present writer, and printed in "Thackeray's Stray Papers" (1901), and again in Macmillan's edition of Thackeray's Collected Works, Vol. IX, "Burlesques . . . Juvenilia," pp. 389-401.

laid the foundation-stone of his future works : "*Now
is the time to lay in stock*," he said in later days to
a young man at college ; "I wish I had had five
years' reading before I took to our trade ";[1] but the
greatest benefits he derived from his stay at the University were those delightful and enduring friendships
that date from this period.

Perhaps never before or since has a college housed
at the same time so many gifted young men as Trinity
boasted in the days when Thackeray was there.
Amongst them were Alfred Tennyson and his
brothers, Charles and Frederick, whose "Poems by
Two Brothers" had appeared in 1827 ; Joseph Williams
Blakesley, afterwards Dean of Lincoln ; James Sped-
ding, the author of the standard Life and Works of
Bacon ; Arthur Hallam and Thomas Sunderland,
whose promising careers were brought to untimely
ends ; Ralph Bernal, afterwards known as Bernal-
Osborne ; Charles Rann Kennedy and Edward
Horsman ; John Sterling, the subject of Carlyle's
memoir ; Edmund Law Lushington, the famous
Greek scholar, and the husband of the sister of
Tennyson, the epilogue to whose "In Memoriam" is
an epithalamium on the marriage ; John, afterwards
Archdeacon, Allèn ; Henry Alford, who became Dean
of Canterbury ; William Hepworth Thompson, sub-
sequently Master of Trinity ; Richard Chenevix
Trench, one day to be Archbishop of Dublin ; Alex-
ander William Kinglake, the future author of
"Eöthen" and historian of the Crimean War ; John
Mitchell Kemble, Richard Monckton Milnes, afterwards

[1] Hannay : *Short Memoir of Thackeray*, p. 23.

first Baron Houghton ; William Henry Brookfield and
Edward FitzGerald. Most of these men had given
some indication of their talents even at this early date,
and, for that reason, it is somewhat surprising to find
Thackeray in the set, for he had come from the
Charterhouse without any particular reputation, and
nothing he did at the University showed promise of
future greatness or even of considerable ability :
"We did not see in him even the germ of those
literary powers which, under the stern influences of
necessity, he afterwards developed," Dr. Thompson
has admitted ; and no other contemporary has come
forward to controvert the statement. Once Thackeray
obtained the *entrée*, however, his invariable good-
temper and his keen sense of humour made his place
secure. With some of them, as it has been said, he
formed an Essay Club, but with the majority his relations were purely social.

> Now the boy has grown bigger. *He* has got
> a black gown and cap, something like the dervish.
> He is at a table, with ever so many bottles on it, and
> fruit, and tobacco ; and other young dervishes come
> in. They seem as if they were singing. To them
> enters an old moollah, he takes down their names,
> and orders them all to go to bed.[1]

Besides his old schoolfellow Venables, who was at
Jesus, Thackeray at Cambridge contracted friendships
that endured through life with James White, of Pem-
broke College, subsequently Vicar of Loxley and
author of "The Eighteen Christian Centuries," "The
Earl of Gowrie : A Tragedy," and many other works.

[1] *De Juventute.*

O Jimmy, and Johnny, and Willy, friends of my
youth ! . . . how should he who knows you, not
respect you and your calling?   May this pen never
write a pennyworth again, if it ever cast ridicule
upon either ![1]

"Willy" was William Brookfield, of whom something will presently be said, and "Johnny" was John
Allen, who subsequently for a while lived in Great
Coram Street, opposite Thackeray, when FitzGerald
sent him a message : "Give my love to Thackeray
from your upper window across the street."

Very pleasant always were the relations between
Thackeray and Richard Monckton Milnes, and
Thackeray was a frequent visitor at Fryston, "a
house," he said to his host, the elder Monckton
Milnes, paying him a compliment for permission to
smoke everywhere but in Richard's own rooms, "a
house which combines the freedom of the tavern with
the elegancies of the *château*."   On Thackeray's return
from Paris, after the failure of the *National Standard*,
Monckton Milnes was one of the first to be informed
of the ex-newspaper's correspondent's arrival.

> The Young Chevalier is arrived, and to be heard
> of at the Bedford Hotel in Covent Garden, or at the
> Garrick Club, King Street. He accepts breakfasts,—
> and dinners still more willingly.[2]

We may be sure many breakfasts and dinners were
offered and taken.   It was to Monckton Milnes more
than to anyone else that Thackeray went for advice
during the years of weary waiting for success, and

---

[1] *The Book of Snobs,* chap. xi.   *On Clerical Snobs.*
[2] Wemyss Reid : *Life of Lord Houghton,* Vol. I, p. 426.

before leaving England to pay his first visit to America he sent his old friend a note of acknowledgment.

> A word and a God bless you ana yours at parting. I was thinking of our acquaintance the other day, and how it had been marked on your part by constant kindnesses, along which I can trace it. Thank you for them, and let me shake your hand, and say *Vale* and *Salve*.[1]

During the Easter Parliamentary recess of 1863, Thackeray went to Fryston for the last time, and on the following Christmas Eve, Monckton Milnes, now Lord Houghton, received a sheet of notepaper, headed Palace Green, Kensington, upon which no words were written, but which bore a little coloured sketch of a robin-redbreast perched upon the coronet of a baron—Thackeray's unconscious farewell, for, ere this greeting reached the newly created peer, the artist had passed away. Monckton Milnes was much grieved by the news of Thackeray's death, and he was very angry that the authorities did not ask permission to bury the novelist within the precincts of Westminster Abbey. He drew an "Historical Contrast" between this behaviour and the conduct of Dr. Sprat, Bishop of Rochester and Dean of Westminster, on the death of Dryden, who

> "Waited for no suggestive prayer,
> But, ere one day clos'd o'er the scene,
> Craved, as a boon, to lay him there;"

and he paid a tribute to the great humorist of his day in the concluding stanzas:

[1] Wemyss Reid: *Life of Lord Houghton*, Vol. II, p 112.

" O gentle censor of our age !
  Prime master of our ampler tongue !
Whose word of wit and generous page
  Were never wrath, except with wrong,—

Fielding—without the manner's dross,
  Scott—with a spirit's larger room ;—
What Prelate deems thy grave his loss?
  What Halifax erects thy tomb?

But, mayhap, he,—who could so draw
  The hidden great,—the humble wise,
Yielding with them to God's good law,
  Makes the Pantheon where he lies." [1]

When, a little before the end of his life, one of his
daughters asked Thackeray which friends he had loved
the best, he replied, " Why dear old Fitz, of course,
and Brookfield."

Thackeray's intimacy with Brookfield was lifelong,
and when in 1841 Brookfield married (the daughter of
Sir Charles Elton of Clevedon), it was eagerly and
heartily extended to his wife.

A friend I had, and at his side—the story dates from seven
  long year—
One day I found a blushing bride, a tender lady kind and
  dear !
They took me in, they pitied me, they gave me kindly words
  and cheer,
A kinder welcome who shall see than yours, O friend and
  lady dear ? [2]

A volume of Thackeray's letters to the Brookfields
has been published, and from a perusal of it may be

[1] *Cornhill Magazine*, February 1864.
[2] Charles and Frances Brookfield : *Mrs. Brookfield and her Circle.*
Vol. I, p. 113.

seen how delightful were the relations between them. The novelist was never too busy to write to " My dear Vieux" and his wife from town, from the Continent, from New York, long chatty letters, often about trifles, sometimes about grave matters. " I tell you and William most things," he said to Mrs. Brookfield. Their house was always open to him ; their regard for him was carried to his children; and Mrs. Brookfield, on the last day of her life, quoted to Thackeray's surviving daughter a passage from the great novelist's works :

> Try to frequent the company of your betters. In books and life that is the most wholesome society ; learn to admire rightly ; the great pleasure of life is that. Note what the great men admired ; they admired great things ; narrow spirits admire basely and worship meanly.[1]

Thackeray portrayed his old schoolfellow in "Travels in London" as the good-natured curate, Frank Whitestock ; and he introduced some traits of Mrs. Brookfield into the composite character of Amelia Osborne (*née* Sedley).

In their earlier years Thackeray and FitzGerald were regular correspondents, and " Old Fitz," or "Cupid," or " Ned," " Neddibus," " Neddikins," or " Yedward," as his friend called him, was able to fill a volume with the drawings sent him by the other, whose habit it was to illustrate his letters. FitzGerald used to stay with his friend in Great Coram Street (Jorum Street, Thackeray called it) and also in Young Street, and the novelist loved to have him in the house. " He is

---

[1] *English Humorists—Pope.*

a delightful companion; the only drawback is we talk so much of books and poems that neither do much work." The poet's diary contains many entries, and his letters many references, concerning his great literary brother. He tells how, in December 1832, Thackeray came to see him before returning to Devonshire. "He came very opportunely to divert my Blue Devils: notwithstanding, we do not see very much of each other: and he has now so many friends (especially the Bullers) that he has no such wish for my society. He is as full of good humour and kindness as ever."[1] Yet they continued to correspond when Thackeray was abroad, and met frequently after his return, though after 1848 or 1849 they saw less of each other.

"I am going to Spedding's rooms this very evening: and there I believe Thackeray, Venables, etc., are to be," FitzGerald wrote to Frederick Tennyson on April 17, 1850. "I hope not a large assembly, for I get shyer and shyer even of those I know." It is in this letter that he said, "Thackeray is in such a great world that I am afraid of him; he gets tired of me, and we are content to regard each other at a distance."[2] But Thackeray never tired of his old college friend. "I am glad *you* like it," he wrote after hearing of the other's approval of "Vanity Fair"—and the explanation of the subsequent irregular correspondence and the rare meetings may be traced to FitzGerald's increasing love of seclusion. But, despite the latter's complaint, there was no coldness in their hearts. "And so dear old Thackeray is really going to America," FitzGerald

[1] *Letters of Edward FitzGerald*, Vol. I, p. 18.
[2] *Ibid.*, Vol. I, p. 295.

exclaimed, hearing the news. "I must fire him a
letter of farewell." And he wrote to him, and told him
of a provision he had made in his will. "You see,"
he said, "you can owe me no thanks for giving what
I can no longer use when I go down into the pit. . . ."[1]
And Thackeray's reply to his "dearest old friend," just
before he sailed, breathes a deep sense of love.

> I mustn't go away without shaking your hand
> and saying Farewell and God Bless you. If any-
> thing happens to me, you by these presents must
> get ready the Book of Ballads which you like, and
> which I had not time to prepare before embarking
> on this voyage. And I should like my daughters to
> remember that you are the best and oldest friend their
> Father ever had, and that you would act as such:
> as my literary executor and so forth. My books
> would yield a something as copyrights: and should
> anything occur, I have commissioned friends in
> good places to get a Pension for my poor little wife.
> . . . Does not this sound gloomily? Well: who
> knows what Fate is in store: and I feel not at all
> downcast, but very grave and solemn, just at the
> brink of a great voyage. . . . The greatest comfort
> I have in thinking about my dear old boy is that
> recollection of our youth when we loved each other
> as I do now while I write Farewell![2]

FitzGerald, late in 1856, went to town, where he
hoped to catch sight of "old Thackeray, who, Donne
wrote me word, came suddenly on him in Pall Mall
the other day; while all the people suppose 'The
Newcomes' was being indited at Rome or Naples."
"Oddly enough," he wrote to E. B. Cowell on
January 26, 1857, "as I finished the last sentence,

---

[1] *Letters of Edward FitzGerald*, Vol. II, p. 10.
[2] *Ibid.*, Vol. II, p. 9.

Thackeray was announced ; he came in, looking gray, grand, and good-humoured ; and I held up this Letter and told him whom it was written to, and he sends his Love ! He goes lecturing all over England ; has fifty pounds for each lecture ; and says he is ashamed of the fortune he is making. But he deserves it." [1]   A few days after FitzGerald went to hear his friend's discourse on George III. " Very agreeable to me, though I did not think highly of the lecture."

This must have been one of the last meetings, if, indeed, it was not the last meeting, of the two men. But the long interval did not deaden their feelings, and news of his friend's death, in 1863, came as a great shock to FitzGerald. " A great figure has sunk under earth," he said to George Crabbe, son of the poet ; and in a letter, dated January 7, 1864, asking Samuel Laurence for particulars of his two portraits of Thackeray, he wrote : " I am surprised almost to find how much I am thinking of him : so little as I had seen of him for the last ten years ; not once for the last five. I have been told—by you, for one—that he was spoiled. I am glad therefore that I have scarce seen him since he was ' old Thackeray.' I keep reading his ' Newcomes ' of nights, and as it were hear him saying so much in it ; and it seems to me as if he might be coming up my Stairs, and about to come (singing) into my Room, as in old Charlotte Street, etc. thirty years ago." [2]

FitzGerald had throughout followed Thackeray's career with great interest, and, as the many criticisms

[1] *Letters of Edward FitzGerald*, Vol. II., p. 52.
[2] *Ibid.*, Vol. II, p. 171.

G

in his letters testify, read all that his friend wrote.
"As to Thackeray's " (books) "they are terrible ; I really
look at them on the shelf, and am half afraid to touch
them," he wrote in 1875 to Samuel Laurence. "He, you
know, could go deeper into the springs of Common
Action than these Ladies (Miss Austen and George
Eliot); wonderful he is, but not delightful, which one
thirsts for as one gets old and dry."[1] And finally, comparing the literary merits of Disraeli with Thackeray,
he said : " The book (' Lothair ') is like a pleasant
Magic Lantern ; when it is over, I shall forget it, and
shall want to return to what I do not forget, some of
Thackeray's monumental figures of *pauvre et triste
humanité*, as old Napoleon calls it : Humanity in its
Depths, not in its superficial Appearances."[2]

Thackeray and Tennyson formed a mutual admiration
society *à deux*. Thackeray, ill in bed, eagerly devoured
"The Idylls of the King." "Oh! I must write to him
now for this pleasure, this delight, this splendour of
happiness which I have been enjoying," he said in a
note to the poet,[3] who declared that this tribute gave
him "more pleasure than all the journals and monthlies and quarterlies which have come across me ;. not so
much from your being the Great Novelist I hope as
from your being my good old friend or from your
being both of these in one."[4]   When the poet-laureate's
"Grandmother" appeared in *Once a Week*, " I wish
I could have got that poem for my *Cornhill*," said

---

[1] *Letters of Edward FitzGerald*, Vol. III, p. 203.
[2] *Ibid.*, Vol. III, p. 17.
[3] *Life and Works of Alfred Lord Tennyson*, Vol. II, p. 287.
[4] *Ibid.*, Vol. II, p 284.

the editor of the magazine to Locker-Lampson. "I would have paid fifty pounds for it, but I would have given five hundred pounds to be able to write it."[1] And numerous were the affectionate notes exchanged. "You don't know how pleased the girls were at Kensington t'other day to hear you quote their father's little verses," Thackeray wrote in 1859; "and he too I daresay was not disgusted."[2]

[1] F. Locker Lampson : *My Confidences*, p. 298.
[2] *Life and Works of Alfred Lord Tennyson*, Vol. II, p. 286.

CHAPTER V

AM RHEIN (1830-1831)

Thackeray goes abroad — Paris — Coblenz — Godesberg — Cologne — Weimar—Weimar in " Vanity Fair "—his flirtations—Dorothea and her prototype—his opinions of the German writers—Mme. Goethe— "Grand old Goethe."

IN the earlier decades of the nineteenth century it was still customary for a young man of means and fashion, after he came down from the University, to make a more or less extended tour through Europe, usually with a "bear-leader" disguised as a tutor, but sometimes alone, when the Young Hopeful had inspired confidence in his steadiness in the bosoms of those members of his family who were responsible for, or who charged themselves with, his welfare. This latter privilege, so much desired by a lad about to enter the broad arena of the world, was secured by Thackeray, about to go abroad when, at the age of nineteen (1830), he left Cambridge. This presupposes he had then secured a reputation for common sense, which he was presently, to some extent, to belie by allowing himself to be victimised in a commercial transaction and to be swindled at the card-table : he was, however, on the whole sensible enough for one of his years. "Be sure," he said years afterwards, "if thou hast never been a fool, thou wilt

68

never be a wise man." The picture of him at this time
is that of a lad of no great intellectual ability, but with
the agreeable qualities of humour, amiability, and
kindness, a love of books and of the lighter branches
of pictorial art, and a considerable talent for satirical
sketches both with pen and pencil that indicate to us,
who can trace from them the development of his
genius, a power of observation unusually acute for so
young a man. In appearance he was, at this time,
according to Dr. Thompson, a tall, thin, large-eyed,
full and ruddy-faced man, with an eyeglass fixed *en
permanence*.

Thackeray prepared himself for his travels by taking
in London a course of German lessons with a Herr
Troppenheger—who, doubtless, would be mightily
surprised to find his name remembered after the lapse
of the greater part of a century—and in July 1830 he
set out for the Continent. Paying a visit to Paris *en
route*, he arrived at the end of the month at Coblenz,
and then, going north, he came to Godesberg, a town
that occupied an important place in his "Legend of the
Rhine." There he stayed a month, noting the habits
and customs of the inhabitants and endeavouring to
supplement his slight knowledge of the German
language, so that, as Mark Twain has happily put
it, he should not make twins out of a dative dog.
Eventually he went on a Rhine steamer to Cologne,
as afterwards did Mr. Titmarsh in company with the
Kickleburys, whose travels he recorded and illustrated.
Thackeray refused to describe the river, which, he
declared, was as familiar to English people as the
Thames, and subsequently Titmarsh made a similar

resolve, to which he adhered until he saw a sunrise at Cologne, when he gave voice to an exquisite prose poem.

> Deutz lay opposite [he wrote in a white heat of enthusiasm], and over Deutz the dusky sky was reddened. The hills were veiled in the mist and the grey. The grey river flowed underneath us; the steamers were roosting along the quays, a light keeping watch in the cabins here and there, and its reflections quivering in the water. As I look, the sky-line towards the east grows redder and redder. A long troop of grey horsemen winds down the river road, and passes over the bridge of boats. You might take them for ghosts, those grey horsemen, so shadowy do they look; but you hear the trample of their hoofs as they pass over the planks. Every minute the dawn twinkles up into the twilight; and over Deutz the heaven blushes brighter. The quays begin to fill with men : the carts begin to creak and rattle, and wake the sleeping echoes. Ding, ding, ding, the steamers' bells begin to ring : the people on board to stir and wake : the lights may be extinguished, and take their turn of sleep : the active boats shake themselves, and push out into the river : the great bridge opens, and gives them passage : the church bells of the city begin to clink : the cavalry trumpets blow from the opposite bank : the sailor is at the wheel, the porter at his burthen, the soldier at his musket, and the priest at his prayers. . . . And lo ! in a flash of crimson splendour, with blazing scarlet clouds running before his chariot, and heralding his majestic approach, God's sun rises upon the world, and all nature wakens and brightens.[1]

Leisurely, by way of Elberfeld, Cassel, and the quaint old town of Gotha, Thackeray proceeded on his travels, and at last on September 29 arrived at Weimar. He

[1] *The Kickleburys on the Rhine.*

came for a few days, but stayed months in the "little, comfortable, Grand-Ducal town of Pumpernickel," as in "Vanity Fair" he styled it—that little town where Sir Pitt Crawley was for years an *attaché* and where that "infernal slyboots of a Tapeworm," the Secretary of the English Legation, showed himself susceptible to the charms of Amelia Osborne.

Pumpernickel [he wrote with satire tempered by the memory of happy days spent there] stands in the midst of a happy valley, through which sparkles— to mingle with the Rhine somewhere, but I have not the map at hand to say exactly at what point— the fertilising stream of the Pump. In some places the river is big enough to support a ferry-boat, in others to turn a mill; in Pumpernickel itself, the last Transparency but three, the great and renowned Victor Aurelius XIV. built a magnificent bridge, on which his own statue rises, surrounded by water-nymphs and emblems of victory, peace, and plenty; he has his foot on the neck of a prostrate Turk— history says he engaged and ran a Janissary through the body at the relief of Vienna by Sobieski,—but quite undisturbed by the agonies of the prostrate Mahometan, who writhes at his feet in the most ghastly manner—the Prince smiles blandly, and points with his truncheon in the direction of the Aurelius Platz, where he began to erect a new palace that would have been the wonder of the age, had the great-souled Prince but funds to complete it. But the completion of Monplaisir (*Monblaisir*, the honest German folks call it) was stopped for lack of ready money, and it and its park and garden are now in rather a faded condition, and not more than ten times big enough to accommodate the Court of the reigning Sovereign.[1]

Thackeray arrived at Pumpernickel-Weimar at the

[1] *Vanity Fair*, chap. lxiii.

beginning of September, and found already settled there Norman MacLeod, the son of the Moderator of the General Assembly and himself afterwards a celebrated Scotch divine, and his old Trinity friend, Lettsom, who was attached to the *suite* of the English Minister; and with these two young men learnt German from Dr. Weissenborn,—"thou wert my instructor, good old Weissenborn."[1] It was a quiet, homely little place in the early thirties, the capital of the Grand-Duchy of Saxe-Weimar-Eisenach, and Thackeray was so happy that he wrote home in December to say he would much appreciate an appointment as *attaché* that would enable him to stay there. "I have never seen a society more simple, charitable, courteous, gentlemanlike, than that of the dear little Saxon city where the good Schiller and the great Goethe lived and lie buried," Thackeray declared in after-life, when he had pictured it in those chapters of "Vanity Fair" where "der Herr Graf von Sedley nebst Begleitung" goes *Am Rhein*.

Everybody in Pumpernickel knew everybody. No sooner was a foreigner seen there, than the Minister for Foreign Affairs, or some other great or small officer of state, went round to the Erbprinz (Hotel), and found out the name of the new arrivals. . . . It was very agreeable for the English. There were shooting-parties and battues; there was a plenty of balls and entertainments at the hospitable Court; the society was generally good; the theatre excellent, and the living cheap.[2]

Thackeray declared that Weimar was the most hospitable place in the world so far as tea-parties were

---

[1] *De Finibus.*   [2] *Vanity Fair*, chap. lxii.

concerned, though he lamented that he was never in one where invitations to dinner were so scarce; but this was the only fault he could find with the place, and if the entertainment was frugal, the welcome at least was hearty. He went to Court, where in his turn he was commanded to balls and assemblies, and —there at least—to dinners. Most of the Germans had a uniform, and, as is their custom, always appeared in it, and those English who had one, diplomatic or military, wore it when paying their respects to the Grand-Duke and Duchess; while those who had not invented one—the *Hof-Marschall* of that day, M. de Spiegel, the father of two beautiful girls, though a martinet so far as the dress of his countrymen was concerned, good-naturedly overlooking the contrivances of the young strangers. Thackeray subsequently told George Henry Lewes that he remembered inventing "gorgeous clothing" for these gatherings; but he wrote home at the time to complain that he was somewhat troubled by his makeshift dress of black coat, waistcoat, and trousers cut down to breeches, in which he declared he looked half a footman, half a Methodist parson; and he begged his stepfather to secure for him a cornetcy in Sir John Kennaway's Yeomanry, so that he might attire himself suitably. The only other grievance he had in these happy days was that all the young ladies at Weimar spoke English so well that he had no opportunity to speak German.

Thackeray visited the theatre which was open two or three nights a week, and where the entire society of Weimar assembled, "a large family party." Besides the regular company, famous artists came from other parts of Germany, and he saw Ludwig Devrient, "the Kean of Germany" he called him, as Shylock, Hamlet, Falstaff, and the hero in "Die Räuber," and the beautiful Schröder in "Fidelio." He drew on his memory of this time when he sent Jos and Emmy and Dobbin to a *Gast-rolle* night at the Royal Grand-Ducal Pumpernickelisch *Hof-Theater*, when they saw "Die Schlacht bei Vittoria," in which the melody of "God save the King" is performed.

> There may have been a score of Englishmen in the house, but at the burst of the beloved and well-known music, every one of them . . . stood bolt upright in their places, and proclaimed themselves to be members of the dear old British nation.[1]

Thackeray had at this time some love-affairs, but, though they lingered in his memory, to judge from the tone in which he wrote about them, they were not very serious.

> Now I see one of the young men alone [he remembered thirty years later]. He is walking in a street— a dark street—presently a light comes to a window. There is the shadow of a lady who passes. He stands there till the light goes out. Now he is in a room scribbling on a piece of paper, and kissing a miniature every now and then. They seem to be lines each pretty much of a length. I can read *heart, smart, dart; Mary, fairy; Cupid, stupid; true, you;* and never mind what more. Bah! it is bosh.[2]

He thoroughly enjoyed his flirtations, humorously bemoaning his fate when a girl was allured from him by the fascinations of a young Guardsman with mag-

---

[1] *Vanity Fair*, chap. lxii.   [2] *De Juventute.*

nificent waistcoats and ten thousand a year, by translating, for the benefit of his mother, poor Thekla's
song in "Wallenstein,"

> This world is empty,
> This heart is dead,
> Its hopes and its ashes
> For ever are fled.[1]

Some ten years after Thackeray was at Weimar Mr.
George Savage Fitz-Boodle, who had followed in his
creator's footsteps, narrated his amorous "Confessions," and it is impossible to put aside the suspicion
that these were based upon the author's experiences.
Whether Thackeray, like Fitz-Boodle, met at Bonn
some "pretty Mina, daughter of Moses Löwe, banker,"
who, after this lapse of time, shall say? and of greedy
Ottilia no trace is to be found in the records of
Thackeray's travels. At Weimar, however, he met
the original of Dorothea, daughter of Herr Ober-Hof-
und-Bau-Inspektor von Speck, and for her sweet sake
learned to dance. He made his first appearance as a
dancer at a Court Ball, secured Dorothea as partner,
and danced with her on a highly waxed floor, danced
—and fell !

> O Dorothea ! you can't forgive me, you oughtn't
> to forgive me ; but I love you madly still.   My next
> flame was Ottilia.[2]

After twenty-three years, Thackeray revisited "the
cheery social little German place," and pointed out to
his daughters the house where his heroine had lived.

---

[1] Merivale and Marzials : *Thackeray*, p. 82.
[2] *Confessions of Fitz-Boodle—Dorothea.*

Dorothea had gone from Weimar, but her erstwhile lover was to see her soon after at Venice, at breakfast in a hotel, a fat woman whom he did not recognise until she was pointed out to him as Madame von Z——. "My poor father turned away, saying in a low, overwhelmed voice, '*That* Amalia! *That* cannot be Amalia!'" his eldest daughter has recorded. "I could not understand his silence, his discomposure. 'Aren't you going to speak to her? Oh, please do go and speak to her,' we both cried. 'Do make sure if it is Amalia.' But he shook his head. 'I can't,' he said; 'I had rather not.' Amalia, meanwhile, having finished her egg, rose deliberately, laid down her napkin, and walked away, followed by her little boy."[1]

In a town that owed its world-wide fame to the welcome it had extended to Goethe, Schiller, Herder, and Wieland, it was natural that the talk in the *salons* should be of letters and art. Thackeray, to whom such conversation was congenial, and who indeed did not require any spur to take him to the company of books, read diligently the standard German authors. Herwegh, now no more than a name even to most of his countrymen, the young Englishman studied, and later wrote of in characteristic Titmarshian manner:

> It is absurd to place this young man forward as a master. His poetry is a convulsion, not an effort of strength; he does not sing, but he roars; his dislike amounts to fury; and we must confess that it seems to us, in many instances, that his hatred and heroism are quite factitious, and that his enthusiasm has a very calculating look with it. Fury, to be effective either in life or in print, should surely only

[1] Lady Ritchie: *Chapters from some Memoirs*, pp. 117-18.

be occasional. People become quite indifferent to wrath which is roaring and exploding all day : as gunners go to sleep upon batteries. Think of the prodigious number of appeals to arms that our young poet has made in the course of these pages ; what a waving and clatter of flashing thoughts ; what a loading and firing of double-barrelled words ; and, when the smoke rolls off, nobody killed ![1]

Uhland, Körner, Von Chamisso, and others he read, and afterwards translated ; and, of course, Goethe and Schiller. "Faust" did not arouse in him great enthusiasm. "Of course I am delighted, but not to that degree I expected" ; but for Schiller's plays and poems he had unbounded admiration.

I have been reading Shakespeare in German [he wrote to his mother]. If I could ever do the same for Schiller in English, I should be proud of having conferred a benefit on my country. . . . I do believe him to be, after Shakespeare, "the poet."[2]

The greatest figure in Weimar in Thackeray's day was Goethe, who had now retired from the direction of the theatre, and, indeed, also from general society, though his daughter-in-law, Madame de Goethe, who kept house for him, occasionally gave a tea-party to some of his favourites. Thackeray and his English friends were frequent visitors, and went there night

---

[1] *George Herwegh's Poems* (*Foreign Quarterly Review*, April 1843). The translations from Herwegh were printed by the present writer in an article on "Thackeray's Ballads" in the *Fortnightly Review* (November 1907) and *Littell's Living Age* (December 1907). The article was first reprinted by Mr. R. S. Garnett in "The New Sketch Book," and it has since been included by Professor Saintsbury in the Oxford edition of Thackeray's Works.

[2] Merivale and Marzials : *Thackeray*, p. 81.

after night to talk, or listen to music, bringing with them books or magazines from England for Goethe to glance at. The Maclise caricatures in the early numbers of *Fraser's Magazine* interested the old man, until there appeared the terrible sketch of cadaverous Sam Rogers, of which Maginn wrote: "*De mortuis nil nisi bonum!* There is Sam Rogers, a mortal likeness, painted to the very death!" "They would make me look like that," Goethe exclaimed angrily. Thackeray, who could fancy "nothing more serene, majestic, and healthy - looking than the grand old Goethe," remembered this remark, and on his return gave Maclise a sketch of the old man, which the artist copied and inserted in the issue of the magazine for March 1832.[1] In those days already it was Thackeray's great pleasure to draw caricatures for children, and when he revisited Weimar more than a score of years after, he was touched to find that several of his sketches had been preserved.

Thackeray naturally regarded as the most memorable day of his stay at Weimar his first meeting with "grand old Goethe," who received him kindly, and, it pleased the young man to think, "in rather a more *distingué* manner than he has used the other Englishmen here." He never forgot the day (October 20) when he met this redoubtable personage—it was like a visit to a dentist, he told Monckton Milnes; and

---

[1] The copy in *Fraser's Magazine* proved a total failure and involuntary caricature, resembling, as was said at the time, a wretched old-clothes-man carrying behind his back a hat which he seemed to have stolen."—Carlyle: *Miscellanies*, Vol. III, p. 93.
The original by Maclise is in the South Kensington Museum.

after a quarter of a century he could recall every detail
of the brief interview.

Of course I remember very well the perturbation
of spirit with which, as a lad of nineteen, I received
the long-expected intimation that the Herr Geheim-
rath would see me on such a morning.   This notable
audience took place in a little ante-chamber of his
private apartments, covered all round with antique
casts and bas-reliefs.   He was habited in a long
gray or drab redingote, with a white neckcloth and
a red ribbon in his button-hole.   He kept his hands
behind his back, just as in Rauch's statuette.   His
complexion was very bright, clear, and rosy.   His
eyes extraordinarily dark, piercing and brilliant.[1]   I
felt quite afraid before them, and recollect comparing
them to the eyes of the hero of a certain romance
called "Melmoth the Wanderer," which used to alarm
us boys thirty years ago ; eyes of an individual who
had made a bargain with a Certain Person, and at
an extreme old age retain these eyes in all their
awful splendour.   I fancy Goethe must have been
still more handsome as an old man than even in
the days of his youth.   His voice was very rich
and sweet.   He asked me questions about myself,
which I answered as best I could.   I recollect I
was at first astonished, and then somewhat relieved,
when I found he spoke French with not a good
accent.

Vidi tantum.   I saw him but three times.   Once
walking in the garden of his house in the Frauen-
platz ; once going to step into his chariot on a sun-
shiny day, wearing a cap and a cloak with a red
collar.   He was caressing at the time a beautiful
little golden-haired granddaughter, over whose sweet
face the earth has long since closed too.[2]

[1] "This must have been the effect of the position in which he sat
with regard to the light.   Goethe's eyes were dark brown, but not very
dark."—G. H. Lewes.
[2] Letter to G. H. Lewes, April 28, 1855, quoted in the *Life of Goethe.*

An artist might well take for the subject of a picture this meeting of the two men, the one on the brink of the grave, renowned as poet and dramatist beyond all living men, the other on the threshold of life, not even dreaming of the greatness he was to attain. The author of "Faust" doubtless did not discern any germ of the still unveiled talent of his young visitor, who all his life was to treasure the memory of this interview. "My only recommendation," Thackeray once humorously remarked, "is that I have seen Napoleon and Goethe, and am the owner of Schiller's sword."

CHAPTER VI

THE TEMPLE (1831-1832)

Thackeray a student of Middle Temple—chambers at No. 2, Brick Court—writes of the literary associations of the Temple—the Temple in his writings—loses money at cards—the original of Deuceace—chambers at No. 10, Crown Office Row—work and play—dislike of the law—goes to Cornwall to canvass for Charles Buller—comes of age—abandons the Law—goes to Paris—loses his patrimony.

O N his return in the autumn of 1831 from his *Wanderjahr*, Thackeray entered himself as a student of Middle Temple, and though he did not look forward with pleasure to practising at the Bar, yet, as he wrote to his mother, he regarded the profession as "a noble and tangible object, an honourable calling, and, I trust in God, a certain fame." He read with the special pleader and conveyancer, Taprell, at No. 1, Hare Court; and he lived at No. 2, Brick Court, and was pleased to recall the fact that his chambers had once been occupied by Oliver Goldsmith.

I have been many a time in the chambers in the Temple which were his, and passed up the staircase, which Johnson, and Burke, and Reynolds trod to see their friend, their poet, their kind Goldsmith—the stair on which the poor women sat, weeping bitterly when they heard that the greatest and most generous of all men was dead within the black oak door.[1]

[1] *The English Humourists—Sterne and Goldsmith.*

81

H

Indeed, the literary associations of the Temple were an abiding interest to the great humorist of the nineteenth century, and he was never weary of conjuring up the ghosts of his predecessors.

> The man of letters can't but love the place which has been inhabited by so many of his brethren, or peopled by their creations as real to us at this day as the authors whose children they were—and Sir Roger de Coverley walking in the Temple Garden, and discoursing with Mr. Spectator about the beauties in hoops and patches who are sauntering over the grass, is just as lively a figure to me as is old Samuel Johnson, rolling through the fog with the Scotch gentleman at his heels on their way to Dr. Goldsmith's chambers in Brick Court; or Harry Fielding, with inked ruffles and a wet towel round his head, dashing off articles at midnight for the *Covent Garden Journal*, while the printer's boy is asleep in the passage.[1]

Subsequently Thackeray shared chambers at No. 10, Crown Office Row, with Tom Taylor, a fact duly commemorated by Taylor at the time the building in which they were situated was pulled down.

> " They were fusty, they were musty, they were grimy, dull, and dim,
> The paint scaled off the panelling, the stairs were all untrim ;
> The flooring creaked, the windows gaped, the door-posts stood awry,
> The wind whipt round the corner with a wild and wailing cry.
> In a dingier set of chambers, no man need wish to stow,
> Than those, old friend, wherein we denned, in Ten, Crown Office Row.

[1] *Pendennis*, chap. xxx, first edition.

No. 2, BRICK COURT, THE TEMPLE

" But *we* were young, if *they* were old, we never cared a pin,
So the windows kept the rain out, and let the sunshine in;
Our stout hearts mocked the crazy roofs, our hopes be-
    decked the wall,
We were happy, we were hearty, strong to meet what
    might befall ;
Will sunnier hours be ever ours, than those which used to
    go,
Gay to the end, my dear old friend, in Ten, Crown Office
    Row.

.   .   .   .

" Good-bye, old rooms, where we chummed years, without
    a single fight.
Far statelier sets of chambers will arise upon your site ;
More airy bedrooms, wider panes, our followers will see ;
And wealthier, wiser tenants, the Bench may find than
    we ;—
But lighter hearts or truer, I'll defy the Inn to show,
Than yours, old friend, and his who penned this Ten,
    Crown Office Row." [1]

As Thackeray, when he turned his hand to fiction,
sent his characters to school at the Charterhouse, so
he utilised his knowledge of the Inns of Court to
people them with fictitious personages.   In Lamb
Court were the chambers of Pendennis and Warrington ; and, near by, Mrs. Bolton and her daughter,
pretty little Fanny, kept the gate of Shepherd's Inn,
where Captain Costigan and Mr. Bows, when they
follow "the Fotheringay" to London, pitched their
tent next door to the chambers of Colonel Altamont
and Captain the Chevalier Edward Strong.   In Pump

[1] " *Ten, Crown Office Row.*"   *A Templar's Tribute* (*Punch*, February
26, 1859).

Court resided the Hon. Algernon Percy Deuceace, who with his scoundrelly neighbour, Richard Blewitt, plucked that most unsuspicious simpleton, Dawkins, who lived on the same stair. The story of these Captains Rook and Mr. Pigeon was based upon an incident in Thackeray's life, for in the Temple social robbers eased him of a good round sum.

When I first came to London, as innocent as Monsieur Gil Blas, I also fell in with some pretty acquaintances, found my way into several taverns, and delivered my purse to more than one gallant gentleman of the road. Ogres, nowadays, need not be giants at all. . . . They go about in society, slim, small, quietly dressed, and showing no especially great appetite. In my own young days there used to be play ogres—men who would devour a young fellow in one sitting, and leave him without a bit of flesh on his bones. They were quiet, gentlemen-like-looking people. They got the young man into their cave. Champagne, *pâté de foie gras*, and numberless good things were handed about; and then, having eaten, the young man was devoured in his turn.[1]

At a sitting Thackeray lost fifteen hundred pounds, probably in the manner described in the "Yellowplush Papers." Many years later he pointed out to Sir Theodore Martin a broken-down but gentlemanly looking man as the original of Deuceace. "I have not seen him since the day he drove me down in his cabriolet to my brokers in the city where I sold out my patrimony and handed it over to him." "Poor devil!" he added, with pity in his voice, "Poor devil! my money doesn't seem to have thriven with him."[2]

[1] *Ogres.*   [2] Merivale and Marzials: *Thackeray*, p. 236.

I go pretty regularly to my pleader's and sit with him until half-past five, and sometimes six; then I come home and read and dine till about nine or past, when I am glad enough to go out for an hour and look at the world.[1]

So he wrote to his stepfather in December 1831; but most of his letters refer to his pleasures rather than to his studies, and his diary is full of entries of visits to the theatre! of happy days spent with "Old Fitz," at this time in lodgings in Charlotte Street, with Tennyson, or with Charles Buller, discussing the poets, upon whose merits they could not agree; of pleasant strolls in Kensington Gardens; of luncheons with friends, and dinners with an uncle, the Rev. Francis Thackeray, to whom subsequently he made appreciative reference,

O saintly Francis, lying at rest under the turf.[2]

The young man was attached to his relative, and his only grievance against him was that this hospitable gentleman would ask him to dinner too often—three times a week—when his nephew would rather have spent an evening in more youthful society.

The picture of those idle apprentices, Pendennis and " Bluebeard " Warrington, was probably drawn from the creator's life at this time, for doubtless, like them, Thackeray and Taylor,

After reading pretty hard of a morning, and, I fear, not law merely, but politics and general history and literature, which were as necessary for the advancement and instruction of a young man as mere

[1] Merivale and Marzials : *Thackeray*, p. 87.
[2] *The Book of Snobs*, chap. xi : *On Clerical Snobs*.

dry law, after applying with tolerable assiduity to letters, to reviews, to elemental books of law, and, above all, to the newspaper, until the hour of dinner was drawing nigh . . . would sally out upon the town with great spirits and appetite, and bent upon enjoying a merry night as they had passed a pleasant forenoon.[1]

Certainly Thackeray did not work hard, and his distaste for the legal profession increased. "The sun won't shine into Taprell's chambers, and the high stools don't blossom and bring forth buds," he lamented in the spring ; and in more serious mood he stated his real objection to the study of the law.

This lawyer's preparatory education is certainly one of the most cold-blooded, prejudiced pieces of invention that ever a man was slave to. . . . A fellow should properly do and think of nothing else than LAW.[2]

Thackeray never overcame this dislike, and expressed it again years after in unmistakable terms.

On the other side of the third landing, where Pen and Warrington live, till long after midnight, sits Mr. Paley, who took the highest honours, and who is a fellow of his college, who will sit and read and note cases until two o'clock in the morning ; who will rise at seven and be at the pleader's chambers as soon as they are open, where he will work until an hour before dinner-time ; who will come home from Hall and read and note cases again until dawn next day, when perhaps Mr. Arthur Pendennis and his friend Mr. Warrington are returning from some of their wild expeditions. How differently employed Mr. Paley has been ! He has not been throwing himself

---

[1] *Pendennis*, chap. xxxi ; (first edition).
[2] Merivale and Marzials : *Thackeray*, p. 88.

away : he has only been bringing a great intellect laboriously down to the comprehension of a mean subject, and in his fierce grasp of that, resolutely excluding from his mind all higher thoughts, all better things, all the wisdom of philosophers and historians, all the thoughts of poets ; all wit, fancy, reflection, art, love, truth altogether—so that he may master that enormous Legend of the law, which he proposes to gain his livelihood by expounding. Warrington and Paley had been competitors for university honours in former days, and had run each other hard ; and everybody said now that the former was wasting his time and energies, whilst all people praised Paley for his industry. There may be doubts, however, as to which was using his time best. The one could afford time to think, and the other never could. The one could have sympathies and do kindnesses ; and the other must needs be always selfish. He could not cultivate a friendship or do a charity, or admire a work of genius, or kindle at the sight of beauty or the sound of a sweet song—he had no time, and no eyes for anything but his law-books. All was dark outside his reading-lamp. Love, and Nature, and Art (which is the expression of our praise and sense of the beautiful world of God) were shut out from him. And as he turned off his lonely lamp at night, he never thought but that he had spent the day profitably, and went to sleep alike thankless and remorseless. But he shuddered when he met his old companion Warrington on the stairs, and shunned him as one that was doomed to perdition.[1]

Delighted with any good excuse to absent himself from Taprell's, in June 1832 Thackeray eagerly accepted an invitation to go to Liskeard to canvass for Charles Buller, who was intimately associated with the school of philosophic radicalism, the friend of Grote,

---

[1] *Pendennis*, chap. xxx (first edition).

Sir William Molesworth, and John Stuart Mill, and the pupil of Carlyle, who described him as a "fine honest fellow, the greatest radical I have ever met." Buller had sat since 1830 for West Looe, Cornwall, but, this pocket borough having been disfranchised by the Reform Bill of 1832, he now offered himself as a candidate for the neighbouring constituency; and being unfortunately too ill to leave London, the task of visiting the voters devolved upon his brother Arthur and Thackeray. The young men worked hard, canvassing farmers, dining with attorneys, writing addresses, and attending meetings; and were rewarded by the return to the first reformed Parliament of Buller, who retained his seat until his death in 1848. "Isn't it an awful sudden summons," Thackeray wrote to Mrs. Brookfield, on hearing the sad news of his friend's demise. "There go wit, fame, friendship, ambition, high repute."[1]

> Who knows the inscrutable design?
> Blessed be He who took and gave!
> Why should your mother, Charles, not mine,
> Be weeping at her darling's grave?[2]

In Thackeray's diary there is an entry on July 18, 1832, "Here is the day for which I have been panting so long"—on this day he attained his majority and came into possession of a patrimony that has been variously estimated at ten thousand pounds and at five hundred a year.

I have been lying awake this morning meditating on the wise and proper manner I shall employ my

[1] *A Collection of Letters of W. M. Thackeray*, p. 34.
[2] *Dr. Birch and His Young Friends—The End of the Play.*

fortune in when I come of age, which, if I live so long, will take place in three weeks. First, I do not intend to quit my little chambers in the Temple, then I will take a regular monthly income, which I will never exceed. . . .[1]

So, from Cornwall, Thackeray of the good intentions had written to his mother, but these, like the earlier and equally praiseworthy resolves of boyhood, were soon abandoned, for no sooner had he attained his majority than he gave up even the pretence of reading for the bar, and went to Paris, where he spent some months learning to speak the language fluently, reading—and criticising in his letters home what he read—drawing, too, and, as a matter of course, frequenting the theatres.

Thackeray returned to England in December (1832), and stayed for a while at Larkbeare before going out into the world to earn a living. A fortune yielding an income of five hundred a year is insufficient to support in idleness a young man with expensive tastes, and from the first Thackeray had realised he must work, not indeed for the necessaries, but for the luxuries of life. So long as it was for the luxuries only, however, he was unwilling to enter any profession uncongenial to him, and he had therefore abandoned his studies for the Bar; but within a short time after he inherited his patrimony he lost most of it; some, as it has been said, went at the card-table, and some to settle his debts at Cambridge, where he had spent a good deal of money; and more in an Indian bank failure, that doubtless suggested the Bundelkund Bank incident

---

[1] Merivale and Marzials: *Thackeray*, p. 92.

in "The Newcomes." An income, therefore, had now
to be earned, and, since there were fewer professions
then, and Thackeray would not read for the Bar, was
too old for the army or navy, and was not attracted to
the Church or to the study of medicine, there was nothing else open to him but the pursuit of art or letters.
Great results spring from small causes, and it is extremely probable that English literature of the Victorian
era would be the poorer by Thackeray's works, if that
author had not lost his money in the days of his
youth.

CHAPTER VII

IN SEARCH OF A PROFESSION (1832-1836)

Thackeray's thoughts incline to literature—becomes proprietor and editor of the *National Standard*—his contributions to that paper— the failure of the *National Standard*—the story of the venture related in " Lovel the Widower "—he proposes to become a painter— and studies ι Paris—his fondness for Paris—his first visit to that city—Eyre F ans Crowe and his family—Thackeray on the artist's life at Paris– abandons painting for caricature—" Flore et Zéphyr " —offers to illustrate " Pickwick "—" Mr. Pickwick's lucky escape "— illustrates mc st of his own books—aware of the limitations of his art —Charlotte Brontë on Thackeray as illustrator.

THACKERAY'S thoughts had often turned to literature, probably in the first instance thereto directed by the appreciation shown by his college friends of his contributions to the *Snob* and *Gownsman*. At Weimar, besides conceiving the project to present Schiller in an English dress, the idea occurred to him to write for the English public a book on Germany and German literature, but he made not the slightest attempt to carry out these schemes ; nor did his acquaintance with " Father Prout," Maginn, and Giffard of the *Standard*, inspire him to literary labours. Yet all the time the notion was at the back of his mind, and it needed but an incentive to set him to work. Charles Buller wrote for the magazines : why not he ! he said to his mother. The idea was fascinating, but he was doubtful of his powers. How can a man know his capabilities, he asked very naturally and very wisely; but in the same breath compared his untried talent with that of Bulwer, then at the zenith of his popularity. Even so did Benjamin Disraeli, seated in the Strangers' Gallery of the House of Commons, mentally measure swords with the parliamentary giants, and decide he could beat them all with their own weapons. But while Disraeli was from the start ambitious, Thackeray, until he lost his money, was well contented with things as they were.

When the necessity for work arose, the opportunity soon presented itself. By a happy accident Major Carmichael-Smyth, perhaps in the hope to retrieve the losses he had suffered in the bank failure, and probably also with the desire to give his stepson an opening in journalism, became connected with the *National Standard and Journal of Literature, Science, Music, Theatricals, and the Fine Arts*. This grandiloquently named weekly was founded by F. W. N. ("Alphabet") Bayley,[1] under whose direction the first number appeared on January 5, 1833. Exactly when Thackeray began to contribute to this periodical cannot be stated, but his first identified contribution appeared in the issue for May 4, about which time he purchased the paper.

> Under the heading of the *National Standard* of ours [so began Thackeray's Address in the nineteenth number, dated May 11], there originally appeared the following : "Edited by F. W. N. Bayley, Esq.,

[1] Frederick William Naylor Bayley (1808-1853), the author of many verses, novels, etc., contributed to the *Times* and the *Morning Post ;* and edited the *National Omnibus* and the *Illustrated London News*.

. . . assisted by the most eminent Literary Men of the Day." Now we have *changé tout cela ;* no, not exactly *tout* cela, for we still retain the assistance of a host of literary talent, but Frederick William Naylor Bayley has gone. We have got free of the Old Bailey, and changed the Governor.

The difficulty under which Thackeray laboured all his life was to begin to work, but, this trouble overcome, the rest was easy. So it was at this early date that, once started as editor of the *National Standard*, his activity was remarkable : he contributed to his paper, verses, drawings, stories, dramatic criticisms, translations of poems and prose, editorial leaders, reviews. Not a tithe of the matter has been identified, and it would be waste of time to attempt to trace his writings : what is known may be taken as representative of the rest, and among this there is nothing remarkable, the verses are crude doggerel, the stories indifferent, and much of the criticism jejune. The last two lines on some verses on Louis Philippe, his earliest identified contribution, are, however, noticeable for the introduction of the word "snob" used in the sense that had not then become common :

> He stands in Paris as you see him before ye,
> Little more than a snob—There's an end of the story ; [1]

and the review of Robert Montgomery's " Woman of Life " has a characteristic Titmarshian conclusion, for, after the quotation of fourteen lines from the poem, is a note :

These are nice verses. On examination we find that the compositor, by some queer blunder, had printed

[1] *National Standard,* May 4, 1833.

them backwards ; but, as it does not seem to spoil the sense, we shall not give him the trouble of setting them up again. They are just as good one way as the other ; and, indeed, the same might be said of the whole book.[1]

Evidently Mr. Charles James Yellowplush saw this review, and was amused by it, for he emulated its humour when he was writing a scathing criticism of "Sawedwadgeorgearllyttnbulwig's" play, "The Sea-Captain," and alluded to a sentence in that long-forgotten play that he had tried "every way, backards, forards, and in all sorts of trancepositions," and found "all which are as sensible as the fust passidge."

Not long after Thackeray entered into possession of the *National Standard* appeared an announcement :— "The Proprietors of the *National Standard* feel that it would be unbecoming to commence their second Volume without acknowledging the extraordinary success which has rewarded their labour ; success they believe unprecedented, the sale of their Journal having quadrupled in the short space of two months. They can now announce, with confidence, that the *National Standard* is established."[2] It is to be hoped, for the sake of the editor's reputation for veracity, that this emanated from the fertile brain of the manager of the paper, for, as a matter of fact, the *National Standard* was at this time established on no firm basis : its circulation was miserable, and advertisements, without which no weekly can be financially successful, were conspicuous by their absence from its columns. Thackeray laboured manfully and spent his days in "writing,

---

[1] *National Standard,* June 15, 1833.   [2] *Ibid.*, July 6, 1833.

puffing, and other delightful employments" for the paper, going frequently to Paris, thinking it looked well for the paper to have its special correspondent in that city. In September he told his mother that the *National Standard* was "growing in repute," but, sad to relate, in a month the circulation rose only by twenty, and then, though he still believed the periodical would eventually provide him with an occupation and an income, he began to realise that the proprietor would probably be ruined before the venture paid its way. A last despairing effort to achieve success was made with the first number of the new year, when the price was raised from twopence to threepence, and the name altered to the scarcely less cumbrous title, the *National Standard and Literary Representative;* but in spite of the confident tone of the "Address" in which these changes were announced, the issue for February 1, 1834, was the last appearance of the *National Standard, etc.*

There can be little doubt that Thackeray was thinking of his connection with the *National Standard* when he wrote of the unfortunate newspaper venture in "Lovel the Widower."

They are welcome . . . to make merry at my charges in respect of a certain bargain which I made on coming to London, and in which, had I been Moses Primrose purchasing green spectacles, I could scarcely have been more taken in. *My* Jenkinson was an old college acquaintance, whom I was idiot enough to believe a respectable man : the fellow had a very smooth tongue, and sleek sanctified exterior. He was rather a popular preacher, and used to cry a good deal in the pulpit. He and a queer wine-merchant and bill-discounter, Sherrick by name, had

1

somehow got possession of that neat little literary paper, the *Museum*, which, perhaps, you remember; and this eligible literary property my friend Honeyman, with his wheedling tongue, induced me to purchase. . . . I daresay I gave myself airs as the editor of that confounded *Museum*, and proposed to educate the public taste, to diffuse morality and sound literature throughout the nation, and to pocket a liberal salary in return for my services. I daresay I printed my own sonnets, my own tragedy, my own verses. . . . I daresay I wrote satirical articles in which I piqued myself on the fineness of my wit, and criticisms, got up for the nonce out of encyclopædias and biographical dictionaries; so that I would be actually astonished at my own knowledge. I daresay I made a gaby of myself to the world : pray, my good friend, hast thou never done likewise? If thou hast never been a fool, be sure thou wilt never be a wise man.[1]

After the failure of the *National Standard* it became necessary for Thackeray in all seriousness to devote himself to a profession by the exercise of which he might support himself. Even when he was writing a considerable portion of each number of the *National Standard*, his thoughts were wandering from journalism to art, and writing from Paris in July 1833 he informed his mother that he was "thinking very seriously of turning artist."

He had to come to London in August in connection with his paper, but two months later he returned to Paris, and settled there with the intention to study art. At first he stayed at the house of his maternal grandmother, but, after a time, he found irksome the restrictions of liberty imposed upon a guest, and rented

[1] Chap. i.

"a little den" in the Rue des Beaux Arts. There
Planché saw him, and, describing him as "a slim
young man, rather taciturn" and "not displaying any
particular love or talent for literature," noted that
drawing appeared to be his favourite amusement, and
that he covered any scrap of paper lying about with the
most spirited sketches and amusing caricatures.

Thackeray, who in London had probably attended
Heatherley's school of painting—the "original" of
Gandish's Academy in "The Newcomes"—at Paris
studied under Brine, the well-known impressionist
painter, and subsequently under Gros, who committed
suicide in June 1835.

Thackeray loved Paris all the days of his life, and
those who hold the mistaken belief that he hated France
and the French have no more reason to do so than
those who assert that he hated the Irish; if he presented some Frenchmen as despicable characters, so he
poured contempt on many Englishmen, and one of the
most exquisite creations of his fancy is that most
charming lady, Madame de Florac. Thackeray went
for the first time to Paris in the Easter vacation of 1830
to join Edward FitzGerald.

I remember as a boy at the Ship at Dover (*imper-
ante Carolo Decimo*), when, my place to London
being paid, I had but 12s. left after a certain little
Paris expedition (about which my benighted parents
never knew anything), ordering for dinner a whiting,
a beef-steak, and a glass of negus, and the bill was,
dinner 7s., a glass of negus 2s., waiter 6d., and only
half-a-crown left, as I was a sinner, for the guard and
coachman on the way to London! And I *was* a
sinner. I had gone without leave. What a long,
dreary, guilty four hours' journey it was, from Paris

to Calais, I remember! . . . I met my college tutor
only yesterday. We were travelling, and stopped
at the same hotel. He had the very next room to
mine. After he had gone into his apartment, having
shaken me quite kindly by the hand, I felt inclined
to knock at his door and say, " Dr. Bentley, I beg
your pardon, but do you remember, when I was
going down at the Easter vacation in 1830, you asked
me where I was going to spend my vacation? And
I said, with my friend Slingsby in Huntingdonshire.
Well, sir, I grieve to have to confess that I told you
a fib. I had got £20 and was going for a lark to
Paris, where my friend Edwards was staying." . . .
The doctor will read it, for I did not wake him up.[1]

This was the first of many visits, and much of his
leisure was spent in this city. He had a great number
of friends there, and nowhere was he more welcome
than at the house of Eyre Evans Crowe, the Paris
correspondent of the *Morning Chronicle*, the father of
Amy, Joseph and Eyre. "Once a week, on Saturdays, my mother received guests in the evening," Sir
Joseph Crowe has recorded. "My mother at her
evenings made everyone bright by playing Irish jigs
or Scotch reels, or accompanying on the piano
Methfessel's students' songs and choruses, the supreme
enjoyment being a song from Thackeray."[2] When
the Crowes settled in 1844 at Hampstead, Thackeray
frequently rode there on his short cob. "Once in our
drawing-room he was apt to forget the hours," says
Sir Joseph; "would stop to partake of an early
dinner, though bound to join a later festivity of the
same kind elsewhere; and I recollect him now, as if
it were yesterday, wiping his brow after trying vainly

---

[1] *Dessein's.*   [2] Sir Joseph Crowe: *Reminiscences.*

to help the leg of a tough fowl, and saying he was
'heaving a thigh.'"[1]   Thackeray, always grateful for
kindness shown him in the days of his struggles, was
delighted later to be able to render the younger members of the family many good services.   When, in
1854, Charles Mackay asked him to go to the seat of
war to furnish sketches for letters for the *Illustrated
News*, he induced the editor to send Joseph in his
place; and on the young man's return, inaugurated
a scheme for him to make money by lecturing on the
war.   Eyre was for a while the great man's secretary,
and went with him on one of the lecture tours to
America.   "Six months tumbling about the world
will do you no harm," he said to the young artist;
and later he took Amy into his house, where she was
treated as a daughter, until she married her host's
cousin, now Colonel Sir Edward Thackeray, v.c., and
went to India, where she succumbed to the tropical
climate.

When Thackeray had been studying art for some
months at Paris, he reported himself satisfied with
his progress, and intimated his belief that in a year,
if he worked hard, he might paint something worth
looking at; but he remarked naïvely that he would
require at least that time to gain any readiness with
his brush!

Until that happy day should arrive when he would
be a full-fledged artist, he, to some extent, threw in his
lot with his low-students, and thoroughly enjoyed
the happy-go-lucky Bohemian existence; albeit he
complained of the impurity of the ideas of the French

[1] Sir Joseph Crowe: *Reminiscences.*   54213

artists, and of the jargon of a corrupt life which they
unwisely admitted into their painting-rooms.[1]

The life of the young (French) artist is the easiest,
merriest, dirtiest existence possible. He comes to
Paris, probably at sixteen, from his province; his
parents settle forty pounds a year on him, and pay
his master; he establishes himself in the Pays
Latin, or in the new quarter of Nôtre Dame de
Lorette (which is quite peopled with painters); he
arrives at his *atelier* at a tolerably early hour, and
labours among a score of companions as merry and
as poor as himself. Each gentleman has his favourite tobacco-pipe; and the pictures are painted in the
midst of a cloud of smoke, and a din of puns and
choice French slang, and a roar of choruses, of
which no one can form an idea who has not been
present at such an assembly. . . . How he passes
his evenings, at what theatres, at what *guinguettes*,
in company with what seducing little milliner, there
is no need to say. . . . These young men (together
with the students of sciences) comport themselves
towards the sober citizens pretty much as the German
bursch towards the *philister*, or as the military man,
during the Empire, did to the *pékin :*—from the height
of their poverty they look down upon him with the
greatest imaginable scorn—a scorn, I think, by
which the citizen is dazzled, for his respect for the
arts is intense.[2]

Then as now Paris was the artist's paradise, for there
more than anywhere else he was appreciated, understood, and well provided with schools wherein to study
his profession.

To account for a superiority over England,—
which I think, as regards art, is incontestable—it
must be remembered that the painter's trade, in

[1] *The Paris Sketch Book—On the French School of Painting.*
[2] J. K. Laughton: *Memoirs of Henry Reeve*, Vol. I, p. 35.

France, is a very good one: better appreciated,
better understood, and, generally, far better paid
than with us. There are a dozen excellent schools
in which a lad may enter here, and, under the eye of
a practised master, learn the apprenticeship of his
art at an expense of about ten pounds a year. In
England there is no school except the Academy,
unless the student can afford to pay a very large
sum and place himself under the tuition of some
particular artist. Here, a young man, for his
ten pounds, has all sorts of accessory instruction,
models, etc. ; and has, further, and for nothing,
numberless incitements to study his profession which
are not to be found in England,—the streets are
filled with picture-shops, the people themselves are
pictures walking about ; the churches, theatres,
eating-houses, concert-rooms are covered with pictures ; Nature herself is inclined more kindly to him,
for the sky is a thousand times more bright and
beautiful, and the sun shines for the greater part of
the year. Add to this incitements more selfish, but
quite as powerful : a French artist is paid very
handsomely ; for five hundred a year is much where
all are poor ; and has a rank in society rather above
his merits than below them, being caressed by hosts
and hostesses in places where titles are laughed at,
and a baron is thought of no more account than a
banker's clerk.[1]

At this time Thackeray was frequently at the picture-
galleries, copying pictures, at one time a Watteau, at
another a Lucas van Leyden ("a better man, I think,
than Albert Dürer, and mayhap as great a composer as
Raphael himself ") ; but he soon discovered it was
extremely unlikely he would ever make any success
as a serious painter, and this opinion his friend, Henry
Reeve, who chanced to be at Paris, could not con-

[1] *The Paris Sketch Book—On the French School of Painting.*

tradict. "Thackeray's drawings, if I may judge by his notebook, are as pure and accurate as any I have seen," said the future editor of the *Edinburgh Review*. "He is a man whom I would willingly set to copy a picture of Raphael's, as far, at least, as the drawing goes; but he does not seem likely to get into a system of massive colouring, if I may judge by what he said."[1] The subject of this criticism bore his disappointment philosophically, and soon after poked fun at himself:

I wish you could see my historical picture of "Heliogabalus in the Ruins of Carthage"; or the full length of "Sir Samuel and His Lady"—sitting in a garden light, reading "The Book of Beauty," Sir Samuel catching a butterfly, which is settling on a flower-pot.

About the time that Thackeray discovered he would never become a good painter, it dawned on him, or perhaps was suggested to him, that the sketches that he used to draw for his friends might have some commercial value. He found one Gibbs, a dealer who offered to try to dispose of his pen-and-ink drawings; and he was fortunate enough to inspire a firm of publishers with the sense of the merits of a series of caricatures, entitled "Flore et Zéphyr," a title probably suggested by a ballet of that name then popular at Paris. The sketches, eight in number, appeared in March 1836 as the work of "Theophile Wagstaffe," though each drawing is signed W. T. (in a monogram). The little book attracted no attention at the time, but the cari-

[1] J. K. Laughton: *Life and Correspondence of Henry Reeve*, Vol. I, p. 35.

catures are most amusing, and the grotesque attitudes
and wonderful contortions of the dancers show that
already the artist's sense of humour was well developed.

In the year that "Flore et Zéphyr" appeared, Thackeray thought to turn an honest penny by furnishing
illustrations to books. A chance soon offered. Robert
Seymour, the creator of the original design of Pickwick,
had completed the drawings of the "Pickwick Papers"
for the first two or three monthly numbers when, in
a fit of temporary insanity, he committed suicide in
April 1836. His place was taken by Robert Buss,
with whose work, however, the author was not satisfied;
and Thackeray, who in May was on a visit to London,
hearing that a new artist was wanted, applied for the
work, and met for the first time his great contemporary.
Years afterwards, at a Royal Academy dinner, rising
after Dickens to respond to the toast of Literature, he
spoke of this offer, to the refusal of which he referred
as "Mr. Pickwick's lucky escape."

Had it not been for the direct act of my friend who
has just sat down, I should most likely never have
been included in the toast which you have been
pleased to drink ; and I should have tried to be, not
a writer, but a painter, or designer of pictures. That
was the object of my early ambition, and I can remember when Mr. Dickens was a very young man,
and had commenced delighting the world with some
charming humorous works, of which I cannot mention the name, but which were coloured light green,
and came out once a month, this young man wanted
an artist to illustrate his writings, and I recollect
walking up to his chambers in Furnival's Inn with
two or three drawings in my hand, which, strange to
say, he did not find suitable. But for that unfortu-

nate blight which came over my artistical existence, it would have been my pride and my pleasure to have endeavoured one day to find a place on these walls for one of my performances. This disappointment caused me to direct my attention to a different walk of art, and now I can only hope to be "translated" on these walls, as I have been, thanks to my talented friend Mr. Egg.

But though Dickens, who also rejected the offers of John Leech and "Crowquill" in favour of Hablot Knight Browne, would not accept Thackeray's aid, Thackeray subsequently found some authors more obliging, and he contributed, besides the illustrations to the little burlesques, "King Glumpus" (1837) and "The Exquisites" (1839), twelve plates to Douglas Jerrold's "Men of Character" (1838), and, for £20, the same number of coloured sketches to Charles Greenstreet Addisons's "Damascus and Palmyra" (1838). Indeed, in spite of the fact that he made no reference to the matter in the speech from which a passage is quoted above, to the end of his days he poured forth drawings in great profusion.

Thackeray stands alone as a great author who illustrated his own books. Besides contributing many hundred sketches to *Punch*, he produced the designs for the "Yellowplush Correspondence", "Major Gahagan's Reminiscences", "Catherine", "The Paris Sketch Book", "The Great Hoggarty Diamond", "The Irish Sketch Book", "From Cornhill to Grand Cairo", "Vanity Fair", "Mrs. Perkins's Ball", "Our Street", "Pendennis", "Dr. Birch and His Young Friends", "The Kickleburys on the Rhine", "The Rose and the Ring", "The Virginians", "Lovel the Widower",

and the "Roundabout Papers."[1]   He had intended to
illustrate "The Newcomes," but eventually he abandoned the idea.

> I have turned away one artist : the poor creature
> was utterly incompetent to depict the sublime, grace-
> ful, and pathetic personages and events with which
> this history will most assuredly abound.[2]

Richard Doyle was entrusted with the task, and the
two sketches designed by Thackeray were adapted and
redrawn by the former.   "He does beautifully easily
what I want to do and can't," Thackeray declared, with
characteristic generosity.   Afterwards, however, he re-
gretted he had entrusted the work to another hard, and
when Whitwell Elwin expressed his admiration for the
conception of the Colonel's face and figure, "Oh, yes,"
said Thackeray, "but I gave it to Doyle.   I drew the
Colonel for him."   Thackeray found it troublesome to
draw on the wood the illustrations for "Philip," and
some of the sketches were made on paper and redrawn
on wood, but not to his satisfaction.   Frederick Walker
was then engaged to redraw some of the sketches, but
soon he declared himself capable of better work, and
declined to continue the task ; so in the end the work
was left in his hands with only written instructions or
sometimes a rough pen-and-ink sketch by the author—
the "Good Samaritans" (in chapter xv.) being the first
illustration executed by Walker on his own responsibility.

All his life Thackeray preferred the pencil to the

[1] The "Fitz-Boodle Papers", "Barry Lyndon" and "Esmond" alone
among Thackeray's works were published without illustrations.

[2] *The Newcomes*, chap. xv.

pen. Often he found writing wearisome and the strain of composition irksome; and there were times even when he almost hated the chain that held him to the desk; but he always turned to the drawing-board with pleasure. "The hours which he spent upon his drawing-blocks and Sketch-books brought no fatigue or weariness: they were of endless interest and amusement to him, and rested him when he was tired," Lady Ritchie has recorded. "It was only when he came to etch upon steel or to draw for the engraver upon wood that he complained of effort and want of ease; and we used often to wish that his drawings could be given as they were first made, without the various transmigrations of wood and steel, and engraver's toil, and printer's ink."[1]

Thackeray was at his best when illustrating his writings, and there has rarely been an artist who could make his drawings so helpful to the text, for the characters are as truly depicted by the pencil as by the pen, and they tell the story together. His drawing may not always have been correct, the perspective may occasionally have been wrong—"Some of my folk have scarcely more legs than Miss Biffin; they have fins instead of hands—they squint almost every one of them!"[2]—but for quaint fancy and humour his illustrations have rarely been surpassed.

Take "Vanity Fair," and study the pictorial work from the opening initial "W" to the tailpiece, at the end of the last chapter, which shows the children shutting up the puppets in the box after the play is played out. Look

---

[1] *The Orphan of Pimlico*: Preface.
[2] *A Grumble About the Christmas Books.*

at the drawings on the cover of the monthly parts and on the title-page—the former portraying the jester, standing on the cask, haranguing the open-mouthed yokels; the latter presenting the jester, lying on the grass, weary and worn, looking into a glass which reflects a countenance that is anything but gay. Look at Becky showing off her doll, "Miss Jemmy," to her father's rather dissolute Bohemian friends; or, all alone, building a house of cards that, we know full well, will sooner or later fall, after the fashion of such unstable structures; or fishing, and trying to hook stupid, hulking, conceited Mr. Jos; or as a governess in the schoolroom, paying just so much attention to her charges as might be expected from a lady with her turn of mind. Why, the slender thread of the story of Miss Rebecca Sharp might be reconstructed from the drawings. Look at Dobbin and Cuff fighting (in a capital C); or at Miss Eliza Styles (better known as Captain Rawdon Crawley) reading a letter from his wife at Mr. Barnet's, saddler, Knightsbridge, near the barracks; or at Moss arresting Rawdon in Gaunt Square, while the bailiff's companion whistles for a hackney coach to convey the trio to the sponging house in Cursitor Street. Glance at the tailpiece to chapter ix —a delightful sketch of that sad jester Thackeray himself. Turn over the pages and, on the eve of the battle of Waterloo, compare Becky, slumbering tranquilly, with Mrs. Major O'Dowd, as Venus, preparing the arms of Mars, her husband, who is sleeping soundly. Turn over again, and observe Miss Horrocks of the ribbons playing the piano with the sycophantic Hester by her side, all admiration; and then glance at

Sir Pitt nursed by Hester, the ill-conditioned bullying attendant.

If space permitted, it would be easy to go through each of the novels and point out sketch after sketch delightful to regard. The "Christmas Books" owe more than half their charm to the plates. Take the portraits of Mr. Titmarsh and Mr. Mulligan of Ballymulligan, of Mr. Flam, of Mr. Larkins; of those famous literary lights, Miss Bunion and Mr. Hicks; of Miss Trotter, whose face brightens at the arrival of the hideous but wealthy Lord Methuselah; of Mr. Beaumoris, Mr. Grig, and Mr. Flanders, and a host of others, all present at "Mrs. Perkins's Ball." "I think that the empty faces of the dance-room were never done better," said Edward FitzGerald, who years earlier had been so pleased with Thackeray's fourteen little coloured drawings in his copy of "Undine" that he wrote to John Allen, asking if he did not think it would make a nice book to publish all the papers about Sir Roger de Coverley alone, with illustrations by Thackeray. "Our Street" contains all sorts and conditions of people duly sketched by the author, from the inquisitive old woman looking out of the window to "the lady whom nobody knows"; from "the lion of the street," Clarence Bulbul, who wrote the Mayfair love-song, "The Cane-Bottomed Chair," to "the happy family," in which plate is depicted the pleasant home-life of the Fairfaxes. The drawings of "The Rose and the Ring" which have delighted several generations of great and small children, were begun at Rome as Twelfth Night pictures for his children. Thackeray revelled in this labour of love : all his life he loved to amuse children, and to his fondness for the " little 'uns " he has left this abiding memorial.

Thackeray suffered from no misapprehension as to the value of his gift, and he was well aware of his limitations. When a man in all good faith said to him, " But you *can* draw," he set him down instantly —and unjustly—as a snob and a flatterer ; and Mr. Corkran found him fretting over a sketch : " Look," he said to the visitor, "now, Cruikshank, by a few touches, throwing some light and shadow here and there, would make this a picture. How it is I know not, but I certainly cannot do it at all." " My pencils don't draw like yours," he said prettily to Marcus Stone ; and, laughing at himself, he wrote in the 'fifties to Edmund Yates :

> You have a new artist on the *Train*, I see, dear Yates. I have been looking at his work, and I have solved a problem. I find there *is* a man alive who draws worse than myself.[1]

Cruikshank claimed Thackeray as a pupil. He taught him etching, and thought him clever with his pencil, though, he declared, " He had not the patience to be an artist with pencil or brush. I used to tell him that to be an artist was to burrow along like a mole, heaving up a little mound here and there for a long distance."[2] Thackeray, indeed, was not ignorant of his lack of technical skill as an etcher, and he asked Henry Vizetelly to find him someone who would etch from his water-colour sketch the frontispiece to

[1] Yates : *Recollections and Experiences.*
[2] Blanchard Jerrold : *Life of George Cruikshank.*

"From Cornhill to Grand Cairo." The work was given to a young man named Thwaites, who subsequently put on the wood a number of the drawings for "Mrs. Perkins's Ball."

I return the drawings after making a few alterations in them (Thackeray wrote to Vizetelly). Present Mr. Titmarsh's compliments to your talented young man, and say M. A. T. would take it as a great favour if he would kindly confine his improvements to the Mulligan's and Mrs. Perkins's other guests' extremities. In your young gentleman's otherwise praiseworthy corrections of my vile drawing, a certain *je ne sais quoi*, which I flatter myself exists in the original sketches, seems to have given him the slip, and I have tried in vain to recapture it. Somehow I prefer my own Nuremberg dolls to Mr. Thwaites's superfine wax models.[1]

Vizetelly said Thackeray was almost as fastidious as Mr. Ruskin in regard to the manner in which his sketches were transferred to the wood; and Thackeray once complained to "Practical John" Hollingshead: "I'm not a first-rate artist, I know; but I'm not half as bad as those fellows, the woodcutters, make me"; and indeed much of the delicacy of expression was lost in the process. But though Thackeray lacked academic correctness and technical mastery, the undeniable originality and humour of his drawings will secure for them a very long lease of life and for him a high place in the ranks of the caricaturists. Charlotte Brontë thought "Thackeray's rude, careless sketches preferable to thousands of carefully finished paintings";[2] and when the question

[1] Vizetelly: *Glances Back Through Seventy Years*, Vol. I, p. 283.
[2] Clement Shorter: *The Brontës*, Vol. II, p. 37.

of an illustrator for one of her novels was raised, "You will not easily find a second Thackeray," she wrote to W. S. Williams on March 11, 1848. "How he can render, with a few black lines and dots, shades of expression so fine, so real; traits of character so minute, so subtle, so difficult to seize and fix, I cannot tell—I can only wonder and admire. Thackeray may not be a painter, but he is a wizard of a draughtsman; touched with his pencil, paper lives. And then his drawing is so refreshing; after the wooden limbs one is accustomed to see portrayed by commonplace illustrators, his shapes of bone and muscle clothed with flesh, correct in proportion and anatomy, are a real relief. All is true in Thackeray. If Truth were again a goddess, Thackeray should be her high priest."[1]

[1] Clement Shorter: *The Brontës*, Vol. I, p. 402.

K

CHAPTER VIII

MARRIAGE (1836–1840)

Major Carmichael-Smyth founds the *Constitutional* newspaper—and appoints Thackeray Paris Correspondent — Thackeray marries Isabella Getkin Creagh Shawe at Paris—works on *Galignani's Messenger*—happy days—" Bouillabaisse "—summoned to London to manage the *Constitutional*—the failure of the *Constitutional*—Thackeray and his wife stay with his mother—takes a house in Great Coram Street, Bloomsbury—the birth of his two eldest daughters—Bloomsbury in his books—the Foundling Hospital—his fondness of children—the British Museum—" Going to See a Man Hanged "—his third daughter born—his wife's illness—the compulsory separation—the happiness of his brief married life—his love for his children.

THACKERAY, who had abandoned journalism for painting, and painting for caricature, was to revert to his first employment. In the spring of 1836 he was summoned to London by Major Carmichael-Smyth to assist at the discussion of a project to establish a new radical daily paper, which should advocate the ballot, triennial parliaments, the complete freedom of the press, and religious liberty and equality. Joseph Hume, George Grote, George Evans, Charles Buller, William Ewart, Sir William Molesworth, John Arthur Roebuck, and other leaders of the advanced party promised their support ; and the Metropolitan Newspaper Company was formed, with a capital of £60,000 in six

thousand shares of £10 each—£6 paid up—with Major
Carmichael-Smyth as chairman.   The *Public Ledger*,
a respectable paper with a small and ever decreasing
circulation, was purchased, renamed the *Constitutional*
(*and Public Ledger*), and the first number under the
auspices of the Company appeared on September 15,
1836, on which day the Stamp Duty on newspapers
was reduced.   Laman Blanchard was installed in the
editorial chair ; to Thornton Hunt, the eldest son of
Leigh Hunt, was entrusted the political department ;
and, through the influence of his stepfather, Thackeray
was appointed Paris Correspondent with a salary of
£400 a year.

"That excellent and facetious being, Thackeray . . .
has fallen in love, and talks of being married in less
than twenty years.   What is there so affecting as
matrimony?" Henry Reeve noted in his diary on
January 16, 1836.   " I dined yesterday with his object,
who is a nice, simple, girlish girl ; a niece of old
Colonel Shawe, whom one always meets at the Stir-
lings."[1]   The "nice, simple, girlish girl" was Isabella
Getkin Creagh Shawe, and Thackeray was married to
her on April 20, 1836, the ceremony being performed
at the British Embassy at Paris by Bishop Luscombe.

Thackeray was at this time mainly dependent on his
salary from the *Constitutional*, but financial considera-
tions were not regarded : he took the step fearlessly,
and neither then nor later would admit its imprudence.
Indeed, he was always an advocate of what the world
calls improvident marriages, and his liking for Harry
Longueville Jones, with whom he was " working on

[1] J. K. Laughton : *Memoirs of Henry Reeve*, Vol. I, p. 59.

Galignani's newspaper for ten francs a day very cheerfully," had its origin in the fact that that young man had "flung up his fellow and tutorship at Cambridge in order to marry on nothing a year."[1] Some sixteen years later, when he had come to forty years, he endorsed the views of his youth.

> I married with £400 paid by a newspaper, which failed six months afterwards, and always love to hear of a young fellow testing his fortune bravely in that way [he wrote to William Webb Follett Synge]. . . . Though my marriage was a wreck, as you know, I would do it again, for behold, Love is the crown and completion of all earthly good. A man who is afraid of his fortune never deserved one.[2]

The young couple rented apartments in the Rue Neuve St. Augustin, not far from the offices of *Galignani's Messenger* in the Rue Vivienne : half-way between these places was No. 16, Rue Neuve des Petits Champs ("The New Street of the Little Fields "), occupied, as an old guide-book gives it, by Terré *jeune*, Restaurateur ; house noted for Spanish dishes, and for good wines, and more especially for the Marseilles dish, "Bouillabaisse." Here the newly married pair came frequently to dine, meeting many friends who also appreciated the *cuisine*. Many years after, when Terré was dead and Gillet reigned in his stead, Thackeray, alone, revisited the eating-house.

> Ah me ! how quick the days are flitting !
> I mind me of a time that's gone,
> When here I'd sit, as now I'm sitting,
> In this same place—but not alone.

[1] *A Collection of Letters of W. M. Thackeray*, p. 36.
[2] Merivale and Marzials : *Thackeray*, p. 240.

A fair young form was nestled near me,
A dear, dear face looked fondly up,
And sweetly spoke and smiled to cheer me
—There's no one now to share my cup.

.   .   .   .

I drink it as the Fates ordain it.
Come, fill it, and have done with rhymes :
Fill up the lonely glass, and drain it
In memory of dear old times.
Welcome the wine, whate'er the seal is ;
And sit you down and say your grace
With thankful heart, whate'er the meal is.
—Here comes the smoking Bouillabaisse ! [1]

These happy days at Paris did not last long. Thackeray's first letter to the *Constitutional* appeared in the issue for September 19, 1836, and neither this nor his subsequent contributions to the journal call for comment: their interest was purely topical, and the predominant note, as readers of "The Paris Sketch Book" would expect, a great dislike of the Government of July.[2] Like the *National Standard* the *Constitutional* never attracted the public, and little good resulted from the announcement on January 2, 1837, that Grote, Ewart, Hume, Roebuck, Molesworth, Buller, and others "do thereby engage to take in such newspaper for a twelvemonth at the least, and we recommend it to the support of our friends, entertaining similar views ; believing that such a newspaper is much wanted as an

[1] *The Ballad of Bouillabaisse* (*Punch*, February 17, 1849).
[2] Thackeray's letters to the *Constitutional* were collected by Mr. W. T. Spencer and published in 1899 in the volume, " W. M. Thackeray in the *National Standard* and *Constitutional*." They were included by the present writer in Macmillan's edition of the Collected Works, Vol. xi, " The Yellowplush Papers, etc." ; 1903.

organ of Uncompromising Liberal Principles and that it will prove extensively useful to the interests of Reform everywhere." Thackeray's last letter from Paris bears the date February 15, 1837; and immediately after this was despatched he, with his wife, came to London to attend a meeting called to discuss the affairs of the Company owning the paper, already in a very unsatisfactory condition. The contributors were unpaid, the correspondent in Portugal, sent out to report on the disturbances there, was destitute, and wrote letters begging for a remittance; and Laman Blanchard, with a wife and five children to support, though writing articles every day, had not been paid for months. Thackeray, of course, could give little advice as to how to run a daily paper without funds and deeply in debt; but, since to wind up the company spelt ruin, it was decided to make a call on the shareholders of £1 a share, and to make every effort to increase the circulation. On March 1, the paper, which had been increased from six to seven columns on each of its four pages, was reduced to its former size; but it dragged on an unprofitable existence until July 1, when the last number (249) appeared with a black border for the death of the King, and an announcement, probably written by Thackeray, explaining the cause of the failure of the paper.

The adverse circumstances have been various. In the philosophy of ill-luck it may be laid down as a principle, that every point of discouragement tends to one common centre of defeat. When the fates do concur in one's discomfiture their unanimity is wonderful. So it has happened in the case of the *Constitutional*. In the first place a delay of some months, consequent upon the postponement of the newspaper

NO. 18, ALBION STREET, HYDE PARK

Where Thackeray and his wife stayed with Major and Mrs. Carmichael-Smyth in 1837

stamp reduction, operated on the minds of many who
were originally parties to the enterprise; in the
next, the majority of those who remained faithful
were wholly inexperienced in the art and practical
working of an important daily journal; in the third,
and consequent upon the other two, there was the
want of those abundant means, and of that wise
application of resources, without which no efficient
organ of the interests of any class of men—to say
nothing of the interests of the first and greatest class
whose welfare has been our dearest aim and most
constant object—can be successfully established.
Then came further misgivings on the part of friends,
and the delusive undertakings of friends in disguise.

So the *Constitutional* went down, and in the wreck
was lost the greater part of the fortune of Major Carmichael-Smyth.

When Thackeray and his wife came to London, they
stayed for a while with Major and Mrs. Carmichael-
Smyth at No. 18, Albion Street, Hyde Park; but soon
"work was abundant and the future promising" enough
to allow of their setting up their home at No. 13, Great
Coram Street,[1] which runs from Woburn Place to Brunswick Square, parallel to the better known Guilford
Street, which connects Russell Square with Gray's Inn
Road. There was born in 1838 the Thackerays' eldest
daughter, Anne Isabella, now Lady Ritchie, but still
affectionately remembered as Miss Thackeray of the
many charming stories; and later another child, Jane
who died in infancy. Readers of "The Great Hoggarty Diamond" will realise how deeply this loss was
felt.

[1] In Great Coram Street at this time lived also, besides John Allen
John Leech and Charles Keene.

Bloomsbury had even then an old-world air and with its many interesting associations made a deep impression upon the future novelist, who again and again introduced the neighbourhood into his stories. Mr. and Mrs. Samuel Hoggarty lived in lodgings in Lamb's Conduit Street, where Mr. and Mrs. Brough called in their splendid carriage and pair; and it was in Hart Street that little George Osborne attended the school of the Rev. Laurence Veal, domestic chaplain to the Earl of Bareacres, who prepared young gentlemen and noblemen for the universities, the senate and the learned professions; whose system did not embrace the degrading corporal severities still practised at the ancient places of education, and in whose family the pupils found the elegancies of refined society and the confidence and affection of a home. In Great Coram Street itself lived Mr. Todd, the junior partner in the firm of Osborne and Todd. Osborne lived in Russell Square, close by the Sedleys, on account of whose daughter he disinherited his son; but it was easier for the old man to turn his son out of his house than to remove him from his heart, and when the young soldier died upon the field of Waterloo he erected a monument on the wall of the church attached to the Foundling Hospital.

The Foundling Hospital, a stone's-throw from his house, attracted Thackeray, always susceptible to the pleasures and sufferings of children.

> There's something, even in his bitterest mood,
> That melts him at the sight of infanthood;
> Thank God that he can love the pure and good.

NO. 13, GREAT CORAM STREET, BRUNSWICK SQUARE
Where Thackeray and his wife lived 1837—1840

Thackeray's love for children was one of his most pleasing characteristics. When James T. Fields, the American publisher, was one day mentioning the various sights he had seen in London, Thackeray, who happened to overhear him, broke in with, "But you haven't seen the greatest one yet. Go with me to-day to St. Paul's, and hear the charity children sing." "So we went," Fields has related, " and I saw the 'head cynic of literature,' the 'hater of humanity,' as a critical dunce in the *Times* once called him, hiding his bowed head wet with tears, while his whole frame shook with emotion, as the children of poverty rose to pour out their anthem of praise. Afterwards he wrote about it."[1]

There is one day in the year . . . when I think St. Paul's presents the noblest sight in the whole world : when five thousand charity children, with cheeks like nosegays, and with sweet, fresh voices, sing the hymn which makes every heart thrill with praise and happiness. I have seen a hundred grand sights in the world—coronations, Parisian splendours, Crystal Palace openings, Pope's chapels with their processions of long-tailed cardinals and quavering choirs of fat soprani—but think in all Christendom there is no such sight as Charity Children's Day. *Non Angli, sed angeli*. As one looks at that beautiful multitude of innocents : as the first note strikes : indeed one may almost fancy that cherubs are singing.[1]

And elsewhere he has written :

To see a hundred boys marshalled in a chapel or old hall ; to hear their sweet fresh voices when they chant, and look in their brave calm faces: I say, does not the sight and sound of them smite you, somehow, with a pang of exquisite kindness ?

[1] *The Four Georges—George the Third.*

Thackeray delighted to play with children, to draw caricatures for them, and, above all, delighted to take them to the pantomime. There is a characteristic tale told of him, that he was once asked by Herman Merivale, whom as a boy he had invited to dinner at his club, if he remembered the occasion. "Oh, yes," said the great man, "and I remember what I gave you. Beefsteak and apricot omelette." The other was delighted that his host should remember even the details, and expressed his pleasure. "Yes," said Thackeray, twinkling in his inimitable way, "I always give boys beefsteaks and apricot omelettes."

Near Great Coram Street was the British Museum, and in the library Thackeray might often have been seen at work.

> Most Londoners—not all—have seen the British Museum Library. I speak *à cœur ouvert* and pray the kindly reader to bear with me. I have seen all sorts of domes of Peters and Pauls, Sophia, Pantheon,—what not?—and have been struck by none of them as much as by that catholic dome in Bloomsbury, under which our million volumes are housed. What peace, what love, what truth, what beauty, what happiness for all, what generous kindness for you and me, are here spread out! It seems to me one cannot sit down in that place without a heart full of grateful reverence. I own to have said my grace at the table, and to have thanked Heaven for this my English birthright, freely to partake of these bountiful books, and speak the truth I find there.[1]

Thackeray appreciated to the full the advantages of the well-conducted library; and when Sir Anthony

[1] *Nil Nisi Bonum.*

Panizzi asked him to give evidence before the Select Committee of the House of Commons, which was ordered on April 24, 1860, "to enquire into the necessity for the extension of the British Museum," he replied that he would gladly come and say on behalf of the British Museum what little he knew— how he once came from Paris to London to write an article on a review about French affairs, and how, when he went to the Bibliothèque du Roi, he could only get one book at a time, and no sight of a catalogue. "But then I didn't go often," he added, "being disgusted with the place, and entering it as a total stranger, without any recommendation."[1]

It was while living at Great Coram Street that Thackeray indulged a morbid desire to see a man hanged. Years before at Paris he had gone to see an execution, but by some mischance had missed the dismal spectacle. He was invited by Monckton Milnes "to make one at the Hanging" of Courvoisier, the murderer of Lord William Russell, in June 1840; and he accepted with some show of eagerness. It was customary then, when the execution took place at five or six in the morning, for the intending spectators to go eastward after a very late supper.

> You must not think me inhospitable in refusing to sit up. I must go to bed, that's the fact, or I never shall be able to attend to the work of to-morrow properly. If you like to come here and have a sofa, it is at your service, but I most strongly recommend sleep as a preparation for the day's pleasure.[2]

[1] Letter to Panizzi, 1860, in the MSS. Department of the British Museum Library.

[2] Wemyss Reid : *Life of Lord Houghton*, Vol. I, p. 427.

The scene made a deep impression on him, and he wrote of it with deep feeling :

There is some talk of the terror which the sight of this spectacle inspires. . . . I fully confess that I came away down Snow Hill that morning with a disgust for murder, but it was for *the murder I saw done* [he wrote after witnessing the scene]. This is the 20th of July, and I may be permitted for my part to declare that, for the last fourteen days, so salutary has the impression of the butchery been upon me, I have had the man's face continually before my eyes; that I can see Mr. Ketch at this moment, with an easy air, taking the rope from his pocket; that I feel myself ashamed and degraded at the brutal curiosity which took me to that brutal sight; and that I pray to Almighty God to cause this disgraceful sin to pass from among us, and to cleanse our land of blood.

Later at Cairo, when invited to witness a similar spectacle, "Seeing one man hanged is quite enough in the course of a life," he replied, "'*J'y ai été*,' as the Frenchman said of hunting." In "The Irish Sketch Book" he repeated the sentiments expressed in the *Fraser* article.

I confess, for my part, to that common cant and sickly sentimentality, which, thank God ! is felt by a great number of people nowadays, and which leads them to revolt against murder, whether performed by a ruffian's knife or a hangman's rope : whether accompanied by a curse from the thief as he blows his victim's brains out, or a prayer from my lord on the bench in his wig and black cap.[2]

Nevertheless he eventually changed his opinion, and when someone praised his "Hanging" article, "I

[1] *Going to see a Man Hanged* (*Fraser's Magazine*, August 1840).
[2] *The Irish Sketch Book*, chap. i.

think I was wrong," he remarked. "My feelings were overwrought. These murderers are such devils, after all." But though he ceased to advocate the abolition of the death-sentence, he never refrained from insisting that the ceremony should be performed in private.

Thackeray's marriage was very happy, but unfortunately the happiness was not of long duration. His third daughter, Harriet Marion, afterwards Mrs. Leslie Stephen, was born on May 28, 1840; and shortly after he went to Belgium to collect material for a Sketch-Book.[1] Mrs. Thackeray had almost recovered her health when he left her, but he was summoned home to find her "in a strange state of languor and mental inactivity," which he at first regarded as a not unusual sequence of an illness that would pass away in course of time. He threw aside all work, sent the children to his mother, and took his wife to her parents in Ireland. Afterwards he went with her to Paris, where for a while she was in a *maison de santé;* and later, hoping against hope that the cloud on her intellect would dissolve, for many months travelled with her from watering-place to watering-place, as the doctors as a last resource had recommended. At last Thackeray was compelled to realise that his wife would never recover sufficiently to undertake the duties of a mother and a wife. Though taking interest in any pleasant things around her, especially in music, she was unable to manage her life, and since it was essential she should be properly cared

---

[1] The Belgian Sketch-Book was never written, but Thackeray used his recollections of this trip in "Little Travels and Roadside Sketches" (*Fraser's Magazine,* May and October 1844, January 1845).

L

for, she was placed with Mr. and Mrs. Thompson at Leigh, in Essex. She outlived her husband by so many years that it was with a shock, since she had already been dead to the world for nearly forty years, that the announcement of her death was read. She was buried at Leigh, not in the graveyard by the church, but in a cemetery farther inland. The memorial stone, surmounted by an Irish cross, bears the following inscription :—

To the Dear Memory of
Isabella Getkin Thackeray.
Born 1818, Married 1836 to
William Makepeace Thackeray.
She died at Leigh, January 11, 1894, aged 76.

How sad, how awful, it was! The man with his great heart, with his yearning for love and affection that, from this time forth, breathes through his letters and his books. To be separated from the woman he had chosen for his companion through life, and whose presence had cheered him when his fortunes were at their lowest ebb, and his reputation was yet to make! How hard it was that she should be taken from him before she could enjoy the great fame! How much he loved her, and how deeply he felt the blow that shattered his happiness and his home, he never divulged. He was not a man to parade his domestic sorrows : he might think of them in solitude, but if a visitor entered he would force himself to look up immediately with a smile and a joke. Once, however, he made a reference in a book, to his bereavement, in a note prefixed to a reprint of the fragment of "A Shabby Genteel Story."

It was my intention to complete the little story of which only the first part is here written. . . . The tale was interrupted at a sad period of the writer's own life. The colours are long since dry; the artist's hand is changed. It is best to leave the sketch as it was when it was first designed seventeen years ago. The memory of the past is renewed as he looks at it

> "*Die Bilder froher Tage*
> *Und manche liebe Schatten steigen auf.*" [1]

"It was written," he said, writing of "The Great Hoggarty Diamond," "at a time of great affliction, when my heart was very soft and humble. Amen. *Ich habe auch geliebt.*"[2] "I was as happy as the day was long with her," he told a cousin after he had returned alone, and worse than alone, to the desolate house in Great Coram Street; and one day when Trollope's groom said to him, "I hear you have written a book upon Ireland, and are always making fun of the Irish. You don't like us," Thackeray's eyes filled with tears as he thought of his wife—born in County Cork—and he replied, turning away his head, "God help me! all that I have loved best in the world is Irish."

Well might Thackeray echo the lines of poor brokenhearted Thekla's song :

> "*Ich habe genossen das irdische Glück,*
> *Ich habe gelebt und geliebet.*"

Yet even in his bitterest moments he did not cry, with Thekla,

> "*Das Herz ist gestorben, die Welt ist leer,*
> *Und weiter gibt sie dem Wünsche nichts mehr,*"

---

[1] *Miscellanies*, Vol. III, 1856. The quotation is from the Introduction to *Faust*.   [2] *A Collection of Letters of W. M. Thackeray*, p. 24.

for even in his most bitter grief he remembered his children and his parents; and set himself resolutely to work to make money so that when his children were old enough he could provide a comfortable home for them, dower them well, and, when he died, leave them, at least, a competency.

From this time, more than ever, the thought of his children was the mainspring of most of his actions; and whether at home or abroad, the "little girls" were always in his thoughts.

> And when, its force expended,
> The harmless storm was ended,
> And as the sunrise splendid
>   Came blushing o'er the sea;
> I thought, as day was breaking,
> My little girls were waking,
> And smiling, and making
>   A prayer at home for me.[1]

"I sat up with the children and talked to them of their mother," he told Mrs. Brookfield. "It is my pleasure to tell them how humble-minded their mother was." He took them to the Colosseum on their birthdays; or the Zoological Gardens, where they amused themselves in finding likenesses to their friends in many of the animals ("Thank Evns!" is Thackeray's expression of gratitude, "both of the girls have plenty of fun and humour"); or went with them to the play "in recompense for their disappointment in not getting to the opening of the Great Exhibition, which they had hopes of seeing."

Nothing in connection with the *Cornhill Magazine*

[1] *From Cornhill to Grand Cairo—The White Squall.*

gave Thackeray so much pleasure as his eldest
daughter's first contribution, "Little Scholars."
"When I read it," he said to Fields, "I blubbered
like a child. It was so good, so simple, and so honest;
and my little girl wrote it, every word of it." "I
assure you that Annie can write ten times more
cleverly than I," he declared enthusiastically to Dean
Hole; but the Dean tacitly declined to accept the
assurance. When a friend expressed admiration for
"The Story of Elizabeth", "I am glad," said Thackeray, "but I can form no opinion of its merits
as I have not read it." "Not read it," came the
echo. "No, I dared not, I love her too much."
When the *Athenæum* attacked the book, Thackeray
was very angry, and quarrelled with Jeaffreson,
whom, erroneously, he believed to have written the
review.[1]

For the sake of his children, Thackeray battled with
his constitutional timidity, and nerved himself to deliver
the two series of lectures—he, to whom public speaking
was misery; and solely on their account made his trips
to America, hating the separation from them, and
longing all the time of his absence for the day of his
return.

It is a painful subject to dwell upon, a picture of
fearful sadness, this dreadful domestic affliction. His
fortune lost, his talents unrecognised, his beloved wife
taken from him! Is it marvellous that Thackeray was
able to see the existence of evil as well as of good in the
world? Yet instead of embittering him, the great
sorrow chastened his soul, and made his later writings

[1] The author was Geraldine Jewsbury.

more sympathetic than his earlier; and the only use he made henceforth of his great gift of sarcasm was to protest with gentle hand against the follies of his fellows, in the endeavour to indicate the path of honour, virtue, goodness and mercy.

CHAPTER IX

IN GRUB STREET (1837-1846)

Writes for the *Times*—and for *Fraser's Magazine*—his earliest contributions to *Fraser's Magazine*—the authorship of "Elizabeth Brownrigge"—and the resemblance between that story and "Catherine"—"Fashnable Fax and Polite Annygoats"—Mr. Yellowplush's other papers—strikes for higher pay—his qualifications as a writer for the periodical press—his knowledge of art and foreign languages—suggests himself for the editorship of the *Foreign Quarterly Review* —and as a contributor to *Blackwood's Magazine*—Sir Henry Cole's tribute to his powers—the *Anti-Corn Law Circular*—"The Pen and the Album"—writes for many periodicals—contributions to *Fraser's Magazine*—"The Paris Sketch Book"—"The Second Funeral of Napoleon"—replies to the *Times'* criticism of that book—"Comic Tales and Sketches"—"The Irish Sketch Book"—stays with Charles Lever at Templeogue—Thackeray on the Irish —the "Life of Talleyrand"—"Barry Lyndon"—"From Cornhill to Grand Cairo"—Carlyle resents Thackeray accepting a free passage —Thackeray's reply—"Titmarsh at Jerusalem"—Thackeray's religion—his indignation with Mrs. Trollope's interpretation of the Scriptures—his dislike of the Jews and the Roman Catholics—his attitude towards "Papal Aggression"—his attack on asceticism— his doubts of the infallibility of the Bible—his deep sense of religion —his fearless outlook on death.

I T was mentioned in the last chapter that when Thackeray came to London early in the year 1837 he found work in plenty: it is now necessary to go back to that time to see what he wrote then, and where he published what he wrote.

Mrs. Thackeray, it has been recorded, used laughingly to say she laid the foundation-stone of her husband's fortune by introducing him to her relative, Thomas Barnes, the editor of the *Times*. Barnes employed Thackeray as a reviewer, and the young man's first identified contribution, a review of Carlyle's " French Revolution," appeared on August 3, 1837. " I understand there have been many reviews of a mixed character," the historian wrote to his brother. " I got one in the *Times* last week. The writer is one Thackeray, a half-monstrous Cornish giant, kind of painter, Cambridge man, and Paris newspaper correspondent, who is now writing for his life in London. . . . His article is rather like him, and, I suppose, calculated to do the book good." This is the only article in the *Times* of 1837 placed to Thackeray's credit by the bibliographers; but as, of the eleven contributions known to be his in the following year, six (filling ten columns) were printed in one month, the natural assumption is that he was writing regularly for the paper. Besides the review of Carlyle's book, the only other identified writings of Thackeray in 1837 are: (i) "The Professor," a tale, in *Bentley's Magazine* for September, (ii) "Fashnable Fax and Polite Annygoats," and (iii) " A Word on the Annuals," in the November and December numbers, respectively, of *Fraser's Magazine*.

The mention of *Fraser's* brings us face to face with the unsolved question that is the stumbling-block of the biographers and the bibliographers of Thackeray: When did Thackeray begin to contribute to this magazine, in which appeared the best of his early work? The subject is the more interesting because, more or less directly, it involves the question of the

THE FRASERIANS

From a drawing by Daniel Maclise, 1835

much - discussed and much - disputed authorship of "Elizabeth Brownrigge : A Tale," printed in this periodical in August and September, 1832.

Dr. John Brown, in an article published in 1864, was the first person to attribute to Thackeray this parody of "Eugene Aram";[1] and then, after an interval, the same opinion was expressed by Mr. Swinburne: "Just before 'Catherine' appeared another burlesque and grotesque horror—'Elizabeth Brownrigge,' a story in two parts, which ought to be Thackeray's, for, if it is not, he stole the idea, and to some extent the style, of his parodies on novels of criminal life, from this first sketch of the kind."[2]   On the strength of the belief of these eminent critics, Mr. Shepherd reprinted the satire in a collection of Thackeray's minor writings, "Sultan Stork," and included it, without a query-mark, in the bibliography appended to that volume. A few years later Mr. C. P. Anderson gave it, also without a query-mark, in his bibliography of Thackeray;[3] and, more recently, Mr. Charles Whibley has expressed his opinion that there is little doubt it is from Thackeray's hand.[4]   In opposition to this view are Mr. J. P. Johnson, who can see in it neither the touch nor the manner of Thackeray,[5] and Mr. M. H. Spielmann, who is inclined to ascribe it to Douglas Jerrold on the ground that it resembles the work of that author in the turns of expression, the handling of sentences and the peculiarities of dialogue.[6]   Certainly Jerrold, who had

[1] *North British Review.*
[2] Letter to Richard Herne Shepherd, printed in *Sultan Stork*, p. vii.
[3] Appended to Merivale and Marzials : *Thackeray*, 1891.
[4] *William Makepeace Thackeray (Modern English Writers)*, p. 28.
[5] *Early Writings of William Makepeace Thackeray.*
[6] *Bookman*, April 1901. A Review of "Thackeray's Stray Papers."

written the "Brownrigg Papers" in the *Weekly Times*, had, not long before the appearance of "Elizabeth Brownrigge," issued a similar parody, entitled "The Tutor Fiend and His Three Pupils."

The present writer, in a work published ten years ago, stated his belief that Thackeray wrote "Elizabeth Brownrigge" (although when reprinting it in "Thackeray's Stray Papers" he was careful to note that the authorship was doubtful). "The satirical 'Dedication to the Author of "Eugene Aram"' and the 'Advertisement' seem to be quite in Thackeray's style," he wrote then. "Indeed, the whole story seems an immature 'Catherine.'" This opinion was, of course, arrived at by a consideration of internal evidence, which is certainly strong, as the following extract from the "Dedication" shows :—

> From the frequent perusal of older works of imagination, I had learned so to weave the incidents of my story as to interest the feelings of the reader in favour of virtue, and to increase his detestation of vice. I have been taught by "Eugene Aram" to mix vice and virtue up together in such an inextricable confusion as to render it impossible that any preference should be given to either, or that the one, indeed, should be at all distinguishable from the other. . . . I am inclined to regard you as an original discoverer in the world of literary enterprise, and to reverence you as the father of a new "*lusus naturæ* school." There is no other title by which your manner could be so aptly designated. I am told, for instance, that in a former work, having to paint an adulterer, you described him as belonging to the class of country curates, among whom, perhaps, such a criminal is not met with once in a hundred years; while, on the contrary, being in search of a tender-hearted, generous, senti-

1846] DISPUTED AUTHORSHIP

mental, high-minded hero of romance, you turned to the pages of the "Newgate Calendar," and looked for him in the list of men who have cut throats for money, among whom a person in possession of such qualities could never have been met at all. Wanting a shrewd, selfish, worldly, calculating valet, you describe him as an old soldier, though he bears not a single trait of the character which might have been moulded by a long course of military service, but, on the contrary, is marked by all the distinguishing features of a bankrupt attorney, or a lame duck from the Stock Exchange. Having to paint a cat, you endow her with all the idiosyncrasies of a dog.

In spite of the Titmarshian flavour of this and other passages, the present writer has, however, abandoned the theory that Thackeray was the author of "Elizabeth Brownrigge." It has been said that the tale appeared in *Fraser's Magazine* in August and September, 1832 : that is to say, it must at latest have been written in July of that year—in which month Thackeray went to Paris, immediately after he came of age. It is not to be denied that if Thackeray did write this, he had special facilities for bringing it to the notice of the editor of the periodical in which it appeared, for he was on intimate terms with the editor in question, William Maginn; but, on the other hand, if he did write "Elizabeth Brownrigge" in July 1832, how is it that he did not follow up this ambitious start? It is true that several articles in subsequent numbers of the magazine are possibly by him, and a set of verses in May 1834 are known to be from his pen : but not even Mr. C. P. Johnson, the most indefatigable of bibliographers, puts forward anything of equal merit until " Fashnable Fax and Polite Annygoats" five years later. Indeed, when "Elizabeth Brownrigge" appeared, Thackeray had, so far as is known, written nothing but the trifles for the *Snob* and the *Gownsman*, and, after it appeared, nothing of any importance until 1837 ; it is scarcely conceivable that Thackeray should have written this clever satirical story, and then have fallen to the low level of his contributions to the *National Standard*. "Elizabeth Brownrigge" must not, therefore, figure among Thackeray's works.

Though Thackeray may not have written "Elizabeth Brownrigge," it is practically certain that he contributed frequently to *Fraser's Magazine* in and after 1834. Merely on the strength of the translation of Béranger's "*Il était un roi d'Yvetot*," which appeared in May of that year, it is highly improbable that even a friendly editor would have ventured in 1837 to *commission* the "Yellowplush Correspondence"—for from the heading, "The Yellowplush Correspondence—Fashnable Fax and Polite Annygoats," it is clear that there was to be a series of articles by Charles Yellowplush, and, we know from a notebook of Thackeray, that these were written, as all his work was then and after, from hand to mouth. There is further proof that Thackeray was a contributor in the frontispiece of the magazine for January 1835, a picture by Maclise showing the principal writers for the periodical dining at the house of the proprietor : Crofton Croker, Lockhart, Hook, Brewster, Moir, D'Orsay, Allan Cunningham, Carlyle, Brydges, Gleig, Mahony, Irving, "Barry Cornwall," Southey, Percival Bankes, Churchill, Murphy, Macwish, Ainsworth,

Coleridge, Hogg, Galt, Dunlop, Jerdan, and, four seats from Maginn, our Mr. Titmarsh.

What Thackeray wrote for *Fraser's Magazine* before November 1837 none now can say. He may have contributed the reviews of Whitehead's "Lives and Exploits of English Highwaymen" (March 1834), of " A Dozen of Novels" including Miss Edgeworth's "Helen" (April 1834), of Ainsworth's "Rookwood" (June 1834, and again on the appearance of the third edition, April 1836), Mrs. Trollope's "Paris and the Parisians" (February 1836); and the "Letters from Cambridge about the Art of Plucking"(June, July, August, 1836). "The Jew of York" (September 1836), and the reviews of James Grant's "The Great Metropolis" (December 1836) and of Landor's "Satire on Satirists" (April 1837) may be from his pen, as well as many other articles. It is sufficient, however, to assume that he contributed to the periodical, and that he scored his first great success with a review of " My Book, or, The Anatomy of Conduct," by one John Henry Skelton, a half-demented West-end linen-draper, who had conceived the idea that it was his mission in life to instruct the world in the canons of etiquette. This review, as all the world knows, was the famous " Fashnable Fax and Polite Annygoats," the first paper written by Mr. Charles Yellowplush, who dated his contribution from " No. — Grosvenor Square, 10th October, (N.B. Hairy Bell)." To this, which appeared in *Fraser's Magazine* for November 1837, was appended a note, written by Thackeray, but initialled O.Y. ("Oliver Yorke," *i.e.*, William Maginn), unaccountably omitted from most reprints :—

He who looketh from a tower sees more of the battle than the knights and captains engaged in it ; and, in like manner, he who stands behind a fashionable table knows more of society than the guests who sit at the board. It is from this source that our great novel-writers have drawn their experience, retailing the truths which they learned. It is not impossible that Mr. Yellowplush may continue his communications, when we shall be able to present the reader with *the only authentic picture of fashionable life* which has been given to the world in our time.

Mr. Yellowplush did continue his communications : in January came " Miss Shum's husband " ; from February to July (with the exception of April) were narrated the adventures of Mr. Deuceace ; and in August the erudite footman made his " Ajew," reappearing on the scene after an interval of more than two years to criticise Bulwer's play, "The Sea-Captain." From the start the "Correspondence" attracted so much attention, that, after three instalments had been printed, the author, who realised the value of the papers to the magazine, felt justified in demanding, at the point of the sword, as it were, higher remuneration for subsequent contributions.

Now comes another, and not a very pleasant point, on which I must speak [he wrote to James Fraser, the proprietor, in February 1838, from Boulogne]. I hereby give notice that I shall strike for wages.

You pay more to others, I find, than to me ; and so I intend to make some fresh conditions about Yellowplush. I shall write no more of that gentleman's remarks except at the rate of twelve guineas a sheet, and with a drawing for each number in which his story appears—the drawing two guineas.

Pray do not be angry at this decision on my part ; it is simply a bargain, which it is my duty to make.

Bad as he is, Mr. Yellowplush is the most popular
contributor to your magazine, and ought to be paid
accordingly : if he does not deserve more than the
monthly nurse, or the Blue Friars, I am a Dutch-
man.

I have been at work upon his adventures to-day,
and I will send them to you or not as you like, but in
common regard for myself I won't work under
price.

Well, I daresay you will be very indignant, and
swear I am the most mercenary of individuals. Not
so. But I am a better workman than most in your
crew and deserve a better price.

You must not, I repeat, be angry, or because we
differ as tradesmen break off a connection as friends.
Believe me that, whether I write for you or not, I
always shall be glad of your friendship and anxious
to have your good opinion.[1]

The sentence, "I am a better workman than most in
your crew," shows very clearly that Thackeray was under
no misapprehension as to the value of his support to
Regina, as members of the staff were pleased to call the
magazine ; and, if further proof is wanted, it shows that
he must have been a frequent contributor for some time
past, since he would scarcely have ventured, even on
the strength of three instalments of the "Yellowplush
Papers," to take up an attitude so independent. Perhaps after some discussion, which would account for
the absence of Mr. Yellowplush in March, the matter
at issue was adjusted, with the result that Thackeray
was a frequent contributor to the magazine for the next
nine years.

Thackeray's connection with *Fraser's Magazine* was
invaluable to him in the early days of his struggle for

[1] *Bookmart* (Pittsburg, Pa.), April 1887 ; Vol. IV, p. 446.

M

bread, since he could rely on it to provide him with a certain, if small, income; and if this periodical was useful to him, there is also no question that he rendered it yeoman's service. He had even at this time qualifications eminently calculated to attract editors: a pleasant, gossipy style, a practical experience with the pencil and the brush that enabled him to write with understanding on art, and an acquaintance with foreign countries and their literatures, rare in a writer for the magazines, in a day when travel was expensive. Indeed, there were not many men who could have volunteered to review French and German books, as Thackeray did when Thomas Longman, the proprietor of the *Edinburgh Review*, approached him as a possible contributor.

> I hardly know what subject to point out as suited to my capacity—light matter connected with art, humorous reviews, critiques of novels—French subjects, memoirs, poetry, history from Louis XV downward and of an earlier period—that of Froissart and Monstrelet—German light literature and poetry—though of these I know but little beyond what I learned in a year's residence in the country fourteen years ago.[1]

It was this first-hand knowledge of the Continent that emboldened Thackeray in 1842, on the eve of his departure for Ireland to write a Sketch-Book for Messrs. Chapman and Hall, to ask that firm for the editorship of the *Foreign Quarterly Review*, which they had just taken over.

> If you have a new editor, as you will, no doubt, and unless you have a great man like Mr. Carlyle

[1] *Letter in the British Museum Library.*

at the head of your undertaking, please to think of your humble servant, who is very anxious to have a calling and regular occupation of some kind, and could really, I think, do your duty very well [he wrote to Messrs. Chapman and Hall]. I know a couple of languages, French and German, and could know Italian in another month, having already a smattering ; and if your intention is not to have a pompous review, but a smart and lively one, I believe I should make as good an editor as another. . . . I need not tell you that I'm not so wedded to the Irish trip but that I would forego it for something more lasting, or for a turn, say in Germany, as ambassador of the *Foreign Quarterly*.[1]

The application was unsuccessful, for John Forster secured the post, but a perusal of Thackeray's contributions to the review show that here, too, his support was valuable.[2]

It was the accomplishments just enumerated that distinguished their possessor from the hack writers of the day, and were of great service to him at the beginning of his career ; though, once he had obtained a footing, his success was mainly due to the fact that he showed himself a master of the art of writing "on subjects relating to society in general, where a writer may be allowed to display the humorous *ego*, or a victim to be gently immolated."[3]

This was the sort of paper he preferred to compose, and he sought an opening in *Blackwood's Magazine*.

Some years back you used to have pleasant papers in *Blackwood* called "The World we live in"

---

[1] *Bookmart*, November 1885, Vol. III, p. 146.
[2] These articles were recently discovered by Mr. Robert S. Garnett, who published them in 1906 under the title of "The New Sketch Book."
[3] *Letter to Thomas Longman in the British Museum Library*.

[Thackeray wrote to Alexander Blackwood in 1840].
I should be glad to do something of like nature if
you are disposed to accept my contributions. No
politics, as much fun and satire as I can muster,
literary talk and criticism of a spicy nature, and
general gossip. I belong to a couple of clubs in
this village and can get together plenty of rambling
stuff. For instance, for next month Courvoisier's
hanging (I'll go on purpose), strictures on C. Phil-
lip's speech, the London Library, Tom Carlyle, the
Times, and account of Willis that may be racy
enough. If the project smiles upon you, as the
French say, please write me word. I can't afford to
begin and send the MSS. in advance, for if you
shouldn't approve the design my labour would be
wasted, as the article would be written for your
special readers, and no good next month.[1]

Blackwood would not have these papers ; and after
" Maga," a little later, declined " The Great Hoggarty
Diamond " Thackeray wooed it no more.

The young writer had a warm friend and eulogist in
Mr. (after Sir Henry) Cole, who introduced him to
Cobden for service in the *Anti-Corn Law Circular*.
" The artist is a genius both with his pen and his
pencil," Cole wrote with enthusiasm. " His vocation
is literary. He is full of humour and feeling.
Hitherto he has not had occasion to think much on
the subject of Corn Laws, and therefore wants the
stuff to work upon. He would like to combine both
writing and drawing when sufficiently primed, and
then he would write illustrated ballads, or tales, or anything. I think you would find him a useful auxiliary."[2]
Thackeray without delay followed up this introduction.

[1] Mrs. Oliphant : *William Blackwood and Sons*, Vol. II, p. 240.
[2] Sir Henry Cole : *Fifty Years of Public Work*.

I shall be glad [he wrote to Cobden, for whom he eventually drew two sketches] to do a single drawing, series, or what you will, for *money*, but I think the one you sent me would not be effective enough for the *Circular*, the figures are too many for so small a sized block, and the meaning mysterious—the river, to be a river, should occupy a deuce of a space [here he introduced a loose sketch]—even this fills up your length almost. What do you think of a howling group with this motto : *Give us this day our Daily Bread?* The words are startling. Of course I will do the proposed design if you wish.

Though it was to *Fraser's Magazine* Thackeray in these early years contributed most largely, he supplied drawings, stories, reviews, burlesques, and art criticism to all quarters where they were acceptable.

> Since he my faithful service did engage,
> To follow him through his queer pilgrimage,
> I've drawn and written many a line and page.
>
> Caricatures I scribbled have, and rhymes,
> And dinner-cards, and picture-pantomimes,
> And many little children's books at times.
>
> I've writ the foolish fancy of his brain ;
> The aimless jest that, striking, hath caused pain ;
> The idle word that he'd wish back again.
>
> I've helped him to pen many a line for bread.[1]

Thackeray contributed to those short-lived periodicals, the *Torch*, the *Parthenon*, and the *Britannia*, and also, it is said, to the *Globe;* he wrote on " Paris Caricatures " and on George Cruikshank's work for the *Westminster Review*, on French and German literature

---

[1] *The Pen and the Album.*

for the *Foreign Quarterly*, and on art for the *Pictorial Times;* he drew political cartoons for the *Anti-Corn Law Circular*, and discoursed on French manners and customs in the *Britannia* and the *Corsair* (New York); to *Bentley's Magazine* he sent "The Professor"; to *Ainsworth's Magazine*, "Sultan Stork"; to the *New Monthly Magazine*, "Mary Ancel", "Major Gahagan" and "The Bedford Row Conspiracy"; to *Cruikshank's Almanacks*, "Stubbs's Calendar" and "Barber Cox"; and to the *Omnibus*, "The King of Brentford's Testament." With the exception of "Major Gahagan," however, his best work went to *Fraser's Magazine*, where, after the "Yellowplush Correspondence," appeared, besides many articles, "Catherine" in 1839, "A Shabby Genteel Story" in 1840, "The Great Hoggarty Diamond" in 1841, the "Fitz-Boodle Papers" in 1842, "Men's Wives" in 1843, and "Barry Lyndon" in the following year.

The publication of the "Yellowplush Correspondence" in *Fraser's Magazine* marks an epoch in Thackeray's literary life, because thereafter he was regarded as one of the best writers for the periodicals. Such attention as it attracted in England, however, was as nothing to the success it achieved in America, where it was pirated before it had run its course, and appeared in book-form without the "Ajew."

The success of the "Correspondence" inspired Thackeray with the desire to offer some of his wares in book-form,[1] and in 1840 he induced John Macrone, who four years earlier had brought out "Sketches by

[1] The article on Cruikshank, signed "θ," in the *Westminster Review* for June 1840 was at once issued in book-form anonymously.

Boz," to publish a collection of articles and tales, more than half of which had appeared in the magazines, under the happy title of " The Paris Sketch Book. By Mr. Titmarsh." The venture met with no particular success, but its failure was not so complete as to deter Hugh Cunningham, Macrone's successor, from publishing "in decent duodecimo" early in the next year, "The Second Funeral of Napoleon," with which was included "The Chronicle of the Drum," which the periodicals had refused to print. Thackeray had gone to Paris with Monckton Milnes in December 1840 to witness the ceremonies in connection with the interment of the remains of Napoleon, brought from St. Helena to rest in the Hotel des Invalides. The little book was practically still-born. With characteristic humour, the author wrote that his future was assured, since he received 7½d. royalty, and if seven hundred and fifty thousand copies were disposed of, he would net no less than £3,125. "One hundred copies have already been sold," he added, "so that you see my fortune is very clear." Eventually the sales rose to one hundred and forty and no more. Possibly an article in the *Times* may account for this : Thackeray thought the affair of the Second Funeral humbug,' and said so, which brought the reviewer down on him.

Disbelief in heroes is very offensive to the world, it must be confessed (Thackeray replied to the attack, in the bantering manner he affected towards adverse criticism). There, now, is the *Times* newspaper, which the other day rated your humble servant for publishing an account of one of the great humbugs of modern days, *viz.*, the late funeral of Napoleon—

which rated me, I say, and talked in its own grave, roaring way, about the flippancy and conceit of Titmarsh.

O, you thundering old *Times!* Napoleon's funeral was a humbug, and your constant reader said so. The people engaged in it were humbugs, and this your Michael Angelo hinted at. There may be irreverence in this, and the process of humbug-hunting may end rather awkwardly for some people. But surely there is no conceit. The shamming of modesty is the most pert conceit of all, the *précieuse* affectation of deference where you don't feel it, the sneaking acquiescence in lies. It is very hard that a man may not tell the truth as he fancies it, without being accused of conceit: but so the world wags. As has already been prettily shown in that before-mentioned little book about Napoleon, that is still to be had of the publisher's, there is a ballad in the volume which, if properly studied, will be alone worth two-and-sixpence to any man.

Well, the funeral of Napoleon *was* a humbug; and being so, what was a man to call it? What do we call a rose? Is it disrespectful to the pretty flower to call it by its own innocent name? And, in like manner, are we bound, out of respect for society, to speak of humbug only in a circumlocutory way— to call it something else, as they say some Indian people do their devil—to wrap it up in riddles and charades? . . . Sacred word! it is kept out of the dictionaries, as if the great compilers of these pub-lications were afraid to utter it. Well then, the funeral of Napoleon was a humbug, as Titmarsh wrote ; and a still better proof that it was a humbug was this, that nobody bought Titmarsh's book, and of the 10,000 copies made ready by the publisher not above 3000 went off. It was a humbug, and an ex-ploded humbug. Peace be to it! *Parlons d'autres choses.*[1]

---

[1] *On Men and Pictures* (*Fraser's Magazine*, July 1841).

The failure of "The Second Funeral of Napoleon" deterred Cunningham from issuing a book by the same author, announced at the end of the other, as "Preparing for Immediate Publication" : "Dinner Reminiscences, or, The Young Gormandizer's Guide at Paris. By Mr. M. A. Titmarsh," whereupon Thackeray, too, abandoned the idea, and used the material he had collected in a paper, "The Memorials of Gormandizing."[1] Cunningham, however, still had enough belief in Thackeray to issue, also in 1841, "Comic Tales and Sketches. Edited and illustrated by Mr. Michael Angelo Titmarsh," which contained the cream of Thackeray's already printed writings, the "Yellowplush Correspondence", "Major Gahagan", "The Professor" and "The Bedford Row Conspiracy." These tales were accompanied by illustrations—the "Correspondence" having a new set in place of those that had appeared in *Fraser's Magazine*—and there was a pictorial title-page on which are depicted Yellowplush, Titmarsh, and Gahagan : "they are supposed to be marching hand-in-hand, and are just on the very brink of Immortality," so Thackeray concluded his preface to the volume : and there, on the brink of Immortality, they stand to this day seventy years later.

Whether Cunningham would have no more of Titmarsh, or Titmarsh would have no more of Cunningham, the fact remains that Thackeray, who never for a moment doubted he had "the right stuff" in him that must sooner or later achieve success, sought elsewhere a market for his manuscripts. He suggested to Messrs. Chapman and Hall that he should write a

[1] *Fraser's Magazine*, June 1841.

book on Ireland, and, the firm liking this idea, he toured through the Emerald Isle in the summer of 1842. Early in the next year the work appeared, not under the title of " The Cockney in Ireland," which the author told Laman Blanchard had been abandoned owing to "the pathetic remonstrances of the publishers,"[1] but as " The Irish Sketch Book," and signed, of course, with the now familiar " Michael Angelo Titmarsh," though in the dedication Thackeray's name appeared for the first time in one of his books :

> Laying aside for the moment the travelling title of Mr. Titmarsh, let me . . . subscribe myself, my dear Lever, Most sincerely and gratefully yours, W. M. Thackeray.

Charles Lever, it may be mentioned, was much blamed by some of his countrymen for accepting the dedication of a book that, according to them, was full of blunders and exaggerations—though Edward Fitz-Gerald wrote from Dublin : "It is all true. I ordered a bath here, and when I got in the waiter said it was heated to 90 degrees, but it was scalding ; he next locked me up in the room instead of my locking him out." Lever, however, ignored these attacks, and, confident that the author had no intention to misrepresent the Irish, reviewed the book favourably in the *Dublin University Magazine*, of which he was then editor. Lever was undoubtedly right in his belief, for Thackeray never desired to do more than poke fun at the eccentricities of the inhabitants of the neighbouring island. If he amused himself by exaggerating their

---

[1] Letter to Laman Blanchard, April 21, 1843 (in Blanchard Jerrold : *A Day with W. M. Thackeray*, p. 328).

pronunciation, he did no harm; and who can help
smiling at the "Lyra Hibernica"?

The noble Chair stud at the stair,
    And bade the dthrums to thump; and he
Did thus evince, to that Black Prince,
    The welcome of his Company.
O fair the girls, and rich the curls,
    And bright the oys, you saw there was;
And fixed each oye, ye there could spoi,
    On GINERAL JUNG BAHAWTHER was!

The Gineral great then tuk his sate
    With all the other ginerals,
(Bedad his troat, his vest, his coat,
    All bleezed with precious minerals);
And as he there, with princely air,
    Recloinin on his cushion was,
All round about his royal chair
    The squeezin and the pushin was.
O PAT, such girls, such Jukes, and Earls,
    Such fashion and nobilitee!
Just think of TIM and fancy him
    Amidst the hoigh gentility.[1]

During the visit to Ireland Thackeray stayed with
Lever at the latter's house at Templeogue, and when
Thackeray died some twenty years after, the other
could still recall "with a heavy heart . . . all our long
evenings together—mingling over plans for the future
many a jest and many a story."[2]   Thackeray had read
Lever's books, but Lever at the outset knew no more
of Thackeray than he had learned from the letter of

[1] *Mr. Molony's Account of the Ball given to the Nepaulese Ambassador
by the Peninsular and Oriental Company.*
[2] Letter to John Blackwood, January 1864 (in E. Downey: *Life and
Letters of Charles Lever*, Vol. II, p. 2.)

introduction that the Englishman brought, and their relations were merely formal. At dinner, however, Thackeray told his host that he would rather have written Harry Lorrequer's rendering of the German student song, " *Der Papst lebt herrlich in der Welt* " ("The Pope he leads a happy life"), than anything he had himself done in literature. When Lever was convinced that Thackeray was sincere, he was very pleased with the handsome compliment, and soon a more cordial tone prevailed. "Thackeray's conversation flowed more easily on the whole, like the deeper current of a river meandering through a cultivated country, and only occasionally quickening its pace and gathering force to dash over some well-selected point," Major Dwyer has written ; " Lever's, on the contrary, resembled a mountain torrent, leaping over rocks and precipices from pool to pool, in clouds of sparkling spray." [1]

"Mr. Titmarsh" had for some time been known to a small and discerning section of the reading public, but, as it has been shown, "The Irish Sketch Book" was his first successful book : though a second edition was not brought out until 1845, the thousand copies of the first edition were soon exhausted. His new publishers were pleased, and they arranged that the first volume of a forthcoming monthly series of original biographical works should be "A Life of Talleyrand. By W. M. Thackeray."

> I will engage to write the volume [Thackeray had written to them on July 16, 1844], and to have the MS. in your hands by December 1, health permitting,

[1] W. Fitzpatrick : *Life of Charles Lever.*

and will sign an agreement to that effect, if you will
have the goodness to prepare one.

This arrangement was first postponed in favour of
another Sketch-Book, "From Cornhill to Cairo," and
then, though Thackeray told his mother he had "read
enormously" for the projected biography, it was
abandoned in favour of another volume for which he
was to be paid £200.   The "little book about the
Mediterranean," as Thackeray referred to it, came to be
written by pure chance.   "Mr. Titmarsh" was dining
at a club on August 20, 1844,[1] and a friend told him he
was going for a tour in the Mediterranean arranged
by the P. and O. Company.   The programme was
alluring : "In the space of a couple of months as many
men and cities were to be seen as Ulysses surveyed and
noted in ten years": Malta, Athens, Smyrna, Constantinople, Jerusalem, Cairo, were to be visited.   The
idea of beholding these famous places took possession
of Thackeray's mind ; and when his friend suggested
he should join the party, he wavered.

> Mr. Titmarsh considered all these things, but also
> the difficulty of the situation ; he had but thirty-six
> hours to get ready for so portentous a journey—he
> had engagements at home—finally, could he afford
> it ?   In spite of these objections, however, with every
> glass of claret the enthusiasm somehow rose, and the
> difficulties vanished.   But when Mr. James, to crown
> all, said that he had no doubt that his friends, the
> Directors of the Peninsular and Oriental Company,
> would make Mr. Titmarsh the present of a berth

[1] In the Preface to the book, Thackeray, with characteristic carelessness, gives wrong dates both for the conversation at the club and his
departure : for July 24 and July 26 we must read August 20 and
August 22.

for the voyage, all objection ceased on his part : to break his outstanding engagements—to write letters to his amazed family, stating they were not to expect him to dinner on Saturday fortnight, as he would be at Jerusalem on that day—to purchase eighteen shirts and lay in a sea stock of Russia ducks—was the work of twenty-four hours.[1]

Though this trip was an agreeable change to the busy literary man, it was not all holiday. He had to make notes for the book he had undertaken to write ; he was sending contributions to *Punch*, notably the "Travelling Notes" and "Punch in the East"; and he finished "Barry Lyndon," which since January had been appearing month by month in *Fraser's Magazine*. The last chapters gave him more trouble than anything he had done, and it was with a feeling of relief that he brought it to a close. He finished it at Malta, where the party was in quarantine, and he noted in his diary : "November 1. Wrote 'Barry' but slowly, and with great difficulty."—"November 2. Wrote 'Barry' with no more success than yesterday." —"November 3. Finished 'Barry,' after great throes, late at night."

Though Thackeray worked hard, not only on "Barry Lyndon" and for *Punch*, but also on the drawings for "Mrs. Perkins's Ball," he enjoyed the tour and thoroughly appreciated the change from town life.

It is worth while to have made the journey for the pleasure : to have walked the deck on long nights, and have thought of home. You have no leisure to do so in the city. You don't see the heavens shine above you so purely there, or the stars so clearly.[2]

[1] *From Cornhill to Grand Cairo—Preface.*   [2] *Ibid.*. chap. xiv.

814.3
F4C 24

920
363 m

_____ of _____

rder to attend Mount Union Co
given your name as one of __

kindly indicate below whethe
d to such aid, the financial
nd whether or not _____ would

ly at your earliest convenie
plication promptly.

truly,

808.3
M112L

820.4
T363e

858
T363m

950
T363b

950
T363d

Thackeray returned to England in December (1844), and during the next year he wrote his account of the tour which, with his own sketches transferred to the wood by Eyre Crowe, appeared in January 1846 under the title of : "Notes of a Journey from Cornhill to Grand Cairo, by way of Lisbon, Athens, Constantinople, and Jerusalem, Performed in the Steamers of the Peninsular and Oriental Company. By Mr. M. A. Titmarsh, Author of 'The Irish Sketch Book,' etc."

When "From Cornhill to Grand Cairo" appeared, Carlyle made no secret of the fact that he thought it undignified of Thackeray to have accepted a free passage, and he compared the transaction to the practice of a blind fiddler going to and fro on a penny ferry-boat in Scotland, playing tunes to the passengers for halfpence.[1] Indeed, he felt so strongly on the matter that he voiced his objection in *Tait's Edinburgh Magazine* (March 1846).

It is that comparison of the blind fiddler who "*sends round his hat*," that ought to be devoted to the indignation of the press of this kingdom [Thackeray wrote in reply]. Your constant reader has never played on the English—or on the Scotch fiddle.

He leaves the sending round of hats to professors of the Caledonian Cremona. He was not "crimped" by the Peninsular and Oriental Company, nor called upon to fiddle for their amusement, nor rewarded with silver spoons by that excellent Company. A gentleman who takes a vacant seat in a friend's carriage is not supposed to receive a degrading obligation, or called upon to pay for his ride by extra joking, facetiousness, etc. ; nor surely is the person who so gives you the use of his carriage

[1] Sir Charles Gavan Duffy : *Conversations with Curlyle.*

required to present you also with a guinea or to pay your tavern bill. The critic, in fact, has shown uncommon keenness in observing the manners of his national violinist; but must know more of them than of the customs of English gentlemen.

If the critic himself is a man of letters and fiddles professionally, why should he abuse his Stradivarius? If he is some disguised nobleman of lofty birth, superb breeding, and vast wealth, who only fiddles for pleasure, he should spare those gentlefolks in whose company he condescends to perform. But I don't believe he's a noble amateur—I think he must be a professional man of letters. It is only literary men nowadays who commit this suicidal sort of impertinence; who sneak through the world ashamed of their calling, and show their independence by befouling the trade by which they live.[1]

Thackeray was made very angry by the attack, as can be seen from the vigour of his rebuke, and his subsequent reference to it in a Postscript added to the book when a second edition was called for in August. Though his friend Charles Buller told Thackeray he agreed with Carlyle, and that it was also his opinion that "Mr. Titmarsh" ought not to have gone fiddling for halfpence or otherwise in any steamboat under the sun,[2] it is not easy to see why all this virtuous indignation and anxiety was felt for the dignity of Thackeray and the literary profession; for not only did the latter not "puff" the Company, but, as he said, the free passage was given to him not by the Company but by one of his friends.

"Titmarsh at Jerusalem will certainly be an era in Christianity," Edward FitzGerald had said when

---

[1] *Punch*, March 14, 1846.
[2] Sir Charles Gavan Duffy : *Conversations with Carlyle.*

Thackeray went "From Cornhill to Grand Cairo." But Jerusalem did not arouse any feeling of mockery in the traveller, who, since there was no false sentiment to excite his satire, was much moved at the sight of the city of many traditions.

From this terrace [he wrote at Jerusalem], whence we looked in the morning, a great part of the city spread before us :—white domes upon domes, and terraces of the same character as our own. Here and there, from among these whitewashed mounds round about, a minaret rose, or a rare date-tree ; but the chief part of the vegetation near was that odious tree, the prickly pear,—one huge green wart growing out of another, armed with spikes, as inhospitable as the aloe, without shelter or beauty. To the right the Mosque of Omar rose ; the rising sun behind it. Yonder steep tortuous lane before us, flanked by ruined walls on either side, has borne, time out of mind, the title of Via Dolorosa ; and tradition has fixed the spots where the Saviour rested, bearing His cross to Calvary. But of the mountain, rising immediately in front of us, a few grey olive-trees speckling the yellow side here and there, there can be no question. That is the Mount of Olives. Bethany lies beyond it. The most sacred eyes that ever looked on this world, have gazed on those ridges ; it was there He used to walk and teach. With shame and humility one looks towards the spot where that inexpressible Love and Benevolence lived and breathed ; where the great yearning heart of the Saviour interceded for all our race ; and whence the bigots and traitors of His day led Him away to kill Him.[1]

Religion was much in Thackeray's thoughts, though there is little mention of it in his books.

"O awful name of God! Light unbearable! Mystery unfathomable! Vastness immeasurable!" he exclaimed

[1] *From Cornhill to Grand Cairo*, chap. xiii.

N

in a white heat of indignation, when writing of
"Madame Sand and the New Apocalypse"; and he
was as angry with Mrs. Trollope, who in her novel,
"The Vicar of Wrexhill," fulminated against those
who interpreted the Scriptures in other ways than she.

> Mrs. Trollope . . . who sees so keenly the follies
> of the other party—how much vanity there is in Bible
> Meetings—how much sin even at Missionary Societies
> —how much cant and hypocrisy there is among those
> who desecrate the awful name of God by mixing it up
> with their mean private interests and petty projects—
> Mrs. Trollope cannot see that there is any hypocrisy
> or bigotry on her part. She, who designates the rival
> party as false, and wicked, and vain, tracing all their
> actions to the basest motives, declaring their worship
> of God to be only one general hypocrisy, their con-
> duct at home one fearful scene of crime, is blind to
> the faults on her own side. Always bitter against
> the Pharisees, she does as the Pharisees do. It is
> vanity, very likely, which leads these people to use
> God's name so often, and to devote all to perdition
> who do not coincide with their peculiar notions. Is
> Mrs. Trollope less vain than they are when she de-
> clares, and merely *declares*, her own to be the real
> creed, and stigmatises its rival so fiercely? Is Mrs.
> Trollope serving God, in making abusive and licen-
> tious pictures of those who serve Him in a different
> way? Once, as Mrs. Trollope has read—it was a
> long time ago!—there was a woman taken in sin ;
> people brought her before a great Teacher of Truth,
> who lived in those days. "Shall we not kill her?"
> said they ; "the law commands that all adultresses
> shall be killed."
> We can fancy a Mrs. Trollope in the crowd, shout-
> ing, "Oh, the wretch ! Oh, the abominable harlot !
> Kill her, by all means—stoning is really too good for
> her !" But what did the Divine Teacher say? He
> was quite as anxious to prevent the crime as any Mrs.
> Trollope of them all ; but He did not make any

allusion to it. He did not describe the manner in which the poor creature was caught, He made no speech to detail the indecencies which she had committed, or to raise the fury of the mob against her. He said, " Let the man who is without sin himself throw the first stone !" Whereupon the Pharisees and Mrs. Trollopes slunk away, for they knew they were no better than she. There was as great a sin in His eyes as that of the poor erring woman,—it was the sin of pride.[1]

Though Thackeray attacked Mrs. Trollope on the score of narrow-mindedness, it must be admitted that he was not always very tolerant of those whose religious beliefs differed from his own. His dislike of the Jews, of whom he always wrote with contempt, was based upon his objection to the race rather than to their religion, of which latter, indeed, he never spoke ; but the Roman Catholics he despised, not as individuals, but because of their religion, and he wrote of that with great harshness.

I once went into a church at Rome at the request of a Catholic friend, who declared the interior to be so beautiful and glorious, that he thought (he said) it must be like Heaven itself. I found walls hung with cheap strips of pink and white calico, altars covered with artificial flowers, a number of wax candles, and plenty of gilt paper ornaments. The place seemed to me like a shabby theatre ; and here was my friend on his knees at my side, plunged in a rapture of wonder and devotion. I could get no better impression out of this most famous Church in the world. The

---

[1] *Our Batch of Novels for December 1837* (*Fraser's Magazine*, January 1838). Shortly after Thackeray had written this article he was invited to a dinner-party at which Mrs. Trollope would be present. " Oh, by Jove ! I can't come," he exclaimed. " I've just cut up her ' Vicar of Wrexhill ' in a review. I think she tells lies." (Richard Bedingfield : *Recollections of Thackeray*.)

deceits are too open and flagrant : the inconsistencies and contrivances too monstrous. It is hard even to sympathise with persons who receive them as genuine ; and though (as I know and saw in the case of my friend at Rome) the believer's life may be passed in the purest exercise of faith and charity, it is difficult even to give him credit for honesty, so barefaced seem to be the impostures which he professes to believe and reverence. It costs one no small effort even to admit the possibility of a Catholic's credulity : to share in his rapture and devotion is still further out of your power ; and I could get from this church no other emotion but those of shame and pain ![1]

In the columns of *Punch* he appeared in active opposition to the " Papal Aggression," though according to Sir Francis Burnand, he had little knowledge of the subject, and subsequently expressed his regret that he had taken part in the attack.

When Thackeray was at Brighton he went to hear a sermon by the Rev. Joseph Sortain, the incumbent of the Countess of Huntingdon's Chapel, upon which he commented :

It was about the origin of nations he spoke, one of those big themes on which a man can talk eternally and with a never ending outpouring of words ; and he talked magnificently, about the Arabs for the most part, and tried to prove that because the Arabs acknowledged their descent from Ishmael or Esau, therefore the Old Testament History was true. But the Arabs may have had Esau for a father, and yet the bears may not have eaten up the little children for quizzing Elisha's bald head.[2]

Thackeray, indeed, had some doubts as to the infallibility of the Bible, and when Richard Bedingfield

[1] *From Cornhill to Grand Cairo*, chap. xiii.
[2] *A Collection of Letters of W. M. Thackeray*, p. 35.

mentioned Thomas Cooper's lecture on Christ, "Oh,
Cooper, the Chartist!" he rejoined. "I suppose he
only makes Christ a reformer! *I don't know what to
think!*" But such expressions were rare with him, and
it seems certain that if he sometimes felt he could not
accept the letter of the Bible, he never ceased to believe
in its spirit. "One Sunday evening in December,"
Dr. John Brown has recorded, "Thackeray was walking with two friends along the Dean Road, to the west
of Edinburgh—one of the noblest outlets to any city.
It was a lovely evening; such a sunset as one never
forgets; a rich dark bar of cloud hovered over the sky,
going down behind the Highland hills, lying bathed
in amethystine bloom; between this cloud and the hills
there was a narrow strip of the pure ether of a tender
cowslip colour, lucid, and as if it were the very body of
heaven in its clearness; every object standing out as
if etched upon the sky. The north-west end of the
Corstorphine Hill, with its trees and rocks, lay in the
heart of this pure radiance, and there a wooden crane,
used in the granary below, was so placed as to assume
the figure of a cross; there it was, unmistakably lifted
up against the crystalline sky. All three gazed at it
silently. As they gazed, Thackeray gave utterance in a
tremulous, gentle, and rapid voice, to what all were
feeling, in the word 'Calvary!' The friends walked
on in silence, and then turned to other things. All
that evening he was very gentle and serious, speaking
as he seldom did, of divine things—of death, of sin,
of eternity, of salvation, expressing his simple faith in
God and in his Saviour."[1]

[1] *Thackeray* (*North British Review*, February 1864).

Like all true men, he had no fear of death, and again and again he expressed his conviction that sympathy was needed not for those who had gone before but for those who remained.

Where can a good and pious man be better than in the presence of God? away from ill, and temptation, and care, and secure of reward [he said in a letter of condolence written to Miss Charlotte Low in 1849]. What a comfort it is to think that he, who was so good and faithful here, must be called away to live among the good and just for ever! There never seems to me any cause for grief at the thought of a good man dying, beyond the sorrow for those who survive him, and trusting in God's mercy and wisdom, infinite here and everywhere, await the day when they too shall be called away.[1]

[1] Canon Irvine : *A Study for Colonel Newcome* (*Nineteenth Century*, October 1893).

CHAPTER X

ON PICTURES AND BOOKS

The savagery of criticism in the earlier decades of the nineteenth century —Thackeray's papers on art—his outspokenness—and the anger of the painters—his opinions of "Christian" or "Catholic" art—and of the historical school of painting—his appreciation of "The Fighting Téméraire"—and of George Cruikshank—miscellaneous criticism of books—on Byron—on the annuals—his attack on Ainsworth— his explanation—on the Newgate school of fiction—"Catherine"— its purpose—and the author's criticism of his book—his savage attacks on Bulwer-Lytton—and his subsequent cry of "Peccavi"— "Mr. Yellowplush's Ajew"—his appreciation of some contemporary writers—Scott and Dumas his favourite novelists—his opinions of Swift, Sterne, Addison, Steele, Goldsmith, Prior and Gay—of Smollett and Fielding—his love for kindly writers—and happy endings.

IN the late thirties and forties of the last century, when Thackeray was a reviewer, the most noticeable feature of contemporary criticism was savagery. Party spirit ran high, and a Tory had as little chance of obtaining justice at the hands of the pundits of the *Edinburgh Review* as a Whig of receiving commendation from the writers of the *Quarterly Review, Blackwood's* or *Fraser's Magazine*. "You have called Hazlitt pimpled, affected, ignorant, a Cockney scribbler, etc.," Maginn wrote to William Blackwood in 1823; "but what is that to what he has said to the most brilliant men of the age? Hook-nosed Wellington, vulture-beaked Southey, hanging-browed Croker, down-looking Jack Murray, and Mudford fat as fleecy hosiery." If Hazlitt led the way, Macaulay and Croker, Lockhart and Maginn were not far behind, and, at a distance, Thackeray followed in their footsteps. A Whig on the staff of a Tory magazine, Thackeray was not asked to exercise his satirical powers on political personages ; and to him fell the more congenial task of reviewing art and letters : in which field he restrained himself not at all, and when he disliked a book or a picture left nothing of his disapproval to the imagination of his readers.

Thackeray's papers on art were certainly as outspoken as they were amusing, and his annual humoristical article on the exhibitions so infuriated the painters that Frank Stone told Edward FitzGerald that "Thackeray would get himself horsewhipped one day by one of the infuriated Apelleses." In art as in literature Thackeray sought the natural, and when he could find only affectation, he wielded the critical flail with no little vigour. The "Christian" or "Catholic" art seemed to him humbug, and he attacked it accordingly.

Here, for instance, is Chevalier Ziegler's picture of "St. Luke painting the Virgin." St. Luke has a monk's dress on, embroidered, however, smartly round the sleeves. The Virgin sits in an immense yellow-ochre halo, with her son in her arms. She looks preternaturally solemn ; as does St. Luke, who is eyeing his paint-brush with an intense, ominous, mystical look. They call this Catholic art. There is nothing, my dear friend, more easy in life. First take your colours, and rub them down clear—bright carmine, bright yellow, bright sienna, bright ultramarine, bright green. Make your costumes as much

WILLIAM MAKEPEACE THACKERAY
From an unpublished water-colour drawing by D. Dighton
Reproduced by permission of Major William H. Lambert

as possible like the costumes of the early part of the fifteenth century. Paint them in with the above colours, and if on a gold ground, the more "Catholic" your art is. Dress your Apostles like priests before the altar ; and remember to have a good commodity of crosiers, censers, and other such gimcracks, as you may see in the Catholic chapels, in Sutton Street, or elsewhere. Deal in Virgins, and dress them like a burgomaster's wife by Cranach or Van Eyck. Give them all long twisted tails to their gowns, and proper angular draperies. Place all their heads on one side, with the eyes shut and the proper solemn simper. At the back of the head, draw, and gild with gold-leaf, a halo, or glory, of the exact shape of a cart-wheel : and you have the thing done. It is Catholic art *tout craché;* as Louis Philippe says.

He had little affection for the historical school, and made cruel fun of Haydon's immense canvases, of one of which he wrote :

Let us hope somebody will buy. Who, I cannot tell ; it will not do for a chapel ; it is too big for a house : I have it—it might answer to hang up over a caravan at a fair, if a travelling orrery were exhibited within.[1]

Thackeray had his likes and dislikes like any other critic, but when he saw fine work he rarely failed to recognise it. The author of the biography of Turner has stated that " Thackeray had more than a finger in lashing the dotage of this great man's genius," but, though the critic did not think highly of " Cicero at his Villa " and other works of the painter, and did not know whether " The Slave-Trader " was sublime or ridiculous, his splendid tribute to " The Fighting

[1] *Picture Gossip (Fraser's Magazine,* June, 1845.)

Téméraire" made amends for his want of appreciation of the other pieces.

I must request you to turn your attention to a noble river piece by J. W. M. Turner, Esq., R.A., "The Fighting Téméraire"—as grand a painting as ever figured on the walls of any academy, or came from the easel of any painter. The old Téméraire is dragged to her last home by a little, spiteful, diabolical steamer. A mighty red sun, amidst a host of flaring clouds, sinks to rest on one side of the picture, and illumines a river that seems interminable, and a countless navy that fades away into such a wonderful distance as never was painted before. The little demon of a steamer is belching out a volume (why do I say a volume? not a hundred volumes could express it) of foul, lurid, red-hot malignant smoke, paddling furiously and lashing up the water about it; while behind it (a cold grey moon looking down on it), slow, sad, and majestic, follows the brave old ship, with death, as it were, written on her. . . . It is absurd, you will say (and with a great deal of reason) for Titmarsh, or any other Briton, to grow so politically enthusiastic about a four-foot canvas, representing a ship, a steamer, a river, and a sunset. But herein surely lies the power of the great artist. He makes you see and think of a good deal more than the objects before you; he knows how to soothe or intoxicate, to fire or to depress, by a few notes, or forms, or colours, of which we cannot trace the effects to the source, but only ac-acknowledge the power. I recollect some years ago, at the theatre at Weimar, hearing Beethoven's "Battle of Vittoria," in which, amidst a storm of glorious music, the air of "God save the King" was introduced. The very instant it began, every Englishman in the house was bolt upright, and so stood reverently until the air was played out. Why so? From some such thrill of excitement as makes us glow and rejoice over Mr. Turner and his "Fighting Téméraire," which I am sure, when the art of translating colours into music or poetry shall be discovered, will be found to be a magnificent natural ode or piece of music.[1]

Thackeray's papers on art are too well known for it to be desirable here, where the object is to describe rather than to criticise them, to embark upon a lengthy discussion, and these brief remarks may conclude with the well-deserved panegyric on one of the greatest of the humoristical artists, upon whose work he was well qualified to speak.

The reader will perhaps wonder at the high-flown tone in which we speak of the services and merits of an individual, whom he considers a humble scraper on steel, that is wonderfully popular already. But none of us remember all the benefits we owe him; they have come one by one, one driving out the memory of the other; it is only when we come to examine them altogether as the writer has done, who has a pile of books on the table before him—a heap of personal kindnesses from George Cruikshank (not presents, if you please, for we bought, borrowed, or stole every one of them), that we feel what we owe him. Look at one of Mr. Cruikshank's works, and we pronounce him an excellent humourist. Look at all, his reputation is increased by a kind of geometrical progression; as a whole diamond is a hundred times more valuable than the hundred splinters into which it might be broken would be. A fine rough English diamond is this about which we have been writing.[2]

Thackeray in these early days of his literary career was, as it has been shown, prepared to write for anybody or on anything, and a glance at the subjects with

---

[1] *A Second Lecture on the Fine Arts* (*Fraser's Magazine*, June 1839).

[2] *An Essay on the Genius of George Cruikshank* (*Westminster Review*, June 1840).

which he dealt recalls the picture he subsequently presented of his young friend, Pendennis.

> The courage of young critics is prodigious : they clamber up to the judgment-seat, and, with scarce a hesitation, give their opinion upon works the most intricate or profound. Had Macaulay's History or Herschell's Astronomy been put before Pen at this period, he would have looked through the volumes, meditated his opinion over a cigar, and signified his august approval of either author, as if the critic had been their born superior, and indulgent master and patron. By the help of the "Biographie Universelle" or the British Museum, he would be able to take a rapid *résumé* of a historical period, and allude to names, dates, and facts, in such a masterly, easy way, as to astonish his mamma at home, who wondered where her boy could have acquired such a prodigious store of reading, and himself, too, when he came to read over his articles two or three months after they had been composed, and when he had forgotten the subject and the books which he had consulted. At that period of his life, Mr. Pen owns that he would not have hesitated, at twenty-four hours' notice, to pass an opinion upon the greatest scholars, or to give a judgment upon the Encyclopædia.[1]

Thackeray was probably not called upon to review an encyclopædia, but he did not hesitate to pronounce judgment upon Carlyle's "French Revolution," Count Valerian Krasinski's "History of the Reformation in Poland," Tyler's "Life of Henry V," Fraser's "Journey from Constantinople to Teheran," and scores of other works upon which he was certainly not able to speak with authority. There were, however, some subjects more congenial to him, and the expression of his opinions on these are of assistance in the task of

[1] *Pendennis*, chap. xxxvi.

presenting his character. We see him from the first tilting with all his powers against affectation, against snobbery and against the degradation of the literary art. With what fire did he attack Byron on the first of these counts.

Give me a fresh, dewy, healthy rose out of Somersetshire; not one of those superb, tawdry, unwholesome exotics, which are only good to make poems about. Lord Byron wrote more cant of this sort than any poet I know of. Think of "the peasant girls with dark blue eyes" of the Rhine—the brown-faced, flat-nosed, thick-lipped, dirty wenches! Think of "filling high a cup of Samian wine"; small beer is nectar compared to it, and Byron himself always drank gin. That man *never* wrote from his heart. He got up rapture and enthusiasm with an eye to the public; . . . Our native bard! *Mon dieu! He* Shakespeare's, Milton's, Keats', Scott's native bard! Well, woe be to the man who denies the public gods![1]

How angry he was with the artists and authors who contributed to the " Keepsake " and other trashy annuals, and how vigorously he attacked them again and again in *Fraser's Magazine* and the *Times!*

Miss Landon, Miss Mitford, or my Lady Blessington, writes a song upon the opposite page [to the plate], about water lily, chilly, stilly, shivering beside a streamlet, plighted, blighted, love-benighted, falsehood sharper than a gimlet, lost affection, recollection, cut connexion, tears in torrents, true love-token, spoken, broken, sighing, dying, girl of Florence, and so on. The poetry is quite worthy of the picture, and a little sham sentiment is employed to illustrate a little sham art. . . . It cannot be supposed that Miss Landon, a woman of genius,— Miss Mitford, a lady of exquisite wit and taste—

[1] *From Cornhill to Grand Cairo*, chap. v.

should, of their own accord, sit down to indite namby-pamby verses about silly, half-decent pictures; or that Jenkins, Parris, Meadows, and Co., are not fatigued by this time with the paltry labour assigned to them. . . . Who sets them to this wretched work?—to paint these eternal fancy portraits, of ladies in voluptuous attitudes and various stages of disha-bille, to awaken the dormant sensibilities of misses in their teens, or tickle the worn-out palettes of rakes and *roués*. What a noble occupation for a poet! what a delicate task for an artist![1]

Even more likely than these ephemeral productions to bring letters into contempt was a manifesto issued by Ainsworth, when that novelist took over the *Monthly Magazine* from Colburn; and this in a vigorous pro-test, unknown to the present generation. Thackeray held up to ridicule.

Mr. Ainsworth, "on whom the Editorship of the *New Monthly Magazine* has devolved," parades a list of contributors to that brilliant periodical, and says he has secured the aid of several writers "*eminent not only for talent,* BUT FOR HIGH RANK."

Are they of high rank as authors, or in the Red Book? Mr. Ainsworth can't mean that the readers of his Magazine care for an author because he happens to be a lord—a flunkey might—but not a gentleman who has any more brains than a fool. A literary gentleman who respects his calling doesn't surely mean to propitiate the public by saying, "I am going to write for you, and—and Lord Fitzdiddle is going to write too."

Hang it, man, *let* him write—write and be—suc-cessful, or write and be—unsuccessful, according to his merits. But don't let us talk about high rank in the republic of letters—let us keep *that* place clear. Publishers have sought for lordlings, we know, and

[1] *A Word on the Annuals* (*Fraser's Magazine*, December 1837).

got them to put their unlucky names to works which they never wrote ; but don't let men of letters demean themselves in this way.

No, William Harrison, trust to your own powers and genius—trust to the harrowing influence of the " Revelations of London "—trust to the contributors "who have shed a lustre over the Magazine," the enterprising and erudite Whatdyecallem ; Thingamy "whose domestic tales have found an echo in every bosom," and the rest. But don't let us hear any more of high rank as a recommendation.[1]

No sooner had these lines gone to the printer than Thackeray felt uncomfortable at the thought of attacking a man he knew from behind the safe shield of anonymity, and he proceeded to avow the authorship.

Of course I'll come to dinner on Sunday, and we are just as good friends as ever [he wrote to Ainsworth, on June 30, 1845]. Wasn't it much better to complain and explain ? I think so—and the imperial house of Titmarsh is now satisfied. There's one thing I regret very much, and must be told to you now in making a clean breast of it—is a certain paragraph in the next *Punch*, relating to a certain advertisement about contributors, " not only of talent, *but of rank*." This moved my wrath ; and has been hardly handled —this was before our meeting and explanation—I always must think it a very objectionable advertisement—but shouldn't have lifted my hand to smite my friend, had explanation come earlier, so that now *you* must be called upon to play the part of forgiver, in which I'm sure you will shine. . . . Your terms are prodigiously good, and if I can see the material for a funny story you shall have it.[2]

[1] *Immense Opportunity* (*Punch*, July 5, 1845). This paper has only been reprinted in Macmillan's edition of Thackeray's Works (Vol. XVII, " Travels in London, etc.").

[2] M. H. Spielmann : *Thackeray's Hitherto Unpublished Contributions to " Punch,"* p. 133.

O

Thackeray, however, did not find material for a "funny story," and he never wrote again for the *New Monthly Magazine*, but it is pleasant to relate that Ainsworth accepted the olive branch, and that henceforth the relations between them were cordial.

To return to Thackeray as a reader and critic of books. Something has already been said of his attitude towards the Newgate school of fiction, and he was never weary of protesting against it.

> Vice is never to be mistaken for virtue in Fielding's honest downright books ; it goes by its name, and invariably gets its punishment. See the consequences of honesty ! Many a squeamish lady of our time would throw down one of these romances with horror, but would go through every page of Mr. Ainsworth's "Jack Sheppard" with perfect comfort to herself. Ainsworth dared not paint his hero as the scoundrel he knew him to be ; he must keep his brutalities in the background, else the public morals will be outraged, and so he produces a book quite absurd and unreal, and infinitely more immoral than anything Fielding ever wrote. "Jack Sheppard" is immoral actually because it is decorous. The Spartans, who used to show drunken slaves to their children, took care, no doubt, that the slave should be really and truly drunk. Sham drunkenness which never passed the limits of propriety, but only went so far as to be amusing, would be rather an object to incite youth to intoxication than to deter him from it, and some late novels have always struck us in the same light.[1]

This clearly expressed the view he held on the subject, and "Catherine," though presented as a story, was, in fact, an attempt to counteract the influence of those books that made heroes of highwaymen and murderers,

[1] Review of Fielding's Works (the *Times*, September 2, 1840).

and created a false sympathy for the vicious and criminal.

We ought, perhaps, to make some apologies to the public for introducing them to characters that are so utterly worthless ; as we confess all our heroes, with the exception of Mr. Bullock, to be [Thackeray wrote at the end of chapter i]. In this we have consulted nature and history, rather than the prevailing taste and the general manner of authors. The amusing novel of "Ernest Maltravers," for instance, opens with a seduction ; but then it is performed by people of the strictest virtue on both sides; and there is so much religion and philosophy in the heart of the seducer, so much tender innocence in the soul of the seduced, that—bless the little dears !— their very peccadilloes make one interested in them ; and their naughtiness becomes quite sacred, so deliciously is it described. Now, if we *are* to be interested by rascally actions, let us have them with plain faces, and let them be performed, not by virtuous philosophers, but by rascals. Another clever class of novelists adopt the contrary system, and create interest by making their rascals perform virtuous actions. Against these popular plans we here solemnly appeal. We say, let your rogues in novels act like rogues, and your honest men like honest men ; don't let us have any juggling and thimblerigging with virtue and vice, so that, at the end of three volumes, the bewildered reader shall not know which is which ; don't let us find ourselves kindling at the generous qualities of thieves, and sympathising at the rascalities of noble hearts. For our own part, we know what the public likes, and have chosen rogues for our characters, and have taken a story from the "Newgate Calendar," which we hope to follow out to edification. Among the rogues, at least, we will have nothing that shall be mistaken for virtues. And if the British public (after calling for three or four editions) shall give up, not only our rascals, but the rascals of all other authors, we shall be content—we shall apply to government for a pension, and think that our duty is done.

A little further on, Thackeray again stopped the narrative to make a further protest.

The public will hear of nothing but rogues; and the only way in which poor authors, who must live, can act honestly by the public and themselves, is to paint such thieves as they are; not dandy, poetical, rose-water thieves, but real downright scoundrels, leading scoundrelly lives, drunken, profligate, dissolute, low, as scoundrels will be. They don't quote Plato, like Eugene Aram; or live like gentlemen, and sing the pleasantest ballads in the world, like jolly Dick Turpin; or prate eternally about $\tau\grave{o}$ $\kappa\alpha\lambda\acute{o}\nu$, like that precious canting Maltravers, whom we all of us have read about and pitied; or die whitewashed saints, like poor Biss Dadsy in "Oliver Twist." No, my dear madam, you and your daughters have no right to admire and sympathise with any such persons, fictitious or real: you ought to be made cordially to detest, scorn, loathe, abhor, and abominate all people of this kidney. Men of genius, like those whose works we have above alluded to, have no business to make these characters interesting or agreeable; to be feeding your morbid fancies, or indulging their own, with such monstrous food. For our parts, young ladies, we beg you to bottle up your tears, and not waste a single drop of them on any of the heroes or heroines in this history: they are all rascals, every soul of them, and behave "as sich." Keep your sympathy for those who deserve it; don't carry it, for preference, to the Old Bailey, and grow maudlin over the company assembled there.[1]

In this satire, which is founded upon an incident narrated in the "Newgate Calendar," Thackeray mitigated as little as possible of the horrors, with the

[1] *Catherine*, chap. ii.

unfortunate result that readers, forgetful or ignorant
of the purpose which inspired it, were absorbed and
fascinated by the realistic narrative, and critics of
little discernment wrote of it as one of the dullest,
most vulgar, and immoral works extant. No doubt
those who were disgusted by "Catherine," later
thought Thackeray an admirer of Barry Lyndon,
Esq., and regarded Henry Fielding as a staunch
sympathiser with the unfortunate Mr. Jonathan Wild.
Irony is a dangerous weapon, and Thackeray realised
that with " Catherine " he had not achieved his purpose.

Thackeray's dislike of Lytton as the author of
"Eugene Aram" was much aggravated by that
author's affectations, and very bitterly did he attack
him in *Fraser's Magazine*. When in after days
Thackeray remarked, "I suppose we all begin by
being too savage : I know *one who did*," it is probable
that he was thinking of this and other attacks on
Lytton, which, indeed, were so violent as to suggest
personal animus, though, as a matter of fact, the
objections he entertained against this author were
purely abstract.

I wish to egsplain what I meant last night with
regard to a certain antipathy to a certain great
author [he wrote to Lady Blessington in 1848]. I
have no sort of personal dislike (not that it matters
whether I have or not) to Sir E. L. B. L., on the
contrary the only time I met him, at the immortal
Ainsworth's years ago, I thought him very pleasant,
and I know from his conduct to my dear little
Blanchard that he can be a most generous and
delicate-minded friend. BUT there air sentiments
in his writings which always anger me, big words
which make me furious, and a premeditated fine

writing against which I can't help rebelling. . . .
My antipathy don't go any farther than this : and it
is accompanied by a great deal of admiration. I
felt ashamed of myself when I came home and
thought how needlessly I had spoken of this. What
does it matter one way or the other, and what cause
had I to select Sir H. Bulwer of all men in the world
for these odious confidences. It was very rude.
I am always making rude speeches and apologising
for them, like a Nuisance to Society. And now I
remember how Sir B. Lytton spoke in a very different manner to a mutual friend about your very
humble servant.

Thackeray was somewhat troubled by these early
onslaughts on Lytton, and, when at the request of
the American publisher, Appleton, he wrote a preface
to an edition of his minor works, he took the opportunity to express his regret.

There is an opportunity of being satiric or sentimental. The careless papers written at an early
period, and never seen since the printer's boy carried
them away, are brought back and laid at the father's
door ; and he cannot, if he would, disown his own
children. Why were some of the little brats brought
out of their obscurity? I own to a feeling of anything but pleasure in reviewing some of these mis-
shapen juvenile creatures, which the publisher
has disinterred and resuscitated. There are two
performances especially (among the critical and
biographical works of the erudite Mr. Yellowplush)
which I am sorry to see reproduced, and I ask
pardon of the author of "The Caxtons" for a
lampoon, which I know he himself has forgiven,
and which I wish I could recall. I had never seen
that eminent writer but once in public when this
satire was penned, and wonder at the recklessness of
the young man who could fancy such personality was

harmless jocularity, and never calculated that it might give pain.[1]

It was some years later that Thackeray told a friend of his and Lytton, that he would have given worlds to have burnt those lampoons, and that he much wished to see the latter and express his contrition. Thackeray gave his friend to understand that he desired his feeling of regret and his admiration for the " Caxton " series of novels to be communicated to the man he had wantonly attacked; and soon after he wrote to Lord Lytton.

> Looking over some American reprints of my books, I find one containing a preface written by me when I was in New York, in which are the following words: [here is copied the passage printed above]. I don't know whether you were ever made aware of this cry of " Peccavi ": but, with the book in which it appears just fresh before me, I think it fair to write a line to acquaint you with the existence of such an apology ; and to assure you of the author's repentance for the past, and the present goodwill.[2]

Bulwer Lytton's reputation, founded mainly upon his later novels, cannot be injured by the reviving of any criticism directed against the early work, and therefore it is permissible to reprint here the delightful burlesque speech which Thackeray put into his mouth, in which he endeavours to dissuade Yellowplush from entering the literary calling.

> " Yellowplush," says he, seizing my hand, "you *are* right. Quit not your present occupation ; black

[1] Preface to *Mr. Brown's Letters to a Young Man about Town*, New York, 1853.
[2] *Life of Lord Lytton*, Vol. II, p. 275.

boots, clean knives, wear plush, all your life, but don't turn literary man. Look at me. I am the first novelist in Europe. I have ranged with eagle wing over the wide regions of literature, and perched on every eminence in its turn. I have gazed with eagle eye on the sun of philosophy, and fathomed the mysterious depths of the human mind. All languages are familiar to me, all thoughts are known to me, all men understood by me. I have gathered wisdom from the honeyed lips of Plato, as we wandered in the gardens of the Academes—wisdom, too, from the mouth of Job Johnson, as we smoked our 'backy in Seven Dials. Such must be the studies, and such is the mission, in this world, of the Poet-Philosopher. But the knowledge is only emptiness; the initiation is but misery; the initiated, a man shunned and banned by his fellows. O," said Bullwig, clasping his hands, and throwing his fine i's up to the chandelier, "the curse of Pwometheus descends upon his wace. Wath and punishment pursue them from genewation to genewation! Wo to Genius, the Heaven-scaler, the fire-stealer! Wo, and thrice bitter desolation! Earth is the wock on which Zeus, wemorseless, stwetches his withing victim—men, the vultures that feed and fatten on him. Ai, Ai! it is agony eternal—gwoaning and solitawy despair! And you, Yellowplush, would penetwate these mystewies; you would waise the awful veil, and stand in the Twemendous Pwesence. Beware as you value your peace, beware! Withdraw, wash Neophyte! for Heaven's sake—O, for Heaven's sake!"—here he looked round with agony—"give me a glass of bwandy-and-water for this clawet is beginning to disagwee with me."[1]

Thackeray might belabour Ainsworth, Madame Sand, Lytton, and the rest honestly believing "Spiridion," "Eugene Aram", "Jack Sheppard" and similar works were harmful; but he was never sparing of praise for

[1] *Mr. Yellowplush's Ajew.*

his contemporaries when he thought it deserved. He wrote enthusiastically of Cruikshank and Leech, who might, in some measure, be regarded as his rivals, and always spoke with great admiration of Doyle; and, both in his writings and letters, expressed, not necessarily unbounded, but certainly not too strictly critical, admiration of Macaulay and Washington Irving, of Tom Hood (whose "Song of the Shirt" he declared the finest lyric ever written), of Charles Lever and Charlotte Brontë; he admired Disraeli's splendid talents, and praised even Lytton for the good example he set by being "thoroughly literate." Of Scott he made frequent mention, and thought "The Bride of Lammermoor" his best novel, and loved "Ivanhoe."

> As for Rebecca, now her head is laid upon Ivanhoe's heart: I shall not ask to hear what she is whispering, or describe further that scene of meeting, though I declare I am quite affected when I think of it. Indeed I have thought of it any time these five-and-twenty years—ever since, as a boy at school, I commenced the noble study of novels—ever since the day when, lying on sunny slopes of half-holidays, the fair chivalrous figures and beautiful shapes of knights and ladies were visible to me—ever since I grew to love Rebecca, that sweetest creature of the poet's fancy, and longed to see her righted.[1]

Next to Scott, if not, indeed, before him, in the list of Thackeray's heroes came Dumas, whom, to his exceeding delight, he had met at the house of Gudin the painter. "Dumas is charming. He is better than Walter Scott," he said enthusiastically to John Esten Cooke. "I came near writing a book on the same

[1] *Rebecca and Rowena*, chap. vii.

subject, 'Les Trois Mousquetaires,' and taking Monsieur D'Artagnan for my hero. D'Artagnan was a real character of the age of Louis XIV, and wrote his own 'Memoires.' I remember picking up a dingy copy of them on an old bookstall in London, price sixpence, and intended to make something of it. But Dumas got ahead of me—he snaps up everything. He is wonderful ! "

Thackeray was always happy when he could pay a compliment in his books to his friends, and never lost an opportunity to do so.

> The young Aja came for a pair of shoes, and his contortions were so delightful as he tried them, that I remained with great pleasure, wishing for Leech to be at hand to sketch his lordship and his fat mamma, who sat on the counter.[1]
>
> There should have been a poet in our company to describe that charming little bay of Glaucus, into which we entered on the 26th of September in the first steamboat that ever disturbed its beautiful waters. You can't put down in prose that delightful episode of natural poetry ; it ought to be done in a symphony, full of sweet melodies and swelling harmonies ; or sung in a strain of clear crystal iambics, such as Milnes knows how to write.[2]

Allusion has already been made to Thackeray's love for the humorous writers of the eighteenth century, which sprang up in him even when he was at the Charterhouse ; and though in his lectures on them, as he was careful to state, it was of the men and their lives rather than of their books that he treated, yet here and there were critical remarks worthy of notice. Swift, he admitted reluctantly, for he hated the man,

---

[1] *From Cornhill to Grand Cairo*, chap. vii.   [2] *Ibid.*, chap. x.

possessed a surprising humour, noble, just, and honest satire, and the power of perfect imagery : "the greatest wit of all times," "an immense genius"; but it is obvious that of all the writings of this author he preferred the "Journal to Stella," than which, he declared, there was "nothing more manly, more tender, more exquisitely touching." He could not refuse to see Sterne's wit, humour, and pathos, but he disliked his pose : "he used to blubber perpetually in his study, and finding his tears infectious, and that they brought him a great popularity, he exercised the lucrative gift of weeping ; he utilised it, and cried on every occasion." He was prejudiced against both these writers, and in a letter to a correspondent who had lent him some Sterne MSS., one reason may be discovered :

I am sorry that reading the Brahmin's letters to his Brahmine did not increase my respect for the Reverend Laurence Sterne.

In his printed letters there is one (xcii.) addressed to Lady P. full of love and despair for my lady, and announcing that he had got a ticket for Miss ——'s benefit that night, which he must use if deprived of the superior delight of seeing Lady P. I looked in the "Dramatic Register" (I think is the name of the book) to find what lady took a benefit on a Tuesday, and found the names of two, one at Covent Garden and one at Drury Lane on the same Tuesday evening, and no other Miss's benefit on a Tuesday during the season. Miss Poyntz, I think, is one of the names, but I'm five miles from the book as I write to you, and forget the lady's name and the day.

However, on the day Sterne was writing to Lady P. and going to Miss ——'s benefit he is *dying* in his Journal to the Brahmine—can't eat, has the Doctor, and is in a dreadful way. He wasn't dying but

lying, I'm afraid. God help him; a falser and
wickeder man it's difficult to read of. Do you know
the accompanying pamphlet (my friend Mr. Cooper
gave me this copy, which he had previously sent to
the Reform Club, and has since given the Club
another copy)? There is more of Yorick's love-
making in these letters, with blasphemy to flavour
the compositions, and indications of a scornful unbelief. Of course any man is welcome to believe as
he likes for me *except* a parson; and I can't help
looking upon Swift and Sterne as a couple of traitors
and renegades (as one does upon Bonneval or poor
Bem the other day), with a scornful pity for them in
spite of all their genius and their greatness.

For Congreve, Wycherley, Farquhar, and their merry
and shameless Comic Muse with the libertine heroes
and the wanton heroines he had no liking. "A touch
of Steele's tenderness is worth all Congreve's finery;
a flash of Swift's lightning, a beam of Addison's pure
sunshine, and his tawdry playhouse taper is invisible."
It was not as the author of "Cato," nor of the poem
celebrating the victor of Blenheim that Addison
attracted him, but as "a Tatler of small talk and a
Spectator of Mankind." "He came in that artificial age,
and began to speak with his noble, natural voice. He
came, the gentle satirist, who hit no unfair blow, the
kind judge who castigated only in smiling." Thackeray loved Steele, whom he declared the founder of sentimental writing in English, and the first author to pay a
manly homage to woman. Naturalness was a short cut
to the heart of the author of "Vanity Fair," and on
this ground he paid tribute to Steele, and to Goldsmith,
with his simple songs of love and beauty. He could
not too highly praise "The Deserted Village", "The

the accompanying pamphlet (My friend Mr
Cooper gave me this copy, w. he had previously
sent to the Reform Club, and has since given the
Club another Copy) — there is more of Yorick's
love-making in these letters, with blasphemy
to flavor the compositions, and indications of a
scornful unbelief. Of course any man is welcome
to believe as he likes for me except a parson:
and I look upon Swift & Sterne as a couple
can't help
of traitors and renegades, as one does upon Bonne
val or poor Bem the other day, with a scornful
pity for them in spite of all their genius and
greatness.
With many thanks for your own believe me dear Sir
very faithfully yours
W M Thackeray.

FACSIMILE OF THACKERAY'S HANDWRITING
*A page of a letter to T. W. Gibbs, September 21, 1851. From the original in the
British Museum*

Vicar of Wakefield," and the two famous plays. Besides
Goldsmith, his favourite poets seem to have been Prior
and Gay: "sweet lyric singers," he styled them.
Prior, he regarded as the easiest, the richest, the most
charmingly humorous of English lyrical poets; while
Gay charmed him by the force of simple melody and
artless ringing laughter. He singled out the six
pastorals called the "Shepherd's Week" and the burlesque poem of "Trivia," and remarked that "these
are to poetry what charming little Dresden figures
are to sculpture: graceful, minikin, fantastic, with a
certain beauty always accompanying them." Pope
he unhesitatingly ranked highest amongst the poets,
brightest among the English wits and humorists, and
the greatest literary artist of the eighteenth century.
Before Fielding and Smollett he bowed low, as a
subject before his sovereign. "Humphrey Clinker"
he thought the most amusing story written since the
goodly art of novel-writing began, and he pronounced
"Peregrine Pickle" "excellent for its liveliness and
spirit, and wonderful for its atrocious vulgarity." He
preferred both these writers to Richardson, though he
admitted that "Clarissa" had one of the best-managed
surprises he had read; but his favourite author was,
of course, Fielding, who may be looked upon as
the literary godfather of his famous successor. He
naturally does not think "Tom Jones" a virtuous
character, and he protests against the author's evident
liking and admiration for his hero, but, he says,

> As a picture of manners, the novel of "Tom
> Jones" is indeed exquisite: as a work of construc-
> tion quite a wonder: the by-play of wisdom; the

power of observation ; the multiplied felicitous turns and thoughts ; the varied character of the great Comic Epic,—keep the reader in a perpetual admiration and curiosity.[1] . . . The public of our day need scarcely be warned that if they are to pass an hour with Fielding they will find him continually in such low company ; those, therefore, who are excessively squeamish and genteel will scornfully keep away from him ; those who have a mind to forgive a little coarseness, for the sake of one of the honestest, manliest, kindest companions in the world, cannot, as we fancy, find a better than Fielding, or get so much true wit and shrewdness from any other writer of our language.[2]

It cannot be contended that Thackeray was a great critic. Indeed there is no doubt that, as a rule, he preferred second-rate books of the first-class to the greatest. For instance, while as a matter of course he admitted that Milton was a great poet, he added that "he was such a bore that no one could read him." Whatever one may think of the discernment of a man who says that, it is impossible to doubt his honesty. He was often led away by the character of the author whose works he was criticising. Because of this he disapproved of Swift and Sterne, and rather grudgingly admitted their qualities ; but he greatly praised Pope, whom he loved because of his infirmity, and because of the love the poet bore his mother. His judgments came from the heart rather than the intellect, and it was fortunate when these coincided. "St. Charles," he said to Edward FitzGerald, in a third-floor in Charlotte Street, putting one of Charles Lamb's letters to his

[1] *English Humourists of the Eighteenth Century.*
[2] Review of Fielding's Works in the *Times*, September 2, 1840.

forehead, remembering his devotion to his afflicted
sister.

I hate Juvenal [he wrote to James Hannay, when
he was preparing his lectures on the Humourists].
I mean, I think him a truculent brute, and I like
Horace better than you do, and rate Churchill much
lower ; and as for Swift, you haven't made me alter
my opinion. I admire, or rather admit, his power as
much as you do ; but I don't admire *that* kind of
power so much as I did fifteen years ago, or twenty,
shall we say? Love is a higher intellectual exercise
than Hatred ; and when you get one or two more of
those young ones you write so pleasantly about,
you'll come over to the side of the kind wags, I
think, rather than the cruel ones.[1]

His own tastes led him to appreciate those books in
which a kindly view of life was taken. He would allow
to Flaubert no credit for " Madame Bovary," which he
pronounced a bad book : " it is a heartless cold-blooded
study of the downfall and degeneration of a woman."[2]
For that sort of study, however excellent artistically, he
had no admiration. Nor could he endure books that
leave the reader sad. He told John Esten Cooke he
could never read " Don Quixote " with pleasure, his
sympathy for the knight made it painful to him ; while
stories with unhappy endings he would not read. He
never dared to re-read " The Pirate " or " The Bride
of Lammermoor " or " Kenilworth ", " because the end
is unhappy, and people die, and are murdered at the
end."[3]

[1] James Hannay : *A Short Memoir of* . . . *Thackeray*, p. 19.
[2] H. Sutherland Edwards : *Recollections*, p. 36.
[3] *De Juventute*

P

The best of your poems, instead of making me laugh, had quite another effect [he wrote to Horace Smith]. All the best comic stuff so affects me. Sancho, Falstaff, even Fielding in "Amelia."

CHAPTER XI

THACKERAY AND THE PUBLIC (1846)

Thackeray's success with the "Yellowplush Papers" in England and America—his opinion of "The Great Hoggarty Diamond"—and John Sterling's appreciation of that story—Thackeray's position in the literary world in 1843—his income—his belief in his gift of writing—some reasons why he did not earlier become famous—his use of pseudonyms—his best work not published in book-form—he runs counter to the feeling of the public—his earlier works considered—the "Yellowplush Correspondence"—"Catherine"—"A Shabby Genteel Story"—the "Fitz-Boodle Papers"—"Barry Lyndon."

WHEN "From Cornhill to Grand Cairo" appeared in January 1846, Thackeray had been writing for about eight years, and it is time to pause and consider what was his position at this time.

At the outset of his career he had achieved considerable success with the "Yellowplush Correspondence," and this and "Major Gahagan" (which attracted little or no attention in this country) were at once pirated in America, where the books circulated widely. His work was much appreciated there, and N. P. Willis, then part proprietor of the New York *Corsair*, coming to London, made it his business to secure Thackeray's services for the weekly paper. "I have engaged a contributor to the *Corsair*," Willis wrote to his co-editor, T. O. Porter. "Who do you think? The author of 'Yellowplush' and 'Major Gahagan.' I have mentioned it in my jottings, that our readers may know all about it. He has gone to Paris and will write letters from there, and afterwards from London, for a guinea a *close column* of the *Corsair*—cheaper than I ever did anything in my life. I will see that he is paid for a while to see how you like him. For myself I think him the very best periodical writer alive. He is a royal, daring, fine creature, too. I take the responsibility of it." It will be seen from this letter that Willis was not only a discerning editor, but also an excellent man of business.

The favourable start made by Thackeray was not followed up by him, so far, at least, as concerns the public. His papers on art and his reviews of books were well written, trenchant, and amusing, and endeared him to editors, who were willing to accept such work from him; but his stories did not find so much favour in their eyes, and attracted little attention from outsiders. Speaking from the point of view of an editor anxious to place before his readers such matter as they liked, "Catherine" was not a success, nor "A Shabby Genteel Story," nor "The Great Hoggarty Diamond," which *Blackwood's Magazine* would not have, and which Fraser would only accept for *Regina* if curtailed. "The best thing I ever wrote," said Thackeray of this story, on the eve of the appearance of "Vanity Fair." The merits of "The Great Hoggarty Diamond" were overlooked by the public, which may have found it pleasant reading, but lacked discernment to see how good it was. One man, however, found in it promise of the author's future greatness: "I have

seen no new book, but am reading your last," John
Sterling wrote to his mother. "I got hold of the two
first numbers of 'The Hoggarty Diamond,' and read
them with extreme delight. What is there better in
Fielding or Goldsmith? The man is a true genius,
and with quiet comfort might produce masterpieces
which would last as long as any we have, and delight
millions of unborn readers. There is more truth in
nature in one of those papers, than in all Dickens'
novels put together." All of which says a great
deal for the critical faculty of the writer, but unfortunately could do nothing to increase Thackeray's
popularity.

Thackeray's position among his literary brethren at
this time was little better than the place he occupied in
the public estimation. When he was in Ireland, he
endeavoured to persuade Lever, for whom he had
a sincere regard, to leave Dublin, where he was
surrounded by third-rate writers, and to come to
London, where he would be able to make much more
money. So much advantage, indeed, did Thackeray
think his fellow - novelist would derive from his
change of residence, that he backed his advice by
offers of pecuniary and other assistance, if such were
needed. Lever, however, for various reasons, declined
his proposal, and afterwards told a friend that Thackeray
was the most good-natured man in the world, "but
that help from him would be worse than no help at
all. . . . He (Thackeray) was like a man struggling
to keep his head above water . . . who offers to teach
his friend to swim." Lever also added that Thackeray
"would write for anything and about anything, and

had so lost himself that his status in London was not good." [1]

There was much truth in Lever's remark, for Thackeray in those days was, apart from the quality of his work, nothing more nor less than a publisher's hack. From the outset, however, he was successful in making money, and in 1838 was doing well enough to refuse a journalistic post worth £350 a year. Few young men who embark in the literary calling make so much, or see their way so clear, in the first or second year of their apprenticeship, as not to be allured by the chance of an assured £350 a year. Thackeray, then, was making so much as this within a year of his settling in London, and, since his output increased, considerably more than this in the following years; but he wanted money, and a good deal of it. He had no house to keep up, owing to the unfortunate illness of his wife; but he had to pay for that lady's accommodation elsewhere, and for his girls' education, as well as to put aside something for the future of those dependent on him; and he had also, there is reason to believe, to contribute to the support of his mother and stepfather.

There is a comfort to think that, however other works and masterpieces bearing my humble name have been received by the public, namely, with what I cannot but think (and future ages will, I have no doubt, pronounce) to be unmerited obloquy and inattention, the present article, at least, which I address to you through the public prints, will be read by every one of the numerous readers of this Magazine. What a quantity of writings of the

[1] Major Frank Dwyer, in W. Fitzpatrick: *Life of Charles Lever*.

same hand have you, my dear friend, pored over!
How much delicate wit, profound philosophy (lurking
hid under harlequin's black mask and spangled
jacket, nay, under clown's white lead and vermilion)
—how many quiet wells of deep, gushing pathos,
have you failed to remark as you hurried through
those modest pages, for which the author himself
here makes an apology!—not that I quarrel with my
lot, or rebel against that meanest of all martyrdoms,
indifference, with which a callous age has visited me—
not that I complain because I am not appreciated by
the present century—no, no!—he who lives at this
time ought to know better than to be vexed by its
treatment of him—he who pines because Smith or
Snooks doesn't appreciate him, has a poor, puny
vein of endurance, and pays those two personages
too much honour.

This passage in "Barmecide Banquets,"[1] though
apparently written in jocular strain, may be taken as a
fairly accurate description of Thackeray's feelings in
1845. He was disappointed that the merits of his work
had not been discovered, and rather sad and perhaps a
little angry that he was spoken of as only a clever
writer for the periodicals. "I can suit the magazines,
but I can't suit the public, be hanged to them!" he
exclaimed, with some bitterness, as, after the failure of
"The Paris Sketch Book" to attract notice, he returned to his pot-boilers.

Poor fellows of the pen and pencil! We must
live. The public likes light literature, and we write
it. Here am I writing magazine jokes and follies,
and why? Because the public likes such, and will
purchase no other.[2]

[1] *Fraser's Magazine*, November 1845.
[2] *May Gambols.*

Nevertheless, although at the moment he "can't suit the public, be hanged to them," Thackeray undoubtedly felt that his day must come sooner or later (only it seemed more likely to be later than sooner), for he was confident of his genius, though perhaps ignorant of its extent. His lightest sketches, even his airiest criticisms, have a ring about them that shows he knew his power, and in "Barry Lyndon" there cannot be detected a trace of mistrust in his capabilities : throughout that romance one feels the hand of the artist working with absolute confidence at his first great masterpiece.

Ainsworth published "Rookwood" when he was twenty-nine ; Disraeli was famous as the author of "Vivian Grey" at two-and-twenty, and, before he was eleven years older, had written "The Young Duke," "Contarini Fleming", "Alroy", "Henrietta Temple" and "Venetia" ; Albert Smith was only twenty-eight when he made his mark with "The Adventures of Mr. Ledbury"; Dickens had written "Sketches by Boz" when he was four-and-twenty, "Pickwick" a year later, and "Oliver Twist", "Nicholas Nickleby", "The Old Curiosity Shop",. "Barnaby Rudge" and "American Notes" before he was thirty. Thackeray in his thirty-sixth year was unknown beyond the narrow circle of men whose business it was to search for talent in the pages of magazines or reviews. What was the reason of this? Certainly it was not because his genius took longer to mature than that of the writers just mentioned—though, of course, the fact that at first he looked to art rather than to letters to provide him with a career gave his literary brethren a few years' start.

Anthony Trollope in his monograph on Thackeray endeavoured to solve the problem. He relates how Thackeray had a marked want of assurance ("I can fancy," Trollope says, "that, as the sheets went from him every day, he told himself, with regard to every sheet, that it was a failure. Dickens was quite sure of his sheet"); how he was "unsteadfast, idle, changeable of purpose, aware of his own intellect, but not trusting it"; and, lastly, how "no man ever failed more than he to put his best foot foremost." Now, this explanation is, on the face of it, most unconvincing, and, what is far worse, misleading. Though Dickens, and Trollope also, we may be certain, felt quite sure of their sheets, this has nothing to do with the question—though if it has, or even if it has not, it is something Thackeray never overcame. But then, perhaps, this dissatisfaction with his work was because, besides being a novelist, Thackeray was an artist to his finger-tips; and because, while lesser men might turn away from their completed work with a self-satisfied smile, he would glance at his pages mournfully, re-read them, perhaps, and think, not whether the public would like them, but how far from perfect in his eyes they were. Indeed, all his life he was conscious that his work might be improved; and it was with a sigh that he sent the sheets to the printer. The charge of idleness may be dismissed, if actual output is meant, for Thackeray's work during the thirty years he devoted to letters is more than sufficient. If intellectual idleness is meant, however, then there is something to be said for Trollope's view; but of this aspect of the case something will be said in a later chapter.

There are, however, good and sufficient reasons to account for the lack of appreciation from which Thackeray suffered until his thirty-eighth year : firstly, he had not given the public a fair chance to discover him; secondly, he had not yet produced much work that appealed to the general reader.

To prove the truth of the first statement, that Thackeray had not given the public a fair chance to discover him, it is only necessary to refer to the number of pseudonyms he employed. Had he elected always to write over any one of them, say, over the signature of "Titmarsh," this would have been another matter : " Titmarsh " would have been as well known as Thackeray should have been ; but this was not the case. " Michael Angelo Titmarsh " wrote reviews and short stories, and also " The Great Hoggarty Diamond " ; " Yellowplush " wrote the " Correspondence " ; " Ikey Solomons " indited " Catherine " ; " Major Gahagan " related his own " Tremendous Adventures ", " The Professor " and " Sultan Stork," and supplied " Mr. Wagstaff " with material for one of the four tales credited to that gentleman ; and " Fitz-Boodle " contributed his " Confessions ", " Professions ", " Men's Wives," and a story no less important than " Barry Lyndon."

Besides, much of Thackeray's work appeared anonymously in the periodicals : and his contributions to *Punch* were signed by all manners of fantastic pseudonyms—to name a few, " Miss Tickletoby," "Spec", " Our Fat Contributor ", " Paul Pindar," " The Mulligan ", " Punch's Commissioner ", " Fitz-Jeames de la Pluche ", " Frederick Haltamont de Mont-

morency."[1] His own name had been appended only
to such unimportant trifles as "Captain Rook and Mr.
Pigeon", "The Fashionable Authoress", and "Going
to see a man hanged." This, it will be seen, rendered
it difficult even for the initiated to recognise all his
work, and to the general reader each name suggested
a different author. Thackeray has explained the necessity that drove him to the use of so many *noms-
de-guerre*.

It may so happen to a literary man that the stipend
which he receives from one publication is not
sufficient to boil his family pot, and that he must
write in some other quarter. If Brown writes articles
in the daily papers, and articles in the weekly and
monthly periodicals too, and signs the same, he surely
weakens his force by extending his line. It would
be better for him to write *incognito*, than to placard
his name in so many quarters—as actors understand,
who do not perform in too many pieces on the same
night; and as painters, who know it is not worth
their while to exhibit more than a certain number
of pictures.[2]

It must not be forgotten, too, that the only books that
Thackeray had published were "The Paris Sketch
Book", "The Second Funeral of Napoleon", "Comic
Tales and Sketches", "The Irish Sketch Book", and
"From Cornhill to Cairo"—all of them good to read,
but not one of them showing Thackeray at his best:

[1] After the beginning of 1846 he used the following, among other,
signatures in *Punch:* "Pleaceman X", "Fitzroy Clarence", "Hibernis
Hibernior", "Leonitus Androcles Hugglestone", "John Corks",
"Folkestone Canterbury", "Brown the Elder", "Mr. Snob", "Solo-
mon Pacifico", "Goliah Muff", "Gobemouche" and "Thaddeus
Molony."

[2] *Proser Papers—On the Press and the Public.*

indeed, to-day, when his genius is recognised, these volumes are among the least read of his writings. " The Great Hoggarty Diamond" and "Barry Lyndon," the best of Thackeray's early work, had appeared only in *Fraser's Magazine*, and it cannot be denied that even modern readers, not specially critical, who know the value of these stories, would not fully appreciate their merits, if they were to peruse them, one in four, the other in a dozen, monthly instalments. This objection, it is true, is somewhat discounted in the case of the "Snob Papers," as they might, without losing their charm, indeed perhaps with advantage, be read singly, being really only so many units, bound together at the fountain head. But this does not weaken the argument, for who, among the public, knew that the Snobographer was "Titmarsh" and "Fitz-Boodle" and "Yellow-plush"?

It is not to be denied [Thackeray wrote, realising the truth of this] that men of signal ability will write for years in papers and perish unknown—and in so far their lot is a hard one : and the chances of life are against them. It is hard upon a man, with whose work the whole town is ringing, that not a soul should know or care who is the author who so delights the public.[1]

The second point, that Thackeray's work until the appearance of "The Snobs of England" would not have greatly attracted the public, is best approached by assuming that everything he had written was known to be from his pen. In this case there would have been a few more to join with Carlyle and Sterling in appre-

[1] *Proser Papers—On the Press and the Public.*

ciation, but, it is contended, the vast majority of readers would have been just as neglectful.

One important reason for this is that, while most of his contemporaries appealed to the gallery, and on occasions were not above playing to it, Thackeray, so far from lowering himself to the level of the public, held it the duty of the artist to educate it to his own intellectual level—a performance painfully slow and not at all remunerative to the tutor. Apart from the high intellectual level in his writings, nothing would induce him to abate one jot of his prejudices to suit the taste of the public, though no one knew better what would suit the majority of novel-readers.[1]

I suppose as long as novels last, and authors aim at interesting their public, there must always be in the story a virtuous and gallant hero, a wicked monster, his opposite, and a pretty girl who finds a champion : bravery and virtue conquer beauty, and vice, after seeming to triumph through a certain number of pages, is sure to be discomfited in the last volume, when justice overtakes him, and honest folks come by their own. There never was perhaps a greatly popular story but this simple plot was carried through it : mere satiric wit is addressed to a class of readers quite different to those simple souls who laugh and weep over the novel. I fancy very few ladies indeed could be brought to like "Gulliver" heartily, and (putting the coarseness and difference of manners out of the question) to relish the wonderful satire of "Jonathan Wild."[1]

Yet, knowing this, and anxious as he was to obtain the approbation of his female readers, Thackeray bravely and deliberately continued in his own way,

[1] *Lectures on the English Humourists.*

preaching his philosophy, and indulging his satiric humour: even the finest work he produced before "Vanity Fair" must be included in the same class as "Jonathan Wild," a work that never has been, and never will be, popular with the general reader. When a critic accuses him—as some few still do—of having preached his cynical philosophy for profit, let him consider how much more profitable it would have been for Thackeray to write in the style of Bulwer, or Lever, or Disraeli, as he has so clearly shown he could have done. To give an example: What success might probably have rewarded "The Second Funeral of Napoleon" had he written to please the public, instead of presenting the work to a hero-loving nation in a form that he knew ran counter to the feelings of the book-buyers? From that volume, read this extract, in which is indicated Thackeray's attitude from the day he began to write until he lay down the pen for the last time.

I feel that you are angry. I can see from here the pouting of your lips, and know what you are going to say. You are going to say, "I will read no more of this Mr. Titmarsh. There is no subject, however solemn, but he treats it with flippant irreverence, and no character, however great, at whom he does not sneer." Ah, my dear, you are young now and enthusiastic; and your Titmarsh is old, very old, sad, and grey-headed. I have seen a poor mother buy a halfpenny wreath at the gate of Montmartre burying-ground, and go with it to her little child's grave, and hang it there over the humble little stone; and if ever you saw me scorn the mean offering of the poor shabby creature, I will give you leave to be as angry as you will. . . . Something great and good must have been in this man (Napoleon), something living and kindly, that has kept his name so cherished

in the popular memory, and gained him such lasting
reverence and affection. But, Madam, one may respect the dead without feeling awestricken at the
plumes of the hearse ; and I see no reason why one
should sympathise with the train of mules and
undertakers, however deep may be their mourning.[1]

The publication of "Vanity Fair" may be regarded
as bringing to a close the first part of Thackeray's
literary career, for the appearance of that book is the
actual line of division drawn between the bright,
humorous, but unrecognised, writer for the magazines
and the successful novelist. Putting aside his reviews
of books and paintings as well as his short stories, there
remain for consideration, as the basis upon which his
earlier reputation was founded, the "Yellowplush Correspondence ", " Major Gahagan ", "Catherine", "A
Shabby Genteel Story ", "The Great Hoggarty Diamond ", the " Fitz-Boodle Papers ", including " Men's
Wives " and " Barry Lyndon."

With the exception of " Major Gahagan," a delightful extravaganza, and far more amusing than " Mun-
chausen," there is not another quite pleasant story.
They are all wonderfully clever ; the literary merit is
astonishing : the style is mature, the word-pictures are
delightful, and there are charming touches and beautiful
tender pictures ; but the predominant feature is intelligence. When has the great reading public admired
a book only because it is intellectual? It must be
admitted that the public is right not wholly to admire
such, for it is a truism that a story which suggests
chiefly the cleverness, the wit, and the brilliancy

[1] *The Second Funeral of Napoleon :* Letter II.

of the writer is not a complete success: it shows there is something wanting in the story. Readers ask more than this; and the taste which demands that the writer's genius shall not be thought of until the book is laid down, finished, is quite sound.

There can be no doubt that for some of these early works Thackeray drew upon some of his own unhappy experiences; and these latter, together with the cynicism affected by most young men, give the stories a certain harshness that makes them compare unfavourably with his more mature productions. His purpose was honest: he fought against snobbishness and vulgarity, against gambling, against swindling company-promoters, against the "Jack Sheppard" class of novels —indeed, against everything that did not appeal to him as simple and honourable. But he did not select his weapons carefully; he fought to the death with the button off the foil, and it is a fact that many of the principal characters in his early books are swindlers, scoundrels, hypocrites, or fools.

Yellowplush, taken from the gutter, sees no reason why he should not listen at keyholes, read his master's letters, pry into his private affairs, or do a hundred other dirty actions. He has no more than a swiftly passing pang of remorse when, for a bank-note, he sells the master, who, with all his faults, has been too good to him. All the people he knows do things of this sort, and he sees no cause for shame. Then comes the picture of the Shum family's wretched life,—the cowardly husband, the bullying wife, the objectionable daughter, though out of the gloom looms Altamont, a good fellow, and the rather lovable Mary. Look at the actors in the Deuceace tragedy—for tragedy it is undoubtedly : the scamp Yellowplush, the sharper Blewitt, the silly and snobbish Dawkins, the revengeful Lady Griffin, the insignificant Jemima, the terrible Earl, Deuceace himself, card-sharper, swindler, fortune-hunter. Only the foolish Matilda remains, and for her loyalty much may be forgiven her : " My Lord, my place is with *him*." The moral, of course, is that roguery comes to a bad end. But the retribution that falls upon Deuceace is planned by his father ; and this occasions a revulsion of feeling which causes the sympathy to be transferred to the swindler until nearly the end—the most sensational Thackeray ever wrote. There is nothing in his works so terrible, except the scenes between the Campaigner and Colonel Newcome. The naturalness of the " Yellowplush Correspondence " is its greatest merit. Perhaps its chief fault against nature is that so many unpleasant people could scarcely be found together. " I really don't know where I get all these rascals for my books," the author said. " I have certainly never lived with such people."

In "Catherine," the history of jail-birds, told by one of them, virtuous folk cannot be expected. Mrs. Cat, Brock, Galgenstein, Thomas Billings, John Hayes, Mrs. Scare, and Ensign Macshane, in their several ways, are as bad as bad can be. So vicious are they, indeed, that the reader is sorry for Catherine : in such company she could hardly be other than she is. It must not be forgotten, however, that "Catherine" was a satire on the "Newgate Novels."

"A Shabby Genteel Story," which shows unmistakable signs of the author's development, presents

Q

another group of objectionable people. It is, perhaps,
the most displeasing, though certainly not the least
clever, of all the earlier tales. It opens with a description of Margate lodging-house society; and concludes
with the entrapping into a mock marriage of a loving,
trusting girl, the family Cinderella. Mr. Gann, a
ruined tradesman, drunk three nights a week with
liquor imbibed at the "Bag o' Nails"; Mrs. Gann,
a virago; the Misses Macarty, her two daughters by
a first marriage, shrews, with genteel pretensions; the
tuft-hunting scoundrel, Brandon; and the blackguard
Cinqbars are the *dramatis personæ;*—the pleasantest
character depicted is that of the honest but vulgar
Fitch.

It is a great relief to turn to "The Great Hoggarty
Diamond," for at last on Thackeray's literary horizon,
though still outnumbered by hypocrites and snobs,
good simple people are sighted. In the story are a
dreadful aunt and a swindling company-promoter; but
pathos and tenderness are to be noted, especially in
the handling of Sam's mother and wife; and the effect
on the parents of the death of a child is beautifully and
reverently described.

Fitz-Boodle, however, is undoubtedly a humorist;
and in his "Confessions" are many touches suggest-
ing the maturer Thackeray. He is a good-hearted
scamp, and amusing enough. His love-affairs are well
told, and though Minna Löwe is a little wretch perhaps she was forced to be mean by her father and
her *fiancé*, scoundrels both; yet Dorothea, silly, sweet
Dorothea, and that sketch for Blanche Amory, Ottilia,
are pleasant and interesting. Certainly they are all

three very real. Most of us have met Dorothea and
Ottilia, though perhaps our Ottilias have not over-
eaten themselves—some of us have known Minnas too.
But Fitz-Boodle cannot be forgiven for writing those
scandalous chronicles of his friends' private lives—
"Men's Wives." One of these is the story of a heartless coquette and a brother's vengeance, "The ——'s
(Executioner's) Wife," but the others tell of mean
lives. The scoundrel Walker, the blackguard Boro-
ski, the humbug Sir George, the foolish Ravenswing
(though she improves with age), the dragon-like Mrs.
Berry, and the selfish, vain, snobbish, and terribly
vulgar Mrs. Dennis Haggarty—the history of Dennis
is a tragedy second only to that of Deuceace—are so
many people whom one would rather not know, and of
whom one would certainly rather not read.

At last comes "Barry Lyndon," the greatest of all
these stories, and the first in which the author's genius
shines unfettered.

In that strange apologue, Jonathan Wild [Thack-
eray said in his lecture on Fielding], the author
takes for a hero the greatest rascal, coward, traitor,
tyrant, hypocrite, that his wit and experience, both
large in this matter, could enable him to devise or
depict; he accompanies this villain through all the
transactions of his life, with a grinning deference
and a wonderful mock respect, and doesn't leave him
till he is dangling at the gallows, when the satirist
makes him a low bow and wishes the scoundrel
good-day.

This is what Thackeray has done in "Barry Lyndon,"
only he lets his scoundrel die of delirium tremens in the
nineteenth year of his residence in the Fleet prison, and

by a most brilliant stroke of genius makes Barry in all good faith tell the story of his own adventures. Not so good or so pure as "The Great Hoggarty Diamond" is "Barry Lyndon," but how much grander a conception! The humour, the satire, the remorseless irony—read the speech where Barry defends cheating at cards—the pictures of life, the varied *dramatis personæ*, place it not far below "Esmond" itself in the list of Thackeray's works. There is no short story in the language more artistically beautiful than "The Princess's Tragedy." But just as "Jonathan Wild" is the most neglected of Fielding's works, so "Barry Lyndon" is the least read of all Thackeray's. Work of genius though it be, it is an unpleasant story, as its author fully realised. "You need not read it," he said to his eldest daughter; "you would not like it."

"Wherever shines the sun, you are sure to find Folly basking in it. Knavery is the shadow at Folly's heels," Thackeray wrote in his character sketch of "Captain Rook and Mr. Pigeon." Yet it seems as if he had not quite grasped the fact that there are things other than folly or knavery to write about, and that a surfeit of rogues has an unpleasant after-affect.

"Oh! for a little manly, honest, God-relying simplicity—cheerful, unaffected, and humble!"[1] he had prayed many years before, in one of his earliest reviews; but it was only with "Vanity Fair" that he began to give it.

[1] *Our Batch of Novels for Christmas 1837.* (*Fraser's Magazine*, January 1838).

CHAPTER XII

MAN ABOUT TOWN

Thackeray, after his wife's illness, leaves Great Coram Street—and lives in apartments in Jermyn Street—becomes a frequenter of clubs—the Garrick—the Reform—the Athenæum—his description of Bohemia—and his visits to it—haunts that have disappeared—the "Coal Hole" —the "Cyder Cellars"—and a description of it in "Pendennis"— "Evans's"—Colonel Newcome at the "Cave of Harmony"—the Fielding Club—Our Club—Thackeray's love of "the play"—some visits to the theatre as a boy—and at Weimar—the theatre in his writings—"The Wolves and the Lamb."

WHEN the illness of his wife deprived him of a home, Thackeray, who was then about thirty years of age, sent his children to his mother, now living at Paris, and himself, of necessity, lived a bachelor life. He gave up the house in Great Coram Street, and rented a room at No. 27, Jermyn Street, close to the Museum of Geology and within a few doors of Regent Street. There Henry Vizetelly, who was then founding the *Pictorial Times*, called on him early in 1843, and happily placed on record his impressions of the visit. "I followed the young lodging-house slavey to the very top of the house," he has written, "and after my card had been handed in, I was asked to enter the front apartment, where a tall, slim individual between thirty and thirty-five years of age, with a pleasant, smiling countenance, and a bridgeless nose, and clad in dressing-gown of decided Parisian cut, rose from a small table standing close to the near window to receive me. When he stood up the low pitch of the room caused him to look even taller than he really was, and his actual height was well over six feet. . . . The apartment was an exceedingly plainly furnished bedroom, with common rush-seated chairs, and painted French bedstead, and with neither looking-glass nor prints on the bare, cold, cheerless-looking walls. On the table from which Mr. Thackeray had risen a white cloth was spread, on which was a frugal breakfast-tray, a cup of chocolate and some dry toast; and huddled together at the other end were writing materials, two or three numbers of *Fraser's Magazine*, and a few slips of manuscript. I presented Mr. Nickisson's letter, and explained the object of my visit, when Mr. Thackeray at once undertook to write upon art, to review such books as he might fancy, and to contribute an occasional article on the Opera, more with reference to its frequenters than from a critical point of view. So satisfied was he with the three guineas offered him for a couple of columns weekly, that he jocularly expressed himself willing to sign an agreement for life upon these terms. I can only suppose, from the eager way in which he closed with my proposal, that the prospect of an additional hundred and sixty pounds to his income was, at that moment, anything but a matter of indifference. The humble quarters in which he was installed seemed at any rate to indicate that, from some reason or other, strict economy was just then the order of the day with him."[1]

[1] *Glances Back through Seventy Years.*

W. M. THACKERAY, M. J. HIGGINS, AND HENRY REEVE

From an unpublished pencil sketch by Richard Doyle, in the British Museum

Thackeray, of course, in these days, became a confirmed clubman. When he came of age he had been elected a member of the Garrick Club, which then had its house in King Street, Covent Garden, the present building in Garrick Street not being completed until a year after his death. This was his favourite club for many years: "We, the happy initiated, never speak of it as the Garrick; to us it is 'the G.', 'the little G.'— the dearest place in the world," he declared in a speech at one of the Shakespeare birthday dinners. Always popular there, in days to come he was the great man of the club, and the immense influence he had was shown when in the late fifties he quarrelled with Edmund Yates. He became a member of the Reform Club in 1840, having been proposed by Martin Thackeray and seconded by Henry Webbe. New members of the Reform are still regaled with descriptions of how the great man used to stand in the smoking-room, his back to the fire, his legs rather wide apart, his hands thrust into the trouser pockets, and his head stiffly thrown backward, while he joined in the talk of the men occupying the semicircle of chairs in front of him.[1] He introduced the club into his novels, and described it in the "Snob Papers" and the letters of "Brown the Elder"; and the club returned the compliment after his death by purchasing a painting of him by Samuel Laurence, and hanging it in a prominent position in the Strangers' Room. An amusing story is told of Thackeray going into the coffee-room of the Reform, and seeing "beans and bacon" on the *menu*. He was

[1] Sir Wemyss Reid: *Some Club Ghosts* (*Cassell's Magazine*, June 1897).

to have dined elsewhere that evening, but he could not resist this alluring dish, and, after hastily writing a note to his host begging to be excused on the ground that he had met an old friend he had not seen for many a long day, he sat down at a table, prepared thoroughly to enjoy himself.

Of the Athenæum Club Thackeray did not become a member till later. His name had been entered in the Candidates' Book in February 1846, when he was proposed by the Rev. William Harness and seconded by Charles Buller. Soon after, however, he became famous, and in 1850, long before he came up for election in the ordinary way, his name was suggested in committee by Dean Milman, supported by Macaulay and Croker, as a person suitable for election under rule ii., which provides for the annual introduction, without recourse to ballot, of a limited number of persons of distinguished eminence in science, literature, art, or the public services. The proposal was opposed by one committee man, and one voice in this matter excludes. Hayward was deputed by Milman to tell Thackeray, who took the rejection in good part.

> Thank you for your kind note [Thackeray wrote to Hayward, on February 1, 1850]. I was quite prepared for the issue of the kind effort made at the Athenæum in my behalf; indeed, as a satirical writer, I rather wonder that I have not made more enemies than I have. I don't mean enemies in a bad sense, but men conscientiously opposed to my style, art, opinions, impertinences, and so forth. There must be thousands of men to whom the practice of ridicule must be very offensive; doesn't one see such in society, or in one's own family? persons whose

nature was not gifted with a sense of humour. Such a man would be wrong not to give me a black-ball, or whatever it is called—a negatory nod of his honest, respectable, stupid old head. And I submit to his verdict without the slightest feeling of animosity against my judge. Why, Dr. Johnson would certainly have black-balled Fielding, whom he pronounced "A dull fellow, Sir, a dull fellow!" and why shouldn't my friend at the Athenæum? About getting in I don't care twopence : but indeed I am very much pleased to have had such sureties as Hallam and Milman, and to know that the gentlemen whom you mention were so generous in their efforts to serve me. What does the rest matter? If you should ever know the old gentleman (for old I am sure he is, steady and respectable) who objects to me, give him my best compliments, and say I think he was quite right to exercise his judgment honestly, and to act according to that reason with which heaven has mercifully endowed him. But that he would be slow, I wouldn't in the least object to meet him ; and he in his turn would think me flippant, etc. Enough of these egotisms. Didn't I tell you once before, that I feel frightened almost at the kindness of people regarding me? May we all be honest fellows, and keep our heads from too much vanity. Your case is a very different one : yours was a stab with a sharp point ; and the wound, I know, must have been a most severe one. So much the better in you to have borne it as you did. I never heard in the least that your honor suffered by the injury done you, or that you lost the esteem (how should you?) of any single friend, because an enemy dealt you a savage blow. The opponents in your case exercised a right to do a wrong ; whereas, in the other, my Athenæum friend has done no earthly harm to any mortal, but has established his own character and got a great number of kind testimonials to mine.[1]

[1] *Correspondence of Abraham Hayward.*

Again in the following year Thackeray's name was brought forward by his friends, and this time he was elected. His name was entered on the roll of the club as a barrister, but he was, of course, proposed for the distinction as "the author of 'Vanity Fair', 'Pendennis,' and other well-known works of fiction."

Thackeray in these days made excursions into Bohemia, and enjoyed himself hugely ; but he was never a Bohemian in the sense that Porson was, or Maginn, belonging rather to the more modern type that wears the "boiled shirt" that provoked the scorn of an earlier generation, sits in the stalls at a theatre, and is a member of at least one reputable club.

A pleasant land, not fenced with drab Stucco like Tyburnia or Belgravia ; not guarded by a huge standing army of footmen ; not echoing with noble chariots ; not replete with polite chintz drawing-rooms and neat tea-tables ; a land over which hangs an endless fog, occasioned by much tobacco ; a land of chambers, billiard rooms, supper rooms, oysters ; a land of song ; a land where soda-water flows freely in the morning ; a land of tin dish-covers from taverns, and frothing porter ; a land of lotus-eating (with lots of cayenne pepper), of pulls on the river, of delicious reading of novels, magazines, and saunterings in many studios ; a land where men call each other by their Christian names ; where most are old, where almost all are young, and where, if a few oldsters enter, it is because they have preserved more tenderly and carefully than others their youthful spirits, and the delightful capacity to be idle. I have lost my way to Bohemia now, but it is certain that Prague is the most picturesque city in the world.[1]

So Thackeray wrote lovingly, tenderly, thinking of

[1] *Philip.*

the visits he had paid to the happy land where for the
time being worries and trouble are thrown aside :—

> Sorrows, begone !
> Life and its ills,
> Duns and their bills,
> Bid we to flee.
> Come with the dawn,
> Blue-devil sprite,
> Leave us to-night,
> Round the old tree.[1]

Thackeray's Bohemia has gone, leaving scarcely a
trace behind.   Gone is the little club on the first floor of
a small old-fashioned tavern in Dean Street, Soho, kept
by Dicky Moreland, the last man in London to wear
a pigtail and topboots, where, to the delight of George
Augustus Sala, Thackeray one night sang "The
Mahogany Tree."   The little establishment in the
Strand, beloved of Thackeray, where two elderly maiden
ladies served fish suppers, has disappeared.   Ranelagh
Gardens has been improved off the face of the map ;
so has Vauxhall Gardens, with its twenty thousand
additional lamps burnt every night, where Arthur Pendennis went with an order that admitted "the Editor
of the Pall Mall Gazette and friend," and there,
rescuing Captain Costigan from an awkward predica-
ment, was rewarded with the acquaintance of pretty
Fanny Bolton !

No longer exists the "Wrekin" in Broad Court,
Drury Lane, famous for Shrewsbury cakes and Tewkesbury ales, where the little coterie of authors, actors,
and artists, calling itself the "Rationals," assembled
on Saturdays to dine at four o'clock ; nor the old

[1] *The Mahogany Tree.*

Gray's Inn Coffee-house, which also had its Thackeray associations. The novelist was at one time seen going eastward at an hour of the day when all the rest of the world was moving towards the west, and once a curious person tracked him to the Gray's Inn Coffee-house, and saw him sit down to dinner there in solitary state. "Ah!" said Thackeray, when years after Cordy Jeaffreson recalled the incident to him. "That was when I was drinking the last of that wonderful bin of port. It was rare wine. There were only two dozen bottles and a few bottles over, when I came upon the remains of that bin, and I forthwith bargained with mine host to keep them for me. I drank every bottle and every drop of that remainder by myself. I shared never a bottle with living man; and so long as the wine lasted, I slipped off to the Gray's Inn Coffee House with all possible secrecy short of disguise, whenever I thought a dinner and a bottle by myself would do me good." [1]

Gone, too, are the "Coal Hole," the "Cyder Cellars," and "Evans's"; but these places deserve more than passing mention. The "Coal Hole," owned by John Rhodes, was situated in a court off the Strand, on the site now occupied by the stage of Terry's Theatre, and here Thackeray would often come about midnight for a Welsh Rarebit. The "Cyder Cellars," managed by John Rhodes's brother William, was in Maiden Lane, between the little Jewish synagogue and the stage-door of the Adelphi Theatre, and it attracted a more distinguished company than the "Coal Hole." Porson had made it his house of

[1] J. C. Jeaffreson: *A Book of Recollections*, Vol. I, p. 288.

call, and night after night would sit there babbling
Greek in his cups : after his death his portrait was
hung in the room. Maginn and most of the "Fraser"
set were visitors, more or less regular; and Charles
Dickens, and "Disraeli the Younger," and Dr.
Maguire, and Napoleon III before he became
President of the French Republic. There in the days
of his youth Thackeray heard Sloman—the "Nadab"
of "The Newcomes"—sing his improvisations; and
to him he referred in the *National Standard*,

> Sloman repeats the strains his father sang,[1]

and appended to this line a note : "It is needless to
speak of this eminent vocalist and improvisatore. He
nightly delights a numerous and respectable audience
at the Cyder Cellars." Here also, in October 1848,
Thackeray went, at least twice, "to hear the man sing
about going to be hanged." This was the once famous
"Sam Hall," sung by the comedian Ross, who drew
the town to the "Cyder Cellars." "Sam Hall" was
the chaunt of a chimney-sweep, who was to be hanged
for murder the next morning, and, having some faint
glimmering of the theory of heredity, endeavoured to
father his crimes on his forbears.

> "My name it is Sam Hall,
>   Chimney-sweep,
>   Chimney-sweep ;
> My name it is Sam Hall,
>   Chimney-sweep.
> My name it is Sam Hall ;
> I've robbed both great and small ;
> And now I pays for all :
>   Damn your eyes."

[1] *Mr. Braham* (*National Standard*, May 11, 1833).

Each verse ended with the same three words, and the expression long survived the song. This popular ditty was given with tremendous effect about two o'clock in the morning. Albert Smith described the "Cyder Cellars" in "The Medical Student" and "The Adventures of Mr. Ledbury"; and Thackeray gave a description of the place, called for the nonce the "Back Kitchen," where George Warrington took Arthur Pendennis, and where Tom Sergeant, Clive Newcome, and Fred Bayham foregathered.

> Healthy country tradesmen and farmers, in London for their business, came and recreated themselves with the jolly singing and suppers at the Back Kitchen,—squads of young apprentices and assistants, the shutters being closed over the scene of their labours—came hither, for fresh air doubtless,—rakish young medical students, gallant, dashing, what is called "loudly" dressed, and (must it be owned?) somewhat dirty,—came here, smoking and drinking and vociferously applauding the songs;—young University bucks were to be found here, too, with that indescribable genteel simper which is only learned at the knees of Alma Mater;— and handsome young guardsmen, and florid bucks from the St. James's Street Clubs;—nay! senators English and Irish; and even members of the House of Peers.[1]

The most famous of all these taverns that were the links between the coffee-houses of Addison's time— the Will's and Button's—and the modern music-halls was Evans's, at the west corner of Covent Garden Piazza—the frontage, unaltered through the centuries, may be seen in Hogarth's picture, "Morning."

[1] *Pendennis*, chap. xxxi.

"Evans's, late Joy's," was the punning inscription on the lamp, though in Thackeray's day the proprietor was John, invariably called "Paddy," Green. This was a great resort of men about town, and among the *habitués* were Douglas Jerrold, Horace Mayhew, Serjeant Ballantine, James Hannay, Lionel Lawson, Albert Smith and his brother Arthur, George Augustus Sala, and John Leech. At one time ribald songs were an element of the programme, as those readers of "The Newcomes" are aware who know that the "Cave of Harmony" had for its prototype "Evans's."

One night Colonel Newcome, with his son Clive, came here "to see the wits." A timely warning to the landlord from Jones of Trinity that a boy was in the room, and a gentleman who was quite a greenhorn, and the songs were so carefully selected that "a lady's school might have come in and, but for the smell of the cigars and brandy and water, have taken no harm by what occurred." The Colonel was delighted, especially when Nadab, the improvisatore, devoted a verse to him and to his son, and he sang a ditty himself, "Wapping Old Stairs." Unfortunately for the peace of the evening, however, Captain Costigan entered, very drunk, and insisted upon singing one of his most ribald songs.

"Silence!" Colonel Newcome roared at the end of the second verse of drunken Captain Costigan's song at the "Cave of Harmony." "'Go on!'" cries the Colonel, in his high voice, trembling with anger. "Does any gentleman say 'Go on'? Does any man who has a wife and sisters, or children at home, say "Go on" to such disgusting ribaldry as

R

this? Do you dare, Sir, to call yourself a gentleman, or to say you hold the King's commission and to sit down amongst Christians and men of honour, and defile the ears of young boys with this wicked balderdash?"

"Why bring young boys here, old boy?" cries a voice of the malcontents.

"Why? Because I thought I was coming to a society of gentlemen," cried out the indignant Colonel. "Because I never could have believed that Englishmen could meet together and allow a man, and an old man, so to disgrace himself. For shame, you old wretch! Go home to your bed, you hoary old sinner! And for my part, I'm not sorry that my son should see, for once in his life, to what shame and degradation and dishonour, drunkenness and whisky may bring a man. Never mind the change, sir!—curse the change!" says the Colonel, facing the amazed waiter. "Keep it till you see me in this place again, which will be never—by George, never!" And shouldering his stick, and scowling round at the company of scared bacchanalians, the indignant gentleman stalked away, his boy after him.

Clive seemed rather shamefaced, but I fear the rest of the company looked still more foolish.

"*Aussi, que diable venait-il faire dans cette galère?*" says King of Corpus to Jones of Trinity; and Jones gave a shrug of his shoulders, which were smarting, perhaps; for that uplifted cane of the Colonel's had somehow fallen on the back of every man in the room.[1]

Before "The Newcomes" was written, however, songs of an equivocal nature had given place to choruses sung by trained choir-boys, whose fresh young voices in the old glees of Purcell, Niedermayer, and Pearsall, were a source of delight to Thackeray.

---

[1] *The Newcomes*, chap. i.

It was outside "Evans's" that Lowell, being on a visit to London, met the novelist looking so haggard and worn that he asked if he were ill. "Come inside, and I'll tell you all about it," said the latter. "I have killed the Colonel." At a table, in a quiet corner Thackeray took the manuscript from his pocket, and read the chapter that records the death of Colonel Newcome. When he came to the end, the tears, that had been swelling his lids, trickled down his face, and the last word was almost an inarticulate sob.

To the last Thackeray loved Bohemian gatherings, and in the last month of his life went with Leech to "Evans's." When he was at the height of his fame, in 1852, he took an active part in the formation of a club, established owing to the impossibility of getting supper at a late hour at the Garrick, and he gave it the pleasant, convivial title of the Fielding Club. Among the members were Arcedeckne, Jullien, George Henry Lewes, Russell the war-correspondent; Tom Macdonald, the

Laughing Tom is laughing yet

of "The Ballad of Bouillabaisse"; Tom Taylor; Pigott, subsequently Examiner of Plays; Shirley Brooks, Charles Lamb Kenney, Talfourd, Baron Huddlestone, Serjeant Ballantine, Leigh Murray, John Leech, and Albert Smith. The last wrote some verses describing the members, some lines of which ran:

"And then there came a mighty man who, 'tis but fair to state,
   Among the small is affable, though great among the great—
   The good Pendennis."[1]

[1] Charles Mackay: *Recollections*, p. 300.

Even so late as 1861 Thackeray joined "Our Club," a literary and social *rendezvous*, next door to Clunn's Hotel, where the members dined. Many of the *Punch* staff, and others of the novelist's friends belonged to "O.C.," as it was called, and here Thackeray was in his element. "I cannot conceive him to have ever been seen to greater advantage than when he was sitting with a party of his congenial comrades at O.C., gossiping tenderly about dead authors, artists, and actors, or cheerily and in the kindliest spirit about living notabilities," Cordy Jeaffreson has written. "It was very pleasant to watch the white-haired veteran, and also to hear him (though at best he sang indifferently), whilst he trolled forth his favourite ballads touching Little Billee and Father Martin Luther. Better still it was to regard the radiant gratification of his face, whilst Horace Mayhew sang 'The Mahogany Tree,' perhaps the finest and most stirring of Thackeray's social songs, or was throwing his soul into the passionate 'Marseillaise.'"[1]

No record of Thackeray's pleasures may omit mention of the theatre, which was one of his abiding joys. No boy had ever derived more pleasure from this form of entertainment; not even little Rawdon Crawley, one of fifty gown-boys in the Chapel of Whitefriars School, "thinking, not about the sermon, but about going home next Saturday, when his father would certainly tip him, and perhaps would take him to the play," can have experienced a deeper thrill of delight. In the schoolboy's diary comes that glorious announcement: "Wednesday, December 27th; Papa took me to the

[1] *A Book of Recollections*, Vol. I, p. 286.

Pantomime." That was the red-letter day of young Thackeray's year, of the years, indeed, for rarely a Boxing-Day came that did not find him at the Pantomime.

Very few men in the course of nature can expect to see *all* the pantomimes in one season, but I hope to the end of my life I shall never forego reading about them in that delicious sheet of the *Times* which appears on the morning after Boxing-Day. Perhaps reading is even better than seeing. The best way, I think, is to say you are ill, lie in bed, and have the paper for two hours, reading all the way down from Drury Lane to the Britannia at Hoxton.[1]

It was only in his later years, however, that he was content to read about them, for in his youth he never missed an opportunity to visit a theatre. In "Vanity Fair" he recalled one blissful night when he and another Carthusian obtained permission to appear on Drury Lane stage when Dowton and Liston played in "The Hypocrite," and a certain august personage was in the audience.

The King! There he was! Beef-eaters were before the august box. The Marquis of Steyne (Lord of the Powder Closet) and other great officers of state were behind the chair on which he sat—He sat—florid of face, portly of person, covered with orders and in a rich curling head of hair. How we sang God save him! How the house rocked and shouted with that magnificent music! How they cheered and cried, and waved handkerchiefs! Ladies wept; mothers clasped their children; some fainted with emotion. People were suffocated in the pit, shrieks and groans rising up amidst the writhing and shouting mass there of his people who were,

[1] *Round about a Christmas Tree.*

and, indeed, showed themselves almost to be, ready to die for him. Yes, we saw him. Fate cannot deprive us of *that*. Others have seen Napoleon. Some few still exist who have beheld Frederick the Great, Doctor Johnson, Marie Antoinette, etc.—be it our reasonable boast to our children that we saw George the Good, the Magnificent, the Great.

At Weimar Thackeray went frequently to the theatre. Opera was given there, though the orchestra, under the direction of Hummel, was, in his opinion, far superior to the singers. During the winter he heard "Medea", "The Barber of Seville", "Il Flauto Magico", "The Battle of Vittoria", and "Fidelio," in the last of which Madame Schröder-Devrient sang. He saw "Hernani," and recommended his family to read it; went with an actor to Erfurt to see Schiller's "Die Räuber" (which play was thought too patriotic and free for the Weimar Court Theatre); and admired Devrient's magnificent performance of "Franz Moor," though he declared, "I never saw anything so horrible in my life." During his early visit to Paris he saw Mlle. Mars in "Valerie" and Madame Dejazet in "*Napoleon à Brienne*," as well as Rachel, who was trying to revive the taste for Racine; but Thackeray thought she could only succeed in galvanising the corpse, not bring it to life: he was glad of this, for, he said, he would rather go to see Deburan dancing on a rope, "his lines are quite as natural and poetical."

When he was reading for the bar, "As for theatres, I scarcely go more than once a week, which is moderate for me," he wrote to his mother. "In a few days come the pantomimes. Huzza!" He was always happy in a theatre. Once he asked a friend if he

THACKERAY AT THE PLAY
From a sketch by Frederick Walker

loved "the play," and receiving the qualified answer,
"Ye-es, I like a good play," "Oh, get out!" the
great man retorted. "I said *the* play. You don't
even understand what I *mean!*" And Edward Fitz-
Gerald went with him in the pit one night to witness
a piece which, with its mock sentiment, indifferent
humour, and ultra-melodramatic scenes bored the poet
so terribly that he was about to suggest they should
leave, when Thackeray turned to him, and exclaimed
delightedly, "By G—d! isn't it splendid?"

In his youth, Thackeray declared, "the stage was
covered with angels, who sang, acted, and danced,"
and "all the dancers were as beautiful as houris"; and
humorously he announced his eventual disillusion.

> What is most certain and lamentable is the decay
> of stage beauty since the days of George IV.
> Think of Sontag! I remember her in "Otello"
> and "Donna del Lago" in '28. I remember being
> behind the scenes at the opera (where numbers of us
> young fellows of fashion used to go) and seeing
> Sontag let her hair fall down over her shoulders
> previous to her murder by Donzelli. Young fellows
> have never seen beauty like *that,* heard such a voice,
> seen such hair, such eyes. Don't tell *me!* A man
> who has been about town since the reign of George
> IV., ought he not to know better than you young
> lads who have seen nothing? The deterioration of
> women is lamentable; and the conceit of young
> fellows more lamentable still, that they won't see this
> fact, but persist in thinking their time as good as
> ours.[1]

The theatre figures largely in Thackeray's writings,
from the days when he began to contribute to *Fraser's*

[1] *De Juventute.*

Magazine. One paper in "The Paris Sketch Book" is entirely devoted to the consideration of "French Dramas and Melodramas," and one of the "Yellowplush Papers" is devoted to a notice of Bulwer Lytton's "Sea-Captain." "Mr. Spec." takes his young friend, Augustus Jones, to the pantomime at Covent Garden Theatre ; and, a dozen years later, Mr. Roundabout describes the pantomime to which he went in company with Bobby Miseltow : while of that once popular dancer Miss Delancy (*née* Budge), and of her daughter Morgiana (so named after that celebrated part in "The Forty Thieves" which Miss Budge performed with unbounded applause both at the "Surrey" and at the "Wells"), the curious may read in the printed "Confessions" of that eminent historian of society, George Savage Fitz-Boodle, Esq.

In the novels there is frequent mention of the theatre, and nearly everyone goes to the play or the opera. In "Vanity Fair," Cuff (whom Dobbin thrashed), the great dandy of the Swishtail seminary, was at an absurdly youthful age acquainted with the merits of the principal actors, preferring Mr. Kean to Mr. Kemble. Little George Osborne, too, with Rawson the footman, visited all the principal theatres of the metropolis, knew the names of all the actors from Drury Lane to Sadler's Wells, and performed, indeed, many of the plays to the Todd family and their youthful friends, with West's famous characters, in their pasteboard theatre.

During the Waterloo campaign, everybody in Brussels went to the opera, where it was almost like being in old England, so many familiar British faces were to be seen ; but the *coup d'œil* of the Brussels opera-house did not strike Mrs. O'Dowd as being so fine as the theatre in Fishamble Street, Dublin, nor was the French music at all equal, in her opinion, to the melodies of her native country. Here it was on a certain memorable evening when Mr. and Mrs. George Osborne, Dobbin, and Mrs. O'Dowd were in a box facing another occupied by Mr. and Mrs. Rawdon Crawley and General Tufto, that Becky played Osborne against the General—and won them both. Becky had her little box on the third tier of the opera-house in London, too, and in the crush-room was cut by Lady Bareacres and Lady de la Mole, both of whom she had known in Brussels, though, after her presentation at Court, she made things equal by refusing to recognise Lady Crackenbury and Mrs. Washington White, whose invitations she had once eagerly sought. She (the daughter of a French opera dancer) acted in the charades at Gaunt House, where she made such a success as Clytemnestra ("Mrs. Rawdon Crawley was quite killing in the part," said Lord Steyne), and, as a French Marquise in the second charade, sang "The Rose upon my Balcony" from Sir George Thrum's opera, "The Brigand's Wife"—this was a favourite song also of "The Ravenswing" (Mrs. Hooker Walker). It is hinted that Becky may have been the Madame Rebecque whose appearance in the opera of "La Dame Blanche" at Strassburg in 1830 gave rise to a furious uproar in the theatre there. Finally, during their continental tour, Amelia and her boy, George, and Dobbin, and Jos were frequent visitors to the Pumpernickel Staats-Theater.

They went to the opera often of evenings—to those snug unassuming dear old operas in the German towns, where the noblesse sits and cries and knits stockings on the one side, over against the bourgeoisie on the other; and His Transparency the Duke and his Transparent family, all very fat and good-natured, come and occupy the great box in the middle; and the pit is full of the most elegant slim-waisted officers with straw-coloured moustachios, and twopence a day on full pay. Here it was that Emmy found her delight, and was introduced for the first time to the wonders of Mozart and Cimarosa. The Major's musical taste has been before alluded to, and his performances on the flute commended. But perhaps the chief pleasure he had in these operas was in watching Emmy's rapture while listening to them. A new world of love and beauty broke upon her when she was introduced to those divine compositions: this lady had the keenest and finest sensibility, and how could she be indifferent when she heard Mozart? The tender parts of " Don Juan " awakened in her raptures so exquisite that she would ask herself when she went to say her prayers of a night, whether it was not wicked to feel so much delight as that with which "Vedrai Carino " and " Batti Batti" filled her gentle little bosom? But the Major, whom she consulted upon this head, as her theological adviser (and who himself had a pious and reverent soul) said that, for his part, every beauty of art and nature made him thankful as well as happy; and that the greatest pleasure to be had is listening to fine music, as in looking at the stars in the sky, or at a beautiful landscape or picture, was a benefit for which we might thank Heaven as sincerely as for any other worldly blessing.[1]

The interest of the earlier part of "Pendennis" is placed almost entirely in stage-land. We are introduced to the full strength of Mr. Bingley's stock com-

[1] *Vanity Fair*, chap. lxii.

pany at the Theatre Royal, Chatteris, from Mr. Bows the first violinist in the orchestra, and Mrs. Dropsicum (Bingley's mother-in-law, great in "Macbeth") who takes the money at the doors, to the leading lady herself, Miss "Milly" Fotheringay. Foker and Pendennis attended a performance of "The Stranger" in which Miss Fotheringay's Mary Haller is supported by the Countess Wintersen of Mrs. Bingley, the Baron Steinforth of Garbetts and the Tobias of Goll. Bingley played the hero and was attired in light pantaloons and Hessian boots and had the stage jewellery on too, and allowed his little finger to quiver out of his cloak with a sham diamond ring covering the first joint of the finger and twiddling in the faces of the pit—this had belonged to George Frederick Cooke, who had it from Mr. Quin, who may have bought it for a shilling. After this Pendennis, falling in love with Miss Fotheringay, went to the theatre nearly every night, and on the occasion of that lady's Benefit took his mother and little Laura and the Rev. Robert Smirke to see "Hamlet." Miss Fotheringay, of course, was the Ophelia, and Mr. Hornbull from London the Hamlet "for this night only," Mr. Bingley modestly contenting himself with Horatio, reserving his full strength for William in "Black Eyed Susan," which was the second piece, and in this the *bénéficiaire* played Susan, Mr. Goll the Admiral, and Mr. Garbetts Captain Boldweather. Later, through the instrumentality of. Major Pendennis, Lord Steyne sent down to Chatteris Dolphin, the London manager, who also figures in "Lovel the Widower" as the employer of the ballet girl, Bessy Bellenden. Dolphin, then running the Museum

Theatre under the patronage of the most noble Marquis, came, attended by his secretary William Minns, saw a performance of "Pizarro," and was so delighted with Miss Fotheringay's impersonation of Cora that he forthwith gave her an engagement to play in London at once. And with her departure Pendennis's interest in the Chatteris Theatre ceased—and so does ours. When Pendennis saw the lady again she was the wife of the old *beau*, Sir Charles Mirabel, and he wondered how he could ever have thought he loved her.

Space forbids reference to the theatre in the other stories, though it figures in all, and especially in "Esmond" and "The Virginians"; but before passing from the subject, a word must be said of Thackeray's first and only serious attempt to write for the stage. After his return from the first American tour he submitted his comedy, "The Wolves and the Lamb," to Buckstone of the Haymarket and then to Wigan of the Olympic; but neither of these managers, despite the popularity of the author, would produce it. "I thought I could write a play," Thackeray said, sadly, "and I find I can't." He was quite right. The play is, of course, well written, the dialogue is amusing, and the characters admirably drawn ; but there is too much talk and too little action. It is essentially for the closet, not for the stage : a novel, with dramatic possibilities, cast in the form of a comedy. Thackeray eventually took this view, for, retaining much of the dialogue, he converted "The Wolves and the Lamb" into "Lovel the Widower." He was never quite convinced, however, that the play might not have been successful.

Is "Lovel the Widower" the story which you propose to dramatise for Miss Sedgwick and Mr. Robson? [he wrote to Cecil Howard, on January 20, 1862]. I wrote it originally as a drama myself, having Mr. Robson in my eye for the principal character. Mr. Wigan, however, did not think the piece suitable for his theatre, and declined it ; as also did Mr. Buckstone, unless I would make alterations, which I did not choose to do.

We are going to have a private representation of this piece by some of my friends and family, and I had it printed to save the trouble of copying. The conversations at the commencement seem needlessly long, and probably are unsuitable for the stage, but these could surely be curtailed ; the last act is so very lively and amusing that I cannot but think Mr. Wigan and Mr. Buckstone were wrong concerning it.

Will Mr. Robson have the kindness to read it over? It seems to me that he and Miss Sedgwick will be excellent representatives of the two principal characters.

CHAPTER XIII

"VANITY FAIR" (1847-1848)

Thackeray's position in literary circles in 1846—his connection with *Punch*—his early contributions to that periodical—the proprietors dissatisfied with "Miss Tickletoby's Lectures"—which were therefore discontinued—Thackeray takes his place at the Round Table, 1843—"Jeames's Diary" attracts attention—"The Snobs of England"—and the influence of these papers on Thackeray's reputation—Thackeray determined to make a bid for fame—"Vanity Fair" begun—the MS. of the novel not "hawked round the town"—accepted by Messrs. Bradbury and Evans—Thackeray's letters to Aytoun in January 1847—"Vanity Fair" published in monthly numbers—its sales increase—Thackeray's works never so popular as those of Dickens—"Currer Bell" dedicates "Jane Eyre" to Thackeray—Abraham Hayward praises "Vanity Fair" in the *Edinburgh Review*—the charge of cynicism brought against Thackeray—his defence—his philosophy—the text from which he preached—"Vanitas Vanitatum"—the gospel of love—Thackeray's character criticised by his contemporaries—he created no heroes or heroines—his desire to draw men and women—his characters human—his portrait gallery—the novelist's depreciators—his faults as a novelist—his asides—his method of writing—his style—his place in English literature.

WHATEVER the cause, it is a fact that at the beginning of 1846 Thackeray's work had attracted little attention beyond the circle of his friends and his literary associates. Indeed, he subsequently remarked that he had nearly "come to forty year" before he was recognised as belonging to a class of writer at all above the ordinary contributor to the magazines. Certainly the

WILLIAM MAKEPEACE THACKERAY

From a drawing by Count D'Orsay.   By permission of. Major William H. Lambert

proprietor of *Fraser's Magazine*, though valuing him as his contributor, never thought he was likely to be anything more than that : " When a little time before ' Vanity Fair ' was published, I had asked for permission to republish some tales from *Fraser's Magazine*, it was given to me with a smile—almost an ironical one, as much as to say ' Much good may you get out of them,'" Thackeray told Sutherland Edwards some years after the novel had made a success, adding complacently, " They bring me in £300 a year."[1] Indeed, before "Vanity Fair" appeared, Thackeray realised his position was such that he must bear in silence and with a good grace such petty rebuffs and discouragement as fell to his lot.

I have just received and acknowledge with many thanks your banker's bill for £21. From them and from you, I shall always be delighted to receive communications of this nature [he wrote on October 16, 1845, to Macvey Napier, the editor of the *Edinburgh Review*, concerning the article on N. P. Willis]. From your liberal payment I can't but conclude that you reward me not only for labouring, but also for being mutilated in your service. I assure you I suffered cruelly by the amputation which you were obliged to inflict upon my poor dear paper. I mourn still—as what father can help doing for his children? —for several lovely jokes and promising *facetiæ*, which were born and might have lived but for your scissors urged by ruthless necessity. I trust, however, that there are many more which the future may bring forth, and which will meet with more favour in your eyes. . . . I quite agree with your friend who says Willis was too leniently used. O, to think of my pet passages gone for ever.[2]

---

[1] H. Sutherland Edwards : *Personal Recollections*, p. 37.
[2] *Selections from the Correspondence of Macvey Napier*, p. 499.

This is very charming in its playfulness, but it is not the letter of a man who has arrived. Consider in what terms Thackeray would have protested three years later against the mutilation of any review written by him! But the time was not far distant when, as John Leech happily put it, Mr. Michael Angelo Titmarsh was to appear in his celebrated character of Mr. Thackeray.

Thackeray owed the opportunity to emerge from his comparative obscurity to his connection with *Punch*. The first number of that famous periodical appeared on July 17, 1841; and soon after, to quote Shirley Brooks, "on a good day for himself, the journal, and the world, Thackeray found *Punch*." Edward Fitz-Gerald, in May of the following year, begged Thackeray "not to go into Punch yet"; but fortunately the latter disregarded this advice—though the advice was good in so far as the paper at the start had been ridiculously undercapitalised by the three owners, and was not on a sound basis until it was taken over by Messrs. Bradbury and Evans.

Within a few weeks of FitzGerald's warning, in the issue for June 18, appeared Thackeray's first contribution, "The Legend of Jawbrahim-Heraudee," a skit on John Abraham Heraud, a minor poet long since forgotten, who was once assistant-editor of *Fraser's Magazine*. "Miss Tickletoby's Lectures on English History," which until recently were thought to be Thackeray's earliest work for the paper, did not begin until a fortnight later. These "Lectures," which suggested to Gilbert à Beckett and John Leech the idea of the "Comic History of England" and the

"Comic History of Rome," were not regarded by the proprietors as of value to the paper, and, receiving a hint of this, Thackeray forthwith discontinued them.

Your letter containing an enclosure of £25 has been forwarded to me, and I am obliged to you for the remittance [he wrote on September 27, to Messrs. Bradbury and Evans, from Halverstown, Kildare, which he was visiting in connection with "The Irish Sketch Book"]. Mr. Lemon had previously written to me to explain the delay, and I had also received a letter from Mr. Landells who told me what I was sorry to learn, that you were dissatisfied with my contributions to *Punch*. I wish that my writings had the good fortune to please every one, but all I can do however is to do my best, which has been done in this case, just as much as if I had been writing for any more dignified periodical.

But I have no wish to continue the original agreement made between us, as it is dissatisfactory to you, and possibly injurious to your work; and shall gladly cease Mrs. [*sic*] Tickletoby's Lectures, hoping that you will be able to supply her place with some more amusing and lively correspondent.

I shall pass the winter either in Paris or in London where very probably I may find some other matter more suitable to the paper, in which case I shall make another attempt upon *Punch*.

Thackeray soon made another attempt upon *Punch*, but not for some time with anything so ambitious as the "Lectures." In 1843 he contributed merely a few short pieces and some pictorial initial letters, but his support was recognised as of value and on December 16 he took Albert Smith's place at the Round Table. For the next ten years he printed in the pages of *Punch* most of his best work (except, of course, his novels), contributing, with a fine indifference, thumbnail drawings, ballads, parodies, caricatures, political skits, social satires, even illustrations to other authors' work.

The next year (1844) was not eventful in the history of Thackeray's connection with *Punch*, for his chief contributions were the "History of the Next French Revolution" and the Fat Contributor's "Travelling Notes"; and it was not until Mr. Yellowplush (who in the meantime had made a fortune by speculating in railway shares) again took up his pen and, over the signature of C. Jeames de la Pluche, told the story of his adventures, that Thackeray was regarded as one of the principal supporters of the periodical. The first of the "Jeames Papers" appeared on August 16, 1845, and the last instalment of the "Diary" on January 31, 1846. The papers were topical in so far as they were a warning against speculating in railway shares in the "boom" engineered by Hudson; but, though this drew attention to them, it was the quaint humour and social satire that made them so successful that, "A witless version of his adventures had been produced at the Princess's Theatre, 'without with your leaf or by your leaf.'"[1]

People began to ask who was the author of "Jeames," and Thackeray's reputation as a humorist was now made; but before the impression made by the "Diary" upon the readers of *Punch* faded away, indeed in the number following that containing the last instalment of the "Diary," began "The Snobs of England," which ran week by week until February 27, 1847. These amusing papers caught the fancy of the public,

[1] *Punch*, January 31, 1845.

and again it was asked who was the writer. When it became known that the author of "Jeames's Diary" and of "The Snobs of England" was one and the same person, Thackeray was regarded as a person of considerable importance in literary circles, and began to taste of the sweets of success. The author never had any great affection for the "Snob Papers," and in later years told Motley he hated them and could not read a word of them; but when he was writing the series he was interested in them, and, because they sent up the circulation of *Punch*, he was persuaded to continue them week by week for a year. It has been said that Thackeray saw snobbishness everywhere and in everyone: there is something in this contention, and colour is given to it by the fact that when "The Snobs of England" were issued in book-form seven papers were suppressed by the author, because, he wrote, "I have found them so stupid, so personal, so snobbish in a word." Of the philosophy of "The Book of Snobs" something will presently be said, but the papers may be read independently of their purpose, for they contain many delightful passages instinct with humour. Is there anything better in its way in any of Thackeray's writings than this conversation between the Club Snob, Captain Spitfire, R.N. ("who has been refused a ship by the Whigs, by the way"), and Mr. Minns, who ever after followed Spitfire about, thinking him the greatest and wisest of human beings?

"Why wasn't the PRINCESS SCRAGAMOFFSKY at LADY PALMERSTON'S party, MINNS? Because *she can't show*—and why can't she show? Shall I tell you, MINNS, why she can't show? The PRINCESS

SCRAGAMOFFSKY'S back is flayed alive, MINNS—I tell you it's raw, Sir! On Tuesday last, at twelve o'clock, three drummers of the Preobajinsk regiment arrived at Ashburnham House, and at half-past twelve, in the yellow drawing-room at the Russian Embassy, before the Ambassadress and four ladies'-maids, the Greek Papa, and the Secretary of Embassy, MADAME DE SCRAGAMOFFSKY received thirteen dozen. She was knouted, Sir—knouted in the midst of England—in Berkeley Square, for having said the Grand DUCHESS OLGA'S hair was red. And NOW, Sir, you tell me LORD PALMERSTON ought to continue Minister?"

MINNS: "Good Ged!"[1]

Having at last made a reputation, Thackeray, who had long since convinced himself of his powers, realised that now, if ever, was the time to lift himself out of the ranks of the magazine writers, and to make a supreme effort to take his place as one of the heads of his calling. "My boy, I think you can write a magazine article, and turn out a pretty copy of verses," Warrington is made to say to Pendennis, to which the latter replies: "By Jove! I'll show you that I am a better man than you think for." For Pendennis may be read Thackeray, who was resolved to show the world there was more in him than it gave him credit for; this resolve resulted in the publication in January 1847 of the first number of "Vanity Fair."

A general belief exists to this day that "Vanity Fair" was hawked round the town, and offered and rejected here and there, before Messrs. Bradbury and Evans, the proprietors of *Punch*, undertook its publication. Statements to this effect have been made by many

---

[1] *The Snobs of England—Club Snobs.*

writers. Anthony Trollope stated that the monthly
nurses of periodical literature did not see their way to
accept "Vanity Fair" as a serial, and that publishers
fought shy of it; Sir Frank T. Marzials has remarked
that "'Vanity Fair' itself, 'Vanity Fair,' one of the un-
questioned masterpieces of English Literature" was
refused by the *New Monthly Magazine;* and Lady
Ritchie speaks of the journeys the manuscript made
to various publishers before it found a firm ready to
undertake the venture. These statements presuppose
that the manuscript was complete, but this was not
the case. The idea of "Vanity Fair" first came to
Thackeray when he and his wife were living in Great
Coram Street, and there, indeed, the story was begun.

So your poor Titmarsh has made another fiasco
[he wrote early in 1841 to the friend who saw "The
Second Funeral of Napoleon" through the press].
How are we to take the great stupid public by the
ears? Never mind; I think I have something which
will surprise them yet.[1]

This, the recipient of the letter remarks, and none
will dispute, was a reference to "Vanity Fair"; but
Thackeray did not make much progress with the book,
for when, some time within the next four years, he
offered it to Colburn for the *New Monthly Magazine,*
he had only drafted some chapters, which were shown
to that publisher as the beginning of a story, of which
even the length was not then determined.[2] "Pencil
Sketches of English Society," it was called then, for
the author had not yet thought of the famous title,

---

[1] *Cornhill Magazine,* January 1866.
[2] J. C. Hotten: *Thackeray.*

which occurred to him suddenly in the middle of the night when he was writing some of the first numbers at the "Old Ship" at Brighton. "I jumped out of bed," he told Miss Perry, "and ran three times round my room, uttering as I went, 'Vanity Fair', 'Vanity Fair', 'Vanity Fair'!"[1]

Thackeray's contributions to the *New Monthly Magazine*, with the exception of "Major Gahagan," had not included any of his best work, and so he was not highly valued by the publisher, who would have nothing to do with "Pencil Sketches of English Society." Thackeray did not abandon the idea of the novel, but he was too busy writing for the periodicals to spend time on a work that might not be lucrative ; and it was only after "The Snobs of England" brought him some degree of popularity, that he made another, and this time a successful, effort to arrange for the publication of the novel. One day late in 1846 Thackeray called at Henry Vizetelly's offices in Peterborough Court, and showed him the manuscript of the first chapters of the book, and some drawings for it, which he had brought with him to show Messrs. Bradbury and Evans. "In little more than half an hour," Vizetelly has recorded in his autobiography, "Thackeray again made his appearance, and, with a beaming face, gleefully informed me that he had settled the business. 'Bradbury and Evans,' he said, 'accepted so readily that I am deuced sorry I didn't ask them for another tenner. I am certain they would have given it.' He then explained that he had named fifty guineas per part, including the two sheets of letter-press, a couple of

[1] *A Collection of Letters of W. M. Thackeray*, p. 178.

etchings, and the initials at the commencement of the chapters. He reckoned the text, I remember, at no more than five-and-twenty shillings a page, the two etchings at six guineas each, while as for the few initials at the beginning of the chapters, he threw those in. Such was Mr. Thackeray's own estimate of his commercial value as an author and engraver, A.D. 1846. I know perfectly well that after the publication commenced much of the remainder of the work was written under pressure for and from the printer, and not infrequently the first instalment of ' copy' needed to fill the customary thirty-two pages was penned while the printer's boy was waiting in the hall at Young Street."[1]

It was arranged that " Vanity Fair," after the manner of the works of Dickens and Lever, should be published in monthly numbers, and that the first should appear in January 1847. Thackeray, while confident of the merits of the novel, was, however, anxious as to its success, and thought an article in *Blackwood's Magazine* might help to increase its circulation.

I think [he wrote on January 2 to William Edmonstone Aytoun—"Sweeter Piper Edina never knew than Aytoun, the Bard of the Cavaliers"[2]] I have never had any ambition hitherto, or cared whether the world thought my work good or bad ; but now the truth forces itself upon me, if the world will once take to admiring Titmarsh, all his guineas will be multiplied by ten. Guineas are good. I have got children, only ten years more to the fore, say, etc.; now is the time, my lad, to make your A when the sun at length has begun to shine.

[1] Henry Vizetelly : *Glances Back through Seventy Years*, Vol. I, pp. 284-5.
[2] *On Alexandrines.*

Well, I think if I can make a push at the present minute—if my friends will shout, Titmarsh for ever ! hurrah for, etc., etc., I may go up with a run to a pretty fair place in my trade, and be allowed to appear before the public among the first fiddles. But my tunes must be heard in the streets, and organs must grind them. Ha ! Now do you read me ?

Why don't *Blackwood* give me an article ? Because he refused the best story I ever wrote ? [" The Great Hoggarty Diamond."] Colburn refused the present " Novel without a Hero," and if any man at Blackwood's or Colburn's, and if any man since— fiddle-de-dee. Upon my word and honour I never said so much about myself before : but I know this, if I had the command of *Blackwood*, and a humouristical person like Titmarsh should come up, and labour hard and honestly (please God) for ten years, I would give him a hand. Now, try, like a man, revolving these things in your soul, and see if you can't help me. . . . And if I can but save a little money, by the Lord ! I'll try and keep it. . . . Between this line and the above a man has brought me the *Times* on " The Battle of Life." 'Appy Dickens ! But I love Pickwick and Crummles too much to abuse this great man. *Aliquando bonus.* And you, young man, coming up in the world full of fight, take counsel from a venerable and peaceful old gladiator who has stripped for many battles. Gad, sir, this caution is a very good sign. Do you remember how complimentary Scott and Goethe were ? I like the patriarchal air of some people.[1]

Thackeray was always willing to help other writers, when it was possible, by reviewing their books in *Fraser's Magazine* or elsewhere ; and his acquaintances were eager to avail themselves of this assistance.

Don't be displeased at my not reviewing you [he wrote to Mr. Bedingfield in 1847]. By jove, I have

[1] Sir Theodore Martin : *Life of W. E. Aytoun*, pp. 132-3.

not time to do half what I ought to do, and have books upon books on my table at this minute—all the works of private friends who want a criticism.

It is one thing to give a puff, however, and another to ask for it ; and when Thackeray, who had written on impulse to Aytoun, reflected upon his request, his pride would not permit that his work should attain success save directly through its merits.

> I have been thinking of the other matter on which I unbosomed myself to you, and withdraw my former letter [he wrote to Aytoun on January 13]. Puffs are good and the testimony of good men ; but I don't think these will make a success for a man, and he ought to stand as the public chooses to put him. I will try, please God, to do my best, and the money will come, perhaps, some day ! Meanwhile a man so lucky as myself has no cause to complain. So let all puffing alone, though, as you know, I am glad if I can have, and deserve, your good opinion. The women like "Vanity Fair," I find, very much, and the publishers are quite in good spirits regarding that venture. This is all I have to say in the solitude of midnight, with a quiet cigar, and the weakest gin and water in the world, ruminating over a child's ball, from which I have just come, having gone as chaperone to my little girls. One of them had her hair plaited in two tails, the other had ringlets and the most fascinating bows of blue ribbon. It was very merry and likewise sentimental. We went in a fly quite genteel, and law ! what a comfort it was when it was over. Adyou.[1]

"I wonder whether this will take, the publishers accept it, and the world read it," Thackeray said when he was writing the early chapters of "Vanity Fair "; and though the publishers accepted, it seemed doubtful

---

[1] Sir Theodore Martin : *Life of W. E. Aytoun*, p. 134.

if the world would read it. The first numbers failed to attract attention, and the question of stopping the publication was actually mooted. Fortunately, later in the year, the sale increased by leaps and bounds, and the success of the venture was assured. There has been much speculation as to the cause of this change from failure to brilliant success ; and many reasons have been suggested. Some have it that the success resulted from a eulogistic article in the *Edinburgh Review* for January, 1848 ; while others insist that it was effected by " Currer Bell's " dedication to Thackeray, prefixed to the second edition of " Jane Eyre." Thackeray thought the publication of his Christmas Book " Mrs. Perkins's Ball " had much to do with it.

No doubt the review, the dedication especially, and the Christmas Book, each and all gave an impetus to the sale of the novel ; but the simplest and most probable explanation of the rise in circulation of the shilling numbers is that the book increases in interest as it goes on. This was FitzGerald's belief. " Thackeray is progressing greatly in his line : he publishes a novel in Nos.—' Vanity Fair '—which began dull I thought, but gets better every number." However, not everyone found the earlier parts dull. " Don't get nervous or think about criticism or trouble yourself about the opinions of friends," Abraham Hayward wrote after two or three numbers had come out ; "you have completely beaten Dickens out of the inner circle already." And Mrs. Carlyle wrote in September (1847) to her husband : "I brought away the last four numbers of ' Vanity Fair,' and read one of them during the night. Very good indeed, beats Dickens out of the world."

People at this time were accustomed to buy their fiction in the green and pink covered monthly parts containing, respectively, the novels of Dickens and Lever ; and they did not at first take kindly to the less exciting, though more artistic, sketches of English society offered in the yellow wrappers. Even during the time of the greatest success of the monthly issue of "Vanity Fair," only about 7000 copies of a number were sold, while the circulation of the parts of Dickens's novels was frequently so much as 20,000 or 25,000. Indeed, Thackeray never approached Dickens in the matter of sales, not even in America where his works have always been popular. Entering a bookstore in South Carolina, Thackeray enquired how many copies of "The Newcomes" had been sold. He was informed that they had taken 300 and that 200 more had been ordered. He then asked how many copies of "Bleak House" had been sold ; and was told that the first order had been for 500, and the repeat order for 600 copies. "I ask these questions wherever I go," he said, "and the answers are the same everywhere." He insisted that five copies of Dickens's books sold for every one of his.

It is quite conceivable that "Currer Bell's" dedication (dated December 21, 1847) hastened the general recognition of the genius of Thackeray ; for the circulation of "Jane Eyre," the book of the year, was very large. The dedication is interesting, not only as being characteristic of the writer, but as one of the first appreciations of Thackeray that appeared in print. "There is a man in our days whose words are not framed to tickle delicate ears : who, to my thinking,

comes before the great ones of society—much as the
son of Imlah comes before the throned Kings of Judah
and Israel; and who speaks truth as deep, with a
power as prophet-like and as vital—a mien as daunt-
less and as daring. Is the satirist of 'Vanity Fair'
admired in high places? I cannot tell; but I think if
some of those amongst whom he hurls the Greek fire of
his sarcasm, and over whom he flashes the levinbrand
of his denunciation, were to take his warnings in time,
they or their seed might yet escape a fatal Ramoth-
Gilead. Why have I alluded to this man? I have
alluded to him, Reader, because I think I see in him
an intellect profounder and more unique than his contemporaries have yet recognised; because I regard
him as the first social regenerator of the day—as the
very master of that working corps who would restore
to rectitude the warped system of things; because I
think no commentator in his writings has yet found
the comparison that suits him, the terms which rightly
characterise his talent. They say he is like Fielding;
they talk of his wit, humour, comic powers. He resembles Fielding, as an eagle does a vulture: Fielding
could swoop on carrion, but Thackeray never does.
His wit is bright, his humour attractive, but both bear
the same relation to his serious genius that lambent
steel lightning playing under the edge of the summer
cloud does to the electric death-spark hid in its womb.
Finally, I have alluded to Mr. Thackeray because to
him—if he will accept the tribute of a total stranger—
I have dedicated this second edition of 'Jane Eyre.'"

After a few numbers of "Vanity Fair" had appeared, it was suggested to Abraham Hayward that

he should write about the novel in the *Edinburgh Review;* but, though willing to do so, he was so busy that he would not bind himself to write the paper : thereupon Mrs. Procter undertook to mark passages that might be usefully quoted ; and at last Hayward consented, basing the review upon the notes supplied to him. There can be no doubt of the service Hayward rendered. The article is on the whole appreciative, though here and there it seems as if the reviewer had been afraid that his enthusiasm was too great. " Full many a valuable truth has been sent undulating through the air by men who have lived and died unknown," he wrote. "At the present moment the rising generation are supplied with the best of their mental aliment by writers whose names are a dead letter to the mass ; and among the most remarkable of these is Michael Angelo Titmarsh, *alias* William Makepeace Thackeray. . . . A writer with such a pen as Mr. Thackeray's is an acquisition of real and high value in our literature. High life, middle life, and low life are (or very soon will be) pretty nearly the same to him ; he has fancy as well as feeling : he can laugh or cry without grimacing : he can skim the surface, and he can penetrate to the core. Let the public give him encouragement, and let him give himself time, and we can fearlessly prophesy that he will soon become one of the acknowledged heads of his own peculiar walk of literature. . . . 'Vanity Fair' is assured of immortality as ninety-nine hundredths of modern novels are sure of annihilation."

It was after the publication of "Vanity Fair" that

T

the charge of cynicism first suggested by "The Second Funeral of Napoleon" was seriously, and for so many years persistently, brought against Thackeray, though it was left for Edmund Yates eleven years later to declare that the novelist "wrote himself 'cynic'—for it pays." To-day, however, Thackeray's admirers are more concerned to defend their literary hero against the charge of sentimentalism than against that of cynicism, yet so often has the latter accusation been repeated, that it is impossible altogether to ignore it. Thackeray smarted under the indictment: "They call the man who wrote that a *cynic*," he exclaimed one evening, when he had read to some young men "The Curate's Walk"; and those who understand him can detect the ring of bitterness in his voice as he asks:

Are authors affected by their own works? I don't know about other gentlemen, but if I make a joke myself I cry; if I am writing a pathetic scene, I am laughing wildly all the time—at least Tomkins thinks so. You know I am such a cynic.[1]

Is the man a cynic who wrote continually in the following strain?

We advance in simplicity and honesty as we advance in civilisation, and it is my belief that we become better bred and less artificial, and tell more truth every day.[2]

Thanks be to Heaven, there are good Samaritans in pretty large numbers in the world, and hands ready enough to succour a man in misfortune.[3]

[1] *On a Peal of Bells.*
[2] *Mr. Brown's Letters—Brown the Younger at a Club.*
[3] *Philip*, chap. xxi.

Is the man a cynic who, waxing satirical at the pomp
of the second funeral of Napoleon, becomes tender at
the thought of the mother spending a few of her hard-
earned *sous* on a wreath for the little child's grave ; or
he who, growling at cringing Nudgit, smiles approval
of the quiet independence of Goldsworthy?[1]   But if it
be cynical to believe that

> Wherever shines the sun you are sure to find
> Folly basking in it ; and Knavery is the shadow at
> Folly's heels ; [2]

if it be cynical to declare that grief for a departed
relative will not last for ever, or that if the deceased
leave you a fortune you will, after the first pangs are
over in some degree, be more reconciled to the loss,
why, if these truisms be cynicisms, then, but then only,
Thackeray was a cynic.

If it is difficult to take this charge seriously, the
statement which often accompanies it, that in Thackeray's eyes all was vanity, though equally indefensible,
cannot be so lightly dismissed, for it opens up the
question of Thackeray's philosophy.   Thackeray looked
upon the world with eyes that saw more than is vouchsafed to the sight of most men ; and from an early age
he saw humbug writ large in many things which less
clear-minded persons took in good faith.

> I read the other day in the papers—*Hier S.M. a
> envoyé complimenter l'Ambassadeur de l'Autriche sur
> la mort du Duc de Reichstadt* [he wrote to his mother
> from Paris just after he came of age].   It is as fine
> a text for a sermon as any in the Bible—this poor
> young man dying, as many say, of poison, and

[1] *Mr. Brown's Letters—Brown the Younger at a Club.*
[2] *Captain Rook and Mr. Pigeon.*

L(ouis) P(hilippe) presenting his compliments on the occasion. Oh, Genius, Glory, Ambition, what ought you to learn from this? and what might I not teach, only I am hungry and going—to breakfast![1]

In this letter may be detected some of the germs from which sprang the feeling that in later days inspired him to preach his weekday sermons against pride of purse, and birth, and place, against haughtiness, and against those who meanly admire mean things.

I am sick of *Court Circulars*. I loathe *haut-ton* intelligence. I believe such words as Fashionable, Exclusive, Aristocratic, and the like to be wicked epithets, that ought to be banished from honest vocabularies. A court system that sends men of genius to the second table I hold to be a Snobbish system. A Society that sets up to be polite, and ignores Art and Letters, I hold to be a Snobbish Society. You, who despise your neighbour, are a Snob; you, who forget your friends, meanly to follow after those of higher degree, are a Snob; you, who are ashamed of your poverty, and blush for your calling, are a Snob; as you who boast of your pedigree, or are proud of your wealth.[2]

From the novelist the reader has no right to demand more than a well-written or interesting tale, but from the satirist he expects more than a story. Thackeray has outlined the aims of the school of authors of which he was so prominent a disciple.

The humorous writer professes to awaken and direct your love, your pity, your kindness—your scorn for untruth, pretension, imposture — your tenderness for the weak, the poor, the oppressed,

---

[1] Merivale and Marzials: *Thackeray*, p. 93.
[2] *The Snobs of England*, chapter last.

the unhappy.   To the best of his means and ability
he comments on all the ordinary actions and passions
of life almost.   He takes upon himself to be the
weekday preacher, so to speak.[1]

What, then, we naturally ask, was the text from
which Thackeray preached? and the answer is to be
found in the verses he wrote when he had come to fifty
years.

O Vanity of Vanities,
   How wayward the decrees of Fate are ;
How very weak the very wise,
   How very small the very great are !

What mean these stale moralities,
   Sir Preacher, from your desk you mumble?
Why rail against the great and wise,
   And tire us with your ceaseless grumble?

Pray choose us out another text,
   O man morose and narrow-minded !
Come turn the page—I read the next,
   And then the next, and still I find it.

Read here how Wealth aside was thrust,
   And Folly set in place exalted ;
How Princes footed in the dust
   While lacqueys in the saddle vaulted.

Though thrice a thousand years are past
   Since David's son, the sad and splendid,
The weary King Ecclesiast,
   Upon his awful tablets penned it,—

Methinks the text is never stale,
   And life is every day renewing
Fresh comments on the old old tale
   Of Folly, Fortune, Glory, Ruin.[2]

[1] *English Humourists—Swift.*   [2] *Vanitas Vanitatum.*

There, in small compass, is the sermon that Thackeray preached day by day from his pulpit. The world seemed to him a sad place, more melancholy than mirthful; and even when in his great prose epic he gives his hero his wish,

Oh! *Vanitas Vanitatum!* [he cries] Which of us is happy in this world? which of us has his desire? or, having it, is satisfied?[1]

Though, it will be seen, he went freely into society, and took his full share of the pleasures of the world, he passed through life a spectator—as someone put it happily, a dignified Dobbin in the larger Vanity Fair —bewailing the faults and follies of mankind, and roused only from the tender chiding of his fellows when he saw a man bullying a woman, a woman taking advantage of her weakness to belabour a man, or any one person taking unfair advantage of another.

People there are living and flourishing in the world . . . with no reverence except for prosperity, and no eye for anything beyond success—faithless, hopeless, charityless. Let us have at them, dear friends, with might and main.[2]

To Thackeray all was not vanity. "He could not have painted 'Vanity Fair' as he has unless Eden had been in his inner eye," George Brimley has written; and it is certain that Thackeray was the first to respect and bow down before such qualities as virtue, simplicity, bravery, and unselfishness. When the Rev. Joseph Sortain sent a volume of his sermons to the novelist, the latter, writing in acknowledgment of the gift, enunciated his aims as a writer.

[1] *Vanity Fair.*   [2] *Ibid.*

I shall value your book very much, not only as the work of the most accomplished orator I have ever heard in my life, but, if you will let me so take it, as a token of good-will and interest on your part in my own literary pursuits [he wrote on May 15, 1850]. I want, too, to say, in my way, that, love and truth are the greatest of Heaven's commandments and blessings to us; that the best of us, the many especially who pride themselves on their virtue most, are wretchedly weak, vain and selfish; and to preach such a charity at least as a common sense of our shame and unworthiness might inspire, to us poor people. I hope men of my profession do no harm, who talk this doctrine out of doors to people in drawing-rooms and in the world. Your duty in church takes them a step higher, that awful step beyond ethics which leads you up to God's revealed truth. What a tremendous responsibility his is who has that mystery to explain ! What a boon the faith which makes it clear to him ! [1]

Five years later, when " The Newcomes " was attacked by the *Times* for its "morality and religion," he invited Whitwell Elwin to defend him in the *Quarterly Review*.

With regard to religion, I think, please God, my books are written by a God-loving man, and the morality—the vanity of success, etc., of all but love and goodness,—is not that the teaching *Domini nostri ?* [2]

In "Vanitas Vanitatum," quoted above, Thackeray perhaps puts forth the more depressing side of his creed, and it is to another set of verses that the student of his philosophy must turn to see the bright side. In "The End of the Play" Thackeray tells

[1] *Memorials of the Rev. Joseph Sortain.*
[2] Whitwell Elwin : *Some Eighteenth Century Men of Letters.*

. . . how fate may change and shift ;
The prize be sometimes with the fool,
The race not always to the swift.
The strong may yield, the good may fall,
The great man be a vulgar clown,
The knave be lifted over all,
The kind cast pitilessly down ;

but, he preached,

Come wealth or want, come good or ill,
Let young and old accept their part,
And bow before the Awful Will,
And bear it with an honest heart.
Who misses, or who wins the prize ?
Go, lose or conquer as you can :
But if you fail, or if you rise,
Be each, pray God, a gentleman.

It has been said, and with truth, that Thackeray
preached from the text that the wisdom of this world is
foolishness with God ; and this undoubtedly was one
of the articles of his creed.   There was, however, another
in which he believed with his whole heart, and this is
best summed up in the words of Jeremy Taylor : "Love
is the greatest thing that God can give us : for Himself
is Love, and it is the greatest thing we can give to
God ; for it will also give ourselves, and carry with it
all that is ours."

Do your duty, he wrote again and again, do your
duty with an honest heart, be truthful, be natural, be
humble, be charitable.   His love of good and contempt
of evil is clearly to be discerned in his books, but especially in "The Newcomes"; and in every story he
wrote he preached the gospel of love.

I cannot help telling the truth as I view it, and describing what I see. To describe it otherwise than it seems to me would be falsehood in that calling in which it has pleased Heaven to place me ; treason to that conscience which says that men are weak ; that truth must be told ; that faults must be owned ; that pardon must be prayed for ; and that Love reigns supreme over all.[1]

In that passage is contained the teaching of Thackeray's life and the epitome of his weekday sermons.

Many bitter attacks have been made upon Thackeray, not only on account of his philosophy but also on account of his characters. Mrs. Jameson declared that every woman resents the selfish and inane Amelia in "Vanity Fair," and regards Laura in "Pendennis" as yet a more fatal mistake ; while Lady Castlewood arouses her anger in no measured degree. "The virtuous woman, *par excellence*, who 'never sins and never forgives'; who never resents, nor relents, nor repents ; the mother who is the rival of her daughter ; the mother who for years is the *confidante* of a man's delirious passion for her own child, and then consoles him by marrying him herself ! O Mr. Thackeray, this will never do !" Charlotte Brontë thought Thackeray "unjust to women—quite unjust"; and Harriet Martineau thought that "the first drawback in his books, as in his manners, is the impression conveyed by both that he can never have known a good and sensible woman." Even as Mrs. Henry Potts could scarcely find a good woman in Shakespeare's plays, so Mr. Frederic Harrison finds it an effort of memory to recall the generous and fine natures in Thackeray, and

[1] *Charity and Humour.*

he complains that all the lovable and affectionate men and women have qualities which lower them and tend to make them either tiresome or ridiculous. Mr. Harrison says that Esmond is a high-minded, almost heroic, gentleman, but glum, a regular kill-joy, and something of a prig; that Colonel Newcome is a noble-hearted soldier, but too good for this world, and somewhat too innocent, too transparently a child of nature; that Warrington, with all his sense and honesty, is rough; that Pendennis is a bit of a puppy; that Clive Newcome is not much of a hero; that Dobbin is almost intended to be a butt. "A more serious defect is a dearth in Thackeray of women to love and honour," he adds. "Though he has given us over and over again living pictures of women of power, intellect, with charm, they are all marred by atrocious selfishness, cruelty, ambition, like Becky Sharp, Beatrix Esmond, and Lady Kew; or else they have some weakness, silliness, or narrowness, which prevents us from at once loving and respecting them. Amelia is rather a poor thing, and decidedly silly; we do not really admire Laura Pendennis; the Little Sister is somewhat colourless; Ethel Newcome runs great risk of being a spoilt beauty; and about Lady Castlewood, with all her love and devotion, there hangs a certain sinister and unnatural taint which the world cannot forgive, and perhaps ought not to forgive."

There is this amount of truth in all these adverse comments, that Thackeray created no heroes or heroines. He knew that human nature, or at least that section of it that reads novels, cries out for sentiment, for pretty ladies and gallant gentlemen making love in the most

romantic manner under the most romantic circumstances.

You would have the heroine of your novel so beautiful that she would charm the captain (or hero, who-
ever he may be) with her appearance ; surprise and
confound the bishop with her learning ; outride the
Squire and get the brush, and, when he fell from his
horse, whip out a lancet and bleed him ; rescue from
fever and death the poor cottager's family whom the
doctor had given up ; make twenty-one at the butts
with the rifle, when the poor captain only scored
eighteen ; give him twenty in fifty at billiards and
beat him ; and draw tears from the professional Italian
people by her exquisite performance (of voice and
violoncello) in the evening—I say, if a novelist would
be popular with ladies—the great novel-readers of
the world—this is the sort of heroine who would carry
him through half-a-dozen editions.

To this desire Thackeray would not pander, for he
held it his duty to present the world and the people in
it as he saw them ; and, though no man liked popularity better, he was not content to purchase it at the
price of his literary conscience.

Since the author of " Tom Jones " was buried, no
writer of fiction among us has been permitted to
depict to his utmost power a MAN [he said, in the
preface to " Pendennis "]. We must drape him, and
give him a certain conventional simper. Society
will not tolerate the Natural in our Art. Many ladies
have remonstrated and subscribers left me because,
in the course of the story, I described a young man
resisting and affected by temptation. My object was
to say that he had the passions to feel, and the manli-
ness and generosity to overcome them. You will not
hear—it is best not to know it—what moves in the
real world, what passes in society, in the clubs,
colleges, messrooms,—what is the life and talk of

your sons. A little more frankness than is customary has been attempted in this story, with no bad desire on the writer's part, it is hoped, and with no ill consequence to any reader. If truth is not always pleasant, at any rate truth is best, from whatever chair—from those whence grave writers or thinkers argue as from that at which the story-teller sits as he concludes his labour and bids his kind reader farewell.

The mistake into which many critics of Thackeray have fallen is one of thinking that the author intended to make his principal characters heroes and heroines ; whereas he presented them merely as men and women whom the reader must like or dislike according to his tastes. He declared that he disliked everybody in " Vanity Fair " except Dobbin and Amelia.

> Our Friend is not Amadis or Sir Charles Grandison [he said of Philip Firmin] ; and I don't set him up for a moment as a person to be revered or imitated, but try to draw him faithfully and as Nature made him.

On the other hand, if no man or woman in Thackeray's books is perfect, all are human. There is no utterly unredeemed scoundrel in any of his books : Sir Francis Clavering is so weak that pity rather than hatred is his portion ; and Dr. Firmin's moral standpoint is so perverted that, like Barry Lyndon, he never realises, and could not be brought to realise, his immorality ; even Lord Steyne, debauched old man as he is, is not without feeling, since he can sympathise with Major Pendennis's distress about Arthur—perhaps Tufton Hunt is the worst man Thackeray ever drew. If Thackeray has not joined pure goodness to pure intellect, if he has not

combined in one person the strength of intellect of a
Becky and the goodness of an Amelia, or the nobility
of a Henry Esmond or a Thomas Newcome with the
brilliance of an Arthur Pendennis, it was certainly not
because he could not do so, or because he was in-
capable of appreciating a perfect man or woman, but
because such folk are rarely, if ever, met with in the
world.

How many novelists are there who have created
such a gallery of characters as can be collected from
Thackeray's stories? Mrs. Peggy O'Dowd, "Jos"
Sedley, Lord Steyne, Becky, Dobbin, and the members
of the Crawley family; Major Pendennis, Captain
Costigan, "the Fotheringay" Bows, Morgan the
valet, Altamont, Strong, Mirobolant, Blanche Amory,
Foker, Warrington, Fanny Bolton, old Pendennis the
apothecary; Beatrix, Lady Castlewood and her husband; Colonel Newcome, Fred Bayham, Charles
Honeyman, Madame de Florac. . . . The list might
be extended almost indefinitely. What admirable
character-drawing! what insight into men and women!
To describe people so truly, so minutely, so humanly
and so humanely, too, as he has done, requires the
unfettered genius of a broad-minded man. Someone
has said that to provide an author for "The Egoist"
God had first to create a gentleman, and then give him
genius; could there be a better basis upon which to
build a criticism of Thackeray's work?

It is not only Thackeray's philosophy that has been
attacked, and his character that has been subjected to
adverse criticism, but there have been and still are
writers who refuse to allot to his works a high place in

the realms of literature. Matthew Arnold did not think him a great writer, though he was impelled to admit, "at any rate, his style is that of one"; all that Ruskin had to say of Thackeray (in "Fors Clavigera") is that "Thackeray settled like a meat-fly on whatever one had for dinner, and made one sick of it"; and to-day, though depreciation of the novelist comes mainly from the decadent school, yet only a few months since one of the most brilliant of the younger novelists stated that he had nothing to learn from Thackeray or Dickens.

It is, of course, easy to point out Thackeray's faults as a novelist. He was often careless; he would kill a character in one chapter and bring him to life again a hundred pages further on, and commit a score of such blunders; and he would often interrupt the narrative to give tongue to his own reflections. "And there is a sermon, and a great deal of love and affection from Papa," he concluded a letter to his daughters; and the same remark applies to his books.

Perhaps of all the novel-spinners now extant, the present speaker is most addicted to preaching. Does he not stop perpetually in his story and begin to preach to you? When he ought to be engaged with business, is he not for ever taking the Muse by the sleeve, and plaguing her with some of his cynical sermons? I cry *peccavi* loudly and heartily. I tell you I would like to be able to write a story which should show no egotism whatever—in which there should be no reflections, no cynicism, no vulgarity (and so forth), but an incident in every other page, a villain, a battle, a mystery in every chapter.

When Allingham said to Thackeray that a certain

story of Dickens might be improved by a man of good taste with a pencil in his hand, by merely scoring out this and that, "Young man," interrupted Thackeray, affecting an Irish brogue, "you're threading on the tail o' me coat. What you've just said applies very much to your humble servant's things." Whereupon Allingham and Father Prout protested there was not a line too much in Thackeray's novels,[1] and, as regards the best works of the author, the protest is true. It would be a dangerous precedent for any writer to follow, but in Thackeray's case, had the story been strictly adhered to, the books would have been less fascinating ; it is the digressions, the personal touches, the little weekday sermons, that invest the novels with much of their charm—" Like the songs of the chorus," says Mr. Andrew Lang, " they bid us pause a moment over the wider laws and actions of human fate and human life."

These exquisite interpolations were certainly in part due to Thackeray's want of method in the construction of his novels. He wrote, as it were, by instinct.

My Pegasus won't fly so as to let me survey the field below me. He has no wings ; he is blind of one eye certainly ; he is restive, stubborn, slow ; crops a hedge when he ought to be galloping, or gallops when he ought to be quiet. He will never show off when I want him. Sometimes he goes at a pace which surprises me. Sometimes, when I most wish him to make the running, the brute turns restive. I am obliged to let him take his time.

His plan was to create mentally two or three of the principal characters, and then to write on from number

[1] William Allingham : *Diary,* p. 78.

to number, with only a general notion of the course
he would be taking a few chapters later. "I don't
control my characters," he told Cordy Jeaffreson; "I
am in their hands, and they take me where they
please."

> I have been surprised at the observations made by
> some of my characters [he wrote in a "Roundabout
> Paper."] It seems as if an occult power was moving
> the pen. The personage does or says something,
> and I ask, "How the dickens did he come to think
> of that?"

Thus, when someone remonstrated with him for
having made Esmond marry "his mother-in-law," he
replied, with a laugh, "*I* didn't make him do it; they
did it themselves." When Whitwell Elwin, suspect-
ing Thackeray wrote by a sort of instinct, without
marking the full import of his narrative, said to him,
"There is probably more in your novels than you are
aware of," "Yes," replied the novelist, "I have no
idea where it all comes from. I have never seen the
persons I describe, nor heard the conversations I put
down. I am often astonished to read it myself when
I have got it down on paper."[1] His characters, none
the less, were very real to him. He was so affected by
the death of Helen Pendennis that he was found in
tears. "I wonder what will happen to Pendennis
and Fanny Bolton," he wrote to Mrs. Brookfield;
"writing and sending it to you, it seems as if it were
true." He told the same correspondent how on a continental trip he had been to the Hôtel de la Terrasse

[1] Whitwell Elwin: *Some Eighteenth Century Men of Letters*, Vol. 1,
p. 155.

where Becky used to stay and had passed by Captain Osborne's lodgings. "I believe perfectly in all the people" he added, "and feel quite an interest in the inn in which they lived."

Thackeray's style was founded upon the masters of the eighteenth century, and in this respect his books bear comparison with Addison and Fielding and Steele. Yet his style, which was born with him and is visible in his early writings, was almost wholly original. "It is more like the result of thinking aloud than the style of any other writer," Professor Saintsbury has put it happily. "But it is also more than this. The writer thinks for himself and for ' the other fellow'—for an imaginary interlocutor who makes objections, spies the ludicrous side of what has been said, and so on."[1]

Very clear is every passage Thackeray wrote, and none can fail to grasp the meaning of his every line. That, indeed, was the object he always kept before him. "The great thing is to make no sentence without a meaning to it," he said ; and he would rewrite pages of manuscript, substituting simpler words for longer ones. Few writers have revised their work more carefully ; and even after the novels were published, when a new edition was called for, the author carefully examined every page, and made many alterations, both trivial and important.

Thackeray hated enthusiastic writing, but he could rise to almost any scene. There are few passages in

[1] Introduction to the Oxford Edition of Thackeray's Works. Vol. I, p. xxxi.

U

English fiction more tender than the last parting of George Osborne and Amelia.

George came in and looked at her again, entering still more softly. By the pale night-lamp he could see her sweet, pale face—the purple eye-lids were fringed and closed, and one round arm, smooth and white, lay outside the coverlet. Good God! how pure she was; how gentle, how tender, and how friendly! And he, how selfish, brutal, and black with crime! Heart-stained and shame-stricken, he stood at the bed's foot, and looked at the sleeping girl. How dared he—who was he, to pray for one so spotless! God bless her! God bless her! He came to the bedside and looked at the hand, the little soft hand, lying asleep; and he bent over the pillow noiselessly towards the gentle, pale face. Two fair arms closed tenderly round his neck as he stooped down. "I am awake, George," the poor child said, with a sob fit to break the little heart that nestled so closely by his own.[1]

A few days later the foolish, weak young man died fighting for his country.

No more firing was heard at Brussels—the pursuit rolled miles away. The darkness came down on the field and city: and Amelia was praying for George, who was lying on his face, dead, with a bullet through his heart.[2]

Thackeray never wrote anything finer than the Waterloo chapters of "Vanity Fair," though very beautifully described are the deaths of Helen Pendennis and Colonel Newcome; and it is necessary to go to "Esmond" to find passages so exquisite. It is hard to find anything to surpass that speech of Lady Castlewood to the Duke of Hamilton, which begins,

[1] *Vanity Fair*, chap. xxix.   [2] *Ibid.*, chap. xxxii.

My daughter may receive presents from the Head of our House : my daughter may thankfully take kindness from her father's, her mother's, her brother's dearest friend ; and be grateful for one more benefit besides the thousands we owe him. [1]

Yet, as is the case with all Thackeray's books, one fine scene conjures up memories of many others, and in "Esmond" there is the interview in which the hero and young Castlewood repudiate the Pretender, and, earlier in the story, the welcone extended to her dear Harry by Lady Castlewood on his home-coming a year after the Viscount's death.

"I knew you would come back . . . and to-day, Henry, in the anthem, when they sang it, 'When the Lord turned the captivity of Zion, we were like them that dream,' I thought, yes, like them that dream—them that dream. And then it went, 'They that sow in tears shall reap in joy ; and he that goeth forth and weepeth, shall doubtless come home again with rejoicing, bringing his sheaves with him' ; I looked up from the book and saw you. I was not surprised when I saw you. I knew you would come, my dear, and saw the gold sunshine round your head. . . . Do you know what day it is ? . . . It is the 29th of December—it is your birthday ! But last year we did not drink it,—no, no. My lord was cold, and my Harry was likely to die : and my brain was in a fever ; and we had no wine. But now— now you are come again, bringing your sheaves with you, my dear." She burst into a wild flood of weeping as she spoke ; she laughed and sobbed on the young man's heart, crying out wildly, "bringing your sheaves with you—your sheaves with you ! " [2]

Only one further quotation may be allowed, and this shall be the description of Esmond's visit to his mother's

---

[1] *Esmond,* Book III, chap. iv.   [2] *Ibid.*, Book II, chap. vi.

grave in the convent cemetery at Brussels, the finest piece of word-painting that Thackeray ever penned.

Esmond came to this spot in one sunny evening of spring, and saw, amidst a thousand black crosses, casting their shadows across the grassy mounds, that particular one which marked his mother's resting-place. Many more of those poor creatures that lay there had adopted that same name, with which sorrow had rebaptised her, and which fondly seemed to hint their individual story of love and grief. He fancied her, in tears and darkness, kneeling at the foot of her cross, under which her cares were buried. Surely he knelt down, and said his own prayer there, not in sorrow so much as in awe (for even his memory had no recollection of her), and in pity for the pangs which the gentle soul in life had been made to suffer. To this cross she brought them; for this heavenly bridegroom she exchanged the husband who had wooed her, the traitor who had left her. A thousand such hillocks lay round about, the gentle daisies springing out of the grass over them, and each bearing its cross and requiescat. A nun, veiled in black, was kneeling hard by, at a sleeping sister's bedside (so fresh made, that the spring had scarce had time to spin a coverlid for it); beyond the cemetery walls you had glimpses of life and the world, and the spires and gables of the city. A bird came down from a roof opposite, and lit first on a cross, and then on the grass below it, whence it flew away presently with a leaf in its mouth : then came a sound as of chanting, from the chapel of the sisters hard by : others had long since filled the place which poor Mary Magdaleine once had there, were kneeling at the same stall, and hearing the same hymns and prayers in which her stricken heart had found consolation. Might she sleep in peace—might she sleep in peace ; and we, too, when our struggles and pains are over ! But the earth is the Lord's, as the Heaven is; we are alike his creatures, here and yonder. I took a little flower off the hillock, and

kissed it, and went my way, like the bird that had
just lighted on the cross by me, back into the world
again.   Silent receptacle of death ! tranquil depth of
calm, out of reach of tempest and trouble !   I felt as
one who had been walking below the sea, and treading
amidst the bones of shipwrecks.[1]

Thackeray once declared frankly that he wished to
rank as classical author.   His desire has been fully
realised.   To-day his name stands for culture and high
intelligence, for delicate humour and exquisite pathos ;
for great understanding of the inner workings of the
minds of men and women ; for literary style and for
pure nervous undefiled English.   As the author of
" Barry Lyndon ", " Vanity Fair ", " Pendennis,"
" Esmond," and the " Roundabout Papers," he has
taken his place among the greatest writers of the nineteenth century, and, indeed, in the history of English
fiction he ranks second only to Henry Fielding.

[1] *Esmond*, Book II, chap. xiii.

CHAPTER XIV

IN SOCIETY

Thackeray lionised by society—his amusement at being so treated—
applause an incentive to him—society provides material for his
writings—speech-making—his " smash " at a Literary Fund Dinner—
and at Manchester—his speech at the banquet given on his departure
for America, 1855—his belief that practice in speaking would enable
him to express his opinions in the House of Commons—charged with
tuft-hunting—the disadvantages of success—he loses old friends—
much improved by success—tributes by Albert Smith, John Hollingshead, Frederick Locker-Lampson, Henry Vizetelly, Dr. John Brown
and the Rev. Whitwell Elwin—attacks on him—his moods—Mrs. J. T.
Fields' opinion of him—his charity—and his kindness—interests himself in Louis Marvy and others—his shyness—and his occasional
savagery—his sense of fun—his conversation—some *bons mots* and
impromptus—sadness the keynote to his character.

EVEN before the last numbers of "Vanity
Fair" were published, Thackeray had become a personage, and his tall figure and
massive head became a familiar sight in the
dining-rooms and drawing-rooms of society.

There is no more dangerous or stupefying position
for a man in life than to be a cock of a small society
[he wrote about this time]. It prevents his ideas
from growing ; it renders him intolerably conceited.
A twopenny-halfpenny Cæsar, a Brummagem dandy,
a coterie philosopher or wit, is pretty sure to be an
ass ; and, in fine, I lay it down as a maxim that it is
good for a man to live where he can meet his betters,
intellectual and social.[1]

[1] *Mr. Brown's Letters—On Friendship.*

Thackeray liked society and felt at home in it; but for a long time he was amused, though certainly not displeased, at the idea of being a great man. "This is true fame," he exclaimed gleefully, on receiving an anonymous present of half a dozen bottles of a fine old brandy; and he was greatly flattered and much moved when Turguéncff called on him without any introduction, simply in the character of a foreign admirer of his works, and without saying a word about his own literary position. At most other tributes, however, he was inclined to smile, being essentially a humble-minded man, and rather astonished at the fuss the world was beginning to make about him.[1]

"I doubt whether Thackeray will be much the happier for his success," his old friend, Monckton Milnes, wrote in May 1849, "though I think people generally are for satisfied ambition." Applause, however, was to Thackeray a glorious incentive. It was what had been wanting during the many years of his struggles; and, now it had come, instead of inclining him to retire on his laurels, it acted as a spur to further effort. Carlyle surmised that since Thackeray had taken to cultivate dinner-eating in fashionable houses, his work would suffer; and perhaps it would have been better for Thackeray if (as with a trifle of exaggeration he told Lady Blessington) he had not "reeled from dinner party to dinner party, wallowed in turtle, and swum in claret and champagne." On the other hand, society was useful and necessary to him. "A social painter must be of the world which he depicts, and native to the manners he portrays," he wrote, when

[1] H. Sutherland Edwards: *Recollections*, p. 37.

comparing the accuracy of Leech's drawings with the many mistakes of Gillray. "If I don't go out and mingle in society, I can't write," he confided to Mrs. Bedingfield. He makes a speech at a Literary Fund Dinner and breaks down : " Of what I said I have not the slightest idea," he told Mrs. Brookfield ; " but the discomfiture will make a good chapter for 'Pendennis.'" He goes to a Sybaritic repast at Spencer Cowper's, and sees a chapter or two in some of the guests. It is all a matter of temperament. Carlyle could probably not have written at all if he had dined out regularly : to Thackeray society was as the breath of his nostrils. "He was a man of sensibility," Locker-Lampson has recorded ; " he delighted in luxuriously furnished and well-lighted rooms, good music, excellent wines and cookery, exhilarating talk, gay and airy gossip, pretty women and their toilettes, and refined and noble manners, *le bon goût, le ris, l'aimable liberté!* The amenities of life and the traditions stimulated his imagination."[1]

There is no doubt Thackeray enjoyed being lion-ised ; but there was one serious drawback : being a prominent personage in literature and society, he had to take the share in speech-making at banquets that falls to the lot of those who have raised themselves above their fellows. Though a finished lecturer, Thackeray was at his worst when he attempted to deliver a speech to a large audience. At the Shakespeare dinners at the Garrick Club and on similar occasions when he felt more or less at home it was not so bad : but elsewhere he was terribly self-conscious,

[1] *My Confidences,* p. 304.

and suffered agonies of nervousness before the hour arrived. The failure itself was not so bad as the anticipation of it, and he could quite light-heartedly laugh at himself when the ordeal was over.

Thackeray, when the "smash" came, as it usually did after the first few sentences of his carefully prepared speech, would sit down so calmly, with such a look of amused bewilderment, that the audience always gave him a kindly smile. Once he made Fields travel with him to Manchester to hear the speech he was going to make at the founding of the Free Library Institution in that city. "All the way down," Fields has recorded, " he was discoursing of certain effects he intended to produce on the Manchester doges by his eloquent appeals to their pockets. This passage was to have great influence with the rich merchants, this one with the clergy, and so on. He said that although Dickens, and Bulwer, and Sir James Stephen—all eloquent speakers— were to precede him, he intended to beat each of them on this special occasion. He insisted that I should be seated directly in front of him so that I should have the full force of his magic eloquence. . . . Sir John Potter, who presided, then rose, and after some complimentary allusions to the author of 'Vanity Fair,' introduced him to the crowd, who received him with ringing plaudits. As he rose, he gave me a half-wink from under his spectacles, as if to say, 'Now for it; the others have done very well, but I will show 'em a grace beyond the reach of their art.' He began in a clear and charming manner, and was absolutely perfect for three minutes. In the midst of a most earnest and elaborate sentence he suddenly stopped, gave a look of comic despair at the ceiling, crammed both hands into his trousers pockets, and deliberately sat down. . . . He continued to sit on the platform in a perfectly composed manner ; and when the meeting was over, he said to me, without a sign of discomfiture, ' My boy, you have accidentally missed hearing one of the finest speeches ever composed for delivery by a great British orator.' "[1] To this occasion he referred in a letter to his youngest daughter :

> Last week I was away at Manchester when I broke down in a speech before three thousand ladies and gentlemen. I felt very foolish, but I tried again at night, and did better ; and as there is nothing more wicked in breaking down in a speech than in slipping on a bit of orange-peel and breaking one's nose, why, I got up again, and made another speech at night without breaking down. It is all custom, and most people can no more do it than they can play the piano without learning.

When George Hodder was acting as Thackeray's secretary, one morning he found the great man still in bed and complaining of a restless night. "I'm sorry you do not seem very well this morning," Hodder said. "*Well*," the unhappy novelist murmured ; "no, I am not well. I have got to make that confounded speech to-night" (at the annual dinner of the General Theatrical Fund)." "Don't let that trouble you ; you will be all right when the time comes," the secretary said soothingly. "Nonsense," Thackeray replied ; "it won't come all right ; I can't make a speech, confound it ! That fellow Jackson let me in for this. Why don't they get Dickens to take the chair ? *He can* make a speech

[1] *Yesterdays with Authors.*

and a good one. . . . *I'm* of no use. . . . They little think how nervous I am ; and Dickens doesn't know the meaning of the word."[1]

Thackeray spoke at the dinners of the Literary Fund, the Theatrical Fund, and other charitable institutions ; and he replied for Literature at a Royal Academy dinner and elsewhere. He was one of the stewards of the banquet given to Macready at the London Tavern on March 1, 1851, on the occasion of the actor's retirement, and he proposed the health of Mrs. Macready and her family.

Thackeray took a great deal of trouble over his speech to be delivered at the farewell banquet given to him on the eve of his departure for the second visit to America. " It is very kind of my friends to give me a dinner," he said, " but I wish it was over, for such things set me trembling. Besides," he exclaimed to Mr. Hodder, " I have to make a speech, and what am I to say ? Here, take a pen in your hand and sit down, and I'll see if I can hammer out something. It's hammering now ; I'm afraid it will be stammering by-and-by." He dictated the speech, and tried to learn it; but the speech as delivered, those who were present have asserted, fell far short of the speech as written, and Thackeray was firmly convinced that he had bungled the business.

My dear fellow [he wrote to Macready from New York, November 20, 1855], it is about that horrible nightmare of a dinner I want to speak to you. You must know I intended to say something funny about Macbeth and Banquo ; and then to finish off with the prettiest compliment and give some notion of the

[1] George Hodder : *Memories of My Time.*

kindness I was feeling—I blundered in the joke, left out the kindness and the compliment—made an awful fiasco. If I lose my head when I try speechmaking, all is up with me. I say what I don't mean, what I don't know afterwards, the Lord forgive me—and you must, if I said aught (I don't know for certain that I did or didn't) which was unpleasing. I am savage sometimes when my heart is at its tenderest, and I want to tell you now—and no other words are authentic, and if I said 'em I deny 'em—that I felt pleased and touch'd by your kindness and apologise hereby for my own blunders and cordially shake you by the hand.[1]

No amount of practice will make a great speaker out of a man who lacks eloquence and the other essential qualities, but it will in course of time enable an intelligent man to say clearly what is in his mind. So Thackeray argued, when he offered himself to the Oxford electors as their representative in Parliament.

As to my own opinions on public questions, you may have heard them pretty frequently expressed on many occasions. I only hope, if you elect me to Parliament, I shall be able to obviate the little difficulty which has been placarded against me—that I could not speak. I own I cannot speak very well, but I shall learn. I cannot spin out glib sentences by the yard as some people can; but if I have got anything in my mind, if I feel strongly on any question, I have, I believe, got brains enough to express it.

Candid friends hinted that Thackeray was becoming a tuft-hunter. "Mr. Thackeray has said more, and more effectively, about snobs and snobbism than any other man," Harriet Martineau has written; "and yet

---

[1] W. M. Thackeray: *Notes for Speech at Dinner, October 11, 1855, etc., printed for Major W. H. Lambert*, Philadelphia, 1896.

his frittered life, and his obedience to the call of the great, are the observed of all observers. As it is, so it must be; but 'O the pity of it, the pity of it!' Great and unusual allowance is to be made in his case, I am aware; but this does not lessen the concern occasioned by the spectacle of one after another of the aristocracy of nature making the Koto to the aristocracy of accident." "Thackeray had grown a little *blasé*," Sir Frederick Pollock wrote in 1849; and some years later: "Thackeray . . . after he became famous, liked no subject so well as himself and his books"; and this, too, after Thackeray had humorously complained to Mr. Brookfield that at a dinner at the "Star and Garter" with the Strutts and Romillys they talked about "Vanity Fair" and "Pendennis" almost incessantly, though he declared he tried to turn the conversation at least ten times, but they would not let him. Very probably these people who complained of Thackeray's conversation turning on his books were the very people who would not permit the subject to be changed.[1] Thackeray was aware of the charges brought against him, and replied to them when, in the person of "Brown the Elder," he was discoursing on Friendship:

> To know young noblemen and brilliant and notorious town-bucks and leaders of fashion, has this great disadvantage; that if you talk about them or are seen with them much, you offend all your friends of middle life. It makes men envious to

[1] It is interesting in this respect to compare an extract from Macaulay's Diary. "I dined at Lady Charlotte Lindsay's with Hallam and Kinglake. I am afraid that I talked too much about my book. Yet really the fault was not mine. People *would* introduce the subject. I will be more guarded; yet how difficult it is to hit the right point! To turn the conversation might look ungracious and affected."

see their acquaintances better off than they themselves are.

Of course he had to pay the inevitable price for his social popularity—the loss of some of his friends of early life. "I like what are called Bohemians and fellows of that sort," he told John Eston Cooke. "I have seen all sorts of society—dukes, duchesses, lords and ladies, authors, actors, and painters—and taken altogether I think I like painters the best, and Bohemians generally. They are more natural and unconventional; they wear their hair on their shoulders if they want, and dress picturesquely and carelessly." [1] That is not like the language of a tuft-hunter, nor is the following sentiment likely to be expressed by an idolater of rank:

> When I see those magnificent dandies yawning out of White's or caracolling in the Park, I like to think that Brummell was the greatest of them all, and that Brummell's father was a footman. [2]

Nevertheless he thoroughly admired the *je ne sais quoi* that marks the gentleman.

> (The Kickleburys) are travelling with Mr. Bloundell, who was a gentleman once and still retains about him some faint odour of that time of bloom. [3]
> It is true poor Plantagenet (Gaunt) is only an idiot . . . a zany . . . and yet you see somehow that he is a gentleman. [4]

[1] *Appleton's Magazine*, September 1879.
[2] Brummell's father, as a matter of fact, was private secretary to Lord Liverpool, and in that capacity amassed a fortune, set up as a country gentleman, and entertained Fox, Sheridan, and other notabilities at Donnington Hall. The *Beau's* grandfather, however, was a small tradesman who let lodgings.
[3] *The Kickleburys on the Rhine*.
[4] *Dr. Birch and His Young Friends*.

These are among the lines that Thackeray has written, expressive of the high value he placed on good breeding. " No doubt a man may be an earl of eleven descents, and yet be a pitifully mean creature," he once said to Cordy Jeaffreson; "all the same for that, I am of opinion that it takes three generations to make a gentleman."[1] But a man may like to be in the company of gentlemen without being a snob!

It cannot be seriously believed that Thackeray neglected the friends of earlier days. We all know how it is. If a social equal or inferior passes us in the street without a word or recognition, it is because he does not see us; but if a person of much higher rank does the same, then it is because he does not wish to see us. The same absurd sensitiveness, which can only arise from a feeling of uncertainty about one's position, may be seen when a family has lost its money. They lose their friends, and then to the end of the chapter grumble at the perfidy of well-to-do people. But is it entirely the fault of the friends? More often it is because the unfortunate people are on the look out for slights and insults in a way that was quite unnatural to them in their days of prosperity. Thus it was, no doubt, with many of those who found Thackeray bored or cold.

When a man gets this character (of being haughty and supercilious to old acquaintances) he never loses it [he defended himself in a letter to his relative, Mrs. Bayne]. This opinion once put forth against a man, all his friends believe it, accommodate themselves to the new theory, see coolness where none is meant. They won't allow for the *time* an immensely

[1] J. C. Jeaffreson: *A Book of Recollections*, Vol. I., p. 250.

enlarged acquaintance occupies, and fancy I am dangling after lords and fine people because I am not so much in their drawing-rooms as in former days. They don't know in what a whirl a man plunges who is engaged in my business. Since I began this work (lecturing), besides travelling, reading, seeing people, dining—when I am forced out and long to be quiet—I write at the rate of five thousand letters a year. I have a heap before me now—six of them are about lectures—one from an old gentleman whom I met on the railroad and who sends me his fugitive poems. I must read them, answer, and compliment the old gentleman. Another from a poor widow, in bad spelling, asking for help. Nobody knows the work until he is in it; and of course, with all this, old friends hint you are changed, you are forsaking us for great people, and so forth, and so forth.[1]

Major Dwyer thought that no man was ever so much improved by success as Thackeray, and testimony to the effect that the novelist was a most agreeable companion in the days of his prosperity has been borne by friends and acquaintances innumerable, both in England and the United States. "He is a very jolly fellow, and no 'High Art' about him," said Albert Smith,[2] and this, coming from a man cast in a very different mould, is high praise; and John Hollingshead has written, "What I saw of Thackeray impressed me with his gentleness and charity. Far from being a cynic, he was more like a good-natured schoolboy."[3] "Thackeray drew many unto him, for he had engaging as well as fine qualities. He was openhanded and kind-hearted. He had not an overween-

---

[1] Merivale and Marizals : *Thackeray*, p. 150.
[2] J. C. Jeaffreson : *A Book of Recollections*, Vol. I, p. 285.
[3] *My Lifetime.*

ing opinion of his literary consequence, and he was generous as regarded the people whom the world chose to call his rivals."[1] Thus Frederick Locker-Lampson, who knew him well; and that practical man of affairs, Henry Vizetelly, has contributed his portion of praise: "His placid temper and pleasant courtesy charmed all who came into contact with him. . . . Thackeray was reticent in expressing his opinion upon people whom he did not like, and very rarely said ill-natured things about anyone."[2] "He is a finer, larger, loveabler man, or rather *fellow*, than ever," Dr. John Brown wrote to Lady Trevelyan;[3] and the Rev. Whitwell Elwin declared, "I can never speak of him without a pang, for I loved him. He was a fine, noble man. His manners were as simple as a child's. He had no assumption, no affectation."[4]

Thackeray had some enemies, of course, as who among the fortunate has not? Has ever a successful man gone through life without stirring up angry feelings or arousing jealousy? Dr. Gordon Hake, Serjeant Ballantine, and others have said unkind things of him; but the majority of those who disliked him did so because they did not understand him. "Those who knew him best," said George Hodder, "loved him best." He was a sick, as well as an overworked, man, often suffering pain from an internal disease, and he could not always be smiling. One day he passed a friend with the curtest nod: "Who

[1] *My Confidences.*
[2] *Glances Back Through Seventy Years.*
[3] *Letters of Dr. John Brown*, p. 113.
[4] Whitwell Elwin: *Some Eighteenth Century Men of Letters*, Vol. I, p. 157.

X

would have thought," said the other, "that we were
up till four o'clock this morning together? He sang
his 'Dr. Luther' and was the liveliest of us all."[1]
Years later he was to meet Anthony Trollope for the
first time at the inaugural dinner given by George
Smith to the contributors of the *Cornhill Magazine*.
Both he and Trollope had looked forward to the
occasion; but when the night came, and the publisher introduced Trollope, Thackeray said abruptly,
"How d'ye do?" and turned on his heel.[2] These are
instances of what Maunsell B. Field called the great
man's "moods of surly incivility"; but in reality they
were merely the outcome of intense physical agony.
It is more pleasant to turn to the picture of him con-
jured up by Mrs. J. F. Fields. "I seem to see one
kindly face—large, full of humour, full of human
sympathy. The face belongs to Thackeray, and I can
recall his goodness to one who, although married
already, was hardly more than 'a slip of a girl,' and
very much afraid of him—afraid, let me say, rather of
the idea of him, the great author and famous lecturer,
who was making his crowded audiences laugh and cry
at his simple word every evening; the great man of
the moment whom everybody was 'running after,'
yet of whom they said that he liked his friends so
much better than all their noise about himself, that
he was always trying to escape from it—and here he
was!—coming to see—whom? Well, it appears it did
not so much matter, for he was bent on kindnesses,

---

[1] Blanchard Jerrold : *The Best of All Good Company*.
[2] G. M. Smith: *Our Birth and Parentage* (*Cornhill Magazine*,
January 1901).

and he took it all in at a glance, and sat down by the window, and drew me to him, and told me about his 'little girls' at home; how he walked down the wrong side of Piccadilly one day, and so lost what money he had had out of his pocket—money which belonged properly to these same dear girls of his; therefore it came about that he made up his mind, though it was hard enough to come away from them, to get something to take back to them in place of what he had lost; and how they were the dearest girls in the world, and when I came to England I should find them more like old friends, and should have somebody, I am sure, he thought, to 'play with,' though, under the circumstances, he could not use just those words! And then, soon after, he went away, leaving a great train of sunshine and kindness behind him which has never faded." [1]

There is the real Thackeray, the Thackeray who was so lavish of kindness, and lavish, too, not only of words, but of money. To be in trouble was a sure passport to his heart. His charity was only bounded by his means; he did not wait to be asked to do a favour; he loved to anticipate, not merely the request, but even the wish. How delicately, too, he dispensed his "loans," as he called the alms he bestowed upon those less fortunate than himself. Lady Ritchie has related how he filled a pill-box with Napoleons, wrote on it "one to be taken occasionally when required," and gave it to his mother to send to a distressed gentlewoman. We are told by Miss Perry how he visited an old acquaintance in very reduced circumstances,

[1] *A Shelf of Old Books.*

administered some little rebuke on the thoughtlessness of not laying by some of the easily gained gold of youth or manhood and, slipping into a blotting-book a hundred-pound note, hurried away. "I never saw him do it," said poor old P——. "I was very angry because he said I had been a reckless old goose—and then a hundred pounds falls out of my writing-book. God bless him!"

> I am sincerely sorry to hear of your position [he wrote to George Hodder, enclosing a cheque], and send this contribution which came so opportunely from another friend, whom I was enabled once to help. When you are well-to-do again I know you will pay it back, and I daresay somebody else will want the money, which is heartily at your service.

The money "which came so opportunely from another friend" was probably a pious fiction invented to spare the recipient's feelings and to make the lender's generosity appear less considerable than it was, for he employed this method more than once. One morning he knocked at the door of Horace Mayhew's chambers in Regent Street, crying from without, "It's no use, Horry Mayhew; open the door." On entering he said cheerfully, "Well, young gentleman, you'll admit an old fogy," and when leaving he remarked: "By the way, how stupid! I was going away without doing part of the business of my visit. You spoke the other day of poor George. Somebody—most unaccountably —has returned me a five-pound note I lent him long ago. I didn't expect it. So just hand it to George, and tell him when his pocket will bear it to pass it on to some poor fellow of his acquaintance. By-bye!"

and he was gone. Trollope has related how he met Thackeray in Whitehall and told him a sad story of a mutual friend who required a loan of £2000 to save him from utter ruin. "Do you mean to say that I am to find £2000?" Thackeray said, with an oath. Trollope hastened to explain that he had not suggested that, he had thought merely that they might discuss the matter. "Then," says Trollope, "there came over his face a peculiar smile, and a wink in his eye, and he whispered his suggestion, as though half ashamed of his meanness, 'I'll go half,' he said, 'if anybody will do the rest.'" [1] Truly, as Trollope remarked, his generosity was overflowing.

Thackeray, who always found pleasure in hearing of kind deeds, and telling of them, was always himself doing kind things, begging somebody to ask a bishop for a living for a curate who wanted to get married, recommending Marguerite Power, the niece of his friend Lady Blessington, for the post of Paris Correspondent of the *Illustrated London News*, or endeavouring to set an impoverished French artist, Louis Marvy, on his feet.

In large gatherings Thackeray, who was an intensely shy man, was inclined to be satirical and severe in his conversation, and Lady Dorothy Nevill has told us how she was afraid of him ever after she heard him administer a terrible verbal castigation to someone who had incurred his displeasure. When, at a dinner party, a dignified man of letters with a broken nose discoursed persistently of love, "What has the world come to?" said Thackeray aloud, "when two broken-nosed old

[1] Anthony Trollope : *Thackeray*, p. 60.

fogies like you and me sit talking about love to each other "; and, in more bitter vein, when a group of members of the Reform Club were gossiping unkindly of another, recently deceased, "That's right," said Thackeray. "Kick him. Trample on him. *He's dead!*" He reserved these onslaughts for those whom he considered stupid people, and as such he classed those who "do not know how to laugh, are always pompous and self-conceited, *i.e.*, bigoted, *i.e.*, cruel, *i.e.*, ungentle, uncharitable, unchristian." When he found he had made a mistake and thought ill of one who deserved otherwise, he was always anxious without delay to make the *amende honorable*. He had always disliked John Wilson Croker, but when, after that unpopular person was dead, someone told Thackeray how Croker had begged his wife to seek out some homeless boys, and let them stay with them from Saturday to Monday, saying, "They will destroy your flower-beds and upset my inkstands, but we can help them more than they can hurt us," Thackeray choked, and forthwith went to Mrs. Croker and asked her pardon for ever having entertained unkindly thoughts of her husband.

Thackeray had a great sense of fun and was always ready to indulge it. This broader humour seldom appears in his writings after "Major Gahagan's Reminiscences," but the source from which that delightful burlesque sprang, never dried up, and his love of buffoonery lasted until the end. Frederick Locker-Lampson remembered seeing him pirouette, wave his arms majestically, and declaim in burlesque—an intentionally awkward imitation of the ridiculous manner that is sometimes met with in French opera; and he also recalled an occasion when he was talking to Thackeray's daughters, their father put on his visitor's hat, many sizes too small for him, and strutted about flourishing it in the old Lord Cardigan style.

Dean Hole has said that Thackeray was the best talker he ever listened to and that when it pleased him to talk, "he said so many good things . . . that they trod down and suffocated each other"; and, wrote Mrs. Browning from Rome in 1854, "If anybody wants small talk by handfuls, of glittering dust swept out of *salons*, here's Mr. Thackeray." He was not a wit in the sense that Sydney Smith and Oscar Wilde were; but there can be no doubt that he must have said far more good things than have been recorded. When he saw in a window off the Strand the legend, "Mutual Loan Fund Association," and a companion wondered what that meant, "Oh, it means," said the novelist, "that they have got no money and lend it to each other." "If that d——d irreligious fish had been to afternoon church," he remarked to Sir Mountstuart Grant Duff, with whom he was angling one Sunday, "we should not have caught him." It was on William Palmer Hale, famous for the quantity of beer he could drink, he pronounced this epitaph: "Take him for half-and-half, we shall not look upon his like again." When outside a shop he saw two tubs of oysters side by side, labelled respectively a shilling and fifteen pence a dozen, "How these," he murmured, looking at the cheaper variety, "must hate the others."

Charles Mackay has put it on record that Thackeray was the best improvisatore of his time, and certainly his fondness for the exercise was perennial. He was always rhyming from his school-days to the end of his life. A lady begged him to write a verse in her album —a practice to which he was always averse. Turning over the pages, however, he found the following :

> "Mont Blanc is the Monarch of Mountains,
> They crowned him long ago,
> But who they got to put it on,
> Nobody seems to know.
>
> "ALBERT SMITH."

Then, yielding to temptation, he took up a pen and wrote immediately underneath :

A HUMBLE SUGGESTION

> I know that Albert wrote in a hurry—
> To criticise I scarce presume ;
> But yet, methinks that Lindley Murray
> Instead of " who " had written " whom."
>
> W. M. THACKERAY.

When he saw the lines that "Soapy Sam" Wilberforce, Bishop of Oxford, had written on the unorthodox Bishop Colenso,

> "There once was a Bishop of Natal,
> Whose doubts on the Deluge were fatal ;
> Said the infidel Zulu,
> ' D'you believe this—you fool, you ? '
> ' No, I don't,' said the Bishop of Natal."

Thackeray at once capped it with :

> There is the bold Bishop Colenso,
> Whose heresies seem to offend so.
> Quoth Sam of the Soap,
> " Bring fagot and rope ;
> For we know he a'nt got no friends, oh ! "

"Little Billee" was chanted off impromptu at a supper-party at Rome; and there are many other, though minor, instances of the kind. When at dinner one day, a neighbour, knowing him to be a *gourmet*, asked him which part of the fowl he preferred, with portentous gravity he answered :

> Oh ! what's the best part of a fowl?
> My own Anastasia cried :
> Then, giving a terrible howl,
> She turned on her stomach and died.

Mere fun, mere farcical nonsense, he did not, of course, value highly. When he was asked if "Vanity Fair" would be funny, he retorted that it would be humorous. He had, indeed, the same keen sense of the ridiculous that he bestowed upon Becky Sharp ; and it was this, probably, that caused him at times to under-estimate the value of even his greatest books : he could not always take himself seriously as a great writer, and he was inclined to doubt the merits of his creations. As with every true humorist, the keynote to his character is sadness. "In much wisdom is much grief." And, above all else, Thackeray was wise and very sad. He told Dr. John Brown how, on one occasion at Paris, he found himself in a great crowded *salon*, and looking from one end, across a sea of heads, being in Swift's place of calm in a crowd ("an inch or two above it"), he saw at the other end a strange visage, staring at him with an expression of comical woebegoneness ; and how, after a little while, he found this rueful being was himself in the mirror. And he liked to relate the pathetic story of the sad-looking man in a decline, who, consulting a great physician, was recommended to go to the pantomime, where the sight of Harlequin would be sure to do him good, and cheer him up. "I am Harlequin," said the patient simply.

Thackeray loved his home and his friends, and books, drawings and music : he enjoyed a good dinner, and sometimes a jovial party ; but Vanity Fair seemed to him a sad place.

A man with a reflective turn of mind, walking through an exhibition of this sort (Vanity Fair), will not be oppressed, I take it, by his own or other people's hilarity. An episode of humour or kindness touches and amuses him here and there ;—a pretty child looking at a gingerbread stall ; a pretty girl blushing whilst her lover talks to her and chooses her fairing ; poor Tom Fool, yonder behind the waggon, mumbling his bone with the honest family which lives by his tumbling ; but the general impression is one more melancholy than mirthful. When you come home, you sit down, in a sober, contemplative, not uncharitable frame of mind, and apply yourself to your books or your business.[1]

The world called to him, as it had done to Cruikshank, and so many others, "Make us laugh, or you and your children starve." He did his best, but he could not assume the *rôle* of *farceur* for very long at a time. He might be cutting the most amusing jokes in a private company, or writing the most amusing verses for the public ; but generally there can be found, under the surface, a touch of pathos, or of melancholy.

[1] *Vanity Fair—Before the Curtain.*

What funny things I've written when fit to hang myself [he said in one letter to Mrs. Brookfield ; and in another] : I did the doggerel verses, which were running in my head when I last wrote you, and they are very lively. You'd say the author must have been in the height of good spirits ! . . . No, you wouldn't, knowing his glum habit, and dismal views of life generally.

This he repeated in "The Pen and the Album":

I've helped him to pen many a line for bread ;
  To joke, with sorrow aching in his heart ;
And make your laughter when his own heart bled.

Fate, dealing harshly with him, had made memory painful, and it distressed him to read his own writings.

Our books are diaries, in which our own feelings must of necessity be set down. As we look to the page written last month, or ten years ago, we remember the day and its events ; the child ill, mayhap, in the adjoining room, and the doubts and fears which racked the brain as it still pursued its work ; the dear old friend who read the commencement of the tale, and whose gentle hand shall be laid in ours no more. I own for my part that, in reading pages which this hand penned formerly, I often lose sight of the text under my eyes. It is not the words I see, but that past day ; that bygone page of life's history ; that tragedy, comedy it may be, which our little home company was enacting ; that merry-making which we shared ; that funeral which we followed ; that bitter, bitter grief which we buried.[1]

[1] *De Finibus.*

CHAPTER XV

PUNCH (1847-1854)

Thackeray's earnings in 1848—success of "Vanity Fair" in book-form
—Thackeray resigns the assistant-editorship of the *Examiner*—and
retires from the staff of *Fraser's Magazine*—his Christmas Books—the
Times' attack on "The Kickleburys on the Rhine"—and Thackeray's
reply, "An Essay on Thunder and Small Beer"—Thackeray sensitive
to criticism—but makes jokes at his own expense—writes again for
the *Morning Chronicle*—his contributions to *Punch* from 1847—
"Punch's Prize Novelists"—"Mr. Brown's Letters to a Young Man
About Town"—the "Proser Papers"—withdraws from *Punch* in
1854—his reference to his withdrawal in his article on John Leech—a
slip of the pen—his letter to the proprietors of *Punch* concerning his
resignation—he attends the dinners to the end—his indebtedness
to *Punch*—*Punch's* tribute to him—and his to *Punch*—his friends on
the staff—Douglas Jerrold—Thackeray's Ballads—"Bow Street
Ballads"—"Lyra Hibernica"—his limitations as a writer of verse—
his sense of parody—and of tenderness—"The Cane-Bottomed
Chair"—"St. Sophia of Kioff"—"The Chronicle of the Drum"—his
merits as a writer of light and humorous verse.

WHEN "Vanity Fair" was coming out
Thackeray told his mother that while
this novel greatly enhanced his reputation, it did not materially increase his
income. That income, however, was not contemp-
tible: "Vanity Fair" alone brought him in fifty
guineas a month, the profits of his Christmas Books
and of the "Snob Papers" and "The Great Hoggarty
Diamond" in book-form were considerable, and he
received a handsome salary from *Punch*, as well as

WILLIAM MAKEPEACE THACKERAY
From a painting by Samuel Laurence in the National Portrait Gallery

remuneration for articles and reviews elsewhere : he must have been earning at least £1000 a year. That he was soon making more than that there can be no doubt, for 1500 copies of "Vanity Fair" in book-form were sold immediately after publication, and for "Pendennis" he received more money than for the earlier story. He was doing well enough in 1848 to resign the assistant-editorship of the *Examiner* which, at a salary of £200 a year, he had held since 1844 under the editorship of Albany Fonblanque.

From *Fraser's Magazine* he had retired on the eve of the publication of "Vanity Fair," and he took his farewell of the readers he had delighted for more than ten years with story, verse, reviews, and sketches, in the following characteristic passage on "the very last page of the very last sheet" of the number for January 1847 :

> Ha ! what have we here ? — M. A. Titmarsh's Christmas Book—*Mrs. Perkins's Ball.* Dedicated to the Mulligan of Ballymulligan. Ballymulligan ! Bally fiddlestick ! What *you*, too, Mr. Titmarsh? You, you sneering wretch, setting up a Christmas-book of your own? This, then, is the meaning of your savage feelings towards "the minor fiddlers" ! Is your kit, sirrah, any bigger than theirs? You, who in the columns of this very Magazine, have sneered at the works of so many painters, look at your own performances !
>
> Some of your folks have scarcely more legs than Miss Biffin ; they have fins instead of hands,—they squint, almost every one of them !
>
> .   .   .   .   .   .
>
> All this is quite true. But see where we have come to ?—to the very last page of the very last sheet ; and the writer is called upon to stop just

at the very moment he was going to cut his own
head off.

So have I seen Mr. Clown (in that Christmas
drama which has been foremost in my thought during
all the above meditations) set up the gallows, adjust
the rope, try the noose curiously, and—tumble head
over heels.[1]

Thackeray's withdrawal from the *Examiner* and
Fraser's Magazine enabled him to devote himself to
work that was more remunerative. He followed his
first Christmas Book, "Mrs. Perkins's Ball," with
others, and in December of each year from 1847 to
1850 he issued, one by one, "Our Street", "Dr.
Birch and his Young Friends", "The Kickleburys on
the Rhine," and "Rebecca and Rowena," the last
founded upon the earlier "Proposals for a Continuation
of Ivanhoe."[2] "The Kickleburys on the Rhine" was
severely handled by the *Times* and, the review happen-
ing to appear just before the second edition went to
press, Thackeray, always sensitive to criticism, took
the opportunity to write a preface, "Being an ᴌssay
on Thunder and Small Beer."

I would rather have a good word than a bad one
from any person : but if a critic abuses me from a
high place, and it is worth my while, I will appeal
[he wrote]. If I can show that the judge who is
delivering sentence against me, and laying down
the law and making a pretence of learning, has no
learning and no law, and is neither more nor less
than a pompous noodle, who ought not to be heard
in any respectable court, I will do so ; and then,

[1] *A Grumble at the Christmas Books.* Thackeray in January 1853
contributed one more paper to *Fraser's Magazine :* "Mr. Thackeray in
the United States. John Small to the Editor of *Fraser's Magazine.*"
[2] *Fraser's Magazine*, August and September, 1846.

dear friends, perhaps you will have something to laugh at in this book.

He reprinted the *Times* review in this preface and made very merry over it.

> Why, a man who can say of a Christmas book [he retorted] that "it is an opuscule denominated so-and-so, and ostensibly intended to swell the tide of expansive emotion incident upon the exodus of the old year," must evidently have had immense sums and care expended on his early education, and deserves a splendid return. You can't go into the market, and get scholarship like *that*, without paying for it: even the flogging that such a writer must have had in early youth (if he was at a public school where the rods were paid for) must have cost his parents a good sum. Where would you find any but an accomplished classical scholar to compare the books of the present (or indeed any other) writer to "sardonic divings after the pearl of truth, whose lustre is eclipsed in the display of the diseased oyster"; mere Billingsgate doesn't turn out oysters like these; they are of the Lucrine lake :—this satirist has pickled his rods in Latin brine. Fancy, not merely a diver, but a sardonic diver: and the expression of his confounded countenance on discovering not only a pearl, but an eclipsed pearl, which was in a diseased oyster! I say it is only by an uncommon and happy combination of taste, genius, and industry, that a man can arrive at uttering such sentiments in such fine language,—that such a man ought to be well paid, as I have no doubt he is, and that he is worthily employed to write literary articles, in large type, in the leading journal of Europe. Don't we want men of eminence and polite learning to sit on the literary bench, and to direct the public opinion?

The culprit was a friend of Thackeray, Charles Lamb Kenney, and very cynically he explained the reason

Y

for the tone in which he had spoken of "The Kickleburys on the Rhine." "My only motive for pitching into the book was to please my employers," he told Jeaffreson. "Thackeray was not liked by them, and I wished them to like me. My friendly regard for the writer of the poor book was overborne by a strong sense of my duty to the public, and a still stronger care for my own interest."[1] If the editor of the *Times* did not like Thackeray, the novelist was unaware of it, for in 1851 when Mark Lemon would not print the "May-Day Ode" in *Punch* because the manuscript arrived late, Thackeray took it to Printing House Square, which took it gladly and paid generously for it. The *Times*, however, attacked "Esmond," and this Thackeray could not forgive.

As for the little hint about Printing House Square [Thackeray wrote in 1858 to Captain Atkinson, the author of "Curry and Rice," in which volume first appeared the verses, "Little Billee"] I know the editor and most of the writers, and, knowing, never think of asking a favour for myself or any mortal man. They are awful and inscrutable, and a request for a notice might bring down a slasher upon you, just as I once had in the *Times* for one of my own books ("Esmond"), of which the sale was absolutely stopped by a *Times* article.[2]

Thackeray, indeed, was often strangely sensitive to criticism, though he would make jokes at his own expense, or, in an aside, would chuckle at his critics. In "Mr. Brown's Letters" we learn that

Horner is asleep in the library at the Polyanthus:

[1] J. C. Jeaffreson: *A Book of Recollections*, Vol. I, p. 296.
[2] *Leisure Hour*, September 1883.

What is he reading? Hah! "Pendennis," No.
VIII.—hum, let us pass on,

and on the previous page is the drawing illustrative
of the episode.

> The heroine is not faultless (ah! that will be a
> great relief to some folks, for many writers' good
> women are, you know, so very insipid),

he said in "Lovel the Widower," probably thinking
of the strictures passed upon Amelia in "Vanity
Fair"; and later in the same novel he wrote:

> Some authors, who shall be nameless, are, I know,
> accused of depicting the most feeble, brainless,
> namby-pamby heroines, for ever whimpering tears,
> and prattling commonplaces.

When Thackeray said, "They have only bought so
many of my new book"; or, "Have you seen the
abuse of my new number?" or, "What am I to turn
my hand to? They are getting tired of my novels,"
Trollope admitted that he could not understand
him. Trollope remarked that he knew authors who
boasted of their thousands of copies sold, but he had
never heard any other writer declare that no one would
read his masterpiece, and that the world was becoming
tired of him; and he was puzzled accordingly. Yet the
cause of such remarks lay but little below the surface.
Thackeray spoke so, not because he was indifferent to
success or the opinion of his contemporaries, but because the pain inflicted by these wounds would have
been greater if he had thought anyone else would
sympathise with him. He preferred to say, "This
book is a failure," rather than let anyone else tell him

he had not succeeded. He was anxious to avoid criticism by himself turning critic. Sometimes he was almost absurdly sensitive, and Frederick Locker-Lampson has related a strange instance of this exaggerated susceptibility to criticism. "I happened to meet him as I was leaving the Travellers' Club. Even now I think I could point out the particular flag-stone on which the dear fellow was standing, as he gazed down on me through his spectacles with that dreary expression of his which his friends knew so well. He said, 'What do you think of the last number?' (No. 2 or 3 of 'The Newcomes.') He himself was evidently not satisfied with it. 'I like it immensely,' was my cordial rejoinder. A word or two more passed respecting the illustrations, which had been sharply criticised, and just as we parted, I was tactless enough to add, 'But, my dear fellow, perhaps there may be some kind people who will say that you did the cuts and Doyle the letter-press.' On this Thackeray's jaw dropped, and he exclaimed bitterly, 'I—Oh! really, that's your opinion, is it?' I saw at once what a mistake I had made, but I could only reply, 'I spoke in fun, pure fun; you know perfectly well how much I admire your writings, and also Doyle's cuts.' But Thackeray would have none of it, and turned wrathfully away in the direction of Pimlico. However, his wrath, I presume, died away in the large and charitable air of the Green Park, for when I met him the day after he was as amiable as ever. The fact is I had so exalted an opinion of Thackeray and of his writing that it seemed impossible such a demi-god should care for aught anybody said;

whereas, like Tennyson, he felt anything that everybody said."[1]

The great mass of Thackeray's miscellaneous
writings after the publication of "Vanity Fair"
appeared in *Punch*. A glance at the Bibliography at
the end of this work will show how numerous were his
contributions both with pen and pencil during the
years that "Vanity Fair" and "Pendennis" were
being published. In 1847, after the "Snob Papers"
were brought to a conclusion in February, began the
series of parodies of contemporary novelists, then
called "Punch's Prize Novelists," and rechristened
"Novels by Eminent Hands." Among his subjects
were to be Dickens and himself, but Mark Lemon
would not have the parody on Dickens, and so neither
was written : Lytton, Mrs. Gore, G. P. R. James, Feni-
more Cooper, were burlesqued ; and Lever, who after
reading "Phil Fogarty" declared he might as well
shut up shop and did actually alter the character of
his novels ; and Disraeli, who never forgave "Cod-
lingsby," and took a belated revenge by maliciously
caricaturing Thackeray as St. Barbe in "Endymion."
The "Prize Novelists" were followed in 1849 by "Mr.
Brown's Letters to a Young Man about Town," so full
of worldly wisdom ; and these, in their turn, by the
"Proser Papers," which in some ways were a continuation of "Mr. Brown's Letters." After 1850
Thackeray wrote less for *Punch*, and his last contribution, "A Second Letter to an Eminent Person,"
appeared in the issue for September 23, 1854, about
which time he severed his connection with the paper.

[1] *My Confidences.*

Four years before, Richard Doyle had retired from the Round Table, and to this and his own resignation Thackeray made reference in his article on that other invaluable contributor to *Punch*.

> Through the violent opinions which Mr. Punch expressed regarding the Roman Catholic hierarchy, he lost the invaluable services, the graceful pencil, the harmless wit, the charming fancy, of Mr. Doyle. Another member of Mr. Punch's cabinet, the biographer of Jeames, the author of the Snob Papers, resigned his functions on account of Mr. Punch's assaults upon the present Emperor of the French, whose anger Jeames thought it was unpatriotic to arouse.[1]

It was unfortunate that just after leaving *Punch* he should have inadvertently written a line that gave offence to his colleagues on the staff of that paper. It occurred in the article on Leech just mentioned.

> There is no blinking the fact that in Mr. Punch's cabinet John Leech is the right hand man. Fancy a number of *Punch* without Leech's pictures! What would you give for it? The learned gentlemen who write the work must feel that, without him, it were as well left alone.

Naturally the *Punch* authors were indignant, and Thackeray could only explain it, when writing to Whitwell Elwin (the editor of the *Quarterly Review*), by saying that he "slipped it over totally in the proof. . . . But we get to write as fast as we talk."[2] To "Professor" Percival Leigh, the author of the "Comic

---

[1] A review of "Picture of Life and Character," by John Leech (*Quarterly Review*, December 1854).

[2] Whitwell Elwin : *Some Eighteenth Century Men of Letters* (Memoir of Elwin. By his Son), Vol. I, p. 155.

HORACE MAYHEW   PERCIVAL LEIGH   GILBERT À BECKETT

W. NEWMAN   RICHARD DOYLE   JOHN LEECH   MARK LEMON   TOM TAYLOR   THACKERAY   DOUGLAS JERROLD

From a drawing by John Leech

MR. PUNCH'S FANCY BALL

"Punch," January 9, 1847

Latin Grammar," and one of the oldest contributors to *Punch*, he unreservedly expressed his regret.

Of all the slips of my fatal pen, there's none I regret more than the unlucky half-line which has given pain to such a kind and valued old friend as you have been, and I trust will be still to me. I ought never to have said " *Punch* might as well be left unwritten but for Leech." It was more than my meaning, which is certainly that the drawing is a hundred times more popular than the writing ; but I had no business to write any such thing, and forgot it so much that I was quite surprised when I first heard I had been accused of sneering at *Punch*. I knew when I came back from Paris, and read the line in the *Quarterly Review*, which I had forgotten as utterly as many another speech which I have made and didn't ought. Jerrold has had his fire into me, and, do you know, I feel rather comforted.

Thackeray, having made the *amende honorable*, asked the *Punch* staff to dinner, and the *Punch* staff came and made merry ; but the blunder, though forgiven, was not forgotten, and it became rumoured that it was owing to this that Thackeray had retired from the paper. Thackeray, hearing this, wrote on March 24, 1855, to " Pater " Evans, and placed the true version on record.

I find a note of yours dated Feb. 5, in which F. M. E. states that my account shall be prepared directly. F. M. E. has a great deal to do and pay and think of, but W. M. T. has also his engagements.

I hope your " Poetry of Punch " will not be published before my collected Ballads—You remember (you wrote me a letter expressly on the subject) that the Copyright of all articles in " Punch " were mine, by stipulation—and my book would be very much hurt by the appearance of another containing ¾ of its contents.

I met Murray the publisher the other day, and cannot help fancying from his manner to me that there is some screw loose with him too about that unlucky Leech article. Lemon, answering one of my letters, said that he personally complained, that my account of leaving *Punch* was not correct.

There was such a row at the time, and I was so annoyed at the wrong that I had done, that I thought I had best leave Lemon's remonstrance for a while and right it on some future occasion.

I recall now to you and beg you to show to him and to any other persons who may have received a different version of the story—what the facts were. I had had some serious public differences with the Conduct of *Punch*—about the abuse of Prince Albert and the Crystal Palace on which I very nearly resigned, about abuse of Lord Palmerston, about abuse finally of L. Napoleon—in all which *Punch* followed the *Times*, which I think and thought was writing unjustly at that time, and dangerously for the welfare and peace of the Country.

Coming from Edinburgh I bought a *Punch* containing the picture of a Beggar on Horseback, in which the Emperor was represented galloping to Hell with a sword reeking with blood. As soon as ever I could after my return (a day or 2 days after), I went to Bouverie St., saw you and gave in my resignation.

I mention this because I know the cause of my resignation has been questioned at *Punch*—because this was the cause of it. I talked it over with you, and Leech saw me coming out of your room, and I told him of my retirement.

No engagement afterwards took place between us; nor have I ever since been a member of *Punch's* Cabinet, so to speak. Wishing you all heartily well, I wrote a few occasional papers last year—and not liking the rate of remuneration, which was less than that to which I had been accustomed in my time—I wrote no more.

And you can say for me as a reason why I should feel hurt at your changing the old rates of payment made to me—that I am not a man who quarrels about a guinea or two except as a point of honour ; *and* that when I could have had a much larger sum than that which you gave me for my last novel—I preferred to remain with old friends who had acted honourably and kindly by me.

I reproach myself with having written ½ a line regarding my old *Punch* Companions—which was perfectly true, which I have often said—but which I ought not to have written. No other wrong that I know of have I done. And I think it is now about time that my old friends and publishers should set me right.

To the last Thackeray would, from time to time, attend the weekly dinners, where a place was always kept for him ; and to the last he cherished kindly thoughts for the paper and all who were connected with it. "Ah, Swain," he said one day, "if it had not been for *Punch*, I wonder where I should be"; and when an old friend on the staff died, he was the first to come forward and suggest that he and his colleagues should offer assistance to the widow and family.

Can't we, his old comrades, do something to show his poor widow and family our sense of his worth? He has a son at Christ Church where, with the family's altered means, it may not be convenient to support the young man. Is the career likely to be serviceable to him, and would he desire to continue it? I shall be heartily glad to give £100 towards a fund for his maintenance at Oxford, should he think fit to remain there. Others of our friends, no doubt, would join in it. It is through my connection with *Punch* that I owe the good chances that have lately befallen me, and have had so many kind offers of help in my own days of trouble, that I would thankfully aid a friend whom Death has called away.[1]

On the sad Christmas Eve when Thackeray died, the *Punch* staff met "round the old tree," mournful and sad. "I'll tell you what we'll do," said Horace Mayhew. "We'll sing the dear old boy's 'Mahogany Tree'; he'd like it." Accordingly they stood up, and with such memory of the words as each possessed, and a catching of the breath here and there by about all of them, the song was sung. "While generous tributes are everywhere being paid to the genius of him who has been suddenly called away in the fullness of his power and the maturity of his fame, some who have for many years enjoyed the advantage of his assistance and the delight of his society, would simply record that they have lost a dear friend," so runs the obituary notice in *Punch*. "At an early period in the history of the periodical he became a contributor to its pages, and he long continued to enrich them; and though of late he had ceased to give other aid than suggestions and advice, he was a constant member of our council, and sat with us on the eighth day from that which has saddened England's Christmas. Let the brilliancy of his trained intellect, the terrible strength of his satire, the subtlety of his wit, the richness of his humour, and the catholic range of his calm wisdom, be themes for others; the mourning friends who inscribe these lines to his memory think of the affectionate nature, the cheerful companionship, the large heart and the open hand, the simple courteousness, the endearing frankness of a

[1] H. Vizetelly: *Glances Back Through Seventy Years*, Vol. II, p. 108.

brave, true, honest gentleman, whom no pen but his
own could depict as those who knew him most desire."[1]
Not less magnificent was the compliment Thackeray
had paid to *Punch* :

> When the future enquirer shall take up your
> volumes, or a bundle of French plays, and contrast
> the performance of your booth with that of the
> Parisian theatre, he won't fail to remark how different
> they are, and what different objects we admire or
> satirise. As for your morality, sir, it does not be-
> come me to compliment you to your venerable face ;
> but permit me to say there never was before pub-
> lished so many volumes that contained so much
> cause for laughing, and so little for blushing, so
> many jokes, and so little harm. Why, sir, say
> even your modesty, which astonishes me more and
> more every time I regard you, is calculated, and
> not a virtue naturally inherent in you, that very
> fact would argue for the high sense of the public
> morality among us. We will laugh in the company
> of our wives and children ; we will tolerate no in-
> decorum ; we like that our matrons and girls should
> be pure.

His colleagues on *Punch* might well deplore
Thackeray's death, for he had been a friend of almost
all of them, from "à Beckett the Beak," who had gone
before, to Sir Francis Burnand, happily still with us, at
whose first dinner at the Round Table "the biographer of Jeames" was present. "Gentlemen," said
the veteran, "allow the old boy to present to you the
new boy !" Tom Taylor and John Leech were friends
of his before he joined the staff, but his acquaintance with the Mayhew brothers, Mark Lemon, Shirley
Brooks, Richard Doyle, Charles Keene, Percival Leigh,

[1] *Punch.*

and Sir John Tenniel, arose out of his connection with
Punch.

Thackeray regarded as his most important rival on
the staff of *Punch* Douglas Jerrold—witty, brilliant
Jerrold, who is little more than a name to-day. On
receiving his early copy of *Punch*, he would hastily
tear off the wrapper to see "what young Douglas has
to say this week," and would read the chapter of the
"Caudle Lectures" or "Miss Robinson Crusoe" or
whatever the contribution might be, before turning to
the remaining contents. They said many sharp and
stinging things about one another and to one another.
When Thackeray saw at the Earl of Carlisle's a
presentation copy of one of Jerrold's books, inscribed,
"To the Right Hon. the Earl of Carlisle, K.G., K.C.B.,
etc., etc., etc.," he remarked, "Ah, this is the style
in which your rigid, uncompromising radical always
toadies to the great!" When it was rumoured that
Thackeray was leaning towards the Church of Rome,
and someone remarked, "Why, they are Romanizing
old Thackeray," "I hope," said Jerrold, "I hope
they'll begin at his nose." "Good Lord," said the
caustic wit, hearing that the other had stood sponsor to
a child, "I hope you didn't present the infant with
your own mug."

"I have known Thackeray for eighteen years, and
I don't know him yet," Jerrold complained one day;
and, on the other hand, when Thackeray was giving
a breakfast party in 1848 to M. de Noé ("Cham"),
though asking several *Punch* men, he did not invite
Jerrold, because if the latter had come, he would have
taken "especial care that his own effulgence should ob-

scure all lesser lights, Cham's included."[1] Still, in spite
of these things, there was some sort of understanding
between them.   In one of his drawings Thackeray has
represented Jerrold and himself in a railway carriage
listening, with most amusing expressions on their
faces, to the other two occupants discussing, with
quite sublime ignorance, the members of the Punch
staff[2]—this does not show ill-feeling.   And it was
clearly an act of friendship when Thackeray ran up to
town one day from Leamington, where he was lecturing, announcing on his return to the astonished
George Hodder, " We've got the little man in "—and
then, noticing his bewilderment, explaining : " Why,
Jerrold ; we've elected him a member of the Reform
Club."   Jerrold's wit had made him many enemies
and Thackeray had gone up to use his influence to
secure his election.   Again, Thackeray rejoiced when
he heard of the increased popularity which *Lloyd's
Newspaper* attained under Jerrold's editorship, and
then characteristically declared, " I am quite pleased
with myself at finding myself pleased at men getting
on in the world."   At Jerrold's death, too, he co-
operated with Dickens to raise a fund for the widow
and children, contributing for his share the lecture on
" Weekday Preachers," in which he made special and
appreciative reference to Jerrold and his writings.   This
lecture was delivered on July 22, 1857, the day after
the declaration of the poll of the Oxford election in
which Thackeray was defeated, and the audience, on
the alert for some allusion to that event, was not dis-

---

[1] Henry Vizetelly : *Glances Back Through Seventy Years*, Vol. I,
p. 286.   [2] *Authors' Miseries.*

appointed, for the opening words of the discourse, delivered with comical solemnity, were, "Walking yesterday in the High Street of a certain ancient city . . ." "So began the lecturer," says the *Times*, in its account of the lecture, "and was interrupted by a storm of laughter that deferred for some moments the completion of the sentence."

Before leaving the subject of Thackeray's connection with *Punch*, something must be said of his ballads, the majority of which appeared in the pages of that paper. It has been remarked that he was always rhyming in private life, and he was devoted to the exercise. The best papers of the little *brochure*, "The Second Funeral of Napoleon," are undoubtedly those given over to "The Chronicle of the Drum"; but as his literary career progressed poetry took its place in his life as a relaxation, for the writing of verses was with him a labour of love. Yet though as a rule he wrote with ease, he was a severe critic of his work, and after publication would sometimes entirely revise the poem. There are two distinct versions of "The King of Brentford"; and no less than three times he materially altered "Lucy's Birthday."

Thackeray wrote in all about one hundred poems. A fifth of this number were based upon political subjects, and of these there is little to say, save that most of them were composed in haste, often with the printer's devil at the door. Their merit consists in a certain humour, but their interest was for the day: they amused the generation for which they were written, and so achieved their object. Clever they are undoubtedly, but few of them bear the hall-mark of the author's individuality ; and, in all probability, the subjects were selected, or at least suggested, by the editor of *Punch*.

The same defects, though in a lesser degree, are noticeable in "The Bow Street Ballads." They also convey in the reading the impression that they were written to order ; and not all the fun of Policeman X 54's queer spelling and phrasing makes them quite acceptable, although here and there the personality of Thackeray emerges from the motley. Notably is this the case in "Jacob Omnium's Hoss," where he gives rein to his indignation against " Pallis Court," with its monstrous scale of costs :—

> Come down from that tribewen.
>   Thou Shameless and Unjust ;
> Thou Swindle, picking pockets in
>   The name of Truth august ;
> Come down, thou hoary Blasphemy,
>   For die thou shalt and must.
>
> And go it, JACOB HOMNIUM,
>   And ply your iron pen,
> And rise up SIR JOHN JERVIS,
>   And shut me up that den ;
> That sty for fattening lawyers in
>   On the bones of honest men.

The " Lyra Hibernica " are better. Carlyle said these Irish ballads were the best things Thackeray ever wrote, and he would quote them and laugh heartily at them. The fun is more spontaneous, the humour of a higher class ; the quaint rhymes amuse, and the swing of the verses delight. It is not worth while, however,

Z

to argue the question of the accuracy of Thackeray's attempt to present phonetically the Irishman's pronunciation of the English language. The catalogue of the exhibits of the Great Exhibition is delightful, and the apparent ease of the versification is not excelled even in the wonderful " White Squall."

There's holy saints
And window paints
By Maydiayval PUGIN ;
Alhamborough JONES
Did paint the tones
Of yellow and gambouge in.

. . . . . .

There's Statue bright
Of marble white,
Of silver and of copper ;
And some in zinc,
And some, I think,
That isn't over proper.

. . . . .

For them genteels
Who ride on wheels,
There's plenty to indulge 'em ;
There's Droskys snug
From Paytersbug
And vayhicles from Bulgium.

There's Cabs on Stands
And Shandthry-danns ;
There's Waggons from New York here ;
There's Lapland sleighs
Have crossed the seas,
And Jaunting Cyars from Cork here.·

Thackeray never attempted the " big bow-wow" kind
of poetry. From the first he recognised his limitations:
and to the end was content to be bound by them. He
might have said with Locker-Lampson, "My aim is
humble. I used the ordinary metres and rhymes, the
simplest language and ideas, I hope flavoured with
individuality. I strove not to be obscure, not to be flat,
above all, not to be tedious." As, indeed, Thackeray
said to the author of the delightful "London Lyrics":
"I have a sixpenny talent (or gift) and so have you ;
ours is small beer, but, you see, it is the right tap."[1]
It is worthy of remark how much in common the verses
of these men had. The poems of Locker-Lampson—
that author thought Thackeray almost as humorous as
Swift, and sometimes almost as tender as Cowper—
often suggest those of the more famous writer. The
dainty "St. James's Street" recalls "The Ballad of
Bouillabaisse," as "Gertrude's Necklace" conjures up
memory of "Lucy's Birthday." Both were artists to
the finger-tips, both had a keen appreciation of humour;
but Thackeray, though he could be dainty, if usually
less elegant, was rather more virile.

Thackeray was strongly imbued with the sense
of parody. He wrote "The Willow Tree," and, seeing
the opportunity, burlesqued it forthwith. "Larry
O'Toole" from "Phil Fogarty" could easily be mistaken for one of the spirited songs with which Lever
adorned his brilliant but more or less unreal stories of
Ireland. Again, the songs of the forties and fifties
were no more sensible than the majority of similar
compositions to-day, and they offered themselves as a

[1] *My Confidences*, p. 300.

good butt for ridicule. Thackeray started a series of parodies with the Mayfair and Oriental Love Songs; but when the turn came of the Domestic Song, the man's sentiment overcame his intention. Though prefaced by a burlesque prose introduction—omitted in most reprints—there is little or nothing of parody in the verse. Humour there is in plenty, but it is that tender humour that is not far away from tears; there is loving kindness in every line; and the picture of the lonely bachelor thinking of the fair young girl whose presence had for a moment relieved the gloom of the dull chambers does not create more mirth than is to be found in a sad smile.

It was but a moment she sat in this place,
She'd a scarf on her neck, and a smile on her face!
A smile on her face, and a rose in her hair,
And she sat there, and bloomed in my cane-bottomed chair.

And so I have valued my chair ever since,
Like the shrine of a saint, or the throne of a prince;
Sweet FANNY, my patroness, sweet, I declare
The queen of my heart and my cane-bottomed chair.

When the candles burn low, and the company's gone,
In the silence of night as I sit here alone—
I sit here alone, but we yet are a pair—
My FANNY I see in my cane-bottomed chair.

She comes from the past and revisits my room;
She looks as she then did, all beauty and bloom,
So smiling and tender, so fresh and so fair,
And yonder she sits in my cane-bottomed chair.

In the same vein of tenderness is the even better-known "Ballad of Bouillabaisse," written in Paris

after a visit to the restaurant where the author and his
wife and friends had been frequent visitors; and the
exquisite "Mahogany Tree," one of the author's favourites, which many a time he sang.

The most ambitious, as well as the longest, of Thackeray's poems was "The Great Cossack Epic of Deme-
trius Rigmarolovicz," founded, so the prefatory note
informs us, on the legend of St. Sophia, whose statue
is said to have walked of its own accord up the river
Dnieper to take its station in the Church of Kiew. It
is good fooling, and amusing enough, but it does not
bear in any marked degree the imprint of Thackeray's
individuality. It was followed by "The Chronicle of
the Drum," which is on quite a different plane, and is
as good as anything Thackeray ever wrote in verse. It
is the narrative of a French drummer, whose ancestors
for the last four generations had rattled the sticks from
the days of Henri of Navarre. In Germany, Flanders,
and Holland

> . . . my grandsire was ever victorious,
> My grandsire and Marshal Turenne;

his father was at Fontenoy and lost his life at Quebec;
while the story-teller was present at Yorktown, helped
to drum down the Bastille, and fought for the Republic
in the days of the Terror.

> We had taken the head of King Capet,
>   We called for the blood of his wife;
> Undaunted she came to the scaffold,
>   And bared her fair neck to the knife.
> As she felt the foul fingers that touched her,
>   She shrank but she deigned not to speak,
> She looked with a royal disdain,
>   And died with a blush in her cheek!

He was in the Napoleonic army and a stout partisan of the Emperor. He was at Marengo, Jena, and Austerlitz; the Hundred Days found him at his post; and he was present at Waterloo.

> A curse on those British assassins,
>   Who ordered the slaughter of Ney;
> A curse on Sir Hudson who tortured
>   The life of our hero away.
> A curse on all Russians—I hate them—
>   On all Prussians and Austrian fry;
> And, O! but I pray we may meet them,
>   And fight them again ere I die.

"The Chronicle of the Drum" presents a fine picture of the wild enthusiasm of the French veterans for their Corsican leader and of the deep-seated hatred of

> . . . . . the red-coated English,
>   Whose bayonets helped our undoing.

The drummer cares nothing for the cause, but everything for the battle; fighting was in his blood, for he loved his country and believed in his General as in his God; yet even when fierce excitement had the better of him, he could spare a thought for the poor woman waiting anxiously for news of her husband, who had marched with the army against Wolfe.

> I think I can see my poor mammy
>   With me in her hand as she waits,
> And our regiment, slowly retreating,
>   Pours back through the citadel gates.
> Dear mammy! she looks in their faces,
>   And asks if her husband has come?
> —He is lying all cold on the glacis,
>   And will never more beat on the drum.

This splendid martial poem contains much satirical humour and just the amount of underlying pathos that adds to the beauty ; while it has many of the qualities that later were to combine in the making of the wonderful, ironical " Barry Lyndon."

" It is easy enough to knock off that nonsense about Policeman X," Thackeray said ; " but to write a good occasional verse is a rare intellectual feat." Yet this, too, he accomplished. He possessed the wit and the fancy, the humour and tenderness, the refinement, without all of which qualities " the real thing " cannot be produced. Nor was the lyrical strain absent from his composition. His verse is easy and possesses the essential merit of apparent spontaneity. He was almost invariably humorous ; yet there was always something more than mere fun. Frequently he was satirical, occasionally he was indignant ; sometimes, as in " The End of the Play " and " Vanitas Vanitatum," he was didactic ; usually he was tender and pathetic. He could be gay ; he could sprinkle his verses with playful or ironic humour ; and upon all his best work his personality is impressed. Of the touch of originality he was proud : " Tom Taylor wrote those verses in *Punch*," he replied to a question of Dr. John Brown. " When I strike the lyre I think it's to a more original tune than that ; it's not the best music, but it's my own." Most of his ballads are good ; all are readable, and many are possessed of distinction. As has been said, his rhymes are often appalling, and his metre is not always perfect ; but his language was as simple and direct as in his prose writings. If he was not underrating his talent when he spoke of it as small beer, he certainly was not guilty of an error of judgment when he declared it was the right tap. No "Lyra Elegantiarum" is complete without the insertion of "The Mahogany Tree", "The Ballad of Bouillabaisse," and "Peg of Limavaddy"; and no anthology of light verse may omit "The Chronicle of the Drum."

CHAPTER XVI

"PENDENNIS" (1849-1850)

Thackeray living at No. 88, St. James's Street—takes a house, No. 13 (now 16), Young Street, Kensington—and has his daughters brought to him there—the greater part of "Vanity Fair" written in that house—his acquaintance with Charlotte Brontë—her appreciation of him—a dismal dinner party—"The Last Sketch"—Thackeray dissatisfied with his financial prospects—endeavours to obtain the cretary-ship of the Post Office—and, failing, tries to get a magistracy—Horace Smith—the Misses Smith and " Pendennis "—the publication of " Pendennis" begun November 1848—interrupted by a serious illness—some opinions of the earlier parts of the novel—Thackeray's recovery—" Pendennis" autobiographical in parts—some prototypes of the characters in "Vanity Fair"—of Sir Pitt Crawley, Lord Steyne, and Becky Sharp—some prototypes of the characters in " Pendennis "—of Warrington, Foker, and Shandon—" The Dignity of Literature "—Thackeray on the responsibility of an author—the literary man's point of honour.

THACKERAY had given up his room in Jermyn Street when he went to Cairo, and on his return had rented chambers at No. 88, St. James's Street, the house at the south-west corner of that street, with a frontage in Cleveland Row, and facing that portion of the palace which is between the Colour Court and the Ambassador's Court. It was next door to the site upon which had stood the old coffee-house, where the fashionable wits of the eighteenth century foregathered, and Swift, not too far away from Esther Vanhomrigh in Suffolk

Street, wrote so frequently to sweet Stella. "He never sends away a letter to her but he begins a new one the same day. He can't bear to let go her little hand as it were."[1] Here Thackeray remained for two years, until the summer of 1846, when he made for himself and his daughters a home at No. 13 (now 16), Young Street, Kensington. He was delighted with the house, and thought its two semi-tower-like embrasures gave it the air of a feudal castle. "I'll have a flagstaff put over the coping of the wall," he said, laughing, "and I'll hoist a standard when I'm at home." His mother brought the children from Paris in the late autumn of 1846; and when things were settled she returned to her husband, and her place was taken by her mother, who remained until her death two years later. Thenceforth Thackeray had his "little girls" constantly with him; and whenever he could snatch an hour or an afternoon, they went for those little outings which he enjoyed as much as they. He was never again separated from them for any length of time except when he went to America; and from this time forth, until he was taken from them, so far as possible they shared the pleasures of his life.

It was when passing by the Young Street house in later days with Fields, the American publisher, that Thackeray exclaimed, with mock gravity: "Down on your knees, you rogue, for here 'Vanity Fair' was penned; and I will go down with you, for I have a high opinion of that little production myself." The house, too, has an association with another great novelist, Charlotte Brontë. Most interesting is the

[1] *English Humourists—Swift.*

WILLIAM MAKEPEACE THACKERAY
From an unpublished water-colour drawing by W. Drummond, 1850
Reproduced by permission of Major William H. Lambert

story of the acquaintance between these notabilities.
It has already been mentioned that "Currer Bell"
dedicated the second edition of "Jane Eyre" to
Thaokeray, and Thackeray later acknowledged the
compliment, before even he knew her name or sex, by
sending her a copy of "Vanity Fair" inscribed with
his "grateful regards." Charlotte Brontë had been
much disturbed by the widespread rumour that she
had drawn Thackeray and his wife as Mr. and Mrs.
Rochester, though she was indifferent to those other
lying reports that said she had been a governess in his
family and subsequently his mistress ; and when she
came to London in December 1849, she eagerly
accepted the offer of George Smith to introduce
Thackeray to her.

When they did meet, she was much astonished. As
the dedication to the second edition of "Jane Eyre"
shows, she had expected to find a fervent prophet, and
Thackeray was simply a quiet, well-bred gentleman,
with nothing in appearance to distinguish him from
hosts of other men. A delightful story has been
related of their meeting. It is worthy of being repeated, for, though probably apocryphal, it is amus-
ingly true of the lady's attitude to her hero. "Behold,
a lion cometh up out of the North !" she quoted under
her breath, as Thackeray entered the drawing-room.
Thackeray, being informed of this, remarked : "Oh,
Lord ! and I'm nothing but a poor devil of an Englishman, ravenous for my dinner." At dinner, Miss
Brontë was placed opposite him. "And," said
Thackeray, "I had the miserable humiliation of seeing
her ideal of me disappearing, as everything went into

my mouth, and nothing came out of it, until, at last, as I took my fifth potato, she leaned across, with clasped hands and tearful eyes, and breathed imploringly, 'Oh, Mr. Thackeray! Don't!'"

Thackeray was an enigma to Charlotte Brontë; she could not understand him; she was never certain whether he was speaking in jest or in earnest; but she was determined to take him seriously. "All you say of Mr. Thackeray is most graphic and characteristic," she wrote to Ellen Nussey, on December 19. "He stirs in me both sorrow and anger. Why should he lead so harassing a life? Why should his mocking tongue so perversely deny the better feelings of his better moods? . . . Mr. Thackeray is a man of very quiet, simple demeanour; he is, however, looked up to with some awe and even distrust. . . . Thackeray is a Titan of mind. His presence and powers impress one deeply in an intellectual sense; I do not know him or see him as a man. All the others are subordinate. . . . I felt sufficiently at my ease with all but Thackeray; with him, I was fearfully stupid."[1]

Charlotte Brontë came again to London in the following June, and Thackeray called on her at George Smith's house, and the host, who was alone with them, afterwards described the interview as "a queer scene." "I suppose it was," the lady wrote to Ellen Nussey. "The giant sat before me: I was moved to speak of some of his shortcomings (literary, of course); one by one the faults came into my head, and one by one I brought them out, and sought some explanation or defence. He did defend himself, like a great Turk

[1] Clement Shorter : *The Brontës.*

NO. 13 (NOW 16), YOUNG STREET, KENSINGTON
Where Thackeray lived, 1846-1853

and heathen; that is to say, the excuses were often worse than the crime itself. The matter ended in decent amity; if all be well I am to dine at his house this evening (June 12)."[1] The dinner, it must be confessed, was not a success. The party included Mrs. Crowe, the Brookfields, the Carlyles, Mrs. Procter and her daughter, and Mrs. Elliot and Miss Perry, and it should have been a bright gathering. Instead it was a gloomy and silent evening, conversation languished, the guest in whose honour all were assembled said nothing, and Thackeray, too much depressed by the failure of the entertainment, but little. Mrs. Brookfield made an effort. "Do you like London, Miss Brontë?" she asked; then, after a pause, the other said gravely, "Yes—no." Charlotte Brontë was the first to leave, and so soon as she had gone Thackeray slipped out of the drawing-room, and his eldest daughter was surprised to see him open the front door with his hat on. "He put his fingers to his lips, walked out into the darkness, and shut the door quietly behind him. When I went back to the drawing-room again, the ladies asked me where he was. I vaguely answered that I thought he was coming back," Lady Ritchie has written. "Long years afterwards, Mrs. Procter, with a good deal of humour, described the situation—the ladies, who had all come expecting so much delightful conversation, and the gloom and constraint, and how finally, overwhelmed by the situation, my father had quietly left the room, left the house, and gone off to his club. The ladies waited, wondered, and finally departed also; and as we were going up to

[1] *Ibid.*, Vol. II, p. 143.

2 A

bed with our candles, after everybody was gone, I
remember two pretty Miss L——'s, in shiny silk
dresses, arriving full of expectation. . . . We still
said we thought our father would soon be back,
but the Miss L——'s declined to wait upon the
chance, laughed, and drove away again almost immediately."[1]

Once more Charlotte Brontë and Thackeray met, and
again a letter of the lady tells the tale. " I came here
(London) on Wednesday, being summoned a day
sooner than I expected, in order to be in time for
Thackeray's second lecture, which was delivered on
Thursday afternoon. This, as you may suppose, was
a great treat, and I was glad not to miss it," she wrote
to Ellen Nussey, on June 2, 1851. "As our party left
the (lecture) Hall, he (Thackeray) stood at the entrance:
he saw and knew me, and lifted his hat ; he offered his
hand in passing, and uttered the words, ' *Qu'en dites-
vous?* '—a question eminently characteristic and re-
minding me, even in this his moment of triumph,
of that inquisitive restlessness, that absence of what
I considered desirable self-control, which were among
his faults. He should not have cared just then to ask
what I thought, or what anybody thought ; but he *did*
care, and he was too natural to conceal, too impulsive
to repress, his wish. Well ! if I blamed his over-
eagerness, I liked his *naïveté*. I would have praised
him ; I had plenty of praise in my heart ; but, alas !
no words on my lips. Who has words at the right
moment? I stammered lame expressions ; but was
truly glad when some other people, coming up with

[1] *Chapter from Some Memoirs*, p. 63.

profuse congratulations, covered my deficiency by their redundancy."[1]

Indeed, though intensely appreciative, Charlotte Brontë proved so severe a critic, both of himself and his works, that Thackeray was not quite pleased with the various letters (printed in Mrs. Gaskell's "Life") in which she expressed her opinions, and he said so much in his "Last Sketch," prefixed to "Emma," when, under his editorship, that fragment appeared in the *Cornhill Magazine.*

I can only say of this lady, *vidi tantum.* I saw her first just as I rose out of an illness from which I had never thought to recover. I remember the trembling little frame, the little hand, the great honest eyes. An impetuous honesty seemed to me to characterise the woman. Twice, I recollect, she took me to task for what she held to be errors in doctrine. Once about Fielding we had a disputation. She spoke her mind out. She jumped to conclusions (I have smiled at one or two passages in the "Biography" in which my own disposition or behaviour form the subject of talk). She formed conclusions that might be wrong, and built up whole theories of character upon them. New to the London world, she entered it with an independent indomitable spirit of her own; and judged of contemporaries, and especially spied out arrogance or affectation, with extraordinary keenness of vision. She was angry with her favourites if their conduct or conversation fell below her ideal. Often she seemed to be judging the London folks prematurely; but perhaps the city is rather angry at being judged. It fancied an austere little Joan of Arc marching in upon us, and rebutting our easy lives, our easy morals. She gave me the impression of being a very pure and lofty, and high-minded person. A great and

[1] Clement Shorter: *The Brontës,* Vol. II, p. 214.

holy reverence of right and truth seemed to be with her always. Such, in our brief interview, she appeared to me.

Though Thackeray was flourishing, he was not satisfied with his prospects, for he feared his popularity might diminish. He was well aware that the earnings of a man of letters are precarious and he was anxious to make provision for his mother and stepfather, for his children, and for himself, should he, in spite of the physicians' opinion, live to be an old man. He had himself called to the bar on May 26, 1848, of course not with any intention to practise, but so as to be able to accept, if fate would only give him a chance, one of the many appointments for which only a barrister is eligible. He heard towards the end of 1848 of a post that he thought would suit him.

But now comes the real and important part of this note [he wrote to Lady Blessington]. *There will be a place vacant in the Post Office soon*, that of Assistant Secretary, at present held by Mr. James Campbell. What a place for a man of letters ! I think if Lord Clanricarde would give it to me I would satisfy my employers, and that my profession would be pleased by hearing of the employment of one of us. I wonder might I write to him, or is there any kind of person who would advocate my cause?

Lady Blessington interested herself on his behalf, but her efforts were in vain. "Another man has got it and deserves it too," Thackeray informed her, but he did not abandon hope of receiving an appointment under Government. In the next year he made another attempt to obtain a vacant magistracy, but again, though this time backed by the influence of Monckton Milnes, he was unsuccessful.

> You are a good and lovable adviser and M.P., but I cannot get the Magistrate's place, not being eligible [he wrote to his friend]. I was only called to the Bar last year, and they require barristers of seven years' standing. Time will qualify me, however, and I hope to be able to last six years in the literary world ; for though I shall write, I daresay, very badly, yet the public won't find it out for some time, and I shall live on my past reputation. It is a pity to be sure. If I could get a place and rest, I think I could do something better than I have done, and leave a good and lasting book behind me ; but Fate is overruling. I have to thank L. for his kind letter, and to beg him to remember me if an opportunity occurs of serving me. I wonder whether Lord Palmerston could? But I would rather be in London. Thank you for thinking of me, and believe me, I am grateful.[1]

Having only his pen to rely on, Thackeray, who had taken his daughters for a holiday abroad, now went with them to Brighton, where he proposed to begin "Pendennis," the publication of which was to begin in a month. He numbered among his friends resident there Horace, part-author of "Rejected Addresses,"

> That good, severe old man, who went out of the world in charity with all in it, and having shown through his life, as far as I know it, quite a delightful love of God's works and creatures ; a true, loyal, Christian man.[2]

[1] Wemyss Reid : *Life of Lord Houghton*, Vol. I, p. 247.
[2] A. H. Beavan : *James and Horace Smith*, p. 305.

To Smith's house in Cavendish Place he went soon
after his arrival at Brighton, and confessed to the
Misses Smith that he was in despair, he had to begin
a new novel without delay, and had not an idea; so
then and there they told him a story of Brighton life.
In return for this favour, he christened the heroine
Laura, after his hostesses' married sister, Mrs. Round,
who, when the story was finished, declared, indig-
nantly, " I'll never speak to you again, Mr. Thackeray.
You know I always meant to marry Bluebeard "—Lady
Rockminster's name for George Warrington.

The first number of " Pendennis," issued by Messrs.
Bradbury and Evans, appeared in November 1848,
and the publication of the story was continued month
by month until the following September, when Thackeray was ill, so ill, indeed, during September, October,
and November that it seemed only too probable that he
would never rise from the sick-bed. Dr. Merriman
attended him, and also Dr. Elliotson, to whom " Pendennis," on its publication in book-form, was dedicated. It was not until December that Thackeray's
recovery was assured; and on the 7th of that month
Edward FitzGerald wrote to Frederick Tennyson : " I
saw poor Thackeray in London, getting slowly better
of a bilious fever that had nearly killed him. . . .
People in general thought " Pendennis " got dull as
it got on ; and I confess I thought so too : he would
do well to take the opportunity of his illness to dis-
continue it altogether. He told me last June he himself
was tired of it, and must not his readers naturally
tire too?"

Fortunately, Thackeray, after being rescued from

illness, was saved from his friends, and the twelfth number of "Pendennis" appeared in January of the new year. FitzGerald, re-reading the novel years later, altered his opinion. "I like 'Pendennis' much," he then said; "and Alfred (Tennyson) said he thought it was quite delicious; 'it seemed to him so mature,' he said. You can imagine Alfred saying this over one's fire, spreading his great hand out." Thackeray, who had a habit of passing remarks on his books, said of this one: "I can't say I think much of 'Pendennis' —at least of the execution, it certainly drags about the middle; but I had an attack of illness at the time I reached that part of the book, and could not make it any better than I did. But how well-written it is!" Well-written it is certainly, and wonderfully interesting, for, like "Vanity Fair," beginning quietly, it gathered force and volume as it proceeded.

"Pendennis," as has already been said, is so autobiographical in parts that most readers acquainted with the social history of the forties of the last century endeavour to trace the "originals," and the curiosity that suggests the enquiry, though it may not be legitimate, is at least natural. It must be borne in mind, however, that Thackeray never wilfully copied anybody; he was, as George Augustus Sala put it, "only gently and skilfully assimilative and combinative in his characters, which passed through the alembic of his study and observation." In "Vanity Fair" the author declared that Sir Pitt Crawley was the only exact portrait in the book: it has lately been asserted that a former Lord Rolle sat for the character; the prototype of "the richly dressed figure of the Wicked Nobleman, on which no expense has been spared," Lord Steyne, undoubtedly was suggested by the second and third Marquises of Hertford, and the inimitable Becky was drawn from the companion of a wealthy and selfish old lady who lived in the neighbourhood of Kensington Square. How far Arthur Pendennis resembled Thackeray has already been discussed, but for the statement that in this story more than any other he drew upon his acquaintances there is the author's authority.

> You will find much to remind you of old talks and faces—of William John O'Connell, Jack Sheehan and Andrew Arcedeckne—in this book [he wrote to George Moreland Crawford, who had nursed him through the illness that nearly left the story a fragment]. There is something of you in Warrington, but he is not fit to hold a candle to you, for, taking you all round, you are the most genuine fellow that ever strayed from a better world into this. You don't smoke, and he is a confirmed smoker of tobacco. Bordeaux and port were your favourites at 'The Deanery' and 'The Garrick,' and War. is always guzzling beer. But he has your honesty, and like you could not posture if he tried. You had a strong affinity for the Irish. May you some day find an Irish girl to lead you to matrimony. There's no such good wife as a daughter of Erin.[1]

"Merry Andrew" Arcedeckne, a member of the Garrick Club, sat for Foker, and it is probably this portrait that was the cause of the author's rejection at the Travellers' Club in 1856. The ballot there is by the members and not by the committee, and the majority gave the reason for their action that they were afraid of seeing themselves in some future novel. It is said that Arcedeckne was often called "Phoca"; hence the name by which he is immortalised; and that he was small in stature, eccentric in his mode of dressing, drove mail-coaches as an amateur, loved fighting dogs, game-cocks, and the prize-ring, and had a large estate in Norfolk. Cordy Jeaffreson states that Foker was no caricature, and that the character was a genial and flattering portrait of the prototype. Arcedeckne resembled Foker, however, in so far that he, too, was no fool. Thackeray had treated him badly by holding him up to ridicule, but he was too sensible to complain: none the less he contrived that the laughter should not all be on one side. Arcedeckne was that member of the Garrick whose presence and speech, Dean Hole observed, "seemed to irritate Thackeray, and who found pleasure in exercising his power as a gadfly on a thoroughbred horse." One night in the club smoking-room Thackeray was in the middle of a story when Arcedeckne entered: Thackeray saw him, hesitated, stopped: whereupon his persecutor with bland smile and gracious manner encouraged him to continue; "Proceed, sweet warbler," he said, "thy story interests me." It was Arcedeckne, too, who congratulated Thackeray on one of his lectures: "Brayvo! Thack, my boy! Uncommon good show. But it'll never go *without a pianner!*"

The noblemen of the staff of the original *Pall Mall Gazette* in "Pendennis" were Lords William and Henry Lennox and a brother of the Duke of St. Albans, and of the last Jack Sheehan used to say, "His name of Beauclerk is a misnomer, for he is

always in a fog, and never clear about anything."
Many of the " Fraserians " sat for the literary portraits
in " Pendennis," the ferocious Bludyer, stout old Tom
Sergeant, and brilliant Charles Shandon. It has been
suggested that Jack Sheehan may have been the
original Shandon, but the character was probably
drawn, in part at least, from Dr. Maginn. But
Maginn was a greater than Shandon. He may have
dictated the prospectus of some *Pall Mall Gazette* from
the Fleet Prison ; he may have written—indeed, he did
write—articles that are models of virulent abuse ; but
he was a parodist of no mean merit, and his Shake-
spearian essays and his Latin versions of " Chevy
Chase " and other ballads extorted praise even from his
enemies.

These and other literary portraits in " Pendennis "
brought in their train great annoyance to Thackeray,
for many members of the Fourth Estate took umbrage,
and declared that the author had set out to hold up to
contempt workers in literature and journalism. So
long as the matter was discussed at the Clubs,
Thackerary took no notice of the comments ; but when
the abuse of him was transferred to the newspapers, in
justice to himself he was compelled to put his case
before the public.

In a leading article of your journal of Thursday,
the 3rd instant, you commented upon literary pensions and the *status* of literary men in this country,
and illustrated your argument by extracts from the
story of " Pendennis," at present in course of publication [he wrote to the Editor of the *Morning
Chronicle*, on January 8, 1850]. You have received
my writings with so much kindness that, if you have

occasion to disapprove of them or the author, I can't question your right to blame me, or doubt for a moment the friendliness and honesty of my critic; and however I might dispute the justice of your verdict in my case, I had proposed to submit to it in silence, being, indeed, very quiet in my conscience with regard to the charge made against me.   But another newspaper of high character and repute takes occasion to question the principles advocated in your article of Thursday, arguing in favour of pensions for literary persons, as you argued against them; and the only point upon which the *Examiner* and the *Chronicle* appear to agree unluckily regards myself, who am offered up to general reprehension in two leading articles by the two writers: by the latter for "fostering a baneful prejudice" against literary men; by the former for "stooping to flatter" this prejudice in the public mind, and condescending to caricature (as is too often my habit) my literary fellow-labourers in order to pay court to "the non-literary class." The charges of the *Examiner* against a man who has never, to his knowledge, been ashamed of his profession, or (except for its dulness) of any single line from his pen—grave as they are—are, I hope, not proven.   "To stoop to flatter" any class is a novel accusation brought against my writings; and as for my scheme "to pay court to the non-literary class by disparaging my literary fellow-labourers," it is a design which would exhibit a degree, not only of baseness, but of folly, upon my part, of which I trust I am not capable.   The editor of the *Examiner* may, perhaps, occasionally write, like other authors, in a hurry, and not be aware of the conclusions to which some of his sentences may lead.   If I stoop to flatter anybody's prejudice for some interested motives of my own, I am no more nor less than a rogue and a cheat: which deduction from the *Examiner's* premises I will not stoop to contradict, because the premises themselves are simply absurd.   I deny that the considerable body of our countrymen described by the *Examiner* as "the non-literary class" has the least gratification in witnessing the degradation or disparagement of literary men. Why accuse "the non-literary class" of being so ungrateful? If the writings of an author give a reader pleasure or profit, surely the latter will have a favourable opinion of the person who so benefits him. What intelligent man, of what political views, would not receive with respect and welcome that writer of the *Examiner* of whom your paper once said that he "made all England laugh and think"? Who would deny to that brilliant wit, that polished satirist, his just tribute of respect and admiration? Does any man who has written a book worth reading—any poet, novelist, man of science—lose reputation by his character for genius or for learning? Does he not, on the contrary, get friends, sympathy, applause—money, perhaps? all good and pleasant things in themselves, and not ungenerously awarded, as they are honestly won. That generous faith in men of letters, that kindly regard in which the whole reading nation holds them, appear to me to be so clearly shown in our country every day that to question them would be as absurd as, permit me to say for my part, it would be ungrateful. What is it that fills mechanics' institutes in the great provincial towns when literary men are invited to attend their festivals? Has not every literary man of mark his friends and his circle, his hundreds, or his tens of thousands, of readers? And has not every one had from these constant and affecting testimonials of the esteem in which they hold him. It is of course one writer's lot, from the nature of his subject or of his genius, to command the sympathies or awaken the curiosity of many more readers than shall choose to listen to another author; but surely all get their hearing. The literary profession is not held in disrepute; nobody wants to disparage it; no man loses his social rank, whatever it may be, by practising it. On the contrary, the pen gives a place in the world to men who had none before—a fair place, fairly achieved by their genius,

as any other degree of eminence is by any other kind
of merit. Literary men need not, as it seems to me,
be in the least querulous about their position any
more, or want the pity of anybody. The money-
prizes which the chief among them get are not so
high as those which fall to men of other callings—to
bishops, or to judges, or to opera-singers and actors;
nor have they received stars and garters as yet, or
peerages and governorships of islands, such as fall
to the lot of military officers. The rewards of the
profession are not to be measured by the money
standard; for one man spends a life of learning and
labour on a book which does not pay the printer's
bill, and another gets a little fortune by a few light
volumes. But, putting the money out of the question, I believe that the social estimation of the man
of letters is as good as it deserves to be, and as good
as that of any other professional man. With respect
to the question in debate between you and the
Examiner as to the propriety of public rewards and
honours for literary men, I don't see why men of
letters should not very cheerfully coincide with Mr.
Examiner in accepting all the honours, places, and
prizes which they can get. The amount of such as
will be awarded to them will not, we may be pretty
sure, impoverish the country much; and if it is the
custom of the State to reward by money, or
titles of honour, or stars and garters of any sort,
individuals who do the country service, and if individuals are gratified at having "Sir" or "My
lord" appended to their names, or stars and ribands
hooked on their coats and waistcoats, as men most
undoubtedly are, and as their wives, families, and
relations are, there can be no reason why men of
letters should not have the chance, as well as men
of the robe or the sword; or why, if honour and
money are good for one profession, they should not
be good for another. No man in other callings
thinks himself degraded by receiving a reward from
his Government; nor, surely, need the literary man
be more squeamish about pensions, and ribands, and

titles, than the ambassador, or general, or judge.
Every European State but ours rewards its men of
letters; the American Government gives them their
full share of its small patronage; and if Americans,
why not Englishmen? If Pitt Crawley is disappointed
at not getting a riband on returning from his diplomatic post at Pumpernickel, if General O'Dowd is
pleased to be called Sir Hector O'Dowd, K.C.B., and
his wife at being denominated my Lady O'Dowd, are
literary men to be the only persons exempt from
vanity, and is it to be a sin in them to covet honour?
And now, with regard to the charge against myself
of fostering baneful prejudices against our calling—
to which I no more plead guilty than I should think
Fielding would have done if he had been accused
of a design to bring the Church into contempt by
describing Parson Trulliber—permit me to say that
before you deliver sentence it would be as well if you
had waited to hear the whole of the argument. Who
knows what is coming in the future numbers of the
work which has incurred your displeasure and the
Examiner's? and whether you, in accusing me of
prejudice, and the *Examiner* (alas!) of swindling
and flattering the public, have not been premature?
Time and the hour may solve this mystery, for which
the candid reader is referred "to our next." That
I have a prejudice against running into debt, and
drunkenness and disorderly life, and against quackery
and falsehood in my profession, I own; and that
I like to have a laugh at those pretenders in it who
write confidential news about fashion and politics for
provincial *gobemouches;* but I am not aware of feeling
any malice in describing this weakness, or of doing
anything wrong in exposing the former vices. Have
they never existed amongst literary men? Have
their talents never been urged as a plea for improvi-
dence, and their very faults adduced as a consequence
of their genius? The only moral that I, as a writer,
wished to hint in the descriptions against which you
protest, was, that it was the duty of a literary man,
as well as any other, to practise regularity and

sobriety, to love his family, and to pay his trades-men. Nor is the picture I have drawn "a caricature which I condescend to," any more than it is a wilful and insidious design on my part to flatter "the non-literary class." If it be a caricature, it is the result of a natural perversity of vision, not of an artful desire to mislead; but my attempt was to tell the truth, and I meant to tell it not unkindly. I have seen the bookseller from Bludyer robbed of his books; I have carried money, and from a noble brother man-of-letters, to some one not unlike Shandon in prison, and have watched the beautiful devotion of his wife in that dreary place. Why are these things not to be described, if they illustrate, as they appear to me to do, that strange and awful struggle of good and wrong which takes place in our hearts and in the world? It may be that I worked out my moral ill, or it may be possible that the critic of the *Examiner* fails in apprehension. My efforts as an artist come perfectly within his province as a censor; but when Mr. *Examiner* says of a gentleman that he is "stooping to flatter a public prejudice"—which public prejudice does not exist—I submit that he makes a charge which is as absurd as it is unjust, and am thankful that it repels itself. And, instead of accusing the public of persecuting and disparag-ing us as a class, it seems to me that men of letters had best silently assume that they are as good as any other gentlemen, nor raise piteous controversies upon a question which all people of sense must take to be settled. If I sit at your table, I suppose that I am my neighbour's equal, as that he is mine. If I began straightway with a protest of "Sir, I am a literary man, but I would have you to know I am as good as you," which of us is it that questions the dignity of the literary profession—my neighbour, who would like to eat his soup in quiet, or the man of letters, who commences the argument? And I hope that a comic writer, because he describes one author as improvident and another as a parasite, may not only be guiltless of a desire to vilify his profession, but may really have its honour at heart. If there are no spendthrifts or parasites amongst us, the satire becomes unjust; but if such exist, or have existed, they are as good subjects for comedy as men of other callings. I never heard that the Bar felt itself aggrieved because *Punch* chose to describe Mr. Dunup's notorious state of insolvency; or that the picture of Stiggins in Pickwick was intended as an insult to all Dissenters; or that all the attorneys in the empire were indignant at the famous history of the firm of " Quirk, Gammon, and Snap." Are we to be passed over because we are faultless, or because we cannot afford to be laughed at? And if every character in a story is to represent a class, not an individual—if every bad figure is to have its obliged contrast of a good one, and a balance of vice and virtue is to be struck—novels, I think, would become impossible, as they would be intolerably stupid and unnatural, and there would be a lamentable end of writers and readers of such compositions.[1]

Thackeray was the last person who should have been charged with an attempt to lower the dignity of letters. He never thought lightly of his profession, and again and again he spoke of the sense of responsibility that an author should feel.

What a place it is to hold in the affections of man ! What an awful responsibility hanging over a writer ! What man, holding such a place, and knowing that his words go forth to vast congregations of mankind —to grown folks, to their children, and, perhaps to their children's children—but must think of his calling with a solemn and a humble heart ! May love and truth guide such a man always ! It is an awful prayer, and may Heaven further its fulfilment ![2]

[1] *Morning Chronicle*, January 12, 1850.
[2] *Mr. Brown's Letters—Brown the Younger at a Club.*

He expressed the same sentiments in his reply to Dr. John Brown, when that gentleman, then unknown to him, presented to him in 1848 a silver statuette of Punch purchased by some Edinburgh admirers of his genius.

> The arms and the man arrived in safety yesterday, and I am glad to know the names of two of the eighty Edinburgh friends who have taken such a kind method of showing their goodwill towards me. If you are grati, I am gratior. Such tokens of regard and sympathy are very precious to a writer like myself, who has some difficulty still in making people understand what you have been good enough to find out in Edinburgh, that under the mask satirical there walks about a sentimental gentleman who means not unkindly to any mortal person. I can see exactly the same expression under the vizard of my little friend in silver, and hope some day to shake the whole octogint by the hand gratos and gratas, and thank them for their friendliness and regard. I think I had better say no more on the subject, lest I should be tempted into some enthusiastic writing of which I am afraid. I assure you these tokens of what I can't help acknowledging as popularity—make me humble as well as grateful—and make me feel an almost awful sense of the responsibility which falls upon a man in such a station. Is it deserved or undeserved? Who is this that sets up to preach to mankind and to laugh at many of the things which men reverence? I hope I shall be able to tell the truth always, and to see it aright according to the eyes which God Almighty gives me. And if, in the exercise of my calling, I get friends, and find encouragement and sympathy, I need not tell you how much I feel and am thankful for this support.—Indeed, I can't reply lightly upon this subject or feel otherwise than very grave when men praise me as you do.[1]

[1] Dr. John Brown : *Thackeray* (*North British Review*, February 1864; Vol. XI, pp. 224-5).

2 B

Thackeray, however, in spite of his reverence for his calling, had no patience with those who prated pompously of their "call" to the work; and he would not allow that even literary genius was an excuse for license.

Men of letters cannot lay their hands on their hearts, and say, "No, the fault" (that caused their intellectual inferiors to sneer at them) "was Fortune's and the indifferent world's, not Goldsmith's or Fielding's." There was no reason why Oliver should always be thriftless; why Fielding and Steele should sponge upon their friends; why Sterne should make love to his neighbour's wives. Swift, for a long while, was as poor as any wag that ever laughed, but he owed no penny to his neighbour; Addison, when he wore his most threadbare coat, would hold his head up and maintain his dignity; and, I dare vouch, neither of these gentlemen, when they were ever so poor, asked any man alive to pity their condition, and have a regard to the weaknesses incidental to the literary profession.[1]

He was always concerned to state what should be the literary man's point of honour. In his struggling days he set it forth as it appeared to him.

To do your work honestly, to amuse and instruct your reader of to-day, to die when your time comes, and go hence with as clean a breast as may be; may all these be yours and ours, by God's will. Let us be content with our *status* as literary craftsmen, telling the truth as far as may be, hitting no foul blow, condescending to no servile puffery, filling not a very lofty, but a manly and honourable part.

[1] *A Brother of the Press on . . . the Chances of the Literary Profession* (*Fraser's Magazine*, March 1846).

Towards the end of his life, when paying tribute to
Tom Hood, as when writing his beautiful appreciation
of Washington Irving and Macaulay, he returned to
the subject.

It may not be our chance, brother scribe, to be
endowed with such merit or rewarded with such
fame [he concluded his appreciation of Macaulay and
Washington Irving].   But the rewards of these men
are rewards paid to *our service*.   We may not win the
bâton or *épaulettes*, but God give us strength to
guard the honour of the flag !

It is pleasing to think that he who wrote these lines
was ever in the foremost rank of those who pressed
forward to fight for the honour of the flag.

CHAPTER XVII

"THE ENGLISH HUMOURISTS" AND "ESMOND"
(1851–1852)

The last number of "Pendennis" issued—Thackeray proposes to lecture—his friends' objections—a subject found in "The English Humourists of the Eighteenth Century"—the first lecture at Willis's Rooms—Thackeray's nervousness—accounts of his reading—the audiences—a *furore* for the lectures—Thackeray invited to deliver them in England and America—he writes "Esmond"—refuses to contribute to "Social Zoologies"—George M. Smith secures the publishing rights of "Esmond"—Thackeray's publishers—Thackeray's comments on "Esmond"—"Esmond's" place in literature—Thackeray and his daughters go abroad—he returns to London—prepares for the American ecture tour.

THE last number of "Pendennis" appeared in December 1850, and early in the following year it was announced that Thackeray would make his *début* as a lecturer. Anthony Trollope in his monograph on Thackeray devoted two pages of his short biographical chapter to the consideration of the effect that lecturing might have had upon Thackeray's fame as a writer, arguing for and against the indignity of the proceedings, and eventually concluding that the money made by the new venture was "earned honestly and with the full approval of the world around him."[1] Who can doubt it? Even the reputation of the author of "Vanity Fair" was not

[1] *Thackeray* (English Men of Letters), pp. 43-5.

WILLIAM MAKEPEACE THACKERAY
From a pencil sketch by Richard Doyle, in the British Museum

likely to be imperilled by reading to an audience "The English Humourists of the Eighteenth Century" or "The Four Georges"; but Thackeray was not happy about it. Sir Edward Hamley and other friends remonstrated with him, arguing that a man of his talents should not waste his time in such a way; and Thackeray told Lady Cullum no one could conceive how it mortified him to have to make money by lecturing : speaking of Carlyle, "*He* would not go round making a show of himself as I am doing," he exclaimed. "But he has lectured ! He did it once, and was done with it." However, he forced himself to overcome his objections, remembering it was his duty, as it was, of course, his desire, to make money to replace his patrimony, and thus to make provision for his family.

But as I don't intend to touch the proceeds of the lectures myself [he wrote to Dr. John Brown] and shall invest all the winnings for my two girls and their poor mother, I'm bolder than I should be otherwise in the business, and determined to carry it through with brazen resolution.

The subject selected for the series of lectures was "The English Humourists of the Eighteenth Century." The writers of this period had always been Thackeray's favourite reading, and at the moment they were much in his mind, owing to the fact that he was studying the eighteenth century, which was to be the scene of the novel upon which he was now engaged.

The first lecture was given on the afternoon of May 22, and the others were delivered on May 29, June 12, 19, 26, and July 3. The price for a reserved seat for the course was two guineas, and seven shillings and sixpence was charged for an unreserved place for a single lecture. Always averse to public speaking, Thackeray's nervousness during the half-hour before the delivery of the first lecture was pitiable. "Going thither (to Willis's Rooms) before the time for his beginning," Mrs. Kemble has related, "I found him standing like a forlorn, disconsolate giant in the middle of the room, gazing about him. 'Oh, Lord,' he exclaimed, as he shook hands with me, 'I'm sick at my stomach with fright.' I spoke some words of encouragement to him, and was going away, but he held my hand like a scared child, crying, 'Oh, don't leave me!' 'But,' said I, 'Thackeray, you mustn't stand here. Your audience are beginning to come in,' and I drew him from the middle of his chairs and benches, which were beginning to be occupied, into the retiring-room adjoining the lecture-room, my own readings having made me perfectly familiar with both. Here he began pacing up and down, literally wringing his hands in nervous distress. 'Now,' said I, 'what shall I do? Shall I stay with you till you begin, or shall I go, and leave you alone to collect yourself?' 'Oh,' he said, 'if I could only get at that confounded thing (the MS.) to have a last look at it!' 'Where is it?' said I. 'Oh, in the next room on the reading-desk.' 'Well,' said I, 'if you don't like to go in and get it, I'll fetch it for you.' And remembering well the position of my reading-table, which had been close to the door of the retiring-room, I darted in, hoping to snatch the manuscript without attracting the attention of the audience, with which the room was already nearly full. I had been used to deliver my reading seated at a very low table, but my friend Thackeray gave his lectures standing, and had a reading-desk placed on the platform, adapted to his own very tall stature, so that when I came to get his manuscript it was almost above my head. Though rather disconcerted, I was determined not to go back without it, and so made a half-jump and a clutch at the book, when every leaf of it (they were not fastened together) came fluttering separately down about me. I hardly know what I did, but I think I must have gone nearly on all fours, in my agony to gather up the scattered leaves, and, retreating with them, held them out in dismay to poor Thackeray, crying, 'Oh, look, look, what a dreadful thing I have done!' 'My dear soul,' he said, 'you couldn't have done better for me. I have just a quarter of an hour to wait here, and it will take me about that to page this again, and it's the best thing in the world that could have happened.' With which infinite kindness he comforted me, for I was all but crying, at having, as I thought, increased his distress and troubles."[1]

In spite of the nervousness which so affected his voice that his daughter did not recognise it when she heard the opening words, "In treating of the English Humourists of the past age, it is of the men and of their lives, rather than of their books, that I ask permission to speak to you," Thackeray gathered courage as he proceeded, and was entirely successful. Very different from Dickens's dramatic readings were Thackeray's lectures ; and, indeed, so far as can

[1] *Records of Later Life.*

be gathered from the reports of those present, the two performances bore the relationship that exists between melodrama and comedy : each admirable of its kind— but there the resemblance ends. Sir Frank Marzials says that the secret of Thackeray's charm "lay in an admirable quiet delivery, that, without undue emphasis or pause for effect, gave the hearer the full value of every sentence." Charlotte Brontë wrote to her father that "Thackeray got up and spoke with as much simplicity and ease as if he had been speaking to a few friends by his own fireside ; the lecture was truly good . . . ; it was finished without being in the least studied,—a quiet humour and graphic force enlivened it throughout"; and Caroline Fox said he read in "a definite dry manner, but makes you understand what he is about." Longfellow recorded that the lectures were "pleasant to hear from that soft, deep, sonorous voice"; and Motley, who some years later heard a lecture on "The Four Georges," wrote : "I was much impressed with the quiet, graceful ease with which Thackeray read—just a few notes above the conversational level,—but never rising into the declamatory. This light-in-hand manner suits well the delicate hovering rather than superficial style of the composition. He skims lightly over the surface of the long epoch, throwing out a sketch here, exhibiting a characteristic trait there, and sprinkling about a few anecdotes, portraits, and historical allusions, running about from grave to gay, from lively to severe, moving and mocking the sensibilities in a breath, in a way which I should say was the perfection of lecturing to high-bred audiences."

The audiences at Willis's Rooms included many of the most famous persons in London.   Besides Charlotte Brontë, Carlyle and his wife went, Harriet Martineau, too, and Monckton Milnes, Hallam, Dickens, Lord Carlisle, the Brookfields, Doyle, Cruikshank, Kinglake, Lord Mahon, Millais, Landseer, Dean Milman, the Duchess of Sutherland, and Lady Ashburton. Macaulay was present at each lecture, and referred to one of them in his diary : " Margaret came to take me to Thackeray's (third) lecture.   He is full of humour and imagination, and I only wish that these lectures may answer both in the way of fame and money.   He told me, as I was going out, that the scheme had done wonders for l...n ; and I told him, and from my heart, that I wish he had made ten times as much." [1]

> The truth is the lectures won't do [Thackeray wrote to Abraham Hayward on May 23].   They were all friends, and a packed house, though, to be sure, it goes to a man's heart to find among his friends such men as you and Kinglake and Venables, Higgins, Rawlinson, Carlyle, Ashburton, Hallam, Milman, Macaulay, Wilberforce, looking on. [2]

But the lectures did do.   They were an undoubted success—" There is quite a *furore* for them," Charlotte Brontë wrote—and Thackeray was invited to repeat them by Young Men's Associations and Literary Clubs all over the country.   " They make me an offer of £150 at the Portman Square Rooms—pretty well for six hours "; he said gleefully, reflecting that an hour's reading would be as profitable as a week's work.

[1] *Life and Letters of Lord Macaulay*, p. 552.
[2] *Correspondence of Abraham Hayward.*

So he accepted many offers—as he put it, "the Titmarsh-Van began its career"—and delivered the "English Humourists" at Oxford and Cambridge, at Edinburgh, Manchester, Liverpool, and a score of other places during the year.

From the United States also came invitations too tempting to be refused, and some of these were entertained, though Thackeray could not be persuaded to sign any contract until he arrived in New York. Before leaving England, however, he had to finish the novel upon which he was engaged, "The History of Henry Esmond, Esquire: A Colonel in the service of Queen Anne, Written by Himself." This was to be published in three volumes. "I have given up and only had for a day or two, the notion for the book in numbers," Thackeray said. "It is much too grave and sad for that." Diligent reading of eighteenth-century memoirs was necessary for "Esmond," and Eyre Crowe, who from April 1851 was Thackeray's secretary and amanuensis, has related how the author, with him in attendance, spent much time in the British Museum Library, where, in a room allotted to him for the purpose by Panizzi, he dictated the General Webb and Marlborough and Cadogan incident. More of the book was written at the Athenæum Club, where one of the side rooms off the large library was placed at his disposal; and much was done at the Bedford Hotel, while his children were with his mother and Major Carmichael-Smyth in Paris, and the Young Street house was in the painters' hands.

Shortly after the publication of the early numbers of "Vanity Fair," Henry Vizetelly, on behalf of

MR. MICHAEL ANGELO TITMARSH,

As he appeared at Willis's Rooms in his celebrated character of Mr. Thackeray.

From a sketch by John Leech in " The Month," July, 1851

Bogue, the publisher, had invited Thackeray to write
as many little volumes as he would undertake
for a series called "Social Zoologies." The first
brochure, "The Gent," by Albert Smith, had been
phenomenally successful; and Bogue very wisely determined to secure the best writers for future volumes.
The terms were liberal : a hundred guineas—just double
the amount paid for a monthly part, including the
etching of two plates, of "Vanity Fair." Thackeray
admitted the offer was tempting, but declined—it was
said, by reason of his disinclination to be associated in
any way with Albert Smith. Vizetelly remarked that
Thackeray could not tolerate Smith's *mauvais goût*,
and that, though showing him outward civility when
brought into contact with him, the occasional observa-
tions which escaped him disclosed his true sentiments
respecting the other's mountebank ways. When
"Pendennis" was nearly finished, Vizetelly again approached Thackeray, this time on behalf of Messrs.
Smith, Elder and Co.; and subsequently George Smith,
the head of the firm, called at Young Street. "There's
a young fellow just come," Thackeray said, as he
burst into the room where his daughters were sitting.
"He has brought a thousand pounds in his pocket:
he has made me an offer for my book: it's the most
spirited, handsome offer, I scarcely like to take him
at his word : he's hardly more than a boy; his name
is George Smith; he's waiting there now, and I must
go back to him." The actual terms were £1200 for an
edition of 2500 copies, to be issued in three volumes
at a guinea and a half.

Thackeray had published his earliest books through

Macrone and Cunningham; but afterwards he had
gone to Messrs. Chapman and Hall and Messrs. Bradbury and Evans, the former issuing "The Irish Sketch
Book", "From Cornhill to Cairo", "Mrs. Perkins's
Ball", "Our Street", "Dr. Birch and His Young
Friends", and "Rebecca and Rowena"; the latter,
"Vanity Fair", "Pendennis", "The Book of Snobs,"
and "The Great Hoggarty Diamond." Messrs. Chapman and Hall had not been satisfied with the sale of
"Dr. Birch" and "Rebecca and Rowena," and were
not eager to issue another Christmas Book: whereupon Thackeray invited Messrs. Smith, Elder and Co.
to issue "The Kickleburys on the Rhine," and the
offer was at once accepted. This was the beginning
of the connection between the novelist and the great
publishing house, which in the course of the next few
years issued "Esmond", "The English Humourists,"
and "The Rose and the Ring." Thackeray, however,
did not desert his old friends, the proprietors of *Punch*,
and Messrs. Bradbury and Evans published "The
Newcomes," the four volumes of "Miscellanies"
(1855-7), and "The Virginians"; and it was not until
after the founding of the *Cornhill Magazine*, by purchasing the rights of the other firms, that Messrs.
Smith, Elder and Co. became Thackeray's sole publishers.

In May 1852 Edward FitzGerald saw Thackeray,
who, he says, "was just in the agony of finishing a
novel" and desirous to go abroad for a brief holiday.
The book was finished on May 28, when Thackeray
gave a dinner party to celebrate the occasion.

"You'll find it dull, but it's founded upon family

papers," Thackeray said of "Esmond" to John (afterwards Canon) Irvine; and to another friend he stated his conviction that the hero is a prig: but probably he expressed his true opinion to Fields, who met him soon after his arrival in Boston with the three volumes of "Esmond" tucked under his arm: "Here is the very best I can do; and I am carrying it to Prescott as a reward of merit for having given me my first dinner in America. I stand by this book, and am willing to leave it where I go as my card."[1] Especially did Thackeray like the chapter where Henry Esmond returns to Lady Castlewood, bringing his sheaves with him, as she says—"I wish the whole book was as good," he added, "but we can't play first fiddle all the time."

Charlotte Brontë might think that in "Esmond" there was "too much history—too little story," and George Eliot might pronounce it "a most uncomfortable book"; historical critics might object that there are blunders: that Thackeray makes the Duke of Hamilton a few years younger than he was, and makes him a widower when, as a matter of fact, he had married a second time in 1698, and was outlived by his wife; that Lady Dorchester was not the daughter of Tom Killigrew but of Sir Charles Sedley; that Esmond and Beatrix refer to "Peter Wilkins" some forty years before that book was published; that the play which Lord Castlewood and Lord Mohun went to see at Drury Lane could not have been "Love in a Wood," because, for one reason anyway, the disguise of a page is not worn by any of the ladies taking part in

[1] J. T. Fields: *Yesterdays with Authors.*

2 C

that comedy ; and so on. Yet, in spite of all who find fault with it, "Esmond" has taken its place in literature, not only as one of the author's masterpieces—for "Vanity Fair" ranks with it—but as one of the best historical novels ever written. "Never could I have believed," said Walter Savage Landor when the book was published, "that Thackeray, great as his abilities are, could have written so noble a story as 'Esmond.'" "A greater novel than 'Esmond' I do not know," Professor Saintsbury has written half a century later, "and I do not know many greater books."

When Esmond was finished Thackeray went abroad again with his children, and he was somewhat amused at the difference in his attitude when travelling *en garçon* and as a family man. They went to Antwerp, then down the Rhine, and then to Switzerland, returning *via* Paris, where Thackeray left his daughters with Mrs. Carmichael-Smyth, feeling very keenly the parting with them.

> You have just parted from the dear ones with bursting heart ; and, lonely man, just torn from your children . . . their little tokens of affection yet in your pocket . . . pacing the deck at evening in the midst of the roaring ocean, you can remember how you were told supper was ready, and how you went down into the cabin, and had brandy and water and biscuit. You remember the taste of them. Yes, for ever. You took them while you and your Grief were sitting together, and your Grief clutched you round the soul.

Before Thackeray could go to America, however, there were more lectures to deliver, "Vanity Fair" to be revised for a cheaper edition, and the proofs of

"Esmond" to be passed for press. The original edition of "Esmond" was printed in the obsolete type of the reign of Queen Anne, and as only a small quantity could be obtained, it took longer than had been expected to set up the book. Then the manuscript of the third volume was mislaid at the printers, and it looked as if the author would have to postpone his journey until he had rewritten the missing chapters. Happily the manuscript was found; but Thackeray only received his bound copies while he was on the pier waiting for the tender to carry him to the ship.

Thackeray went to Liverpool to deliver a course of lectures at the Athenæum in that city on the Tuesdays and Thursdays, September 28 and 30, and October 5, 7, 12 and 14; and to Manchester at the Philharmonic Hall on the Wednesdays and Fridays of the same weeks. Then he returned to London, going again to Liverpool on October 29, in company with Eyre Crowe, who was to accompany him to America. That night they dined at the house of Mr. Ratcliffe; the *pièce de résistance* of the meal being roast sucking-pig—a surprise for the great man, who loved only beans and bacon better. On the following morning Thackeray and Eyre Crowe, with their fellow-travellers, Lowell, just returned from Italy, and Arthur Hugh Clough, embarked on the R.M.S. Canada (Captain Lang).

The lectures were as highly approved in the provinces as in London. At Oxford, where he stayed with his old friend Stoddart, the readings were worth thirty pounds apiece; and Cambridge showed itself nearly as appreciative as the sister university. At Edinburgh, too, they were a great success—a hundred subscribers, and two hundred other people for the first lecture. Indeed, the audiences there were so large that the visit to America, at this time arranged for May, hung in the balance. It was not, however, abandoned. "I must and will go, not because I like it, but because it is right I should secure some money against my death for your mother and you two girls,' he told his daughters. "And I think, if I have luck, I may secure nearly a third of the sum I ought to leave behind me by a six months' tour in the United States."

CHAPTER XVIII

FIRST VISIT TO THE UNITED STATES
(1852-1853)

Thackeray attacked in an American paper before he sails—a fair chance given him on arrival—his first dinner at Boston—in New York—his great popularity in the United States—his books better known there than in England—on pirated editions—Thackeray likes America and Americans—his objections to personal journalism in the United States—" Mr. Thackeray in the United States "—his lectures in New York—and elsewhere—" Charity and Humour "—tired of acting the lion—his sudden departure for England.

THACKERAY prepared for his American trip in no hilarious frame of mind, and while lecturing in Liverpool he was further depressed by seeing in a New York paper a bitter attack on him. It was, indeed, very doubtful what reception he would meet with from the Americans, who, still smarting under the castigation inflicted by Dickens in his " American Notes," and thinking of the "Boz" Tableaux and the Dickens Ball at the Park Theatre, not unnaturally said : "Thackeray will come and humbug us, eat our dinners, pocket our money, and go home, and abuse us like Dickens." The instinct of fair-play, however, is in all English-speaking races, and it was tacitly agreed that Thackeray in the United States should have his chance.

"The passage is nothing now it is over," Thackeray, on his arrival at Boston on a frosty morning, said to Fields, who at once carried him off to dinner, where a joke was played upon him. "In London," Fields has related, "Thackeray had been very curious in his enquiries about American oysters, as marvellous stories, which he did not believe, had been told him of their great size. We apologised—although we had taken care that the largest specimen to be procured should startle his unwonted vision when he came to the table —for what we called the extreme *smallness* of the oysters, promising that we would do better next time. Six Falstaffian bivalves lay before him in their shells. I noticed he gazed at them anxiously, with fork up-raised; then he whispered to me with a look of anguish, 'How shall I do it?' I described to him the simple process by which the free-born citizens of America were accustomed to accomplish such a task. He seemed satisfied that the thing was feasible, selected the smallest one in the half-dozen (rejecting a large one, 'because,' he said, 'it resembled the High Priest's servant's ear that Peter cut off'), and then bowed his head as if he were saying grace. All eyes were upon him to watch the effect of a new sensation in the person of a great British Author. Opening his mouth very wide, he struggled for a minute, and then all was over. I shall never forget the comic look of despair he cast upon the other five over-occupied shells. I broke the perfect stillness by asking him how he felt. 'Profoundly grateful,' he gasped, 'and as if I had swallowed a little baby.'"[1]

[1] J. T. Fields: *Yesterdays with Authors.*

Thackeray had been advised to open his tour in New York, and he repaired to that city on November 16, being amused in the train by "a rosy-cheeked little peripatetic book-merchant" crying "Thackeray's Works!" from whom he bought "A Shabby Genteel Story" to read on the journey. Prescott was his first visitor in New York. "The historian is delightful," he wrote to English friends; adding that society at New York was like that of "a rich cathedral - town in England — grave and decorous, and very pleasant and well-read." One evening he heard Bancroft lecture before the New York Historical Society; and on another he was initiated into the mysteries of spirit-rapping and table-turning at a *séance* conducted by the notorious Home. He met Horace Greeley, the proprietor of the *Daily Tribune*, in the columns of which he had been welcomed to the United States by Henry James, father of the novelist.

The impartiality with which the United States had determined to receive Thackeray was, before a week was over, turned into a great enthusiasm. "The popular Thackeray-theory before his arrival was of a severe satirist who concealed scalpels in his sleeves and carried probes in his waistcoat pocket; a wearer of masks; a scoffer and sneerer and general infidel of all high aim and noble character," said a writer in *Putnam's Monthly Magazine* for June 1853. "Certainly we are justified in saying that his presence among us quite corrected this idea. We welcomed a friendly, genial man; not at all convinced that speech is heaven's first law, but willing to be silent when there was nothing to say—who decidedly refused to be lionised, not by sulking, but by stepping off the pedestal and challenging the common sympathies of all he met. . . . We conceive . . . the chief merit of Thackeray's visit to be that he convinced us of his intellectual integrity, he showed us how impossible it is for him to see the world and describe it other than he does. He does not profess cynicism, nor satirise society with malice, and his interests are human and concrete, not abstract."

Within a few days of his arrival in New York Thackeray was being *fêted* as he had never been before, and luncheons, dinners and suppers in his honour were so numerous that he laughingly spoke of his visit as "one unbroken round of indigestion." He was the most popular man in the city: to shake hands with him even was regarded as a pleasure, to converse with him an honour. Judging from the innumerable records of Thackeray in America,[1] nearly everyone who was with him for half an hour must have written down his impressions; and to this day those surviving men and women who knew him cherish his memory. "For years I was constantly hearing gossip about Thackeray from those who had met him during his visits to us," the present American Ambassador to this country (the Hon. Whitelaw Reid) recently remarked in the course of his speech when he was in the chair of the English Titmarsh Club, of which he is a member.[2] "Their

---

[1] Many of these records have been collected by General James Grant Wilson, and printed in his interesting volume on "Thackeray in the United States."

[2] This speech was subsequently printed as an Introduction to the edition of *Vanity Fair* in "Everyman's Library."

accounts all ran one way. They admired his talk and
they loved him. They pictured him as big, hearty,
and very human. They didn't find him playing the
lion the least little bit. . . . They pointed out the
corner in the Century Club where he used to sit ex-
changing literary chat, or, in Yankee, parlance, 'swap-
ping stories,' with a group of club men about him.
They could tell you years afterwards what had been
Thackeray's favourite chair, and some had even been
so observant of the least trifles about the great man as
to know what particular concoction in a club tumbler
had been his favourite ' night-cap.' "

It is not surprising that, when the distrust of
him had vanished, Thackeray should have become
immensely popular. Long before there was any
thought of his visiting the United States, his writings
were better known, and more widely appreciated
than in his own country. In England he only
"arrived" with "Vanity Fair," in America his
"Yellowplush Correspondence" and "Major Gahagan"
had attracted attention and his career had been followed
with interest by a considerable public from this time
forth. The " Yellowplush Correspondence," which
appeared in *Fraser's Magazine* in 1837 and 1838, and
" Major Gahagan," which was printed in the *New
Monthly Magazine* in the same years, were issued at
once in book-form in America, though here they were
not collected until 1841; and other of his works, including "Stubbs's Calendar", "The Irish Sketch Book"
and "From Cornhill to Cairo," were pirated immediately after publication. "Jeames's Diary," which
was not issued in book-form in England until 1856,

was at once collected there; and similar honours of publication earlier than in the country of their origin were accorded to "The Great Hoggarty Diamond" and, indeed, to all the works prior to "Vanity Fair." "Vanity Fair", "Pendennis" and "Esmond" were to be had in America almost as soon as in London. This, no doubt, is directly attributable to the fact that in the United States there was then no protection for English authors; and, as there was no royalty to pay, their works could be produced more cheaply, and so made more accessible to the public. Some publishers, however, took the honourable course of · paying Thackeray a fee; and among these, to its credit, may be mentioned the great house of Harper, which paid respectively £150, £100, and £480 for the advance sheets of "The Newcomes", "Esmond" and "The Virginians." Putnams, too, would willingly have done the right thing by him, but their offer could not be entertained.

Messrs. Harpers, who have published my larger books and have paid my London publisher for my last work, have offered me a sum of money for the republication of my lectures, and all things considered, I think it is best that I should accept their liberal proposal. I thank you very much for your generous offer; and for my own sake, as well as that of my literary brethren in England, I am sincerely rejoiced to find how very kindly the American publishers are disposed to us. . . .[1]

Thackeray, who liked money as well as most men, was annoyed that piracy was possible, but, since noth-

[1] *Putnam's Magazine*, Vol. IV, p. 681.

ing he could do would alter the state of things, he put a good face on it.

That extreme liberality with which American publishers have printed the works of English authors has had at least this beneficial result for us—that our names and writings are known by multitudes using our common mother tongue, who never had heard of us or our books, but for the speculators who have sent them all over this continent.

It is, of course, not unnatural for the English writer to hope that some day he may share a portion of the profits which his works bring at present to the persons who vend them in this country; and I am bound gratefully to say myself that since my arrival here I have met with several publishing houses who are willing to acknowledge our little claim to participate in the advantages arising out of our books; and the present writer, having long since ascertained that a portion of a loaf is more satisfactory than no bread at all, gratefully accepts and acknowledges several slices which the book-purveyors in this city have proffered to him of their own free-will.

If we are not paid in full and in specie as yet, English writers surely ought to be thankful for the very great kindness and friendliness with which the American public receives them; and if we hope some day that measures may pass here to legalise our right to profit a little by the commodities which we invent and in which we deal, I, for one, can cheerfully say that the goodwill towards us from publishers and public is undoubted, and wait for still better times with perfect confidence and good-humour.[1]

If the Americans were delighted with Thackeray, he in his turn was most agreeably astonished. "You know what a virtue-proud people we English are. We

---

[1] Preface to Appleton's edition of *Mr. Brown's Letters*, 1853.

think we have got it all to ourselves," he replied to the
Hon. William B. Reed (sometime the United States
Minister to China), who had asked for his candid
opinion of the United States. "Now that which
most impresses me here is, that I find homes as pure as
ours, firesides like ours, domestic virtues as gentle ;
the English language, though the accent be a little
different, with its homelike melody ; and the Common
Prayer Book in your families. I am more struck by
pleasant resemblances than anything else." [1]

> You are more tender-hearted, romantic, senti-
> mental, than we are [he wrote later to Reed]. I
> keep on telling this to our fine people here, and
> have so belaboured your country with praise in
> private that I sometimes think I go too far. I keep
> back some of the truth, but the great point to ding
> into the ears of the great stupid virtue-proud English
> public is, that there are folks as good as they in
> America. That's where Mrs. Stowe's book has done
> harm, by inflaming us with an idea of our own
> superior virtue in freeing our blacks, whereas you
> keep yours. Comparisons are always odorous, Mrs.
> Malaprop says.[2]

There was one thing, however, to which Thackeray
strongly objected : the personal journalism, then
happily almost unknown in England, but already
rampant in the United States. He could not escape
the reporters, and had to bear the trial as good-
humouredly as possible : he had his tit-for-tat with
them by satirising the American newspapers in an
article entitled "Mr. Thackeray in the United States,"
which appeared in *Fraser's Magazine*, January 1853.

[1] W. B. Reed : *Haud Immemor—Thackeray in the United States.*
[2] *Ibid.*

You cannot help perceiving that the lion in
America is public property and confiscate to the
common weal.   They trim the creature's nails, they
cut the hair off his mane and tail (which is distributed
or sold to his admirers), and they draw his teeth,
which are frequently preserved with much the same
care as you keep any memorable grinder whose
presence has been agony and departure delight.

Bear-leading is not so in vogue across the Atlantic
as at your home in England ; but lion-leading is
infinitely more in fashion.

Some learned man is appointed Androcles to the
new arrival.   One of the familiars of the press is
despatched to attend the latest attraction, and by this
reflecting medium the lion is perpetually presented
to the popular gaze.   The guest's most secret self
is exposed by his host.   Every action, every word,
every gesture, is preserved and proclaimed—a sigh,
a nod, a groan, a sneeze, a cough, or a wink, is each
written down by this recording minister, who blots
out nothing.   No *tabula rasa* with him.   The portrait is limned with the fidelity of Parrhasius, and
filled up with the minuteness of the Daguerre process itself.   No blood-hound or Bow-street officer
can be keener or more exact on the trail than this
irresistible and unavoidable spy.   'Tis in Austria
they calotype criminals ; in the far West the public
press prints the identity of each notorious visitor to
its shores.

The article was anonymous, but it was almost immediately recognised as from his pen.   It caused as much
amusement in America as in England, and if in the
former country some sensitive persons felt a touch of
annoyance, it was removed when they came to the last
page, where Thackeray printed the tribute to this land
which he had delivered at the conclusion of the last
lecture of the first course of " The English Humourists
of the Eighteenth Century."

In England it was my custom after the delivery of these lectures to point such a moral as seemed to befit the country I lived in, and to protest against an outcry, which some brother authors of mine most imprudently and unjustly raise, when they say that our profession is neglected and its professors held in light esteem. Speaking in this country, I would say that such a complaint could not only not be advanced, but could not even be understood here, where your men of letters take their manly share in public life; whence Everett goes as Minister to Washington, and Irving and Bancroft to represent the republic in the old country. And if to English authors the English public is, as I believe, kind and just in the main, can any of us say, will any who visit your country not proudly and gratefully own, with what a cordial and generous greeting you receive us? I look round on this great company, I think of my gallant young patrons of the Mercantile Literary Association, as whose servant I appear before you; and of the kind hands stretched out to welcome me by men famous in letters, and honoured in our country as in their own, and I thank you and them for a most kindly greeting and a most generous hospitality. At home, and amongst his own people, it scarce becomes an English writer to speak of himself, his public estimation must depend upon his works; his private esteem on his character, and on his life. But here among friends newly found, I ask leave to say that I am thankful; and I think with a grateful heart of those I leave behind me at home, who will be proud of the welcome you hold out to me, and will benefit, please God, when my days of work are over, by the kindness which you show to their father.

Thackeray in the United States found many congenial companions, he met Washington Irving, Prescott, Ticknor, and Longfellow; and struck up an intimacy with William B. Reed and the Baxter family, with whom he corresponded during the rest of his life. "By

jove ! how kind you all were to me," he wrote to Reed.
"How I like people and want to see 'em again." Certainly everybody conspired to make his tour agreeable.

The business arrangements for the lecturing were
made so far as possible without troubling him with
details of the negotiations, and the tour was carried out
under the auspices of the Mercantile Literary Association, of which institution the president was Millard L.
Felt. The first lecture was delivered on the evening of
November 19, in the Church of the Unity, on the east
side of Broadway, near Prince's Street, a Unitarian
chapel of which Dr. Chapin (who had recently succeeded
the Rev. Henry Bellows) was the pastor. Thackeray
had to read from a rostrum fronting the pulpit, and he
pretended not to be at his ease until he received the
assurance that the organ would not accompany his
utterances. Twelve hundred people were assembled,
and these included such literary celebrities as Ticknor,
Bancroft, Bryant, and Greeley. "He is a stout,
healthful, broad-shouldered specimen of a man, with
cropped greyish hair and bluish-grey eyes, peering
very strongly through a pair of spectacles that have a
very satiric focus," he was sketched by one of the
audience. "He seems to stand strongly on his own
feet, as if he would not be very easily blown about or
upset either by praise or pugilists—a man who scents
all shams or rumours, straightening them between his
thumb and finger as he would a pinch of snuff."

All the tickets for the first course had been sold before
he landed ; and, thus encouraged, the organisers had
arranged a second course to begin on December 6. So
successful was this, too, and the c urse delivered at

Brooklyn, that before leaving New York, Thackeray placed to his credit at his bankers the sum of five thousand dollars. A minimum estimate of the lecturer's receipts during the first American tour is £2500; but it is probable that double the amount was realised.

From Brooklyn, where he met the great Barnum, who wanted him to write something in the first number of a paper in imitation of the *Illustrated London News*, just about to make its appearance, Thackeray went to Boston. "I remember," Fields has recorded of the first reading at the great Melodeon Music Hall in that city, "his uproarious shouting and dancing when he was told that the tickets to his first course of lectures were all sold; and when we rode together from his hotel to the lecture-hall, he insisted on thrusting both his long legs out of the carriage window, in deference, as he said, to his magnanimous ticket-holders."[1]

"At Boston there is very good literary society indeed," he remarked; and indeed the fact must have been very apparent to him when he saw in his first night's audience the faces of Longfellow, Whittier, Emerson, Holmes, Prescott, and Ticknor. He supped with Longfellow; and went to Cambridge to see Lowell who promised: "You shall either be carried back to Boston, or spend the night with us." He became intimate with Ticknor, especially on his second visit. He invited himself to eat a Christmas dinner with the historian and his family; and on New Year's eve watched the New Year in by their fireside, rising on the stroke of twelve, with tears in his eyes, to exclaim: "God bless my girls, and all who are kind to them."

[1] J. T. Fields: *Yesterdays with Authors.*

That prince among humorists, Oliver Wendell Holmes, naturally attracted him. "A dear little fellow, a true poet," he said. "I told him how much I liked his verses, and what do you think he did? *His* eyes began to water. Well, it's a comfort to have given pleasure to that kind soul."

After visiting Philadelphia and Baltimore, Thackeray went to Washington, where he was the guest of the British Minister, Mr. (afterwards Sir John) Crampton, "most hospitable of envoys," Thackeray dubbed him, and described his stay in that city as "an interminable succession of balls, parties, and banquets." He dined with President Filmore, and that personage came to his lecture in company with General Pierce, the President-Elect. "Two Kings of Brentford smelling at one rose," Washington Irving murmured to the lecturer as they appeared. In one of the "Snob Papers" Thackeray said the height of rapture must be to walk down Pall Mall arm-in-arm with a couple of dukes ; lecturing before two Presidents was surely only one degree less magnificent.

From Washington Thackeray returned to New York to give a lecture on January 31, in the Church of the Messiah, for the benefit of a Sewing Society of a Unitarian Church, in which some of his friends were interested. He composed for the occasion a special discourse on "Charity and Humour," in which he compared the humorists of the eighteenth with their successors of the nineteenth century.

Charleston was reached, after many other places had been visited, on March 8 ; and three discourses were read in the Hibernian Hall. Thackeray met

2 D

Professor Agassiz, who was also there to lecture: "a delightful *bonhommious* person, as frank and unpretending as he is learned and illustrious in his own branch." Savannah followed, where he was the guest of Andrew Low, the British Consul; but the lectures were not a financial success, and the attendance was smaller than anywhere else on the tour, with the exception perhaps of Pittsburg. In April he was back at the Clarendon Hotel, New York. He went for a couple of days to Albany; and intended to go to Canada—indeed, his appearance at Montreal was announced—but he never crossed the border.

Long before the tour was over Thackeray was heartily sick of it and the attendant publicity. Only the thought of the benefit that was accruing to his children enabled him to continue so long. "Even when I am reading my lectures, I often think to myself 'What a humbug you are, and I wonder people don't find you out,'" he exclaimed one day to Bayard Taylor; and he wrote to Mrs. Elliot to say how much he desired a week's holiday without his "dem'd lecture-box." Suddenly he made up his mind he must return. On the morning of April 20 he astonished Eyre Crowe, who had arranged for him to visit several towns in the middle and western states, by saying: "I see there's a Cunarder going this morning. I'll go down to Wall Street to see whether I can secure berths in her." His quest was successful. He scribbled on a card: "Good-bye, Fields; good-bye, Mrs. Fields; God bless everybody, says W.M.T."—there was no time for personal farewells—hurried down Broadway, got into a boat on the east river, reached the Europa to be greeted with the cry, "Hurry up—she's starting!" and landed at Liverpool almost exactly six months after his departure.

The story of his arrival at his house has been charmingly told by his eldest daughter in the following words: "When the long summer and winter were over, and the still longer spring, suddenly one day we heard he was coming back much sooner than he had expected. I believe he saw a steamer starting for home and could stand it no longer, and then and there came off. I can still remember sitting with my grandparents, expecting his return. My sister and I sat on the red sofa in the little study, and shortly before the time we had calculated he might arrive came a little ring at the front door-bell. My grandmother broke down; my sister and I rushed to the front door, only we were so afraid that it might not be he that we did not dare to open it, and there we stood until a second and much louder ring brought us to our senses. 'Why didn't you open the door?' said my father, stepping in, looking well, broad, and upright, laughing. In a moment he had never been away at all."[1]

[1] *Chapters from some Memoirs*, p. 171.

CHAPTER XIX

"THE NEWCOMES" (1853-1855)

Thackeray moves from No. 13, Young Street, Kensington, to No. 36, Onslow Square, Brompton—Green carpets and curtains—his plans for the future—he goes abroad with his daughters—his accounts of his travels—he begins to work at " The Newcomes " in Switzerland—his illness on his return to London—applies for the Secretaryship of the British Legation at Washington—his disappointment at being refused the post—"The Rose and the Ring "—prepares the lectures on " The Four Georges " for delivery in America—George Hodder acts as his amanuensis—a dinner given to him prior to his departure for America—Charles Dickens in the chair—the second American tour— acquires valuable information for " The Virginians "—the weariness of the lecture tour—revives " The English Humourists "—again departs suddenly for England—" The Four Georges " in England—another illness—accused of disloyalty—his defence—offers himself as Parliamentary candidate at Oxford—the election—he is defeated—invited Dickens to canvass for him—Yates' article on Thackeray in *Town Talk*—Thackeray's letter to Yates—Dickens supports Yates—further correspondence —Dickens v. Thackeray—Thackeray's praise of Dickens.

AFTER his return Thackeray removed from Young Street to No. 36, Onslow Square, Brompton, next door to his friend Baron Marochetti, the sculptor. " The result of my father's furnishing was a pleasant, bowery sort of home, with green curtains and carpets looking out upon the elm trees," Lady Ritchie has told us. Thack--

eray lived here nine years, and in this house wrote
"The Four Georges," the latter part of "The Newcomes", "The Virginians", "Lovel the Widower," the
opening chapters of "Philip," and the earlier "Roundabout Papers." Immediately after the removal to
Onslow Square, he went abroad with his daughters.

Three weeks of London were more than enough for
me, and I feel as if I had had enough of it and pleasure [he wrote to W. B. Reed, from Neuchatel, on
July 21, 1853]. Then I remained a month with
my parents; then I brought my girls on a little
pleasuring tour, and it has really been a pleasuring
tour. We spent ten days at Baden, when I set
intrepidly to work again ; and have been five days in
Switzerland now ; not bent on going up mountains,
but on taking things easily. How beautiful it is !
How pleasant ! How great and affable, too, the
landscape is ! It's delightful to be in the midst of
such scenes—the ideas get generous reflections from
them. I don't mean to say my thoughts grow moun-
tainous and enormous like the Alpine chain yonder ;
but, in fine, it is good to be in the presence of this
noble nature. It is keeping good company ; keeping
away mean thoughts. I see in the papers now and
again accounts of fine parties in London. *Bon Dieu!*
is it possible anyone ever wanted to go to fine London
parties, and are there now people sweating in Mayfair
routs? The European continent swarms with your
people. They are not all as polished as Chesterfield.
I wish some of them spoke French a little better. I
saw five of them at supper at Basle the other night
with their knives down their throats. It was awful !
My daughter saw it, and I was obliged to say, " My
dear, your great-great-grandmother, one of the finest
ladies of the old school I ever saw, always applied
cold steel to her wittles. It's no *crime* to eat with a
knife," which is all very well : but I wish five of 'em
at a time wouldn't. . . .

I am about a new story, but don't know as yet if it will be any good. It seems to me I am too old for story-telling; but I want money, and shall get 20,000 dollars for this, of which (D.V.) I'll keep fifteen.[1]

The story referred to in the letter was "The Newcomes," the idea of which occurred to him when he was abroad.

Two years ago, walking with my children in some pleasant fields, near to Berne in Switzerland, I strayed from them into a little wood [he wrote in the postscript to the novel]; and, coming out of it presently, told them how the story had been revealed to me somehow, which for twenty-three months the reader has been pleased to follow.

Much of "The Newcomes" was written abroad, at Rome, in Germany, and Switzerland, and at the Château du Brecquerecque at Boulogne. In the autumn of 1854 he was in London, where he had a bout of illness.

I am to-day just out of bed after another, about the dozenth, severe fit of spasms, which I have had this year [he wrote to W. B. Reed from Onslow Gardens on November 8]. My book would have been written but for them, and the lectures begun, with which I hope to make a few thousand more dollars for those young ladies. But who knows whether I shall be well enough to deliver them, or what is in store for next year?[2]

In the same letter he mentioned another, and last, attempt to enter the Government service.

The secretaryship of our legation at Washington was vacant the other day, and I instantly asked for it;

---

[1] W. B. Reed : *Haud Immemor—Thackeray in America.*
[2] *Ibid.*

NO. 36, ONSLOW SQUARE, BROMPTON
Where Thackeray lived 1853—1862

but in the very kindest letter Lord Clarendon showed
how the position was impossible. First, the place
was given away; next, it would not be fair to appoint
out of the service. But the first was an excellent
reason, not a doubt of it. So if ever I come, as I
hope and trust to do this time next year, it must be at
my own cost; and not the Queen's.

The first number of "The Newcomes" appeared in
October 1853, and the last in August 1855. When the
novel was finished in the summer of the latter year,
Thackeray again went abroad, and at Rome caught a
fever, from the effects of which he never entirely
recovered. It was just before this illness that he began
to write that glorious nonsense, "The Rose and the
Ring."

After his recovery, Thackeray returned to London to
prepare the second course of lectures, which were to be
delivered first in America. He had thought of "Men
of the World" as a subject, but this was eventually
abandoned for "The Four Georges." The work was
begun in September, when the author dictated it to
George Hodder. Thackeray was one of the few men
of genius who could dictate their work, and the commencement of this habit may probably be traced so far
back as 1849, when, after his illness, he was too weak to
sit long at a desk, and was compelled to employ an
amanuensis. At the house in Onslow Square he
usually wrote in his bedroom, for his study, a small
room on the ground-floor, was exposed to the noises
from the street. Mr. Hodder has recorded how Thackeray was sometimes in doubt as to whether he should
commence operations sitting or standing or walking

about or lying down ; how often he would light a cigar, and after pacing the room for a few minutes, would put the unsmoked remnant on the mantelpiece, as if he had gathered fresh inspiration from the "gentle odours" or the "sublime tobacco"; and how, when he made a humorous point, which caused Mr. Hodder to laugh, his own countenance would be quite unmoved.[1]

The famous lectures are only three quarters done [Thackeray wrote on October 11], and I must trust to luck and the voyage and my previous knowledge of his "heroic" character for finishing George IV.

A farewell dinner, to which allusion has already been made, was given to him by his literary brethren on October 11, at the London Tavern, with Dickens in the chair ; and on the 13th he sailed for the second time Westward Ho !

The second American tour was in most essentials a repetition of the first. Again he was *fêted*, again the lectures were applauded, and again he made money— only this time far more than before.

I have been wanting to send you a line ever since I have been here, and waiting for a day's quiet when I could have leisure to send a letter big enough to travel 3000 miles—but there never *is* a day's quiet here. It is day after day skurry and turmoil, friends calling, strangers calling, newspaper articles bawling out abuse or telling absurd personalities—you know the life well enough, and have undergone the persecution in your time. The dollars hardly compensate for it ; nor the extraordinary kindness and friendliness of the real friends on whom one lights [he wrote to Macready on November 20].

As far as money goes I am doing great things here

[1] George Hodder, *Memories of My Time.*

and the dollars are rolling in.   I shall make all but
£1000 in 5 weeks—though not, of course, to continue
at this rate.   At first the papers didn't like the lectures:
but they are better pleased with the second reading,
and the public likewise, who begin to find that what
seems very easy is not done in a hurry.   What the
people like is sentiment, and I could not give them
any of this article except about old George III whom
they received very tenderly.   I finish him off with an
image taken from the death scene of an old king . . .
you used to know in times when you wore crowns,
and of whom, being dead, it was said, Vex not his
ghost, and let him pass, he hates him who would
upon the rack of this tough world stretch him out
longer.[1]

The tour was extensive—New York, Boston, and
Baltimore, from which last city he wrote to W. B. Reed
to complain of "wicked weather, and an opera company which performed on the first two lecture nights,
and made the audiences rather thin."   At Baltimore in
1853 he had made the acquaintance of John P. Kennedy,
and on this visit he was the guest of that gentleman,
who gave him valuable information concerning Virginia, and even took him to that State so that he might
see things for himself.   The knowledge acquired was
used in "The Virginians," and on the strength of this,
apparently, for no further evidence has been adduced,
several friends of Mr. Kennedy claimed that he wrote all
or part of the fourth chapter of the second volume
of "The Virginians"!   Unfortunately for those who
advance this statement the manuscript of the novel is
in Thackeray's handwriting.   "No doubt Mr. Kennedy

---

[1] W. M. Thackeray : *Notes for Speech at Dinner, October 11, 1855:
etc.—printed for Major W. H. Lambert.*   Philadelphia, 1896; pp. 22, 26.

gave my father some facts about the scenery," Lady
Ritchie has said; "but I am sure my father wrote his
own books, for nobody else could have written them for
him." From Baltimore, Thackeray went to Richmond,
Charleston, Augusta, Savannah, Montgomery, Macon,
Mobile, New Orleans, Buffalo, Cincinnati, etc.; and
then back to New York, where he stayed with three
bachelor friends at the "Bower of Virtue," as he styled
the house, No. 604, Houston Street.

When Thackeray was in New York, a young bookseller offered him a large sum to repeat the course of
lectures on "The English Humourists." This he was
unwilling to do, but eventually yielded, partly at the
request of friends, and, no doubt, somewhat persuaded
by the handsome terms. The course was a failure
from the pecuniary point of view: it was too late in
the season for the thing; and the lectures had been
printed and everyone was familiar with them. "I
don't mind the empty benches; but I cannot bear to
see that sad, pale-faced young man as I come out, who
is losing money on my account," he said to Reed,
through whose agency the bookseller remitted the
money. Reed received no acknowledgment of the
draft, and was not a little annoyed, especially when he
learnt that Thackeray had sailed for home. The next
morning, however, came a letter from the novelist,
containing a certificate of deposit in a New York bank
for an amount sufficient to make up the bookseller's
loss.

When you get this, . . . remummum-ember me
to kick-kick-kind friends . . . a sudden resolution—
to-mummum-morrow . . . . in the Bu-Bu-baltic.
Goodbye, my dear kind friend, and all kind friends

WILLIAM MAKEPEACE THACKERAY
From a drawing by Samuel Laurence. By permission of Major William H. Lambert

in Philadelphia.   I didn't think of going away when
I left home this morning ; but it's the best way. . . . I
think it is best to send back 25 per cent to poor
——.   Will you kindly give him the enclosed.[1]

The second visit terminated in the same abrupt
manner as the first.   "The process of saying Goodbye
is horrible to me—as I shook kind hands and walked
away out of hospitable doors at Philadelphia for the
last time I felt quite sad and guilty as it were,"
Thackeray declared.   "Where was the need of pro-
longing these *adieux?*   So Friday, 25th (April 1856),
as I walked down Broadway seeming very bright,
warm, and cheery, I went with my usual sudden
impetus straight to Collin's office, and was off the next
day, before I knew I was gone."   His good-byes were
made by letter.

I tell you writing is just as dismal and disgusting
as saying goodbye [he wrote to William Duer
Robinson, "On Board, Last Day," May 7, 1856].
I hate it, and but for a sense of duty I wouldn't write
at all—confound me if I would.   But you know after
a fellow has been so uncommonly hospitable and
kind and that sort of thing, a fellow ought, you see,
to write and tell a fellow that a fellow's very much
obliged and—in a word you understand.   Sir, you
made me happy when I was with you, you made me
sorry to come away, and you make me happy now
when I think what a kind, generous W.D.R. you
are.   You have Davis back in the Bower of Virtue
—you'll fill that jug when you one day drink my
health, won't you? and when you come to Europe
you'll come to me and my girls mind, and we'll see
if there is not some good claret at 36, Onslow Square.
. . . We have had a dreary, rough passage—yesterday the hardest blow of all.   I have been ill with

[1] W. B. Reed: *Haud Immemor—Thackeray in the United States.*

one of my old intermittent attacks, after which my mouth broke out with an unusually brilliant eruption, and I am going to Liverpool with a beard eight days long. It is not becoming in its present stage. I have not been seasick, but haven't been well a single day. Wine is ojus to me, segars create loathing—couldn't I write something funnier and more cheerful? Perhaps I may when we are fairly in Liverpool—perhaps we may be there to-night, perhaps not till to-morrow morning, for it blew a hurricane in our face last night, and the odds are we shall not have water enough to pass the bar.

We did pass the bar [he added, when he reached Onslow Square]; and didn't I have a good dinner at the Adelphi, and wasn't I glad to get back to town yesterday, and wasn't there a great dinner at the Garrick Club (the annual Shakspeare dinner, which ought to have come off on the 23rd ult., but was put off on account of the naval review), and didn't I make a Yankee speech, and oh lor', Robinson, haven't I got a headache this morning? I'm ashamed to ask for a sober-water, that's the fact—And so here's the old house, the old room, the old teapot by my bedside—the old trees nodding in at my window: it looks as if I'd never been away, and that it's all a dream I have been making. Well, in my dream I dreamt there was an uncommonly good fellow, by name W D R, and I dreamed that he treated me with all sorts of kindness, and I send him and J C B D (i.e., J. C. Bancroft Davis) and D D (Dening Duer) and what's his name, (Samuel E. Lyons) downstairs? my heartiest regards, and when my young women come home I shall tell them what a good deal of kindness their papa had across the water.[1]

Soon after his arrival in London, Thackeray, through the agency of Mr. Hodder, made arrangements to deliver the lectures on the "Four Georges" in London

Academia, February 19, 1868.

and the provinces for the sum of fifty guineas each. Mr. Beale, of Messrs. Cramer and Beale, had suggested the terms, which Thackeray accepted without showing any special elation, or letting the impresario see that he thought the offer anything exceptional, though as soon as Beale had left he remarked: "Fifty guineas a night! Why, I shouldn't have received half that sum for an article in *Fraser's Magazine* a few years ago." He was always careful never to lower the market-price of his works, and after the success of "Vanity Fair" had placed him in the front rank of men of letters, he invariably demanded the full pecuniary value of his literary labours. "Always ask enough," he said; "they can but drop you down a bit if they don't like it."

After the lectures had been delivered in London, Thackeray went with George Hodder (who acted throughout as agent for Messrs. Cramer and Beale) to Exeter, Plymouth, Clifton, Birmingham, and Oxford, at which city he was very well received by the under-graduate audience, and was so delighted at the enthusiasm of the young men that he exclaimed: "There's an audience for you! Gad, I'd lecture to those young fellows for nothing"; and he received many of them in his private room, where he thanked them for the sympathy and encouragement they had given him. "Lewis Carroll" met him there at breakfast. "I was much pleased with what I saw of him," wrote the author of "Alice in Wonderland." "His manner is simple and unaffected: he shows no anxiety to share in conversation, though full of fun and anecdote when drawn out. He seemed delighted with the reception

he met with last night—the undergraduates seem to
have behaved with most unusual moderation."[1] Norwich
was the last place in England where the lectures were
to be given, and here Thackeray was seized with one
of the violent attacks to which he was subject, which
delayed his journey northwards.   Though Professor
Aytoun advised him to " Let the Georges alone, and
stick to the Jeameses,"[2] the lectures were well attended
—in Edinburgh by actually three per cent. of the whole
population : " Ah ! " exclaimed the great man, " if I
could but get three per cent. of London."

In connection with these lectures on the Georges,
the charge of disloyalty was brought against the
author.   While they were being delivered in America,
many English newspapers and people asserted that
he would never dare to read them in England,
and when, nothing daunted, he made arrangements for their delivery, a certain class or school
of persons waxed exceeding wroth.   Amongst these
the place of honour must most certainly be given
to a rector (whose father had been presented to a
valuable living by George IV) who was so enraged
that he wrote to a newspaper : " An elderly, infidel
buffoon of the name of Thackeray has been lecturing
in town on the subject of the Four Georges, etc.,
etc."   At Edinburgh, Thackeray, replying to a toast
at a public dinner given in his honour, made his
defence.

I had thought that in these lectures I had spoken
in terms, not of disrespect or unkindness, but in

[1] *The Journal of Lewis Carroll.*
[2] Charles Mackay : *Recollections*, p. 99.

feelings and in language not un-English, of her Majesty the Queen ; and whenever I have had to mention her name, whether it was upon the banks of the Clyde or upon those of the Mississippi, whether it was in New England or in Old England, whether it was in some great hall in London to the artisans of the suburbs of the metropolis, or to the politer audiences at the western end—whenever I had to mention her name, it was received with shouts of applause, and with the most hearty cheers. And why was this? It was not on account of the speaker ; it was on account of the truth, it was because the English and the Americans—the people of New Orleans a year ago, and people of Aber-deen a week ago—all received and acknowledged with due allegiance the great claims to honour which that lady has, who worthily holds that great and awful situation which our Queen occupies. It is my loyalty that is called in question, and it is my loyalty I am trying to plead to you. Suppose, for example, in America—in Philadelphia or in New York—I had spoken of George IV in terms of praise or affected reverence, do you suppose they would have hailed his name with cheers or have heard it with anything like respect? They would have laughed in my face if I had so spoken of him. They know what I know and what you know, and what numbers of squeamish loyalists who affect to cry out against my lectures know, that that man's life was not a good life—that that king was not such a king as we ought to love or regard or honour. And I believe, for my part, that in speaking the truth as we hold it of a bad sovereign, we are paying no disrespect at all to a good one. Far from it. On the contrary, we degrade our own honour and the Sovereign's by unduly and unjustly praising him : and the mere slaverer and flatterer is one who comes forward, as it were, with flash notes, and pays with false coin his tribute to Cæsar. I don't disguise from you that I feel somehow or other on my trial here for loyalty, for honest English feeling.

"To what is it the people are objecting?" Mrs. Browning asked, after hearing the lecture on George III, and indeed the question is not easy to answer. How could it have been deemed even bad taste, much less disloyalty, to discuss the failings of four sovereigns who had been dead respectively for a hundred and twenty-five, ninety-five, thirty-five, and twenty-five years? Surely it is perfectly legitimate, without violating any of the canons of decency, to criticise the acts and life of a public character, however highly placed, who has been dead for a quarter of a century. Progress would indeed be slow if it were necessary to wait more than a century and a quarter after the death of a man before we might discuss his doings and argue the question of his morality. Thackeray might have spoken even in harsher terms of George IV, and he must have been inclined to do so, for when he spoke of the lectures to Sir Charles Gavan Duffy, he said he sometimes wondered whether "every soul of these people he had to speak of was not damned in the end."

The lectures on the Georges delivered, Thackeray, who for some time past had thought of standing for Parliament, was invited to contest Oxford in the Liberal interest in June 1857, when Professor Neate was unseated for what Thackeray called, "a twopennyworth of bribery which he never committed." Though never a keen politician, he held strong views on some subjects, and expressed himself in favour of the ballot and reform. He told Sir Mountstuart Grant Duff the chief reason he wished to be in the House of Commons was that he might stand up once a year and tell his countrymen what would happen "when the French invade us."[1] But this was *à propos* of the fiery Colonels, and must have been a passing desire.[1] Thackeray dated his Address to the electors from the Mitre, July 9, 1857.

I should be unworthy of the great kindness and cordiality with which you have received me to-night, were I to hesitate to put your friendship to the test and ask you to confirm it at the poll. . . .

I would use my best endeavours, not merely to popularise the Government of this country. With no feeling but that of goodwill towards those leading aristocratic families who are administering the chief offices of the State, I believe it could be benefitted by the skill and talents of persons less aristocratic, and that the country thinks so likewise.

I think that to secure the due freedom of representation, and to defend the poor voter from the chance of intimidation, the ballot is the best safeguard we know of, and would vote most hopefully for that measure. I would have the suffrage amended in nature, as well as in numbers, and hope to see many educated classes represented who have now no voice in elections. . . .

The usefulness of a member of Parliament is best tested at home ; and should you think fit to elect me as your representative, I promise to use my utmost endeavour to increase and advance the social happiness, the knowledge, and the power of the people.

Edward Cardwell was the Tory candidate, and, as was only to be expected from two such men, the contest was conducted with much courtesy. When Lord Monck came down to address the electors for the Peelite candidate, and met Thackeray, he said, "May the best man win." "I hope not," said the other, smiling. Lord Monck in his speeches spoke in high terms of Thackeray ; and the latter on the hustings chided his

[1] Sir M. E. Grant Duff: *Diary*, April 4, 1858.

supporters for hissing when the name of his opponent was mentioned. A characteristic anecdote was told by a friend of Thackeray's, who was staying with him at the hotel. One day during the election he was looking out of a window when he saw a crowd hustling and hooting some of Mr. Cardwell's supporters. Thackeray started up with an oath, and rushed down the street, notwithstanding the efforts of some old electioneerers who wished to hold him back. He was next seen towering above the crowd, dealing about him right and left, in defence of his opponent's partisans, and in defiance of his own friends.[1]

Thackeray fought hard but, probably owing to the fact that he supported the Sunday opening of museums —a measure for which the country was not then ready —he was defeated by 1085 to 1018 votes. The result was eminently satisfactory : Cardwell went to the House of Commons, where he was the right man in the right place ; and Thackeray returned to his desk. It is extremely unlikely that Thackeray would have achieved any remarkable success in the House of Commons. His candid friend, Anthony Trollope, believed he would have been a disastrous failure ; but that is an extreme to which it is unnecessary to subscribe. It must be admitted, however, that there was much against him. His health was bad ; his habits irregular ; and, though he would have done his duty, it would doubtless soon have become irksome to him. He was not a man unhesitatingly to have obeyed the orders of his party's whip ; he was the very last person in the world

---

[1] The speeches made by Thackeray during the progress of the election are printed in the Appendix.

WILLIAM MAKEPEACE THACKERAY

From a crayon drawing by E. Goodwyn Lewis, in the Kensington Public Library

to have believed his friends to be always right, and
his opponents always wrong ; and he would certainly
have voted against his party whenever he thought they
were in error. By his defeat the party whip was saved
much annoyance. Anyhow, whether as a politician he
had been good, bad, or indifferent, with regard to his
defeat, remembering that it left him free to pursue his
literary labours, we can only remark, as did Carlyle to
his wife after the lady who claimed to be the prototype
of Blanche Amory had paid a visit to Cheyne Walk
and left, "Oh! my dear, we cannot be sufficiently
grateful!"

> Come down and make a speech, and tell them who
> I am [Thackeray wrote to Dickens from Oxford], for
> I doubt whether more than two of the electors have
> ever heard of me, and I think there may be as many
> as six or eight who have heard of you.

This was probably the last friendly letter exchanged
between the two novelists, for in the following year
they quarrelled. The cause of the quarrel was Edmund
Yates, who in 1858 printed in his paper *Town Talk* a
character-sketch of Thackeray :—

> Mr. Thackeray is forty-six years old, though from
> the silvery whiteness of his hair he appears some-
> what older. He is very tall, standing upwards of
> six feet two inches ; and as he walks erect, his height
> makes him conspicuous in every assembly. His face
> is bloodless, and not particularly expressive, but
> remarkable for the fracture of the bridge of the nose,
> the result of an accident in youth. He wears a small
> grey whisker, but otherwise is clean shaven. No one
> meeting him could fail to recognise in him a gentle-
> man : his bearing is cold and uninviting, his style
> of conversation either openly cynical or affectedly

good-natured and benevolent; his *bonhommie* is forced, his wit biting, his pride easily touched—but his appearance is invariably that of the cool, suave, well-bred gentleman, who, whatever may be rankling within, suffers no surface display of his emotion. . . . His success, commencing with "Vanity Fair," culminated with his "Lectures on the English Humourists of the Eighteenth Century," which were attended by all the court and fashion of London. The prices were extravagant, the Lecturer's adulation of birth and position was extravagant, the success was extravagant. No one succeeds better than Mr. Thackeray in cutting his coat according to his cloth : here he flattered the aristocracy, but when he crossed the Atlantic, George Washington became the idol of his worship, the "Four Georges" the objects of his bitterest attacks. These last-named Lectures have been dead failures in England, though as literary compositions they are most excellent. Our own opinion is, that his success is on the wane ; his writings never were understood or appreciated even by the middle classes ; the aristocracy have been alienated by his American onslaught on their body, and the educated and refined are not sufficiently numerous to constitute an audience ; moreover, there is a want of heart in all he writes, which is not to be balanced by the most brilliant sarcasm and the most perfect knowledge of the workings of the human heart.

The article was certainly in bad taste, and some of it mighty offensive. Thackeray, who hated "personal" journalism at all times, saw in this particular instance a gratuitous insult from a young fellow-clubman to whom he had held out a friendly hand, and he did not hesitate to express his indignation.

I have received two numbers of a little paper called "Town Talk," containing notices respecting myself, of which, as I learn from the best authority, you are the writer [he wrote to Yates on June 14]. In the first article of "Literary Talk" you think fit to publish an incorrect account of my private dealings with my publishers. In this week's number appears a so-called "Sketch" containing a description of my manners, person, and conversation, and an account of my literary works, which of course you are at liberty to praise or condemn as a literary critic. But you state, with regard to my conversation, that it is either "frankly cynical or affectedly benevolent and good-natured"; and of my works, that in some I showed "an extravagant adulation of rank and position," which in other lectures ("as I know how to cut my coat according to my cloth") became the object of my bitterest attack. As I understand your phrases, you impute insincerity to me when I speak good-naturedly in private; assign dishonourable motives to me for sentiments which I have delivered in public, and charge me with advancing statements which I have never delivered at all.

Had your remarks been written by a person unknown to me, I should have noticed them no more than other calumnies; but as we have shaken hands more than once, and met hitherto on friendly terms (you may ask one of your employers, Mr. ——, of ——, whether I did not speak of you lately in the most friendly manner), I am obliged to take notice of articles which I consider to be not offensive and unfriendly merely, but slanderous and untrue.

We meet at a Club, where, before you were born, I believe, I and other gentlemen have been in the habit of talking without any idea that our conversation would supply paragraphs for professional vendors of "Literary Talk"; and I don't remember that out of that Club I have ever exchanged six words with you. Allow me to inform you that the talk which you have heard there is not intended for newspaper remark; and to beg—as I have a right to do—that you will refrain from printing comments upon my private conversations ; that you will forego discussions, however blundering, upon my private affairs ; and that you will henceforth please to consider any question of my personal truth and sincerity as quite out of the province of your criticism.[1]

The castigation was severe ; but it was in some measure deserved. Yates, however, was no coward, and he immediately wrote an apologetic reply, in which, however, while urging that he had not meant all that Thackeray had read in his article, he reminded him of similar misdemeanours committed against fellow-clubmen in his youth—against Dr. Lardner and Sir Edward Bulwer Lytton in the "Yellowplush Papers"; against Stephen Price, Wyndham Smith, and Captain Granby Calcroft, in the "Book of Snobs"; and, above all, in later days, against Andrew Arcedeckne in "Pendennis." Had this letter been sent, the matter would probably have dropped, and the men, in course of time, might have come together again. Unfortunately Yates showed his letter to Dickens, who considered it too flippant, and drafted another, which was neither dignified nor wise to be sent by a man who was an offender.

Yates's reply, as amended by Dickens, infuriated Thackeray, who sent the correspondence to the Committee of the Garrick Club, and appealed to them

to decide whether the complaints I have against Mr. Yates are not well founded, and whether the practice of publishing such articles as that which I enclose will not be fatal to the comfort of the Club, and is not intolerable in a society of gentlemen.

[1] J. C. Hotten : *Thackeray*, pp. 159-161.

Here, it must be admitted, Thackeray put himself in the wrong, for, despite the provocation he had received, it was an extreme and perhaps unjustifiable step, as, indeed, Thackeray subsequently saw, for years later he told Hamstede, the honorary secretary of "Our Club," that "he had already driven one man out of a club for a personal reason, and was not so satisfied with the consequences of the affair as to be in a humour to repeat the operation." [1]

Yates protested that the Committee was incompetent to enter into the matter since there was no mention of the Club in the article, but the objection was overruled, and the offender was called upon to apologise to Thackeray or resign his membership. Yates, after consulting Dickens, John Forster, W. H. Wills, and Albert Smith, determined to appeal to a General Meeting. This was summoned for July 10, and, while neither Thackeray nor Yates was present, the latter sent a letter to be read, in which he expressed his willingness to express regret "for any unpleasant feeling that I may have awakened in the Club by the publication of the unfortunate article"; but he added that he considered Thackeray had placed it out of his power to apologise to him. In spite of the efforts of Dickens and Wilkie Collins, backed by Robert Bell, Samuel Lover, Palgrave Simpson, Sir James Ferguson, and others, the resolution to support the Committee was carried by seventy against forty-six. Yates was allowed until July 20 to apologise, and then, no communication being received from him, the Secretary of the Club wrote to inform him that the Committee

[1] J. C. Jeaffreson : *A Book of Recollections*, Vol. I, p. 323.

had erased his name from the list of members. There the matter rested for some months, when Dickens reopened it by offering his services as a mediator. The correspondence explains itself.

TAVISTOCK HOUSE,
TAVISTOCK SQUARE,
LONDON, W.C.,
Wednesday, 24th November, 1858.

MY DEAR THACKERAY,

Without a word of prelude, I wish this note to revert to a subject on which I said six words to you at the Athenæum when I last saw you.

Coming home from my country work, I find Mr. Edwin James's opinion taken on this painful question of the Garrick and Mr. Edmund Yates. I find it strong on the illegality of the Garrick proceeding. Not to complicate this note or give it a formal appearance, I forbear from copying the opinion ; but I have asked to see it, and I have it, and I want to make no secret from you of a word of it.

I find Mr. Edwin James retained on the one side ; I hear and read of the Attorney-General being retained on the other. Let me, in this state of things, ask you a plain question.

Can any conference be held between me, as representing Mr. Yates, and an appointed friend of yours, as representing you, with the hope and purpose of some quiet accommodation of this deplorable matter, which will satisfy the feelings of all concerned ?

It is right that, in putting this to you, I should tell you that Mr. Yates, when you first wrote to him, brought your letter to me. He had recently done me a manly service I can never forget, in some private distress of mine (generally within your knowledge), and he naturally thought of me as his friend in an emergency. I told him that his article

was not to be defended; but I confirmed him in his
opinion that it was not reasonably possible for him
to set right what was amiss, on the receipt of a
letter couched in the very strong terms you had
employed. When you appealed to the Garrick Committee and they called their General Meeting, I said
at that meeting that you and I had been on good
terms for many years, and that I was very sorry to
find myself opposed to you; but that I was clear
that the Committee had nothing on earth to do with
it, and that in the strength of my conviction I should
go against them.

If this mediation that I have suggested can take
place, I shall be heartily glad to do my best in it—
and God knows in no hostile spirit towards any one,
least of all to you. If it cannot take place, the
thing is at least no worse than it was; and you will
burn this letter, and I will burn your answer.

Yours faithfully,

CHARLES DICKENS.

W. M. Thackeray, Esq.[1]

36, ONSLOW-SQUARE,
26th November, 1858.

DEAR DICKENS,

I grieve to gather from your letter that you
were Mr. Yates's adviser in the dispute between me
and him. His letter was the cause of my appeal to
the Garrick Club for protection from insults against
which I had no other remedy.

I placed my grievance before the Committee of
the Club as the only place where I have been accustomed to meet Mr. Yates. They gave their opinion
of his conduct and of the reparation which lay in his
power. Not satisfied with their sentence, Mr. Yates
called for a General Meeting; and, the meeting which
he had called having declared against him, he declines
the jurisdiction which he had asked for, and says he
will have recourse to lawyers.

---

[1] J. C. Hotten: *Thackeray*, pp. 162–163.

You say that Mr. Edwin James is strongly of opinion that the conduct of the Club is illegal. On this point I can give no sort of judgment: nor can I conceive that the club will be frightened, by the opinion of any lawyer, out of their own sense of the justice and honour which ought to obtain among gentlemen.

Ever since I submitted my case to the Club, I have had, and can have, no part in the dispute. It is for them to judge if any reconcilement is possible with your friend. I subjoin the copy of a letter which I wrote to the Committee, and refer you to them for the issue.
Yours, &c.,
W. M. THACKERAY.

C. Dickens, Esq.[1]

36, ONSLOW-SQUARE,
GENTLEMEN,
Nov. 28, 1858.

I have this day received a communication from Mr. Charles Dickens, relative to the dispute which has been so long pending, in which he says:—

"Can any conference be held between me as representing Mr. Yates, and any appointed friend of yours, as representing you, in the hope and purpose of some quiet accommodation of this deplorable matter, which will satisfy the feelings of all parties?"

I have written to Mr. Dickens to say, that since the commencement of this business, I have placed myself entirely in the hands of the Committee of the Garrick, and am still as ever prepared to abide by any decision at which they may arrive on the subject. I conceive I cannot, if I would, make the dispute once more personal, or remove it out of the court to which I submitted it for arbitration.

If you can devise any peaceful means for ending it, no one will be better pleased than
Your obliged faithful servant,
W. M. THACKERAY.
The Committee of the Garrick Club.[2]

[1] J. C. Hotten: *Thackeray*, pp. 163-164.   [2] *Ibid.*, pp. 164-165.

The feud between Thackeray and Yates did not end here. Thackeray, it was said, made veiled allusions to the novelist in "The Virginians," and the other fed the flame by sarcastic reference to his opponent in the *Illustrated Times*. When the *Cornhill Magazine* was established, however, Yates made an overture of peace by sending a poem as a contribution; but this was merely answered by a curt note from a clerk stating he was "desired by Mr. Thackeray to return the enclosed." For this slight Yates revenged himself by a spiteful article in the *New York Times*, which disgusted Dickens, and drew from Thackeray a reply in "On Screens in Dining Rooms."

It was always the impression of Yates, who it is but fair to mention, on hearing of Thackeray's death, wrote a charming obituary notice of his foe, that after the first Thackeray was more angry with Dickens than with him, and that the affair, much to his detriment, was made a trial of strength between the novelists. Jeaffreson supports this opinion by declaring that Thackeray said to him, "You must not think, young 'un, that I am quarrelling with Mr. Yates. *I am hitting the man behind him.*"[1] This unfortunate quarrel has led to much speculation as to whether any real friendship existed between the rivals—for as rivals they will be considered to the end of the chapter. If Thackeray envied Dickens his early success and greater popularity, as he may well have done, at least he gave no sign of it: indeed, he never missed an opportunity to pay graceful tribute to the other's books, and many appreciations of the author of "Pickwick" may be

[1] J. C. Jeaffreson: *A Book of Recollections*, Vol. I, p. 269.

culled alike from his writings, his lectures, and his correspondence.

> Get "David Copperfield," by Jingo, it's beautiful ; it beats the yellow chap ("Pendennis") of this month hollow;[1]

he wrote to the Brookfields ; and of the same book he said in *Punch :*

> How beautiful it is, how charmingly fresh and simple ! In those admirable touches of tender humour —and I shall call humour, Bob, a mixture of love and wit—who can equal this great genius? There are little words and phrases in his book which are like personal benefits to the reader.[2]

Of "A Christmas Carol" he wrote : "It seems to me a national benefit, and to every man or woman who reads it a personal kindness "; and he referred to "The Battle of Life" and the other Christmas stories as "these charming little books of Mr. Dickens's which are chorales for Christmas executed in prose." In the lecture on "Charity and Humour," which he delivered in England in 1855, he introduced the following story against himself.

> All children ought to love Dickens; I know two that do, and read his books ten times for once they peruse the dismal preachments of their father. I know one who, when she is happy, reads "Nicholas Nickleby"; when she is un- happy, reads "Nicholas Nickleby"; when she is tired, reads "Nicholas Nickleby"; when she is in bed, reads "Nicholas Nickleby"; when she has nothing to do, reads "Nicholas Nickleby"; and when she has finished the book, reads "Nicholas

[1] *A Collection of Letters of W. M. Thackeray*, p. 54.
[2] *Mr. Brown's Letters.*

Nickleby" again. This candid young critic, at ten years of age, said, "I like Mr. Dickens's books better than your books, papa," and frequently expressed her desire that the latter author should write a book like one of Mr. Dickens's books. Who can?

But Thackeray, though keenly appreciative of the other, was too clear-sighted a critic unduly to depreciate his own writing, or overrate Dickens'. Indeed, he was constrained to admit that Dickens was not a deep thinker, though he had "a clear and bright-eyed intelligence, which is better than philosophy: I think he is equal to Fielding and Smollett—at any rate to Smollett: he is not such a scholar as Fielding was." This, then, was the greatest difference between them, that other things being equal, Thackeray's literary culture was far wider. He was thereby enabled thoroughly to appreciate the many beauties of Dickens's works. Dickens, unfortunately, was not a discerning critic of writings other than those of his own kind, and he read little and thought less of the books of the master stylist of his day. "He knows that my books are a protest against his—that if the one set are true, the other must be false," so said Thackeray; and it may confidently be assumed that he had not much doubt as to which set were right.

CHAPTER XX

THE CORNHILL MAGAZINE (1860–1863)

Thackeray undertakes to write another novel—various plans for it—
" The Virginians "—his desire to found a magazine—the early shilling
magazines—accepts an offer to contribute novels to the *Cornhill
Magazine*—and later is invited to edit it—goes abroad—his circular
letter to likely contributors—asks Longfellow to write for it—" the
regular cabs "—contributors to the *Cornhill Magazine* under Thack-
eray's editorship—success of the venture—" On Some Late Great
Victories "—Thackeray as editor—" Lovel the Widower " and
" Framley Parsonage "—he resigns the editorship—refuses Mrs.
Browning's " Lord Walter's Wife "—" Thorns in the Cushion "—his
kindness—his earnings in his last years—his contributions to the
Cornhill Magazine.

AFTER returning from the second visit to America,
Thackeray undertook to write another novel
to be published in numbers by Messrs.
Bradbury and Evans; but when he entered
into this engagement he had not made up his mind
what it would be. He began a story, was dissatisfied
with it, and burnt what he had written. " I can't jump
further than I did in ' The Newcomes,' but I want to
jump as far," he told Whitwell Elwin; adding that
the manuscript he had destroyed ran in "the old track,"
and lamenting that he had exhausted all the types of
character with which he was familiar. He thought of
a story in the days of Dr. Johnson, but abandoned the
scheme; and then for a moment reverted to his hint in

" The Newcomes " that one day he would relate the history of " J. J." "I intended to show J. J. married, and to exhibit him with the trials of a wife and children. I meant to make him in love with another man's wife, and recover him through his attachment for the little ones."[1] Eventually he turned to the idea that he had mentioned in America to John Esten Cooke. "I shall lay the scene of the novel in Virginia. There will be two brothers who will be prominent characters ; one will take the English side in the war, the other the American, and they will both be in love with the same girl. . . . I shall give it the title of ' The Two Virginians.' " The first number of "The Virginians" was issued in November 1857, and the novel appeared month by month until October 1859.

It had long been Thackeray's ambition to establish a magazine, as Ainsworth had done, and Douglas Jerrold and Cruikshank, Hood and Dickens. The failure of the periodicals with which he had in earlier days been connected had in no wise damped his ardour. Two years after the failure of the *Constitutional* he had asked Jerdan if the *Literary Gazette* was for sale, and about the time "Esmond" was published he had suggested to George Smith a small daily print after the style of the *Tatler*, to be called *Fair Play*. He was now in 1860 to satisfy his ambition in this direction.

In those days the price of periodical literature was high, and the only shilling monthlies had been Douglas Jerrold's *Shilling Magazine*, long since defunct, the series of booklets, edited by Edmund Yates, called

[1] Whitwell Elwin : *Some Eighteenth Century Men of Letters.* (Memoir. By his Son.)

the *Train*, and its rival, the *Idler*, the principal supporter of which was James Hannay. The publishing house of Messrs. Smith, Elder and Co. thought the time ripe to found a high-class shilling magazine, and began to make preparations accordingly. George Smith deemed it highly desirable to secure for the first numbers a novel by Thackeray, and he offered to pay at the rate of £350 per monthly instalment for the serial, American, and colonial rights and the edition in volume form at the original price : the profits on cheaper editions to be divided. The offer was accepted, and the founder of the periodical then set out to find an editor. He had made up his mind that Thomas Hughes, the author of "Tom Brown's Schooldays," was the man ; but when he approached Hughes he learnt that the latter had undertaken to contribute to the forthcoming shilling *Macmillan's Magazine*, and was unable to accept any offer for a similar production. After further consideration Smith offered Thackeray the editorship at a salary of £1000 a year, and the offer was accepted.

Thackeray, however, was busy with "The Virginians," and it was decided not to bring out the new magazine until January 1860. The novel was finished on the previous September 7 at Folkestone—" I am surprised I have finished 'The Virginians' so well— and what a load off my mind ! " he announced the fact from Folkestone to George Smith. Thackeray then went abroad with his daughters, passing a week in September

> in the little old town of Coire or Chur, in the Grisons, where lies buried that very ancient British

WILLIAM MAKEPEACE THACKERAY
From a crayon drawing by Samuel Laurence

king, saint, and martyr, Lucius, who founded the
Church of St. Peter, which stands opposite the
house No. 65, Cornhill.[1]

He called on St. Lucius to help him to find a title,
and his prayer was effective, for a few days later he
wrote to suggest the *Cornhill Magazine:* "it has," he
said, "a sound of jollity and abundance about it."[2]
The suggestion could not be improved upon, and this
title was used for the magazine.

Our Store-House being in Cornhill, we date and
name our Magazine from its place of publication
[he wrote in a circular letter sent to George Henry
Lewes and other likely contributors]. We might
have assumed a title more startling : for example,
"The Thames on Fire" was a name suggested ;
and, placarded in red letters about the City and
Country, it would no doubt have excited some
curiosity. But, on going to London Bridge, the
expectant rustic would have found the stream rolling
on its accustomed course and would have turned
away angry at being hoaxed. Sensible people are
not to be misled by fine prospectuses and sounding
names ; the present writer has been for five-and-
twenty years before the world, which has taken his
measure pretty accurately. We are too long acquainted to try and deceive one another; and, were
I to propose any such astounding feat as that above
announced, I know quite well how the schemer
would be received, and the scheme would end.

You, then, who ask what the *Cornhill Magazine* is
to be, and what sort of articles you shall supply for
it ; if you were told that the Editor, known hitherto

[1] *Roundabout Papers—On a Bad, Idle Boy.*
  Messrs. Smith, Elder and Co.'s offices were then at No. 65,
Cornhill.
[2] Lady Ritchie : *The First Number of the " Cornhill"* (*Cornhill
Magazine*, July 1896).

only by his published writings, was in reality a great
reformer, philosopher, and wiseacre, about to ex-
pound prodigious doctrines and truths until now
unrevealed, to guide and direct the peoples, to pull
down the existing order of things, to edify new social
or political structures, and, in a word, to set the
Thames on Fire; if you heard such designs as-
cribed to him—*risum teneatis?* You know I have
no such pretensions : but, as an Author who has
written long, and had the good fortune to find a
very great number of readers, I think I am not
mistaken in supposing they give me credit for experience, observation, and for having lived with
educated people in many countries, and seen the
world in no small variety; and, having heard me
soliloquise, with so much kindness and favour, and
say my own say about life and men and women,
they will not be unwilling to try me as Conductor of
a Concert, in which I trust many skilful performers
will take part.

We hope for a large number of readers, and must
seek, in the first place, to amuse and interest them.
Fortunately for some folks, novels are as daily bread
to others ; and fiction of course must form a part,
but only a part of our entertainment.   We want, on
the other hand, as much reality as possible—discussion, and narrative of events interesting to the
public, personal adventure and observation, familiar
reports of scientific discovery, description of Social
Institutions — *quicquid agunt homines* — a Great
Eastern, a battle in China, a Racecourse, a popular
Preacher—there is hardly any subject we *don't* want
to hear about, from lettered and instructed men who
are competent to speak on it.

I read the other day in the *Illustrated London
News* (in my own room at home), that I was at that
moment at Bordeaux, purchasing first-class claret for
first-class contributors, and second-class for those of
inferior *crû*.   Let me continue this hospitable simile ;
and say that at our contributors' table, I do not ask
or desire to shine especially myself, but to take my

part occasionally, and to invite pleasant and instructed gentlemen and ladies to contribute their
share to the conversation.   It may be a Foxhunter
who has the turn to speak ; or a Geologist, Engineer,
Manufacturer, Member of the House of Commons,
Lawyer, Chemist—what you please.   If we can only
get people to tell what they know, pretty briefly and
good-humouredly, and not in a manner obtrusively
didactic—what a pleasant ordinary we may have,
and how gladly folks will come to it !   If our friends
have good manners, a good education, and write in
good English, the company, I am sure, will be all
the better pleased ; and the guests, whatever their
rank, age, sex be, will be glad to be addressed by
well-educated gentlemen and women.   A professor
ever so learned, a curate in his country reti ·ment,
an artisan after work-hours, a schoolmaster or
mistress when the children are gone home, or the
young ones themselves when their lessons are over,
may like to hear what the world is talking about, or
be brought into friendly communication with persons
whom the world knows.   There are points upon
which agreement is impossible, and on these we
need not touch.   At our social table, we shall suppose the ladies and children always present ; we
shall not set rival politicians by the ears ; we shall
listen to every guest who has an apt word to say ;
and, I hope, induce clergymen of various denomina-
tions to say grace in their turn.   The kindly fruits
of the earth, which grow for all—may we not enjoy
them with friendly hearts?   The field is immensely
wide ; the harvest perennial, and rising everywhere ;
we can promise competent fellow labourers a welcome and a good wage ; and hope a fair custom
from the public for our stores at the *Cornhill
Magazine*.[1]

Having settled the title of the magazine and the
style of the contributions, Thackeray cast around for

[1] *Cornhill Magazine*, January 1860.

contributors, throwing his net so far as America, and begging Longfellow to rally round his standard.

> Has Hiawatha ever a spare shaft in his quiver, which he can shoot across the Atlantic? How proud I should be if I could have a contribution or two from you for our *Cornhill Magazine*.
> I should like still better to be driving to Cambridge in the snow, and expecting a supper there. Two or three months ago I actually thought such a scheme was about to come off. I intended to shut up my desk for a year—not write a line—and go on my travels. But the gods willed. otherwise. I am pressed into the service of this Magazine, and engaged to write ever so much more for the next three years. Then, if I last so long, I shall be free of books and publishers; and hope to see friends to whose acquaintance I look back with—I can't tell you how much gratitude and kind feeling.[1]

The *Cornhill Magazine*, like the *Pall Mall Gazette* in "Pendennis," was to be written by scholars and gentlemen. New blood was eagerly sought by the editor and the proprietor, but with very little success; and at the inaugural dinner given to the contributors by George Smith at his house in Gloucester Place, Hyde Park, the familiar faces were everywhere to be observed. "I see," said Thackeray, "there are only a certain number of regular cabs upon the stand, and whether they are bad or good, rickety or otherwise, we must make the best of them." Anthony Trollope, "Father Prout," Robert Bell, G. A. Sala, E. F. Dallas, "Jacob Omnium," James Hannay, John Oxenford, G. H. Lewes, Sir John Burgoyne, Frederick Greenwood, and John Hollingshead, with Godfrey

[1] *Life of H. W. Longfellow*, Vol. II, p. 346.

Sykes, who designed the cover, Millais and Leighton for artists, formed the original staff; while among occasional contributors during Thackeray's editorship were Tennyson, Thomas Hood, Monckton Milnes, Charles Lever, W. H. Russell, Herman Merivale, Mrs. Gaskell, Mrs. Browning, Locker-Lampson, Dean Hole, Lord Lytton, Adelaide Procter, Matthew Arnold, Ruskin, Fitzjames Stephen, George Macdonald, and Miss Thackeray (now Lady Ritchie).

From the start a hearty welcome was accorded by the public to the *Cornhill Magazine*. Of the first number 110,000 copies were sold, of the second over 100,000 ; and some months later, when the circulation had reached its normal level, 80,000 to 85,000 were required to supply the demand. Immediately after the issue of No. 1, Thackeray went to Paris—as it happened, for the last time. He had been overwhelmed with manuscripts, not only at the office—which was all very well —but actually at "the editor's private residence to which, in spite of prayers, entreaties, commands, and threats, authors, and ladies especially,"[1] would send their communications. Even against this he held up manfully ; but when the intending contributors began to call on him in Onslow Square, then, he said, he packed a portmanteau and ran away. "The darlings demanded that I should rewrite, if I could not understand their nonsense, and put their halting lines into proper form. I was so appalled when they set upon me with their 'ipics' and their 'ipicacas' that you might have knocked me down with a feather, sir. It was insupportable, and I fled away to France."

[1] *Second Circular Letter to Contributors to the Magazine.*

This he told Fields, the American publisher, who has further confided to the public how, when he called on Thackeray at his hotel in the Rue de la Paix, he found him almost delirious with joy at the news from London of the immense sale of the magazine and full of enthusiasm for George Smith. "London is not big enough to contain me now, and I am obliged to add Paris to my residence! Great Heavens" (said he, throwing up his long arms) "where will this tremendous circulation stop? Who knows but that I shall have to add Vienna and Rome to my whereabouts? If the worst comes to the worst, New York also may fall into my clutches, and only the Rocky Mountains may be able to stop my progress."

"Those days in Paris were simply tremendous," says Fields. "We dined at all possible and impossible places together. We walked round and round the glittering courts of the Palais Royal . . . and all my efforts were necessary to restrain him from rushing in and ordering a pocketful of diamonds and 'other trifles' as Thackeray called them; 'for,' said he, 'how can I spend the princely income which Smith allows me for editing the *Cornhill* unless I begin instantly somewhere?' If he saw a group of three or four persons talking together in an excited way . . . he would whisper to me with immense gesticulation, 'There, there, you see, the news has reached Paris, and perhaps the number has gone up since my last accounts from London.' His spirits during these few days were colossal, and he told me he found it impossible to sleep for counting subscribers."

Thackeray in mock-heroic strains expressed his de-

WILLIAM MAKEPEACE THACKERAY
From a statuette by Sir Edgar Boehm, 1864, in the National Portrait Gallery

light at the success of the magazine in a "Roundabout
Paper" that appeared in it, "On Some Late Great
Victories":

> The Victories which I wish especially to com-
> memorate in this paper are the six great, complete,
> prodigious, and undeniable, victories, achieved by
> the corps which the editor of the *Cornhill Magazine*
> has the honour to command. . . . Up the Hill of
> Ludgate, around the Pauline Square, by the side
> of Chepe, until it reaches our own hill of Corn, the
> procession passes. The Imperator is bowing to
> the people. . . . I fancy the Imperator standing on
> the steps of the Temple (erected by Titus) on the
> Mons Frumentarius, and addressing the citizens.
> "Quirites!" he says, "in our campaign of six
> months we have been engaged six times, and in
> each action we have taken near upon *a hundred
> thousand prisoners*. Go to! What are other maga-
> zines compared to our magazine? (Sound trumpets.)
> What banner is there like that of Cornhill? You
> philosopher yonder!" (He shakes under his mantle.)
> "Do you know what it is to have a hundred and ten
> thousand readers? a hundred thousand readers? a
> hundred thousand *buyers?*" (Cries of "No!"
> "Pooh!" "Yes, upon my honour!" "O come!"
> and murmurs of applause and derision.) "I say
> more than a hundred thousand purchasers—and I
> believe *as much as a million readers?*" (Immense
> sensation.) "To these have we said an unkind
> word? We have enemies; have we hit them an
> unkind blow? Have we sought to pursue party
> aims, to forward private jobs, to advance selfish
> schemes? The only persons to whom, wittingly,
> we have given pain are some who have volunteered
> for our corps—and of these volunteers we have had
> *thousands.*" (Murmurs and grumbles.) "What com-
> mander, citizens, could place all these men—could
> make officers of all these men?" (cries of "No, no!"
> and laughter), "could say, 'I accept this recruit,
> though he is too short for our standard, because

2 G

he is poor, and has a mother at home who wants
bread?' could enrol this other, who is too weakly
to bear arms, because he says, 'Look, sir, I shall
be stronger anon'? The leader of such an army
as ours must select his men, not because they are
good and virtuous, but because they are strong and
capable. To these our ranks are ever open; and
in addition to the warriors who surround me "—(the
generals look proudly conscious)—"I tell you,
citizens, I am in treaty with other great and most
tremendous champions, who will march by the side
of our veterans to the achievement of fresh victories.
Now, blow trumpets! Bang, ye gongs! and drummers, drub the thundering skins! Generals and
chiefs, we go to sacrifice to the gods."

The question with which a biographer of Thackeray
is concerned in the matter of the *Cornhill Magazine*,
is how far the editor was responsible for the success
of the venture. George Smith has avowed that the
reason he did not think of offering the editorship in
the first place to Thackeray was because he did not
"attribute to him the business qualities which go to
make a good editor," and Anthony Trollope went so
far as to say that "a man so susceptible, so prone to
work by fits and starts, so unmethodical, could not
have been a good editor." That Thackeray was not a
man of business there can be no doubt, and that
George Smith had himself largely to thank for the
success of the *Cornhill Magazine* cannot be questioned;
but as the tree is judged by its fruit, so must the editor
be judged by his periodical, and perhaps there has
never been any monthly more brilliant than the *Cornhill
Magazine* when Thackeray was sitting in the editorial
chair. It is easy to admit he was unmethodical as an

editor, since his want of method as a writer is an open secret; but then much admirable work is sometimes done by the unmethodical.

Thackeray, however, was not quite so unmethodical as Trollope thought. That latter most delightful story-teller once stated that the editor had intended in the first number of the magazine to print one of his great novels, but that he put off writing it until too late, and that at the eleventh hour he, Trollope, was asked to write a story. " ' Lovel the Widower ' was commenced at the same time as ' Framley Parsonage,' " he continued, " but ' Lovel the Widower ' was not sub-stantial enough to appear as the principal joint at the banquet." [1] This was an amiable delusion on Trollope's part. He had written to Thackeray offering to con-tribute some short stories, and to his surprise received in reply an invitation to contribute a novel to begin in the first number.

Smith and Elder have sent you their proposals; and the business part done, let me come to the pleasure, and say how very glad indeed I shall be to have you as a co-operator in our new magazine [Thackeray wrote to him on October 28, 1859]. And looking over the annexed programme, you will see whether you can't help us in many ways besides tale-telling. Whatever a man knows about life and its doings, that let us hear about. You must have tossed a good deal about the world, and have count-less sketches in your memory and your portfolio. Please to think if you can furbish up any of these besides a novel. When events occur, and you have a good lively tale, bear this in mind. One of our chief objects in this magazine is the getting out of novel spinning, and back into the world. Don't

[1] Anthony Trollope : *Thackeray*, p. 53.

understand me to disparage our craft, especially your wares. I often say I am like the pastrycook, and don't care for tarts, but prefer bread and cheese ; but the public love the tarts (luckily for us), and we must bake and sell them. There was quite an excitement in my family one evening when Paterfamilias (who goes to sleep on a novel almost always when he tries it after dinner) came downstairs into the drawing-room wide awake and calling for the second volume of "The Three Clerks." I hope the *Cornhill Magazine* will have as pleasant a story.[1]

Thackeray, however, had made no default, for "Lovel the Widower" was the story he had intended to contribute, and the invitation to Trollope arose from the proprietor's belief that a second serial would strengthen the magazine. "Framley Parsonage" was given the place of honour in the new periodical, indeed, and it was this that led Trollope to a mistaken conclusion ; but that was by Thackeray's own arrangement on grounds of courtesy. "He would not claim the first place in his own magazine," George Smith has explained. "He looked upon himself as a host, and upon Trollope as his guest."[2]

Though Thackeray contributed to the *Cornhill Magazine* until his death, he retired from the editorship in April 1862, when, in its pages, he bade farewell to his contributors :—

> Ladies and gentlemen (who *will* continue, in spite of the standing notice below, to send papers to the Editor's private residence), perhaps you will direct the postman to some other house, when you learn

[1] Anthony Trollope : *An Autobiography.*
[2] G. M. Smith : *Our Birth and Parentage* (*Cornhill Magazine*, January 1901.)

WILLIAM MAKEPEACE THACKERAY
From a painting by Samuel Lawrence, in the Strangers' Room
of the Reform Club

that the editor of the *Cornhill Magazine* no longer lives in mine.

My esteemed successor lives at Number —, but I will not intrude upon the poor man's brief interval of quiet.   He will have troubles enough in that thorn-cushioned Editorial Chair, which is forwarded to him this day by the Parcels (Happy) Delivery Company.

In our first number, Ladies and Gentlemen, I, your obedient servant, likened himself to the captain of a ship, to which and whom I wished a pleasant voyage.   Pleasant !   Those who have travelled on shipboard know what a careworn, oppressed, uncomfortable man the captain is.   Meals disturbed, quiet impossible, rest interrupted ; such is the lot of captains.   This one resigns his commission.   I had rather have a quiet life than gold-lace and epaulets ; and deeper than ever did plummet sound, I fling my speaking-trumpet.   Once, in a voyage to America, I met a sea-captain who was passenger in the ship which he formerly commanded.   No man could be more happy, cheerful, courteous than this.   He rode through the gale with the most perfect confidence in the ship and its captain ; he surveyed the storm as being another gentleman's business ; and his great delight was to be called at his watch to invoke a blessing on the steward's boy who woke him, and to turn round in his crib and go to sleep again.   Let my successor command the *Cornhill*, giving me always a passage on board ; and if the printer's boy rings at my door of an early morning with a message that there are three pages wanting or four too much, I will send out my benediction to the printer's boy and take t'other half-hour's doze.

Though Editor no more, I hope long to remain a contributor to my friend's Magazine.   I believe my own special readers will agree that my books will not suffer when their Author is released from the daily task of reading, accepting, refusing, losing and finding the works of other people.   To say No has often cost me a morning's peace and a day's work.   I tremble *recenti metu*.   Oh, those hours of madness spent in searching for Louisa's lost lines to her dead Piping Bullfinch, for Nhoj Senoj's mislaid Essay! I tell them for the last time the (late) Editor will not be responsible for rejected communications, and herewith send off the Chair and the great *Cornhill Magazine* Tin-box, with its load of care.

Whilst the present tale of "Philip" is passing through the press I am preparing another, on which I have worked at intervals for many years past, and which I hope to introduce in the ensuing year; and I have stipulated for the liberty of continuing the little Essays which have amused the public and the writer, and which I propose to contribute from time to time to the pages of the *Cornhill Magazine.*

The reason usually assigned as the cause of Thackeray's resignation is that he found the work too troublesome. He made it the harder by his inability to say "No" curtly, and it was terrible to him to have to refuse to print the work of a friend. It cost him hours of agony to write to decline Mrs. Browning's poem, "Lord Walter's Wife," which he did not think suitable for the *Cornhill Magazine.* He was, indeed, too sensitive to do the work with comfort.

Ah me [he cried] we wound where we never intended to strike; we create anger where we never meant harm; and these thoughts are the thorns in our cushion. Out of mere malignity, I suppose, there is no man who would like to make enemies. But here in this editorial business you can't do otherwise, and a queer, sad, strange, bitter thought it is that must ever cross the mind of many a public man. Do what I will, be innocent or spiteful, be generous or cruel, there are A and B, and C and D who will hate me to the end of the chapter—to the chapter's end—to the finis of the page—when hate and envy, fortune and disappointment, shall be over.[1]

[1] *Thorns in the Cushion.*

"How can I go into society?" he said. "I dined
out the other day, and at the table were four gentlemen
whose masterpieces of literature I had declined with
thanks." The letters that accompanied the proffered
contributions were frequently of a nature to distress him.
Referring to one of these, sent with a poem,

> Here is the case [he said] put with true female
> logic. "I am poor; I am good; I am ill; I work
> hard; I have a sick mother and hungry brothers and
> sisters dependent on me. You can help us if you
> will." And then I look at the paper with the
> thousandth part of a faint hope that it may be suitable,
> and I find it won't do; and I knew it wouldn't do;
> and why is this poor lady to appeal to my pity, and
> bring her little ones kneeling to my bedside, and
> calling for bread which I can give them if I choose?
> No day passes but that argument *ad misericordiam*
> is used. Day and night that sad voice is crying out
> for help. Thrice it appealed to me yesterday. Twice
> this morning it cried to me : and I have no doubt
> when I go to get my hat I shall find it with its piteous
> fate and its pale family about it, waiting for me in
> the hall. One of the immense advantages which
> women have over our sex is, that they actually like
> to read these letters. Like letters? O mercy on us !
> Before I was an editor I did not like the postman
> much :—but now ! [1]

Well, the poem was useless ; it was entirely without
merit or value, and could never appear in the *Cornhill
Magazine*, or, for the matter of that, in any other
magazine. Yet the manuscript in question—and who
knows how many others also—because of the pathetic
letter, was probably never returned to its authoress, who,
instead, received a brief and formal note. I can see the

[1] *Thorns in the Cushion.*

dear, great man writing it in secret, and hurriedly thrusting the letter into a drawer at the sound of approaching footsteps, stating that the editor of the *Cornhill Magazine* had much pleasure in accepting the little verses, and enclosing a cheque, quite out of proportion to the length, let alone the merits of the poem. And if that cheque could be shown we should notice that, by some error, it was drawn on Mr. Thackeray's own banking-account, and not on that of Messrs. Smith, Elder and Co., the proprietors of the magazine. And then, too, the poem would never appear in the periodical. Still more strange, and most astonishing of all, when his successor examined the manuscripts accepted, and not yet printed by his predecessor, there would be no trace of the poem, and no record of it in the books of the firm—but then, all the world knows how unmethodical Thackeray was.

Thackeray told Mr. James Payn how a young man had sent him a long story, for which he demanded particular attention from "the greatest of novelists," upon the ground that he had a sick sister entirely dependent upon him for support, and how, touched by the appeal, he wrote to his correspondent a long letter of advice, enclosing also some pecuniary assistance. "I feel for your position," he said, "and appreciate your motive for exertion ; but I must tell you at once that you will never do anything in literature. Your contribution is worthless in every way, and it is the truest kindness, both to her for whom you are working, and to yourself, to tell you so straight. Turn your mind at once to some other industry "—and how this produced a reply couched in the most offensive terms

conceivable, and ending by telling "the greatest of
novelists" that, although he had attained by good luck
the top of the tree, he would one day find himself,
where he deserved to be, at the bottom of it. " For my
part," said Thackeray (upon Mr. Payn showing some
preliminary symptoms of suffocation), " I see little to
laugh at. What a stupid, ungrateful beast the man
must be! And if ever I waste another half-hour writing to a creature of that sort, call me a horse, or
worse!"[1]

What *Punch* had been to Thackeray in his struggling
days, the *Cornhill Magazine* was to him in the hour of
his success. He had years before it was founded been
relieved from the eternal want of pence that troubles
the soul of most men of letters. " Now, the dear girls
are provided for, the great anxiety is taken from my
life, and I can breathe freely for the little time that is
left for me to be with them," he said to Bayard Taylor
after the second visit to America. He calculated his
receipts from his pen in the twenty years ending in 1859
to have amounted to £32,000. "Vanity Fair" had
brought in £2000, and "Esmond" about the same;
"The Newcomes" £4000, and "The Virginians"
£6000 ; while the profits of the lecture tours were about
£9500. His annual expenses had averaged £1000, and
he had contrived to save £13,000, and hoped within the
next three years to replace the rest of his patrimony.
Thanks to the *Cornhill Magazine* he did better than he
expected. Apart from his novels, he received the record
price for short articles, twelve guineas a page, and,
when the success of his periodical was assured, the pro-

[1] James Payn : *Literary Recollections.*

prietor most generously doubled the editorial salary. Naturally Thackeray was in high spirits.

How dy do, my dear old Davus? [he wrote to Sir Henry Davidson early in 1860]. Read the *Cornhill Magazine* for May ; the article " Little Scholars " is by my dear old fat Annie. She sends you her love, so does Minnie. We're going out to drive. We've got two horses in our carriage now. The Magazine goes on increasing, and how much do you think my next twelve months' earnings and receipts will be if I work? £10,000. Cockadoodleoodloodle. We are going to spend four thousand in building a house on Palace Green, Kensington. We have our health. We have brought Granny and G. P. to live at Brompton Crescent, close to us, and we are, my dear old Davus's
Faithful W. M. T., A. T., and H. M. T.[1]

To the *Cornhill Magazine* in its first year Thackeray contributed " Lovel the Widower " and " The Four Georges," and in 1861 began " Philip," which ran until August 1862 ; while throughout these years he wrote from time to time those inimitable little essays, the " Roundabout Papers," in which he is autobiographical, impersonal, fanciful, angry, tender, exulting, sad, preaching always the gospel of Love and deploring the *Vanitas Vanitatum*. The number of the magazine for December 1863 on the orange-coloured fly-leaf bore the announcement that " a new serial story by W. M. Thackeray would commence early in the new year."

I intend [he had written to Motley in 1858] to write a novel of the time of Henry V, which will be my

[1] F. St. John Thackeray : *Reminiscences of W. M. Thackeray* (*Temple Bar*, July 1893).

capo d'opera, in which the ancestors of my present characters, Warringtons, Pendennises, and the rest shall be introduced. It will be a most magnificent performance, and nobody will read it.[1]

This idea, however, had been abandoned in favour of "Denis Duval," and that part of it which was finished appeared posthumously from March to July, 1864. It had been said that Thackeray was exhausted, and unkindly critics suggested that for the sake of his reputation he had better write no more novels : it is true that "The Virginians" and "Philip" were not on the same level as stories that came before ; but "Denis Duval" came as the answer to those who thought Thackeray was played out, for this story was nearly as good as anything he had ever done, and there are few things in his books more perfect than the description of Madame de Saverne's sorrows and madness and death.

[1] J. L. Motley : *Correspondence.*

CHAPTER XXI

LAST YEARS (1862-1863)

Further reasons for Thackeray's resignation of the *Cornhill Magazine*—
his failing health—his "dragons"—his convivial habits—his hard
work—his appearance in 1858—his standard of comfort—his weariness—his mode of writing—rebuilds No. 2, Palace Green—and goes
to live there—the house-warming—the History of Queen Anne—
realises that his days are numbered—the last months of his life—the
Cruikshank Exhibition—Founder's Day at the Charterhouse, 1863—
his death—and burial.

IT was not editorial worries that induced Thackeray to resign the editorship of the *Cornhill
Magazine* so much as failing health. He was
only fifty-one, but he had had many severe ill-
nesses, and he had, too, an internal disease that
frequently racked him with pain. He should have
husbanded his strength; but to take care of himself was
the last thing he would do. He had the best medical
advice, and was often to be seen in Sir Henry Thompson's
consulting-room, but, as he said, "What is the use
of advice if you don't follow it? They tell me not
to drink, and I do drink. They tell me not to eat, and
I do eat. In short I do everything I am not to do,
and, therefore, what is to be expected?" How true
this was may be gathered from a story told by Bayard
Taylor, who went with Thackeray to pay a visit to
Baron Marochetti. The sculptor gave a small engrav-

ing of Albert Dürer's "St. George and the Dragon" to Thackeray, who accepted it with great pleasure, but suddenly became grave. "I shall hang it near the head of my bed, where I can see it every morning," he said. "We have all our dragons to fight. Do you know yours? I know mine: I have not one, but two. Indolence and luxury . . . I am serious. I never take up the pen without an effort. I work only from necessity. I never walk without seeing some pretty useless thing which I want to buy. Sometimes I pass the same shop window every day for months, and resist the temptation and think I am safe; then comes the day of weakness, and I yield. My physician tells me that I must live very simply, and not dine out so much; but I cannot break off the agreeable habit. I shall look at this picture, and think of my dragons, though I don't expect to overcome them." Cordy Jeaffreson one day said to him, "You have drunk a good deal in your time." "Enough to float a 74-gun ship," the novelist answered. "Since I came out of my poverty, a bottle has been my daily minimum, and on three out of every four days I have taken a second bottle. I may be called a two-bottle man; and that takes no account of the two or three glasses of wine at midday, nor of the punches and grogs in the hours about midnight."[1] Thackeray had, indeed, lived hard, especially in the years before success came to him. In the early forties Edward FitzGerald told Frederick Tennyson how their friend wrote half the day: "Reviews and newspapers all the morning; dining, drinking, and talking of a night; managing to preserve a fresh colour and perpetual flow

[1] J. C. Jeaffreson: *A Book of Recollections*, Vol. I, p. 301.

of spirits under a wear and tear of thinking and feeding that would have knocked up all the other men I know two years ago, at least."

This combination of work and play undermined Thackeray's health, and about the time of the publication of "Vanity Fair" he told Brookfield he had something which prevented his being able to insure his life. Illness and hard work and his mode of living had worn him out prematurely, and he was an old man before his time. "He has the appearance," Motley wrote to his wife in the summer of 1858, "of a colossal infant—smooth white shiny ringletty hair, flaxen, alas! with advancing years, a roundish face, with a little dab of a nose, upon which it is a perpetual wonder how he keeps his spectacles, a sweet but rather piping voice with something of the childish treble about it, and a very tall, slightly stooping figure."

Except in regard to the lamentable tragedy of his married life—and what a cross that was for any man to bear!—there is no occasion to pity Thackeray. He had to work hard as a young man, and during that period he had disappointments and may well have been angry that the public did not realise that the author of "Barry Lyndon" had genius; but fame came to him at seven-and-thirty, a world-wide fame. Still, however, he worked as hard as ever : it is said because he desired to make provision for his children. That undoubtedly was his object, but it could have been achieved if he had done only half the work and lived more economically. Writing to his mother he told how "Tom Carlyle lives in perfect dignity in a little £40 house at Chelsea, with a snuffy Scotch maid to open the door,

WILLIAM MAKEPEACE THACKERAY
From a portrait by Sir John Gilbert, in the Garrick Club

and the best company in England knocking at it"; but it was not in him to emulate the example of his great contemporary. Unfortunately for himself his standard of comfort was high, and rather than reduce this, and live more economically, he preferred to work double shifts to the end of his days.

Thackeray must have his man-servant, a big house, a good cellar, his horse, and, later, his brougham. Every man may order his life in his own way, and none have the right to blame : but because a man, to use Thackeray's expression, "takes too many crops out of his brain" to provide himself and his with luxuries, none should waste pity upon him in the matter of his labour.

As the years passed he became very weary. "All I can do now," he said towards the end of his life, "is to bring out my old puppets, and put new bits of ribbon upon them. I have told my tale in the novel department. I only repeat old things in a pleasant way, but I have nothing fresh to say. I get sick of my task when I am ill, and think 'Good Heavens! what is all this story about?'" Even when "Vanity Fair" had only just appeared he required rest and quiet, and he was urged by his friends to work less. One of them, indeed, went so far as to offer him facilities to do so. At last, he found he could not work at will. "My number is nearly due," he said to Miss Henrietta Corkran when he was editing the *Cornhill Magazine*, "but I cannot make it come. . . . I would like to rest my head in some quiet corner ; I had a nice scene this morning, and I cannot call to mind a bit of it now."

There is no doubt his method of work was injurious to his health, for he could only write at high pressure. "I cannot write comfortably in my own room. I do most of my composition at hotels or at a club. There is an excitement in public places which sets my brain working. I can write anywhere better than at home, and I write less at home than anywhere. I did not write ten pages of 'The Newcomes' in that house at Brompton." He had his stated hours for writing. He would take a quiet table at the Athenæum Club, and cover a few of those little slips of papers upon which he wrote his stories; and later in the day he would go to the Garrick Club, and write a few more pages; but he was easily tempted to go for a walk, or to join in an interesting conversation, and to put his sheets away until another time. "I can conceive nothing more harassing in the literary way," Motley wrote in June, 1858, to his wife, "than Thackeray's way of living from hand to mouth. I mean in regard to the way he furnishes food to the printer's devil. Here he is just finishing the number that must appear in a few days. Of course, whether ill or well, stupid or fertile, he must produce the same amount of fun, pathos, or sentiment. His gun must be regularly loaded and discharged at command. I should think it would wear his life out." It did wear his life out; and Dickens told Fields that when he looked at Thackeray lying in his coffin, he wondered that the figure he had known in life as of such noble presence could seem so shrunken and wasted; his hands were quite thin, like those of an old man of eighty.

Thackeray in 1859 had taken a long lease of a rather

dilapidated house in Palace Green. It was his intention to repair and improve the existing structure; but,
after careful consideration, he pulled it down; and, in
its place, from his own drawings, erected a handsome
mansion of red brick with stone facings, in the style of
Queen Anne. Thackeray looked upon the house as
a judicious investment; and when a friend playfully
reminded him of what Horace said of those who, forgetful of death, built houses, he replied cheerfully :
" No, I am *memor sepulchri*, for this house will always
let for so many hundreds a year." He was thoroughly
satisfied with his " lordly dwelling-house." " Well,
upon my word, it is one of the nicest houses I have
ever seen," he declared; and he was enthusiastic
about the old green and the old palace and the magnificent trees before the windows at which he wrote.

He moved from Onslow Square to Palace Green
early in February 1862, and a few weeks later gave
a house-warming. "The cards of invitation," Canon
Irvine has recorded, "were for ' W. Empty House,'
denoting at once its unfurnished condition and the
initials of its owner; and the bill proclaimed the fare
of our host's play of ' The Wolves and the Lamb' (to
be enacted by Herman Merivale, Sir Charles Young,
Morgan O'Connell, Follett Synge, Quintin Twiss,
Mrs. Caulfield, two daughters of Sir Henry Cole, and
Thackeray's younger girl), to be followed by a farce
entitled ' A Desperate Game,' by J. Maddison Morton,
the author of ' Box and Cox,' who, curiously enough,
ended his days as a Charterhouse Codd. I see in the
play-bill that Mr. Thackeray is announced as Mr.
Bonnington, but in fact he only appeared upon the

stage just before the fall of the curtain to say, ' Bless you, my children.' "

Installed in his new house, Thackeray finished "Philip," the last instalment of which appeared in the *Cornhill Magazine* in August 1862 ; and there he also wrote many "Roundabout Papers." He had been asked to continue Macaulay's History of England, and this offer he neither refused nor accepted at the moment.

> Queen Anne has long been my ambition [he wrote to Dr., afterwards Sir John, Skelton], but she will take many a long year's labour, and I can't ask any other writer to delay on my account. At the beginning of the year I had prepared an announcement stating that I was engaged on that history ; but kept it back, as it was necessary that I should pursue my old trade of novelist for some time yet to come. Meanwhile her image stands before St. Paul's, for all the world to look· at ; and who knows but some one else may be beforehand with both of us, and sketch her off while we are only laying the palette.[1]

Thackeray, hoping one day to undertake the task, stocked his library with the necessary books. "Here," he said, "here, I am going to write my greatest work —a 'History of the Reign of Queen Anne.' There are my materials "—pointing to a collection of volumes in various bindings, which occupied a separate place on the shelves. "Probably" (I shall begin it) "as soon as I am done with 'Philip'; but I am not sure I may not have to write another novel first. But the history will mature all the better for the delay. I want to *absorb* the authorities gradually, so that when I come

[1] *The Table-Talk of Shirley.*

NO. 2, PALACE GREEN, KENSINGTON
Where Thackeray lived from 1862 until his death

to write, I shall be filled with the subject, and can sit down to a continuous narrative, without jumping up every moment to consult somebody. The History has been a pet project of mine for some years past. I'm slowly working up to the level of it, and know that when I once begin I shall do it well." But even as the unexpected journey to the East caused the abandonment of the "Life of Talleyrand," so another and more untimely voyage to a more distant land deprived the world of Thackeray's "History of the Reign of Queen Anne."

> Now we are half a century old, and the kind hand which wrote the name in the books in the fine, well-remembered writing is laid under the grass which will cover us old gentlemen too ere long, after our little life's journey is over [he wrote in 1861 to an old Charterhouse friend]. And the carriage is going down hill, isn't it? Mine is, after having had some pleasant travelling, after being well-nigh upset, after being patched up again, after being robbed by footpads, etc., etc. The terminus can't be far off—a few years more or less. I wouldn't care to travel over the ground again, though I have had some pleasant days and dear companions.[1]

The months passed uneventfully, except for the fact that in November, 1862, Thackeray had another serious illness, and realised that his days were numbered. When William Follett Synge had left England in the previous year to take up the duties of Commissioner for the Sandwich Islands, Thackeray told him: "I want to tell you that I shall never see you again. I feel that I am doomed. I know that this will grieve

[1] H. Vizetelly: *Glances Back through Seventy Years*, Vol. II, p. 108.

you ; but look in that book and you will find something that I am sure will please and comfort you." The "something" was a prayer in which "he prayed that he might never write a word inconsistent with the love of God, or the love of man ; that he might never propagate his own prejudices to pander to those of others : that he might always speak the truth with his pen, and that he might never be actuated by a love of greed. And I particularly remember," Mr. Synge has written, "that the prayer wound up with the words, 'For the sake of Jesus Christ, our Lord.'"[1] Thackeray was doubtless thinking of himself when in a "Roundabout Paper" he wrote of Dr. London and Dr. Edinburgh, for, like the former, knowing the end was approaching, he

> made up his accounts with heaven. . . . And he said not a word to his family at home ; but lived among them cheerful and tender, and calm and loving ; though he knew that the night was near when he should see them and work no more. . . . And he died ; and his family never knew until he was gone that he had long been aware of the inevitable doom.[2]

It is also legitimate to suppose that he was thinking of his sentence when in another "Roundabout Paper" he made his peace with the world.

> In former days, I too have militated, sometimes, as I now think, unjustly ; but always, I know, without personal rancour. Which of us has not idle words to recall, flippant jokes to regret? Have you never committed an imprudence? Have you never

---

[1] Merivale and Marzials : *Thackeray*, p. 247.
[2] *On Letts's Diary.*

had a dispute and found out you were wrong? So
much the worse for you. Woe be to the man (*qui
croit toujours avoir raison*) . . . As I write . . . I
think about one or two little affairs of my own. . . .
Never mind, old Squaretoes : never mind, Madame
Pomposa ! Here is a hand. Let us be friends, as
we once were, and have no more of this rancour.

There is little to record of these last months of
Thackeray's life, save that he was writing " Denis
Duval " and occasionally composing a " Roundabout
Paper." During May 1863, Cruikshank was exhibiting
his cartoon, " Worship of Bacchus, or, The Drinking
Customs of Society," to a generation that knew him
not and paid little attention to the picture, until, anxious
to show consideration for an old friend, " Kind
Thackeray," as the artist's biographer has put it,
" came with his grave face, and looked through the
little gallery, and went off to write one of his charming
essays," which appeared in the *Times* of May 15.

Thackeray kept his last Founder's Day at the Charterhouse on December 12, looking very well, we have
been told. " He was there in his usual back seat in
the quaint old chapel," wrote one who was present.
" He went thence to the oration in the Governor's
room ; and as he walked up to the orator with his contribution, was received with such hearty applause as
only Carthusians can give to one who has immortalised
their school. At the banquet afterwards he sat at the
side of his old friend and artist-associate in *Punch*,
John Leech ; and in a humorous speech proposed, as
a toast, the noble foundation which he had adorned by
his literary fame, and made popular in his works."

Anthony Trollope saw him on December 14, and sat with him talking for half an hour : "I never knew him pleasanter, or more at ease as to his bodily ailments"; and two days later Thackeray was dining cheerfully at the Garrick Club, "pretending," one of the company has narrated, "to incite one very old friend to give a party of an excessively gay description, in order, as he said, that we might fancy ourselves all young again." On the next day, Thursday, December 17, with his elder daughter, he dined at the house of Dr. Merriman, who, with Dr. Elliotson, had watched him through his dangerous illness in 1849. "As he entered," Dr. Merriman has recorded, "I saw he was not well, and with his usual kindness he said, 'I would only have turned out to come to you as an old friend.' I remember saying, 'Oh ! but you, like every Englishman, will be better for your dinner. Do you know Jean Ingelow?' 'No—the woman in all London whom I am most anxious to know,' was the reply. 'Do you know the quondam Miss Croker?' 'No, but she is not here,' he replied. They were both present, and I had the great pleasure of introducing him to them. He soon revived under this mental pleasure. Ere we reached the dining-room he was himself again, and, falling in with an old Carthusian, Sir George Barrow, all went as pleasantly as possible. . . . My friend stayed late, his daughter going on to some other party, and I strolled up Young Street with him ; we halted by 'No. 13,' when he alluded to old times and happy days there ; he told me 'Vanity Fair' was his greatest work, and 'The Cane-Bottomed Chair' his favourite ballad ;

WILLIAM MAKEPEACE THACKERAY
From a bust by Nevill Burnard, 1867

and we parted at the top of 'Our Street,' never to meet again alive in this world."[1]

Carlyle has related how on December 20 he "was riding in the dusk, heavy of heart, along by the Serpentine and Hyde Park, when some human brother from a chariot, with a young lady in it, threw me a shower of salutations. I looked up—it was Thackeray with his daughter : the last time I was to see him in this world." On the 21st Thackeray attended the funeral of a relative, Lady Rodd ; and on that day or the next he went to the Athenæum. There he and Dickens passed each other on the stairs as usual, since the Yates affair, without giving any sign of recognition ; then Thackeray turned back, and with outstretched hand went up to Dickens and said he could no longer bear to be on any but the old terms of friendship. "I saw him shortly before Christmas at the Athenæum Club," Dickens has recorded, "when he told me he had been in bed three days—that after these attacks he was troubled with cold shiverings which quite took the work out of him, and that he had it in his mind to try a new remedy which he described. He was very cheerful and looked very bright." A few days later Dickens was looking down into the other's grave.

On the evening of Thursday, December 23, Thackeray went into his study and worked on the proofs of "Denis Duval"; but feeling ill, he retired at an early hour. It was noticed afterwards that the last words he revised were, "And my heart throbbed with an exquisite bliss." The next morning he was found dead in his bed, effusion into the brain having taken place.

[1] *St. Mary Abbott's Parish Magazine*, September 1889.

I lay the weary pen aside,
And wish you health, and love, and mirth,
As fits the solemn Christmas tide,
As fits the holy Christmas birth,
Be this, good friends, our carol still,—
Be peace on earth, be peace on earth
To men of gentle will![1]

The Middle Temple of which he was a member asked to be allowed to bury Thackeray in the Temple, where Goldsmith lies, but the offer was declined ; and the mortal remains of him who was, perhaps, the greatest novelist of his time were laid at rest in the cemetery at Kensal Green, under a plain stone bearing the simple but sufficient record :—

WILLIAM MAKEPEACE THACKERAY
BORN JULY 18, 1811
DIED DECEMBER 24, 1863

[1] *The End of the Play.*

PRINTED IN GREAT BRITAIN BY PHOTOTYPE LIMITED, BARNET, HERTS.

INDEX

References to characters and places (fictitious and real) to Thackeray's books mentioned in this work are marked *.

"Virginians, The," 221, 361, 405
—— designs for, 104
—— in America, 348
—— material for, 365, 383, 387, 388
—— publication of, 338
"Vivaldi," 34
Vizetelly, Henry, 109
—— on Thackeray, 110, 271
—— secures Thackeray for *Pictorial Times*, 201
—— "Glances Back Through Seventy Years," 232, 233, 294 note, 297 note
—— approaches Thackeray for "Social Zoologies," 337

Wagner, 77
"Wagstaffe, Theophile" (pseudonym of Thackeray), 102, 190
Walker, Frederick, 105, 199
*Walker, Mrs. Hooker, 219
Walpole House, Chiswick, 20
"Wapping Old Stairs," 211
*Wapshot, Rev. F., 44
*Warrington, George, 83, 85, 86, 210, 230, 248, 251, 316
Washington, U.S.A., 352, 355, 362
Washington, George, 376
Waterloo, 218, 305
Watteau, 101
Webb, Amelia, 8, 14
Webb, General, 336
Webb, Lieut.-Col. Richmond, 8
Webb, Sarah Richmond, 17
Webbe, Henry, 203
"Weekday Preachers," 297
Weekly Times, 132
Weimar, Thackeray at, 70–80, 216
Weissenborn, Dr., 72
Wellington, Lord, 159
Western Luminary, 402
West Looe, Cornwall, 88
Westminster Abbey, 60
Westminster Review, 141, 142
—— Essay on the Genius of Cruikshank, 163
Weyer, Van der, 71 note
Weynendal, 365

Whewell, Dr., 49
Whibley, Charles, 36, 131
White, James, 58
*White, Mrs. Washington, 219
Whitehead, Charles, "Lives and Exploits of English Highwaymen," 135
"White Squall, The," 33, 126, 300
*Whitestock, Frank, 62
Whittier, J. G., 354
Wieland, 76
Wigan, Horace, 222
Wilberforce, Bishop, 278, 335
Wilde, Oscar, 277
Williams, W. S., 111
Willis, N. P., 140
—— secures Thackeray for the *Corsair*, 183
—— Thackeray's article on, 225
Willis's Rooms, Lectures in, 332, 335
"Willow Tree, The," 301
Will's Coffee-house, 210
Wills, W. H., 279
Windsor, 6
Wolfe, General, 304
"Wolves and the Lamb, The," 222, 411
Woodward, John, 5
"Word on the Annuals, A," 130, 166
Wycherley, William, 178

Yates, Edmund, 109, 203
—— declares Thackeray a cynic, 240
—— offends Thackeray, 375–79
—— *The Train*, 387
"Yellowplush Papers," 84, 94, 104, 134, 135, 136, 142, 172, 174, 183, 190, 195, 196, 218, 228, 347, 413
—— "The Sea Captain," 136, 218
"Yorke, Oliver" (pseudonym of Maginn), 135
Yorktown, U.S.A., 303
Young, James Reynolds, 25 note, 53, 54
Young, Sir Charles, 411

Date Due